Prisoners of Myth

Prisoners of Myth

THE LEADERSHIP OF THE TENNESSEE VALLEY AUTHORITY, 1933–1990

Erwin C. Hargrove

THE UNIVERSITY OF TENNESSEE PRESS

KNOXVILLE

Preface for the Paperback Edition copyright © 2001 by
The University of Tennessee Press / Knoxville.
All Rights Reserved. Manufactured in the United States of America.
First Edition.

The paper used in this book meets the minimum requirements of
ANSI/NISO Z39.48-1992 (R 1997) (Permanence of Paper). The
binding materials have been chosen for strength and durability.

LIBRARY OF CONGRESS CATALOGING-IN-PUBLICATION DATA

Hargrove, Erwin C.
    Prisoners of myth: the leadership of the Tennessee Valley Authority,
1933–1990/Erwin C. Hargrove.
        p.   cm.
Originally published: Princeton, N.J.: Princeton University Press, c1994.
Includes bibliographical references and index.
ISBN 1-57233-117-8 (pbk. alk. paper)
1. Tennessee Valley Authority—Management—History.
2. Electric utilities—Tennessee River Valley—Management—History.
3. Corporations, Government—United States—Management—History.
4. Leadership. I. Title.
HD9685.U6 T219 2001
333.91'62'097680904—dc21   00-049095

This book is dedicated to my father,
Erwin C. Hargrove, in his ninety-second year,
from whom I have learned so much.

Men commit the error of not knowing when to limit their hopes.

—Niccolo Machiavelli

Contents

Preface to the Paperback Edition

THE FIRST EDITION of this book has been received differently by historians and political scientists. Historians see the story of development, maturation, and the aging of the TVA. They anchor their ideas about the authority in the politics of the New Deal and the ebb and flow of ideas about planning and regional development. Political scientists are more likely to look for a "theory" about bureaucratic organizations in American government. I hope that I have satisfied both audiences. The two approaches are complementary, even though each discipline would follow its own modes of thought.

I have tried to combine both approaches because for me the theory is implicit in the narrative. How and why did the changing organization and the changing political context present quite different tasks to organizational leaders? My central theoretical question, seen in the title *Prisoners of Myth*, is to ask how and why organizations which seek new successes according to strategies developed in past glories may fail. This inquiry opens the door to many further questions about the conditions for organizational achievement and decline.

Historians will place the TVA in the New Deal and its politics, recording the subsequent decline of progressive politics as a political resource for the authority. This is good, straightforward research which stands on its own merits. Political scientists are likely to complicate the issue by trying to pull general propositions out of the history of the TVA. A special kind of theoretical approach is required; that is, the use of historical narrative as a basis for theory can yield insights that a study of any organization at one time cannot produce. Time itself does not produce change, but the analysis of changes across time may tell one about the consequences of those changes for the functioning of the organization. Leadership of the authority during the New Deal could bank on strong political resources that were not available a generation later. The defensive politics of opposition to the Eisenhower administration's efforts to curb the TVA were very different from the New Deal years, and both periods were hardly recognizable in the 1970s and 1980s when the authority was sued by the Environmental Protection Agency and lost the support of many of its Tennessee Valley constituencies.

The study of change thus permits one to develop generalizations that cannot be captured in a study of the present TVA and its politics. Not all political science research should be historical inquiry, but history with an eye to theory should be celebrated. I have tried to build on the analysis of institutions as agents which develop cultures and folkways so that past decisions are very likely to influence new decisions according to an organizational bias (March and Olsen 1989).

My work on organizational leadership, which is fully expressed in this study, has, without any conscious intention on my part, enriched my understanding of leadership in the American presidency. The idea of the practice of presidential political "skill" in historical "context" developed out of my work on the leadership of the TVA and of other organizational entrepreneurs (Doig and Hargrove 1987; Hargrove 1998). The eight chairmen of the TVA, who are analyzed in this book, faced quite different tasks in changing environments. For example, David Lilienthal used his ability to articulate and preach a national mission for the TVA and similar authorities that was sustained by New Deal politics. S. David Freeman, who sought to emulate Lilienthal's leadership a generation later, could not find the national missions that he might articulate to supportive audiences. Personal political skill and a favorable political environment reinforce each other so that each is stronger than it would be alone. And, by the same token, limited political skills and an adverse environment will cause an organization to flounder. Most cases, of course, are somewhere in between those two poles. A rolling history of the leadership of an organization can capture these variations and assess the relative importance of organizational leadership across time.

I began this study without a "covering law" that might have been used as a guide to description and analysis. Philip Selznick's pioneering study of the TVA in the 1940s produced such a theory (Selznick 1966). His focus was on how the agency needed to win the political support of the large farmers in the valley if it wished to carry out its agricultural missions. He developed a theory of "cooptation" which explains how government bureaucracies must coopt, and perhaps surrender to, their immediate constituencies in the very programs they present to those constituencies. I did not use Selznick as a model because my questions were different. But it has occurred to me in retrospect that one could have asked his questions of my material. For example, the TVA began to develop real political trouble in the 1970s when the distributors of electric power in the valley vocally opposed experiments with solar power, the conservation of energy, and other projects introduced by David Freeman. That story is in my narrative, but I did not try to squeeze the theoretical richness out of it because my attention was on other questions.

By the same token, my study provides snapshots of the TVA bureaucracy over time which, if further explored, might contribute to theories of organization quite apart from the particularity of the TVA. Principal-agent approaches ask about "moral hazard" in the difficulty organizational leaders may have in winning compliance with their directives lower in the organization. I make a strong argument that the organizational culture of the TVA, with its very strong emphasis on delegation of operational authority to its several bureaus, prevented the TVA board from getting control of the practices that eventually led to the shut down of the agency's nuclear reactors. But a former TVA director, Richard Freeman, disagrees and argues that the problem could have been resolved if only Congress had permitted the agency to pay higher salaries to managers in the nuclear power program. At bottom, this is both an empirical and a theoretical disagreement, but a potentially profitable one.

One could study the politics of the TVA without ever looking at the agency itself by asking how the members of the Congress have combined to protect the organization and its missions from interference from any source. One could also explore why the chairmanship of the agency has ceased to be an office about which the White House cares much. Such studies would complement and broaden the kind of study that I have attempted here.

I now lay down my pen and invite others to seize my unanswered questions and do what they will with them. One wishes to have one's work recognized in the stream of inquiry, and I hope that my provocations will stimulate that effort.

WORKS CITED

Doig, Jameson W., and Erwin C. Hargrove, eds. *Leadership and Innovation: A Biographical Perspective on Entrepreneurs in Government.* Baltimore: Johns Hopkins Univ. Press, 1987.

Hargrove, Erwin C. *The President as Leader: Appealing to the Better Angels of Our Nature.* Lawrence: Univ. Press of Kansas, 1998.

March, James G., and Johan P. Olsen. *Rediscovering Institutions: The Organizational Basis of Politics.* New York: Free Press, 1989.

Selznick, Philip. *TVA and the Grass Roots: A Study in the Sociology of Formal Organization.* New York: Harper, 1966.

Preface

MY INTEREST in TVA began in 1979 when I was invited to become one of several social scientists who were asked to advise the TVA board on what were then referred to as the "nonpower" programs of TVA. The goal was to generate ideas for exciting new missions in regional development. David Freeman, the chairman of the board, and Richard Freeman, the only other director at the time, were explicit in their determination that TVA be more than a power company.

We met with the board, talked with TVA staff members, and wrote papers that were eventually assembled in a book published by TVA.[1] My assignment was to provide a rough design of a policy-planning staff operation within TVA. I did a great many interviews and learned three things about TVA. First, it had no tradition of formal policy analysis by staff members reporting directly to the board or general manager. All analysis of policy alternatives and program evaluation was in the operating arms of engineering, power, agriculture, etc. Second, the strong operating divisions differed greatly in their responsiveness to the idea of centralized policy analysis. The Offices of Engineering and Power had no use for it. Various nonpower regional development programs were congenial to the idea because of the belief that analysis might help them win support in Washington for their programs, which lived by appropriations. Third, the Freemans hoped to use analysis as the catalyst to knit the several parts of TVA, especially engineering and power, back together by using a policy-planning process to foster ideas for new cross-departmental programs of regional development. Dam building is inherently a multipurpose activity. The Freemans were looking for equivalents to dam building for the 1970s and '80s. These three insights emerged from interviews with TVA people and were the stepping stones to my next learning experience.

My interest in TVA led to a conference at the Vanderbilt Institute for Public Policy Studies in 1981, and my contribution to the book that resulted was a study of the leadership of the seven TVA board chairmen from 1933 to 1981.[2] A new round of interviews of past and present TVA professionals permitted me to develop seven portraits of leadership at different times in the agency's history. I began to understand that the effectiveness of leadership depended, in large part, on the reinforcement of personal skill by historical conditions congruent with that skill. Thus, David Lilienthal's rhetorical abilities were perfect for dramatizing the TVA idea in the context of the New Deal. By the same token, David Freeman's attempt to repeat Lilienthal's achievement was only partially successful, in part because the historical context was much less favorable to a highly innovative TVA.

These reflections led me to other work on "entrepreneurial" government leaders in which the combination of skill, task, and political environment was found to be crucial for substantive achievement. Again, variations in the relation of skill to the work to be done and the political context became the basis for my generalizations about the effective leadership of government organizations.[3] The analysis of variations among skill, task, and historical context had been the theme of my portraits of cycles of politics and policy in the American presidency. I had articulated the idea that in effective presidential leadership, talent is well matched to the historical tasks and the political climate.[4] Not all presidents should try to be heros, like Franklin Roosevelt. And it was a mistake to try to do so in unheroic times. My study of Jimmy Carter as president strengthened this belief.[5] As a result of this work, I developed an interest in returning to the study of TVA in order to explore relationships between organizational leadership and changing historical contexts.

A stroke of luck had occurred in 1981 when I had learned that the political scientist Herman Finer had done a study of TVA in 1937–38 that was never published. The Social Science Research Council (SSRC) had sponsored the study under its program to "capture and record" New Deal agencies. Finer, then at the London School of Economics and later at the University of Chicago, was given an office and a research assistant by TVA. The assistant was Herman Pritchett, who was writing his dissertation on TVA and later published it as a book.[6] Finer spent a year in Knoxville observing and doing interviews. He attended meetings of the TVA board. His manuscript proved to be very controversial, although there is no record in TVA files of the controversy.[7] Finer had sided in a polemical way with TVA's first chairman, Arthur E. Morgan, in Morgan's conflict with the other two directors, Harcourt A. Morgan and David E. Lilienthal. The SSRC had sent Finer's manuscript and interviews to the National Archives with the stipulation that no one was to read any of the material until all three members of the first board had died.[8] After David Lilienthal died in 1981, I inspected the Finer material, which included his manuscript, typed summaries of his many interviews, and interviews conducted by the Draper Committee, a three-man team sent by President Roosevelt to the valley in 1937 to find out what all the fighting was about on the TVA board.[9]

In January 1989 I embarked on the TVA project in earnest. I conducted more interviews with past and present TVA officials, and I mined a rich lode of documentation in the U.S. Archive at East Point, Georgia, where TVA papers up to 1959 are deposited. The papers of board members, other than the chairmen, through 1985 are also there. TVA mistakenly sent some papers from David Freeman's chairmanship years to East Point, which I was able to read. More contemporary papers are in the TVA Technical Library in Knoxville, and after a sparring match with TVA lawyers, I was able to see specific files that I requested, although a TVA official had to read whatever I copied in case the material was privileged.[10] A good many documents from Charles H. Dean's board, which were still in current TVA files, were also in David Freeman's papers at East Point through 1984 when he left the board.

Another rich source was the oral history interviews of TVA officials conducted by Charles Crawford, a historian at Memphis State University. These interviews cover the period of founding through the 1960s, and they provide the link between Finer's interviews and my interviews about the 1970s and '80s. However, my interviews reach across the entire span of TVA history, so there is considerable redundancy in the people interviewed and the themes covered. As a result, I have a continual stream of reporting about TVA by its leaders, the upper level of professionals from the founding in 1933 to 1990. In addition to interviews and documents, I have relied on published and unpublished scholarship and on journalistic studies and reports.

All of this material has been the raw data for my study. My method of interpretation is that of configurative reasoning. I look for patterns and support generalizations about them with evidence from documents, interviews, and any other useful source. Interpretation is inductive. I build up a portrait of an individual or a group from direct interviews, reports from others, and documents describing thinking and action. For example, in trying to understand the nine chairmen, I have used their own words, accounts of those who worked with them, and the paper record to make inferences about their goals and strategies of action. Such conclusions must also take account of the political context at any given time which presented problems the chairmen were trying to solve. By the same token, I sketch rolling portraits of parts of TVA, such as the power program, by showing how the programs kept a certain identify even as they changed over time. I also describe the changing relationship of TVA to its environment by drawing pictures of TVA actions in changing historical contexts. The research strategy that animates this book is therefore one of "biography," by which I mean portraiture of individuals, groups, and organizations across time. One must grasp the inner logic of the parts of TVA as well as the logic that has held the whole together and given it support from its environment. This research strategy is based on the assumption that the organization is not a machine in which the whole can be understood in terms of the parts, but rather an organism in which the whole and the parts have a dynamic relationship. One does not ask "How much of this part affects that part?" but "What does the whole look like as it moves and changes?"[11]

I have observed the spirit of that insight by deliberately amassing redundant evidence to support the propositions I develop so that different pieces of evidence will reinforce and complement the pictures of the organization across time that I draw. The mode of thought here is thus descriptive and inductive. There was no prior deductive framework of covering laws or hypotheses to be tested. There is a "theory," but it is initially immanent in the story as it unfolds, which is one of organizational success, stabilization, and failure. The truth of the story is plausible only if the evidence, in its many layered richness, is convincing.

My story is intended to be a theoretical one. My purpose is not only to write an interesting history of TVA, although I hope I have done that, but to understand why organizations fail by attempting to repeat the glories of the past in new form. One cannot test a new theory against the case study from which it is derived, so the merits of my theory about organizational failure will have to be tested against other similar historical stories. As you enjoy the story that follows, also look for the theory that guides it and judge the author accordingly.

Acknowledgments

MANY PEOPLE have helped along the way in the writing of this book. The National Endowment for the Humanities, the Alfred P. Sloan Foundation, the American Philosophical Society, the Vanderbilt University Research Council, and the Vanderbilt Institute for Public Policy Studies all provided funds for research travel and expenses. Gayle Peters, director of the National Archives, Southeast Region, and his staff were extremely helpful in my several visits to Atlanta. Gail Cox and Michael Patterson, public information officers at TVA, were efficient in getting me permission to copy material in the TVA archives in Knoxville. Ed Best of the TVA Technical Library was always resourceful in his help. Kalpana Chatterjee of the TVA record center assisted me greatly in finding materials. Michelle Fagan of the Mississippi Valley Historical Archive at Memphis State University introduced me to the oral histories of TVA employees and copied material for me. Christie Solomon was a most efficient research assistant, and the book could not have been completed at all without the wonderful work of Peter Carney, a secretary extraordinaire, of the Vanderbilt Political Science department. I also thank my friends John Stewart and Alan Pulsipher, both formerly of TVA, who were my mentors into the TVA labyrinth. The library of Missouri Western College was a most welcome home in the summer of 1991 when I began to write, and I am grateful for the courtesies of the library staff.

Sections of chapters 2 and 3 are drawn from my essay on David Lilienthal in *Leadership and Innovation: A Biographical Perspective on Entrepreneurs in Government*, edited by Jameson W. Doig and Erwin C. Hargrove (Baltimore: Johns Hopkins University Press, 1987), and I thank the Johns Hopkins University Press for permission to use that material. The entire book was originally one chapter in *TVA: Fifty Years of Grass-roots Bureaucracy*, edited by Erwin C. Hargrove and Paul K. Conkin (Urbana: University of Illinois Press, 1983). I wish to acknowledge the origins of this book.

I am grateful to the many people at TVA, past and present, as well as all those others who agreed to be interviewed for this study, often more than once. The book could not have been written without them. My friend and colleague Paul Conkin read the manuscript with great care and made many good suggestions, for which I thank him. Two anonymous reviewers for the Princeton University Press provided invaluable help.

Liz Pierson was a painstakingly thorough and yet delightful copy editor. And finally, my wife Julie was always there when I needed her.

This book surely has shortcomings, and they all belong to me.

Erwin C. Hargrove
Nashville, Tennessee
July 1993

Prisoners of Myth

CHAPTER 1

History and Theory

ORGANIZATIONS may fail in their missions when they seek to repeat glories of the past in changed conditions. Old missions may not match new problems. Political failure may also follow as new demands on the organization are frustrated. We usually think of such failures as occurring in rigid, hidebound organizations that are caught up in past habits and devoid of innovative leadership. But there is an interesting variation in the story. The organization may continue to be highly innovative but still fail. It will not simply cleave to old programs and missions but will actually become more inventive in those missions. This will be a failing attempt to capture past glory. The new, inventive missions will not win support because they are out of kilter with the changed environment. The very dynamism and inventiveness of the effort will have been the organization's undoing.

Such organizations may have had highly creative and dynamic beginnings. The organizational culture will carry stories of past heroism in which the organization is depicted as special and unique, having been created as a response to a bold historical challenge that only a heroic organization could meet. The memory of past greatness is the dynamic that drives the organization to seek new glory. It carries solutions seeking problems.

Of course, organizations do not act as such. They are led, at many levels and in many ways. Leadership provides the link between organizational history and the present. Leaders have the task of interpreting and articulating the organization's purposes to its own people and to constituencies in its environment. For the most part, organizational leaders see only dimly into possible futures and continually grope for ways to relate past, present, and future. They experiment as they act. Purposes emerge in action, and the sense of purpose, of how to enhance organizational missions, is often uncertain. For this very reason, leaders rely heavily on past examples for inspiration, even as they seek to adapt that spirit to new work. Past glories are invoked as the basis for new achievements. To abandon that spirit and the ideology that supports it is to face the world naked, without resources.

The history of the Tennessee Valley Authority reveals the drama of glory, renewal, and failure that we seek to understand. TVA has undergone three distinct periods in its historical development and is now in the early years of a fourth period. The first period was that of creation, from 1933 to 1945, in which TVA was organized, fought off legal challenges to its power program, and developed the missions of generating and selling hydroelectric power, flood control and navigation, farm demonstration programs and fertilizer development, and forestry and other strategies for developing natural resources and improving the economy of the Tennessee valley. The central TVA figure in those years was David Lilienthal, who as one of the three directors, organized the legal fight against the private utilities, created the embryo network of municipal and rural distributors of electric power, and sold the people of the valley on the uses of electricity, all in the name of a "grass roots democracy" in which TVA worked in cooperation with the governments and people of the valley. The ideology of action at the grass roots by a multipurpose public authority, which Lilienthal fashioned, grew out of TVA experience and became a resource for internal cohesion and sense of purpose as well as a justification for TVA autonomy within the federal government.

The second period, from 1945 to approximately 1970, saw the development of an imbalance among TVA programs as TVA became a large power company. The construction of coal-fired steam plants for generating electricity signaled that TVA had become the power company of the valley and the federal government, since half of TVA's power for industrial users in the postwar years went to the Atomic Energy Commission facilities in Oak Ridge, Tennessee, and Paducah, Kentucky. The demonstration of techniques for the use of fertilizer on home demonstration farms gradually receded in favor of a scientific effort to produce new fertilizers for the industry. Improvements for navigation and flood control on the Tennessee River were achieved. And there was more than a hint of uncertainty within TVA about how the mission of regional development, which was always conceived in multipurpose terms, was to be carried out by a power company. It was an article of faith, from the founding, that TVA had to be more than a power company if it were to be true to itself and its origins. The most important event in these years, aside from the decision to build steam plants, was congressional action in 1959 to permit TVA to finance its power program by the marketing of bonds. After that time, congressional oversight of TVA focused primarily on the low-budget programs funded by appropriations.

The third period, from roughly 1970 to 1988, was characterized by the search for new missions to keep TVA heroic and by the technological and political failure of those missions. TVA leaders were prisoners of myths about the organization that had developed through practice and had been celebrated by Lilienthal. But the leaders could not duplicate the technological and political successes of Lilienthal's time because a changed environment was not receptive to new forms of heroic action. In 1985 TVA's Office of Power, with board concurrence, shut down five nuclear reactors at two plants because it did not believe it could meet the Nuclear Regulatory Commission's impending regulations. This was also a problem in the other two plants then under construction, which has delayed their completion. These technical issues reflected an organizational pathology that TVA leadership did not detect until it was too late.

A fourth period began in 1988 when Marvin Runyon became chairman of the TVA board. A former automobile executive, he brought in a new management team and sought to infuse TVA with the goals and procedures of a private corporation: profit, cost control, service, and accountability for results. Runyon left in mid-1992 to become postmaster general of the United States, and his effort to refashion TVA culture has an uncertain future. But the discontinuity arising from organizational failure in 1985 created opportunities for a break with the past.

The conception of organizational leadership that I have employed is stated by Philip Selznick.[1] He defines the paramount task of leadership as the articulation of institutional purpose. An organization becomes an institution when its skeletal, mechanical form receives the flesh of purposes, norms, and habits. Leaders must infuse the organization with values beyond the technical tasks at hand if the institution is to thrive. Values guide technical work and give consistency to organizational actions, making debate about what to do and how to do it less necessary than in an organization in which there is uncertainty or conflict about purposes.

Leadership of this kind is, for Selznick, most important for organizations in times of uncertainty about their missions. The task of leadership is to clarify ambiguity and chart directions for the future. The chief resource that leaders fashion and then draw upon for this task is what Selznick calls an organizational "myth." Myths are beliefs about the purposes of the organization and the ways it should go about accomplishing them. Organizational myths are not falsehoods but aspirations of purpose and ideals for action. They are a reality insofar as they influence beliefs and actions in the organization and among its constituents. There is always a gap between myth and reality. Some institutions may use myths as propaganda for defense against external control, but a myth is more than a rationale. It is believed.

Selznick's study of TVA identified a core ideology with which TVA justified its structure and missions.[2] The ideology had three tenets:

1. TVA could make important decisions by itself in operational areas without control from Washington.

2. The people of the valley had to be active participants in TVA programs. "People" encompassed state and local governments as well as private groups.
3. TVA was to coordinate the work of federal, state, and local agencies in accomplishing missions shared by all.

These beliefs matched the organizational structure mandated by the TVA Act. In his message to Congress asking for creation of TVA, President Franklin Roosevelt described "a corporation clothed with the power of Government but possessed of the flexibility and initiative of a private enterprise."[3]

Implicit in the ideal was the assumption, as well as the fact, that the several purposes of TVA would be complementary. Damming the rivers for navigation and flood control also permitted developing hydroelectric sites. The manufacture of fertilizer, using waterpower, helped farmers through demonstration projects. The condition of the soil was affected by forest cover and, in turn, influenced water quality in the river. Engineering, agriculture, and forestry were complementary disciplines for carrying out TVA missions. Incidental tasks such as malaria control on TVA reservoirs, water recreation, or commercial use of the river were offshoots of the core enterprise.

Selznick's, study focused on TVA's agriculture programs. He showed that TVA's delegation of its assistance programs to farmers to the seven land-grant agricultural colleges of the valley states and to the county agent system did not really constitute grass roots democracy as defined by the myth. Instead, the agricultural programs were coopted by the colleges and county agents to serve the needs of those organizations. Selznick saw this cooptation as a political necessity if TVA was to have the support of the valley agricultural establishment. He also acknowledged that TVA was organized differently in other programs. For example, the power division kept strong controls over TVA electrical distributors.[4] In both forms of cooptation, language about the "grass roots" often substituted for thought. But the myth was extremely useful for the socialization of TVA employees, as a defense against outside control, and as a genuine guide to several of TVA operations.[5]

In this study I will explore the fit between myth and reality across TVA history. I will not examine the validity of Selznick's theory of cooptation in the TVA agricultural program because I accept it. I will build on Selznick's understanding of organizational leadership to explore the extent to which various TVA myths influenced the actions of TVA leaders. Such myths were a great resource for action in the early and even middle TVA years. But they have became an obstacle to organizational learning in recent years. TVA leaders have been prisoners of myth.

Selznick depicts one myth as the core of TVA ideology, the gospel of grass roots democracy. The conception of multiple purposes within one organization is consistent with the grass roots ideal. But other myths developed from TVA experience and became part of the core ideology, thus influencing the thinking and actions of TVA leaders. From the beginning TVA leaders claimed that they would be nonpartisan in staff appointments and free of political controls in decision making. The most often repeated story in the TVA mythology was about how TVA built the Douglas Dam in 1942 over the opposition of Tennessee senator Kenneth McKeller. TVA thus began its contribution to war production with the lesson that engineers must do what their expertise tells them is right rather than capitulate to politicians.[6]

The Douglas Dam story contains an implied warning against assaults on TVA autonomy and is thus linked to the core ideology. But it also celebrates professional engineering judgment over politics. There is a tension between the proclamation of such expertise and the grass roots ideal. TVA experts and constituents may disagree in a political sense, whether or not engineers wish to admit it. The post–World War II period brought a widening gap between expertise and the grass roots principle in TVA, especially in a power program in which centralized bureaucracy matched centralized technology. Of course, the mission of generating electricity for local distributors was represented as TVA cooperation with grass roots institutions, but the TVA power people set the terms of cooperation.

Electricity itself had a mythic character in early TVA history. Two practical maxims became almost religious tenets. The first was the assumption that the cheaper the cost to the consumer, whether residential or industrial, the greater the use of electricity. This proved to be true in the early years of the power program. The second tenet was that the supply of electricity should always precede the demand for it, otherwise economic development of the valley would falter. This may have been true for much of TVA history, but it proved to be disastrous when applied to ambitious plans for nuclear power.

More than one myth has been at work in TVA history, but the several strands of myth are closely related and often complementary even when in tension with each other. The grass roots ideal thrived, declined, and then revived in the 1970s and 1980s. Belief in professional excellence and autonomy was strong from the beginning and grew stronger as TVA became a giant power company. But the nuclear debacle of the 1980s shattered that belief. By the same token, different parts of the TVA bureaucracy were havens for different myths. The divisions of engineering, power, and fertilizer production took pride in their high professional standards. Staffs in the various nonpower programs, such as navigation, forestry, and economic development, kept the grass roots myth alive.

TVA leaders, particularly board members and general managers, attempted to incorporate the several mythic themes into their actions as well as their words. This was apparent in their continual attempts to keep the various nonpower programs alive in order to affirm TVA's multipurpose character. But one also sees how TVA leaders were captivated with the idea of an electric valley in which technology would produce a good life for all people. They assumed that TVA could do excellent work on a more massive scale than any other organization in the world. TVA engineers basked in the glow of countless visitors from third world countries who saw TVA as a model to emulate.

A study of the TVA leadership across time therefore requires an analysis of the complex tasks of articulating purposes and values, reconciling the tensions among values, and matching ideals to the invention, operation, and adaptation of programs. In this analysis I will build upon the insights of an "institutionalist" perspective within political science.[7] According to those who adhere to this persuasion, institutions are much more than aggregates of rational utility-seeking individuals. Institutions embody ideals, values, and norms, as well as cognitive styles, across time. Institutions have varying degrees of autonomy and are not necessarily always in harmony with the society they inhabit. Because institutions are the carriers of values, decision makers are inclined to follow earlier precedents in making new decisions. This may make institutions less "efficient" in response to historical change. The task of institutional leadership is to mediate between an institution and a changing environment. In an institutionalist approach, one engages in historical analysis of organizations in order to see if continuing decisions were influenced by past choices. Old patterns may reappear even after sharp breaks with the past. But new departures are also possible, and the capacity of institutional leaders to learn about their environments so as to create new precedents is crucial.

This study draws on the institutionalist perspective in an effort to understand how TVA leaders combined personal styles of leadership, organizational purposes, and demands from the political environment. The principal task of leadership was to bring these factors into harmony. The thesis of the book is that in the early TVA, David Lilienthal brilliantly matched TVA capacities to environmental demands. TVA leaders of the 1970s and 1980s, Aubrey J. Wagner and David Freeman, failed in their strenuous attempts to put new wine in old bottles. They could not recapture past glories, largely because the environment gave conflicting and discordant signals. Wagner and Freeman, both highly innovative, became prisoners of myth. The 1985 nuclear debacle and new leadership provided an opportunity to recast organizational culture and perhaps create a new myth.

CASE STUDIES AND THEORY

The history of an organization is like the unfolding plot in a novel. What were the principal characters trying to achieve and why? What did they believe and reject and what did they know and fail to see and why? The portrait must capture the characters in the plot as it enfolds in order to identify the prevailing uncertainties and avoid a post hoc imposition of total rationality on people who were, in fact, trying to understand what the best actions might be. Theda Skocpol suggests three ways in which historical case studies can contribute to social science theory.[8] A case can be used to test and illustrate the validity of a prior theoretical model. Thus Selznick's study of TVA was an application of theories of cooptation that he took to the Tennessee Valley with him. A second approach is to provide a meaningful historical interpretation of a phenomenon that illuminates contemporary problems. An analysis of the mistakes made in recent history by General Motors might help explain the difficulties of American automobile companies today. Of course, the sequences of cause and effect in such a study are a matter of interpretation without the benefit of comparison of the importance of key variables to other organizational histories. This is why Skocpol prefers the third approach, which is to discover causal regularities by comparing organizational histories.

This study of TVA initially takes the second approach, telling a story with implications for the present, but with the aspiration of developing propositions about causal regularities that can be the building blocks for theories of organizational success and failure. This second strategy, which Skocpol calls "interpretive historical sociology," focuses, in her words, upon "the culturally embedded intentions of individuals or group actors."[9] One looks at TVA as a public authority, created out of the progressive impulse in American government to separate politics from government and thus given a charter that grants great autonomy to the organization to conduct its business within a loose framework of accountability. The subject is relevant for questions of accountability of public bureaucracies to democracy at any time. I will explore such questions about TVA and American government because important normative issues are raised here. One limitation to the interpretive approach is that general knowledge about institutions is not likely to emerge from such studies which emphasize the unique characteristics of single institutions.[10] The application of abstract, theoretical models or the extraction of generalizations are in tension with the rich particularity of the story.

The primary justification for this study and those like it, for political science, is to develop hypotheses about organizations in action that will explain a number of similar and different organizational stories. Skocpol calls this "analytical historical sociology."[11] Historical cases are compared in an effort to "establish causal regularities." Such comparisons may properly focus on organizational similarities in order to test hypotheses about causal regularity or analyze organizational differences in order to understand the reasons for historical variations.[12] One must go beyond interpretation, as in the second approach, and attempt to develop theory that will apply to several cases. The strength of this approach as that it combines a historical analysis with a reach for theory through comparison. On the one hand, the search for causes is more analytic than in interpretive historical sociology and, on the other hand, the grounding in evidence is more particularistic than in the application of a model to a single case in which the evidence primarily illustrates the theory.[13]

This study is an example of interpretive historical sociology as a point of departure for building analytic historical theory. At the conclusion, theoretical insights from partial theories are applied to the story as a step toward theoretical development. But because it is a point of departure, the presentation of evidence in one case is different than would be the case in analytical historical sociology. One looks for organizational patterns over time in which the parts form more or less stable configurations among themselves. One recognizes the institution just as one recognizes the subject of an individual biography at any point during his or her life. The character of a part is strongly influenced by its relation to the whole.[14] Change takes place and is observed and documented, but the larger, more or less coherent configuration is maintained. I do test the validity and reliability of pieces of evidence, but I also ask you, the reader, to affirm the plausibility of the larger pattern, which is presented and illustrated through elaborate redundancy.[15] One sees persistence in continuity and can then identify the times and possible causes of changes from the pattern. Such studies rely on the richness of the evidence—interviews, primary documents, descriptions of actions taken. The institutional patterns depicted in such interpretive analysis are often incomplete. There will be unresolved puzzles and loose ends, just as there are in writing the biography of an individual. Explanations consist of joining otherwise puzzling items in insights that makes sense of the puzzles in terms of a thesis. This interpretive historical approach is carried over, to a great extent, as one reaches for the comparative analytic method, much as personality theory is developed from comparison of cases. Clinical psychology and cultural anthropology reveal analogical approaches as theorizing grows out of cases.[16] One jumps back and forth between theory and cases until the generalizations explain a good deal. Particular events in several settings can be seen as illustrations of shared "historical predicaments." We are not looking for statistical generalizations in such research but for incomplete, but plausible, patterns susceptible to general explanations.

But such explanations are likely to be very open-ended. The use of narrative in the presentation of such analysis permits a description of the dynamic processes at work in the interplay of institutions and social processes.[17]

ORGANIZATIONAL LIFE CYCLES

One must reject any deterministic theory of either the individual or the institutional life cycle in which developmental stages are posited quite independently of internal freedom or contextual developments. But different periods in the history of an organization may present different problems, each of which must be addressed in its own terms. Creating, stabilizing, maintaining, reforming, and reconstructing an organization are very different activities which occur at different points in organizational history.

The best analytic concept to use in trying to understand such dilemmas and choices is to look at organizations in terms of the idea of an organizational life cycle, not as a number of predetermined stages but as a delineation of the diverse challenges to the organization over time. If we take time, history, and context seriously, we must explore the organization's early history and its changing context and identify the sources and consequences of adaptation and sluggishness.[18] The important theoretical questions are: How do organizations develop "mechanisms that set them on particular life courses from which deviation is difficult? What are these mechanisms? How can we account for exceptions?"[19] Leadership would seem to play a crucial role, not only in creating organizations and in maintaining established routines and relationships with the environment but in articulating the need to adapt to a changing environment. One kind of leader might be more appropriate for one problem than for others.[20] And it is an open question whether leadership is more or less difficult at the time of the organization's founding or during crucial periods of adaptation.

Organizational learning is thus crucially important for survival and health. Key people must keep the windows open to the environment while at the same time encouraging critical self-evaluation by those within the house. In "enactive learning," understanding follows behavior. This is especially true in the early years of an organization's history when alternative conceptions of structure and missions are tested in the real world by trial and error experience.[21] Eventually the organization develops an identity based upon what has worked in the initial founding period. This is how Lilienthal and H. A. Morgan proceeded in the early TVA years. By implication, an organization that would thrive would keep a capacity for enactive learning throughout its life so that adaptation might continue. The alternative is "proactive learning," in which the organization is created and led by ideas about what it should do derived from past experience, organizational blueprints, accountability to superiors, and other forms of standardization.[22] No organization can do without proactive learning, but creativity and adaptation may require a high degree of enactive learning. We will see a struggle between Aubrey Wagner and David Freeman in which the former favored proactive learning and the latter was struggling to repeat Lilienthal's feat of feeling one's way to new missions by enactive learning.

Proactive organizations are in danger of succumbing to a dominant coalition's definition of a situation, and early successes, which created such a coalition, may hinder later learning. Enactive learning must be more widely distributed in an organization than proactive learning if the organization is to be effective, and there is no guarantee that agreement on effective adaptation strategies will emerge.[23] Such a fear is an impediment to learning itself.

A special problem with which this study of TVA is concerned is what Robert Miles calls "organizational persistence in the face of success."[24] In such instances organizations may have succeeded in accomplishing the missions set out at their founding. But they either continue to press the old missions or invent new ones. Routinization and conservatism are attacked by organizational leaders as they assert the need for the organization to continue to be dynamic. The strength of their leadership may, however, cause more problems than it resolves because there may be good reasons why the organization should no longer exist or be dynamic. A more conserving leadership may be more appropriate. Leaders may become prisoners of organizational myths in order to infuse the organization with new vitality.

Mary Douglas, the anthropologist, understands that "in a complex hierarchy, a combination of coercion, multiple cross-ties, convention and self-interest explain a lot but not everything about the commitment of individuals to the larger group."[25] She describes the "entrenching of an institution" as based on more than economic and social interests and as requiring a justification in "reason and nature," by which she means that the institutions we value are seen by us as appropriate and natural for the human condition as we understand it. Thus the U.S. Constitution is believed to reflect the nature of people, and its tenets are therefore grounded in what appears to be the nature of things. Of course, some institutions are largely matters of convenience, but their staying power is therefore limited.[26] Institutions, for Douglas, represent the desire to create public goods. The way we think and the values we seek come to us from our enculturation in institutions. "The most profound decisions about justice are not made by individuals as such, but by individuals thinking within and on behalf of institutions . . . it would appear that the rational choice philosophers fail to focus at the point at which rational choice is exercised. Choosing rationally . . . is not choosing intermittently among . . . private preferences, but choosing continually among social institutions."[27]

Self-knowledge is so elusive because the premises in our thinking are guided by institutions. Individuals seldom take moral stands on individual rational grounds but decide within implicit frameworks set by institutions. This is how collective goods are created as individual preferences are harmonized by a process of give and take within institutions.[28] For Douglas, "institutions create shadowed places in which nothing can be seen and no questions asked. . . . History emerges in an unintended shape as a result of practices directed to immediate, practical ends. To watch these practices establish collective principles that highlight some kinds of events and obscure others is to inspect the social order operating on individual minds."[29]

And as a result, "in most forms of society hidden sequences catch individuals in unforseen traps and hurl them down paths they never chose."[30] This insight, and others expressed by Douglas, about "how institutions think" will be seen in concrete form in this study of TVA. The animating myths that fueled TVA's early creativity were also its undoing in the end.

Several insights about the politics of institutions can be found in the body of institutionalist work that may provide clues to the history of TVA. Institutions receive legitimacy from shared values in their environment, but they also manipulate those values to increase their autonomy vis a vis the polity.[31] Organizational cultures may be so complex that subcultures develop as by-products of bureaucratization. Conflicts within the organization may thus be between subcultures, and there may be a struggle about which group defines the larger purposes of the organization.[32] Organizations may cope with this problem by decoupling the hierarchy and granting considerable autonomy to its parts. But this does not solve the problem of justifying the organization as a whole. The organization's formal structure symbolizes meaning and order in terms of the institution's purposes even when such ideas have limited influence over parts of the whole.[33] The effort to foster unity in such complex organizations, in terms of overriding purposes or central myths, may foster a situation in which the organization has not only problems looking for solutions but solutions, derived from past history and the justifying charter, looking for problems.[34] Dynamic, innovating organizational leadership may thus see its task as one of inventing new missions that will hold the organization together.

INSTITUTIONAL LEADERSHIP

Leaders bring their abilities to tasks of institutional leadership in historical contexts that favor or hinder skillful leadership to carry out those tasks. Skill varies in its capacity to discern opportunities for leadership, and high skill can make a difference even in unpropitious times. But for the most part, skill and an environment favorable to creative abilities reinforce each other. The environment does not produce the leaders necessary for given tasks, but it can help or hurt them greatly. Institutional leaders must also select tasks and responsibilities that permit them to play to their abilities. A mismatch between skill and task can be the undoing of an organizational leader who is unable to give the institution what it needs at a given time.[35]

I therefore conclude that the most important skill for a "political" leader is discernment of what it is necessary and possible to achieve in a given historical context. Of course, we only acknowledge discernment after the fact and even then cannot be sure what might have been possible. Some situations are beyond the power of leaders to change, and perhaps the leaders should withdraw, but few do because discernment is an imperfect faculty and we value the will to act more than we do the wisdom to realize the futility of action. Discernment must then be joined to imagination, for skillful leadership is an act of imagination. Effective leaders must be able to clarify the ambiguity and uncertainty in a historical situation by discernment and then use their imaginations to articulate and propose plausible actions that will reduce the uncertainty that many feel.[36] The conventional political skills of coalition building and conflict management are important, but without the political capital that comes from the effective use of discernment, these skills will have limited reach. Leadership is most empowered when skill, task, and context are congruent in a positive fashion.[37]

However, it does not necessarily follow that all institutional leadership must be heroic in the sense that the institution is mobilized by the leader to achieve great missions. In fact, the need for congruence among skill, task, and context follows from the importance of discernment of what the context requires and will permit. The founders of institutions may have heroic qualities which require imaginative vision and rhetorical faculties to establish the myths by which the institution will be legitimized. But successor leaders may need only to manage supportive coalitions to keep an equilibrium among the organization's missions and capacities and its external constituents. One may assume that highly imaginative, rhetorical leaders are then required to adapt the institution to a changing environment, but there is also an alternative possibility. Rather than seeking new missions, it might be wise for institutional leaders to find a niche in the environment that would permit their institution to continue to do what it has always done well but without heroics. Of course, such a seemingly passive strategy goes against the grain of the American belief that institutions must always be bigger and better.

No matter which style and strategy institutional leaders choose, depending upon the context they must all lead by managing events to teach followers the importance of what they are doing.[38] Thus, if one is convinced that retrenchment is more important than expansion because the latter is unrealistic, one must fasten on an organizational shortcoming to teach the importance of doing less but doing it well. Or failure may provide the opportunity to preach reform. Without the "superb politician" who can lead in this fashion, complex institutions would be immobilized.[39] A high order of political skill is necessary to play any of the leader roles. Institutional leaders must therefore be no one's captive and must rely upon their own inner resources as the basis of their strength, even as they listen and learn from others. To do otherwise is to risk becoming a pawn.[40]

Leadership through interpreting events is an exercise in the interpretation of culture.[41] It requires skills that are not in the armory of the leader who works within a rational choice framework who must generate individual rewards for others so they will comply with his or her policies. Things get done through exchanges and trades, and the inability to bargain is a fatal flaw. Such leaders do not appeal to the higher interest of their associates but to their private incentives. Collective goods emerge out of private bargains.[42] This is part but not all of the task of institutional leadership. The web of interests must be lifted by an appeal to purpose and meaning, or the institution will flounder. However, by the same token, highly imaginative leadership that can articulate shared values through insights that only the leader sees initially may be led astray by that leader's reliance upon his or her inner resources. This is unavoidable if leadership is to be creative.

It is therefore important to ask how organizations get their leaders. Are there mechanisms for estimating the kind of leadership that is needed for a given time and therefore trying to match skill, task, and context? If such processes are more sensitive to one aspect of leadership—for example, technical knowledge is valued, but political skill is slighted and the institution faces great political problems—then failure is likely to be the result. The discernment of historical requirements and possibilities must therefore be a faculty shared by those who would select the leaders who would exercise such discernment. This is not always the case, as the TVA story reveals.

PART I

The Founding Generation

CHAPTER 2

Visions of an Institution

THE TENNESSEE VALLEY AUTHORITY was the manifestation of many historical threads, not all of which were woven into one fabric.[1] Proposals for federal action to improve navigation on the Tennessee River were long-standing. The Army Corps of Engineers first recognized the potential number of dam sites on the river, not only for improving navigation but for generating hydroelectric power. However, the corps had no mandate for the latter purpose and would have had to integrate its plans with public or private utilities.

The open question from World War I until 1933 was how best to develop the hydroelectric capacities of the waterpower at Muscle Shoals, Alabama, on the Tennessee River. The National Defense Act of 1916 authorized the federal government to use waterpower at Muscle Shoals to produce nitrates for ammunition. This action had been preceded by efforts to exploit the site commercially for the development of power to manufacture fertilizer. However, the conservationist movement in politics, led by Theodore Roosevelt and Gifford Pinchot, the first head of the Forest Service, prevented private development of the site. Conservationists regarded such prime locations as properly in the public domain. President Woodrow Wilson responded to the 1916 act by authorizing the construction of a dam at Muscle Shoals which was named Wilson Dam when it was completed in 1925. Private companies were given contracts to produce nitrates.

There was no agreement about postwar uses of the dam. A Wilson administration bill devised a public Fixed Nitrogen Corporation which would manufacture and sell fertilizer to farmers and the fertilizer industry and also sell surplus hydroelectric power generated by the dam. Southern farmers and their representatives favored the bill, which passed the Senate, but opponents of public power were able to kill it. However, the corporate model of organization—the corporation was to be managed by a board—persisted in all subsequent plans. Designers were reaching for some combination of government and business.

During the next decade several efforts were made to combine hydropower and the capacities of Muscle Shoals to make nitrates for fertilizer. Henry Ford offered to lease the facilities and build a new Detroit in the south, but southern private utilities and public-power politicians combined to block Ford. Senator George W. Norris, a Nebraska Republican progressive and chairman of the Agriculture Committee, inherited the controversy by virtue of his post. A strong advocate for public power, he gradually inched his way in the 1920s toward a public-power and fertilizer corporation, supported by a coalition of conservationists like himself and southern agriculturalists. But vetoes by presidents Coolidge and Hoover of bills that had passed Congress produced stalemate.

The election of Franklin Roosevelt ensured that an entity would be created, but the new president's imagination ranged far beyond the workaday ideas of Norris and his southern allies. The Democratic party had committed itself to public ownership of the site for the development of waterpower. But FDR added long-standing interests in the conservation of natural resources, regional development, and the creation of urban settlements, all understood by him as means to a fresh start in developing an urban society that would harmonize the machine with nature. After a trip to the area with Senator Norris, FDR called for a Tennessee Valley Authority that would be an example for the nation in the union of agriculture, forestry, and flood prevention. Public hydroelectric power was justified in this vision as a means for the decentralization of industry in which the hydro capacity of the river would be the skeleton for areawide planning. TVA was to be a model for the nation in how to organize and plan for the use of natural resources. A three-member board was to manage a public corporation which would be, in FDR's words, "a corporation clothed with the power of government but possessed of the flexibility and initiative of a private enterprise."[2] FDR's language made very clear that he had something far grander in mind than a power and fertilizer corporation:

> It [TVA] should be charged with the broadest duty of planning for the proper use, conservation and development of the natural resources of the Tennessee River drainage basin, and its adjoining territory for the general social and economic welfare of the Nation. This authority should also be clothed with the necessary power to carry these plans into effect. Its duty should be the rehabilitation of the Muscle Shoals development and the coordination of it with a wider plan. Many hard lessons have taught us the human waste that results from lack of planning. Here and there a few wise cities and counties have looked ahead and planned. But our Nation has "just grown." It is time to extend planning to a wider field, in this instance comprehending in one great project many States directly concerned with the basis of one of our greatest rivers.
>
> This in a true sense is a return to the spirit and vision of the pioneer. If we are successful here we can march on, step by step, in a like development of other great natural territorial units within our borders.

FDR was in love with a vague idea of planning, but it was the idea he loved rather than the particulars. He envisioned forest, soil, and water linked in a complementary endeavor. He had been much influenced by city and regional planning ideas, and they were strengthened in his mind by the facts of depression and unemployment in the cities. He hoped that new cities and factories in the country would be created to which unemployed urban workers and their families would come for work and a better life. The Tennessee Valley Authority would be a machine-driven Arcadia in the countryside. FDR's personal knowledge of the poverty of the rural south, gained from long residence in Warm Springs, Georgia, reinforced his desire for a bold experiment.

The great forester and conservationist Gifford Pinchot was a link between the two Roosevelts, and he spoke for the union of conservationist ideas and progressive politics to which both presidents adhered.[3] An example of this union was the Appalachian Report of 1901 which called for comprehensive regional planning. FDR's uncle, Frederic Delano, who was later head of the National Resources Committee in his nephew's administration, gave a copy of the report to FDR.[4] There is no question that the young FDR had been influenced by the regional planning movement of the 1920s and had imbibed the ideas of Lewis Mumford and Patrick Geddes secondhand. In an informal talk to the Roundtable on Regional Planning at the University of Virginia, FDR, then governor of New York, spoke in a vague and general way of using planning as a means of modernizing the south.[5] His talk reflected, in the words of one observer, his "instinct to return industry directly to the soil."[6]

Clearly FDR's ideas about planning and regional development, as they applied to the nascent TVA, were too loose and general to be much of a guide to the first TVA directors.[7] FDR was a bold opportunist who took advantage of the historical moment to create an institution that would symbolize his aspirations for the south and the nation. But his language, and the ideas hovering behind it, had no perceptible effect on the politics of passage of the TVA Act.[8]

The act that finally emerged was the result of legislative bargaining with no reference to the president's language. It was a broader version of Norris's Muscle Shoals corporation with a few words about planning that were added on advice from two land-use planners of the Brookings Institution.[9]

A three-member board was to govern, with one member acting as chairman. The board was to carry out the purposes cited in the preamble to the act: improved navigation and flood control, reforestation, and reclamation of marginal land for agricultural and industrial development. The construction of dams and the sale of hydroelectric power were authorized as by-products of the central purposes which clearly fell within federal authority. There was also a provision for the manufacture, demonstration, and sale of fertilizers. Section 22 authorized the president to make surveys and general plans for the proper physical, economic, and social development of the river basin, and FDR subsequently assigned that responsibility to TVA by executive order. Section 23 directed the president to recommend appropriate legislation to maximize navigation, flood control, and the production of power consistent with the first two objectives. Such action was also to include the reclamation and use of marginal lands and was to seek the "economic and social well being of the people living in the said river basin."[10]

Sections 22 and 23 were not debated and were appendages that were not linked to the statutory powers of TVA to build dams, improve navigation and flood control, and make fertilizer. This is an important point for our story because the aspirations for coherent regional development that were expressed in sections 22 and 23 were not embedded in specific powers. There was no ready path in the act to the romanticism of regional planning. FDR's election made the creation of TVA possible, but his rhetoric may have contributed to future uncertainty about whether TVA was an organization to do specific things for the development of natural resources or an agency for comprehensive planning for regional development. In fact, TVA was a Rooseveltian device to create hope, for the south and the nation, that economic recovery and a better life were within reach. TVA was thus a child of the first New Deal and resembled the National Recovery Administration in the hope for cooperation, planning, and recovery. Specific questions about administrative mechanisms were left for later. These two acts were not unlike the Appalachian Regional Commission and the Office of Economic Opportunity a generation later. All four measures revealed the willingness of reforming presidents to leave questions of implementation for others. The presidency is a place for political and moral leadership, not administrative planning.

FDR's love for ad hoc improvisation was visible in the origins of TVA. The political artistry of coalition creation, in which opposites were often married, reflected not only his cast of mind but his style of leadership, in which continuing conflicts were brought to him for resolution. It was not long before his style was put to the test as the quarreling TVA directors appealed to him for a definitive definition of their work. However, FDR was content to let them struggle for a time until he could feel his way to a solution. He may even have shared their confusion and therefore have been unable to clarify it. The struggle between Arthur E. Morgan, TVA's first chairman, and his two colleagues, Harcourt A. Morgan and David E. Lilienthal, appealed to both the romantic and pragmatic sides of FDR. It was not until 1937 that he sided with Lilienthal and H. A. Morgan and did so as a practical politician, thus undercutting his more utopian hopes.

Nor did FDR help the first directors resolve the ambiguities in the act. There was no priority among the stated purposes. The only clear subordination of tasks was in regard to hydroelectric power which was to be presented as a by-product of dams built for navigation and flood control.

The only integrating principle was the carryover of older Army Corps of Engineers proposals for integrating control of the river throughout the watershed. TVA thus became a multipurpose organization without an explicit plan for integrating its several purposes. Congress did not discuss the administrative aspects of the new organization.[11] Congress is as inclined as presidents to neglect administrative and implementation questions. TVA was to produce hydroelectric power, but was it practical to subordinate that goal to navigation and flood control? Was the power to be sold to private utilities in the region, or was TVA to have its own distributors? If the policy were the latter, who would finance the creation of distributorships? Would TVA compete or cooperate with private utilities? The right to turn nitrates into fertilizer was clear, but how was TVA to make the benefits of fertilizer known to farmers? How were farmers to be assisted in developing "modern" agriculture techniques and by whom? Possible relations with the private fertilizer industry were left open. If TVA was to plan for the region, as sections 22 and 23 implied, for whom was it to plan and how? How was planning to mesh with state and local governments of the region? How were the several TVA missions to be ranked in the competition for federal appropriations? By what criteria was the flooding of reservoirs for dams to be reconciled with the reclaiming of land for farming? Was urban or rural electrification to be preferred? TVA's place in the federal firmament of competing agencies, especially in the Departments of Agriculture and Interior, was not clear.

FDR did not appear to consider such questions when he appointed the three board members. It was not clear whether his first choice for chairman was A. E. Morgan, but Morgan was a reasonable choice. He was a construction engineer of national reputation who had built a series of innovative earthen dams on the Ohio River, the Miami Conservancy Project. He was also an apostle of regional planning and of the creation of small communities as vehicles for virtuous civic life. FDR told Morgan that he had read his *Antioch Notes*, philosophical musings written when Morgan was president of Antioch College.[12] It is more likely that Mrs. Roosevelt read *Antioch Notes*. But Morgan's ideals and FDR's mood meshed in 1933, and the Ohio engineer came away convinced that he and the president both wanted TVA to be a model for ways to organize American life for the future.

FDR entrusted Morgan with the assignment of finding the other two directors, stipulating that one should be a southern agriculturalist and the other conversant with power and electricity. After sifting through names and rejecting some possibilities, Morgan presented two names to FDR. Harcourt A. Morgan, president of the University of Tennessee, was a sixty-five-year-old agriculturalist who had spent his career advising southern farmers how to improve their product. David E. Lilienthal was a thirty-three-year-old lawyer and a crusading member of the Wisconsin

Public Service Commission. FDR apparently wished to have Lilienthal appointed and may have ensured that he was interviewed.[13]

FDR made no effort to find out if the views of these three men were compatible. He never called them together to clarify his purposes for TVA. A. E. Morgan was convinced that he understood FDR's mind, and this misunderstanding on A. E.'s part was to cause havoc once the board went to work. Of course, TVA was not the only innovative New Deal agency without a blueprint for action. The entire New Deal was such an effort, so it was not reasonable to expect that the new president would devote time to implementing any agency designs. H. A. Morgan remembered years later how clean the slate was: "We got into TVA with no tradition. We didn't have a pattern. . . . Nobody had ever set up the idea of integration of natural resources, water, land, air and everything else, including human ability. The result was that there was nobody that could give us advice from the outside."[14]

A. E. Morgan on the one side, and H. A. Morgan and Lilienthal on the other, each believed that they were in tune with FDR's ideas about TVA. Raymond Moley, manager of FDR's "brains trust" in 1933, remembered that FDR tried to reconcile the irreconcilable in the TVA appointments.[15] Moley believed it typical of FDR that "when confronted with several objectives [he] embraced all of them."[16] But it is likely that FDR did not see the incipient conflict, and it seems even more probable that he had not thought through the implicit tension between the TVA of his romantic vision and the TVA that Congress had actually created.

The conflicts within the first board were inevitable given the differences in values and style among the directors. It was also predictable that A. E. Morgan would lose the fight because he lacked the ability to anchor the new organization in its political environment. Indeed, he would have regarded such an effort as a form of prostitution. And yet his stamp is all over TVA even today.

A. E. Morgan

A. E. Morgan once wrote of himself that "since boyhood I have had the prophetic urge."[17] He belonged to a generation of "ministers of reform."[18] Like Charles Beard, Jane Addams, John Dewey, and other midwesterners of his generation, A. E. converted the evangelical piety of his family origins into a secular passion to make the world over. A period of uncertainty and searching in young adulthood, in which he rejected formal religious ties, was followed by a sense of affirmation and purpose in a secular calling.

A. E.'s father was a Wisconsin land surveyor with a scientific outlook who left his church and enjoyed liquor. His mother was a Minnesota

Baptist who disapproved of her husband's drinking and preached moral perfectionism to young Arthur. His biographer records that "he drove himself unmercifully to please her."[19] His youthful diaries reveal a constant effort at self-discipline and moral improvement.[20] He worried continually about his health, and an analysis of his diaries suggests that he used illness to excuse himself from his mother's demands for performance. Indeed, for the rest of his life he would plead sickness whenever he ran into trouble or conflict.[21] The parent's marriage was not happy. A. E. was committed to the scientific outlook of his father, which included the search for truth, and to the piety of his mother, and he began his adult life with the effort to bring the two together in himself. He rejected conventional religion in favor of a vague transcendentalism that was to take the form of moral purity. A. E. held himself and others to very high moral standards, which he knew by intuition. The combination of religion and science produced a perfectionism in which scientific method was guided by moral certainties.[22]

A. E. went to college briefly but was largely self-taught, even in the fields of surveying and engineering which he learned from his father. Contemporaries often commented that he lacked the sense of intellectual give-and-take that might have been learned in a university. His ideas were anchored in his own search for identity, particularly in the effort to combine science and moral reform.[23]

He sought reform but had only disdain for politicians who he felt cared for only short-term, selfish benefits. He wished government to have its eye on the long view. In his view, social reform was dependent upon the moral transformation of individuals.[24] He favored cooperation based on moral agreement rather than conflict. People should be able to reason together and come to agreement on the good of the whole.[25] A. E. relied on his intuition to tell him an action was consistent with the whole and fashioned for the long run. People who disagreed with him were often castigated for not reasoning in good faith.[26] He was not a democrat but believed in enlightened leadership which would point the way for others to follow.[27]

A. E.'s professional life before he came to TVA embodied these values. His biographer saw them as the basis for his inventiveness: "he had an institutionalized way of fighting custom, bureaucracy and narrow thinking. He had talent for seeing the whole of a project and an almost uncanny intuition about interactions and effects."[28] His early work in land reclamation made him critical of the patchwork of county established drainage laws in Minnesota. He came to believe that rivers must be treated as holistic units.[29] His most important project was in the 1920s when his engineering firm designed and built a series of earthen dams on the Ohio River, known as the Ohio Conservancy Project. Several precedents for TVA were set there: innovative dam design, enlightened labor policy, vocational and general educational programs for construction workers, and an absence of political patronage.[30] In 1921 he became president of Antioch College in Yellow Springs, Ohio. A. E. transformed the failing school into a model for work/study programs in which students took time off from academic studies to work at real jobs. He saw the model as a device for transforming American culture by combining learning and work.[31] He was to see TVA as a model for the nation on how to organize society. But the same tragic denouement was acted out at both Antioch and TVA. A. E. got ahead of his followers, reproached them for failing to live up to his ideas, and eventually saw opposition to him as unprincipled.[32] His efforts to dictate moral standards to Antioch students and faculty were resisted, but at the same time his goals for Antioch were somewhat vague. He wished goals to be set by consensus but could not bargain or resolve disagreement.[33] The same thing happened at TVA. He hoped for agreement with his fellow directors but interpreted their disagreement as opposition. And yet he never presented a clear blueprint of his goals. His vagueness invited disagreement because it seemed unrealistic to others. He did not wish to impose his ideas but to engage others in the search for the ideal. Therefore he often simply advanced first thoughts as a basis for discussion. But when others criticized these ideas without engaging him in dialogue, he assumed they had bad motives. But once he had taken a position, he was immovable because of his belief that reason and intuition had led him to the right decision.[34]

A. E. Morgan acted out on a public stage his inner need to perfect himself. Political scientist Herman Finer, who studied him closely and sympathetically at TVA, understood this: "The key to Arthur Morgan's character is an enormous dissatisfaction with himself, combined with the tenacious austere purpose of self-improvement."[35] A. E.'s search for self-improvement was projected onto a life-long search for the good society which he would be instrumental in creating. He never gave up. In his nineties he was traveling to Africa, with a nurse in attendance, to oversee development projects.[36] We can see how A. E. Morgan appeared to FDR to be a good agent for the realization in TVA of FDR's belief in regional planning, small communities, and return to the land.[37] There was a sympathy between them.

HARCOURT A. MORGAN

Harcourt A. Morgan cut his professional eyeteeth in Louisiana helping farmers fight the boll weevil. His years as dean of agriculture at the University of Tennessee had been spent persuading farmers that row crops, that were planted every year, like corn and cotton, damaged the soil. He advocated pasture and stock for southern farmers. His experience had convinced him that deliberate change could only be successfully implemented by farmers themselves. This was the basis for his belief in implementing programs at the grass roots level through self-help. Neil Bass, H. A.'s assistant at TVA, remembered:

> He was a natural leader. People followed him because they respected his vision for the valley, ability and honesty. He was the most popular man in the region. It was due to H. A. that people accepted TVA. People don't like outsiders telling them what to do, So H. A. formulated the idea of letting the people decide. For example, he got a Nashvillian, the president of Rotary International Bill Manier, to organize and lead the Tennessee Valley Association to promote TVA programs. They served their purpose and went out of existence in four or five years. That was typical of H. A.'s leadership. He persuaded Bill that he should lead the effort.[38]

As president of the University of Tennessee, H. A. Morgan had not been particularly progressive. He watched the state pass a law forbidding the teaching of evolution without saying a word.[39] Nor did he fight for higher faculty salaries. He was good at cultivating the politicians who supplied the appropriations.[40] But H. A. did have a public philosophy, to which he gave the name "a common mooring." The idea was simple. People and nature were dependent on each other, and the parts of nature were interdependent. Water and land were linked negatively in soil erosion and positively in care for the soil. Agriculture and industry should be balanced so that industrial growth did not tip the ecological balance against self-renewing nature.[41]

But H. A. Morgan was not articulate. He would often give chalk talks illustrating how everything was related to everything else, but this approach often confused others as much as it enlightened them. His papers were filled with such diagrams. For this reason his TVA colleagues saw him less as an administrator than a preacher.[42] An associate remembered that H. A. "was forever trying to think out ways of stating his philosophy and how TVA's programs could fit into it."[43] The concept of the common mooring and the grass roots were important for H. A.'s leadership of the natural-resource programs at TVA. He was responsible for the TVA practice and philosophy of working through state and local agencies whenever possible. The national government was too remote, but TVA could work in the area between national and state and local governments to try to integrate all government functions in a given area.[44] Lilienthal was to learn and borrow this philosophy in his articulation of "democracy at the grass roots." Both A. E. and H. A. were critical of unrestrained individualism which despoiled nature. In this sense H. A.'s belief in the common mooring made him cautious about industrial growth in the valley and its possible adverse affects on water and land. The main difference between the two men was that H. A. thought that ideals could only be achieved through the work of citizens themselves, and A. E. thought that ordinary people required moral and intellectual leadership. John Ferris, an early TVA staff member who worked closely with all three directors, remembered that H. A. and Lilienthal had the idea of giving people the tools with which to improve their lives, whereas A. E. had the idea of the elite inspiring the mass. Ferris felt that A. E. did not understand that the American people did not think that way. In Ferris's view, it was because of A. E. that TVA survived in the first years.[45]

David E. Lilienthal

David Lilienthal's leadership style emphasized rhetoric, in speech and writing, as the chief means of winning support and creating cohesion within the organizations he led. At several stages of his career he wrote books popularizing the issues and principles he had articulated in that particular mission. The book on TVA was the first example. He also kept a journal from his TVA years through the rest of his life until he died in 1981. It was his way of giving significance to his life and career.[46] He was very inventive and creative and wanted the world to know of his uniqueness. When he was eighty, he recalled his inventiveness at TVA as an expression "of a creative impulse, wanting to do something that had not been done before."[47]

When a professor of Lilienthal's at DePauw University offered to make any of his students a great man or woman, Lilienthal challenged him to "try it on me."[48] He was consciously grooming himself to be a leader. After delivering a well-received talk at a DePauw chapel assembly, he recorded: "I had a taste this morning of what some day may be my customary diet."[49] He had thrown himself into the preparation of the talk with great intensity, working on it for months. The preparation of speeches was to receive the same close attention throughout his career. He became a college debater and won many competitions.

He also went out for football at DePauw and recorded his love of "the fighting spirit."[50] But he especially liked boxing. Many years later he told an interviewer that he would not have put himself in so many controversial positions in his career if he had not been a combative person. But he did not regard boxing as an expression of combativeness for its own sake: "I think I considered competence at defending yourself as a means of preserving your personal independence. I learned that from my father. 'Be your own man' he used to say."

Lilienthal went on to add that "there's something missing when you don't have a McKellar laying it on the line any more. The moral equivalent of that for me is taking on challenges, different kinds of McKellars."[51] Ambition, rhetorical skill, and combativeness all served a developing idealism, derived in part from the New Freedom of Woodrow

Wilson, which Lilienthal carried into the conservatism of the 1920s. By 1919 Lilienthal knew he wished to be a lawyer in order to study the industrial conditions of labor, become an expert, and write on labor problems. He entered the Harvard Law School in 1920. He had only been there a few months when he confided to his diary the wish that he "could get such a man as [Louis B.] Brandeis or [Frank P.] Walsh interested in me and my ambitions so that I could get some bit of personal guidance and encouragement from them."[52] And indeed, in 1921 Lilienthal wrote Walsh, a prominent industrial-relations attorney, about his ambitions, which led to an extensive correspondence between them.[53] He also met Justice Brandeis, through Professor Felix Frankfurter of Harvard, after graduating from law school. For the rest of his life, Lilienthal was to cultivate important people. It became a vital resource for his leadership because he had friends who knew of his work and could give him advice, help him build alliances, and speak out publicly on behalf of his issues. At TVA, he was to cultivate both Senator Norris and President Roosevelt this way. This was not simply currying favor. One of Lilienthals's close TVA associates caught it: "His obvious qualities of mind impressed the people with whom he dealt. . . . Look at his career as combining idealism and opportunism. He impressed people of great discrimination—Brandeis, Frankfurter, FDR, Acheson. He could take a difficult task and carry it out."[54]

After graduating from Harvard in 1923, Lilienthal went to work for Chicago lawyer Donald Richberg who was general counsel for the national railroad unions. Frankfurter and Walsh had recommended Lilienthal to Richberg.[55] In addition to practicing law, he wrote articles for highbrow magazines such as *The New Republic* and the *American Review*. He eventually formed his own law firm in Chicago, specializing in public-utility law. As special counsel to the city of Chicago, he helped the city win a refund of $20 million for telephone company customers. His law-review articles on utility issues and his founding editorship of a national information service on utility regulation complemented his national recognition as a utility attorney.[56]

In 1931 the new governor of Wisconsin, Philip F. LaFollete, appointed Lilienthal to the state Public Service Commission. Lilienthal was an aggressive member of the commission who attracted national attention by his advocacy of utility regulation. One student of regulation wrote that the young commissioner's accomplishment "must be offset to a degree by the friction he created in the relations between the utilities and the Commission . . . such an attitude is not completely in the negotional procedure which characterizes much of the regulatory process."[57] Lilienthal's own belief was that too many public-service commissions were captives of the utilities they regulated.[58]

He worked with concentration and intensity all his career, as the few entries from his journal in the Wisconsin years reveal. One admitted, "My tendency to overwork and get all intense about phases of my work must be a nuisance" to his wife.[59] Another time: "It is the driving of others and yourself that seems to take the kink out of you."[60]

Lilienthal put heavy pressure on himself and others to get work done, and the intensity of his efforts periodically brought him to the point of exhaustion, so that he required regular rest and vacations, a habit he continued all his life.

One can see the elements of a mature leadership style in the young Lilienthal. He was ambitious for achievement and recognition both for himself and for reform. His administrative style involved intensive homework, the combative pressing of advantages and opportunities, and the cultivation of patrons and alliances. He had learned to use rhetoric to good effect in Wisconsin. His appointment to the TVA board gave him the opportunity to develop fully and to express his leadership style as a director of the most innovative creation of the New Deal.

A. E. Morgan chose Lilienthal after a brief meeting in Chicago. A. E. had received a note from an associate who reported that, "his shortcomings are reported to be personal ambition and publicity seeking."[61] But evidently the interview was smooth. However, if the two men had really known each other, or if FDR had know much about either, the combination might have been avoided on psychological, if not ideological, grounds. Both A. E. and Lilienthal were driven men who would seek to make TVA a projection of themselves, and it was psychologically inevitable that they would clash even if there had been substantive agreement, which was anything but the case. Protagonists in a conflictual situation may generate their opposite by projecting their hatreds onto an opponent. The emotional quality of the exchange between A. E. and Lilienthal suggests that something of that kind may have occurred.

But one must separate personal antagonisms from conflicting philosophies of what TVA should be. In this case personality and principle reinforced each other. I will describe the competing conceptions of TVA and then depict the drama of the conflict between the two men, H. A. Morgan siding with Lilienthal, with the final act being A. E. Morgan's dismissal from the board by FDR.

CONCEPTIONS OF TVA

A. E. Morgan wanted TVA to be a laboratory for the nation for the organization and conduct of social life. TVA was to carry out social and economic demonstrations and experiments that would be of general value. The scope of TVA operations was thus of less importance to A. E. than their quality. A TVA engineer who worked with him remembered that "his conception was artistic and intellectual. TVA would act like a limited scope model that would be so perfect that the utilities would copy it. No need for large scope. One demonstration farm and one democratic cooperative and one TVA municipal power company would be enough. The yardstick would exemplify the right way of doing things."[62]

In an August 1933 nationwide radio talk on NBC, A. E. spoke of his hopes:

[T]he Tennessee Valley Authority is established in an effort to bring about an orderly wholesome development of economic and social life.

It will undertake to secure a balance between agriculture and industry by promoting the small scale endeavor, to balance "foreign" trade by developing industries peculiar to the region. Some of these will be large-scale mass production projects based on the presence of mineral resources and cheap power. Others should be in the nature of . . . fine textiles, fine furniture or scientific instruments, which can be produced in small communities by intelligent craftsmanship and organization.[63]

These words suggest an implicit TVA effort to plan for the most productive use of valley resources in some coherent way. It was anything but a conception of a free market guided solely by profit. A. E. told Herman Finer in 1937 of his hope that ideal, small communities would be built by TVA, of which Norris, Tennessee, had been the first: "All can be brought into relation with each other, so that the community as a whole will function. . . . It is the kind of thing I have been wanting to do all my life."[64]

Finer commented to himself that for all three directors TVA had "become the progressive realization of their larger selves. Is it not surprising that the thing went to their heads, now that they have the levers, money and power, to act?"[65] A. E. never succeeded in articulating a coherent picture of a TVA program of regional development. He desired several kinds of planning—small communities, dam construction with thought for the effect on the countryside and human settlement, education, agriculture, forestry, navigation—but the overall shape of the effort was never expressed.[66] This was perhaps to be expected because the idea of planning, which permeated progressive thinking and New Deal rhetoric, was vague. Planning was a symbol to use against the failure of markets.[67]

A. E.'s response to this conclusion was that it would be a mistake to plan definitively. A moral community does not develop from a blueprint but from insights derived from collective experience. TVA was an experimental body which would evolve. A. E. advocated deliberate trial and error, and his pragmatism was scientific. One learned from experience in systematic ways. It was anything but ad hocery. His seeming authoritarianism often took the form of insistence on right procedure, which he saw as moral, more than of demand for any particular ideas. Any departure from a moral and scientific conception must be resisted. He told Finer that "wherever I worked, I made up my mind that I was going to be the person who was the master of policy. I am not going to make vital concessions of moral principle." Finer added that "in a moment of mutual confession he explained to me that his ambition was 'to banish caprice from human affairs.' "[68]

A. E.'s speeches called for social and economic planning against waste, duplication of effort, selfishness, and taking a short-sighted view of social development. Reform must come by reason and vision, not fiat. He told Finer that he regarded himself as a pioneer or inventor, which required the readiness to break loose from known patterns.[69] For this reason A. E. was reluctant to establish a clear and definite organizational form for TVA, or any new organization. Premature stabilization might inhibit creativity.[70] It was better to appoint good people and let them create because administrative form should grow out of action. A. E. had never worked in a conventional organization but had always built his own.[71] He believed that a science of administration would block the creative leader.[72] He was therefore suspicious of public administration orthodoxy of the kind advocated by Louis Brownlow of the Public Administration Clearing House in Chicago. The dominant model of the day linked hierarchy and accountability. A. E. disliked hierarchy and wanted a free flow of views within an organization.[73] His resistance to hierarchy was seen in his policy, as chief construction engineer, of encouraging engineers to revise the plans for dams at the site in response to newly perceived conditions. Such discretion became a part of TVA culture.[74] At the same time, A. E. directed that land planners, not engineers, draw the "taking line" for Norris Dam reservoir. This was a new principle which advanced social criteria for dam construction.[75]

A. E. Morgan was not simply a technocrat. Professionalism was to be harnessed to larger goals. TVA in subsequent years, at its best, institutionalized A. E.'s ideas in this respect. Indeed, Lilienthal's paean to grassroots democracy praised the high amount of professional cross-fertilization and dialogue throughout the TVA organization, and much of that spirit could be attributed to A. E. Morgan.

It was A. E.'s habit to throw out untested ideas as a basis for discussion. But discussion seldom followed because the ideas themselves often seemed peculiar to others. A. E. was very disappointed by the failure of H. A. and Lilienthal to pick up the dialogue, for he found their thinking to be utterly conventional without any contribution to the remaking of American society. They wanted to accept society as it was in its basic outline and just make it work better.

A. E. was not happy with H. A.'s plan to delegate the program of technical assistance to farmers to the land-grant agricultural colleges and the county agent system, preferring to find more creative conduits such as

Peabody College for Teachers in Nashville.[76] But A. E. was not a confrontationist who wished to challenge established institutions. For example, he hoped to get along peacefully with private utilities in the region by demarcating a TVA service area for the sale of electric power in which superior methods would be demonstrated without open conflict with private utilities. TVA was to be a model which others would copy. For A. E., excellent professionalism was to be joined to imaginative approaches to resource development. TVA was to be a collection of experiments and demonstrations.[77] As the first head of TVA regional planning put it:

> I will say this for A. E. Morgan, there was hardly any program that we developed that he didn't look around to see if he could make a contribution to it. And that wasn't true of the others. We [regional planning] would have to find out about the other programs, particularly the agricultural program. They wanted no part of any plans at all. They had their paths determined. The county agents were working with them. They were working on programs the way they always did.[78]

In later years, when TVA leaders were to search for new experiments and missions, it was to A. E.'s restlessness and idealism that they looked. This was one of A. E.'s legacies to TVA organizational culture. Whether it was a practical restlessness was another matter. A. E. could be very peculiar at times. John Ferris remembered an evening in which A. E., after a day of conflict with H. A. over the organization of the agricultural program, introduced a talk by Vice-president Henry Wallace. During the talk A. E. appeared to be deep in thought, but immediately afterward he told Ferris, "There has never been a chair with three legs. . . . we ought to develop a chair with three legs for manufacture in the valley." Ferris added, "There is something odd about a state of mind that could produce results like that."[79]

H. A. Morgan

Toward the end of H. A.'s life, his daughter recorded and transcribed informal conversations with him about TVA in which it was apparent that he, too, had a holistic vision of what TVA should have been. His disappointment is clear if somewhat cloudy:

> I thought we did wrong when we didn't utilize some of the income from the power to build the land; to save the water; to increase the power. . . . if you would say here, we are going to determine what is the value of this cover of grass, cover of winter legume, etc. . . . How much, what returns do we get out of that in power? Well, of course engineers, with all their multiplying precision, they just said that there's no, you can't get any data, you can't do anything with that.[80]

H. A. always resisted the separateness of the TVA power program and thought that power-revenue money should help support other programs. He concluded: "I gave up a long time ago that the valley was going to be an integrated agency by the staff."[81]

The prose is opaque, but the idea is clear. The health of the power program depended on the health of land and water. H. A. thought that TVA had failed to explain this to the people of the valley, who saw only the power aspect of TVA. Nature's contribution had not been announced. It was all paraded as human achievement, but "I don't feel that you can carry on the process of democracy without a full understanding of nature's contribution."[82]

H. A. was even critical of his close ally Lilienthal: "They just grab nature in order to make their own personal promotions. . . . Dave was as bad in that as anybody, grand as he is."[83] He complained that Lilienthal's book contained no conception of the common mooring, but "simply looked at the administrative . . . there was nothing to it except that it was a fine, exciting sort of topic . . . he didn't get what I was after at all. But he got what I couldn't get."[84]

Notice the implied compliment to Lilienthal's political talents. H. A. had to side with Lilienthal because H. A. thought A.E. was a paternalist and not a democrat. H. A. taught Lilienthal about grass roots democracy, but he seems to have feared that the technology of power would undermine that concept. H. A. told Finer that he would regularly tell Lilienthal that he would oppose more development of electricity for industry because it would "ruin and wash away the earth containing phosphates." No matter how much power could be sold, electricity must be used as a productive factor, not just for the consumption of appliances.[85]

H. A.'s primary contribution to TVA was the creation of administrative forms for grass roots democracy. The best-known example was delegation of the agricultural program to the agricultural colleges. The deans of the colleges were worried that TVA would develop its own services to farmers and that their programs would fall by the wayside. H. A. thought that the colleges had "mediocre ideas and were not at all partial to Roosevelt and the New Deal" and "that was a handicap, but we have always felt that these barriers would eventually be of great value to us. . . . We had to set a pattern then in spite of these things . . . so that the program had to evolve step-by-step through experience."[86]

TVA had to work though the institutions that had ties with the people of the valley, or else its programs would not be accepted.[87] H. A. applied this principle to all TVA nonpower programs. On October 3, 1933, he sent a memo to his fellow directors which was one of the most important documents in TVA history. H. A. pointed out that TVA had two sets of functions, the statutory authority to build dams, etc., and the authorization, under section 22 of the TVA Act, to make surveys and plans for the development of the valley. TVA could act on its own for the first tasks, but the second should always be carried out in cooperation with state and local governments. Surveys and plans could only be implemented by local governments which should therefore be in on their preparation. This memo focused only on plans and surveys, but H. A. applied it to all of TVA's nonpower programs, including forestry, public health, education, and economic development. As a result, TVA developed the practice of trying whenever possible to work through state and local agencies for this range of programs.

David Lilienthal

David Lilienthal's chief contribution to TVA in the first decade was to develop a system for the distribution and sale of electric power. He fostered the creation of publicly-owned distributorships to which TVA sold power. He fought the challenge of the private utilities to this policy in the courts and won. And he sold the people of the valley on the uses of electricity. He was a man of action and less of a theorist than either of the Morgans. He was above all a realist. He did not share A. E.'s faith that the utilities would permit TVA to exist within its own sphere. Therefore he opposed a demarcated service area for power at the outset. TVA should build its programs and then settle on an area, working from strength. He did not believe in TVA planning for the people of the valley. The task was to give people the instruments with which they could act to improve their lives as they wished. He had no desire to refashion American society beyond the hope of greater abundance for all. Lilienthal accepted H. A.'s ideal of the common mooring but, according to John Ferris, in a realistic fashion:

> H. A. Morgan always had the idea that business and industry . . . had never really found their role. They had never properly related their operations to the fundamental ecological realities. . . . Dave Lilienthal realized that . . . but he felt that realities were such that industries were going to have to go on exploiting resources, the way they had done . . . for quite a while before we came in America to a situation in which the role of industry was better adapted to the limitations of resources.[88]

Barrett Shelton, longtime editor of the Decatur, Alabama, *Daily*, described Lilienthal's first meeting with Decatur community leaders to discuss what could be done to arrest the decline of Decatur's economy:

> Into this dismal, perplexed economic setting one late mid-winter afternoon came David Lilienthal. . . . We were frankly hostile to him, for he represented to us another way of thought and another way of life. And our conversation might be summarized in this fashion, "All right you're here. You were not

invited but you're here. You are in command. Now what are you going to do?"
Dave leaned his chair back against the wall and a twinkle of a smile came into
his eyes and he said, "I'm not going to do anything. You're going to do it." . . .
He went on to say that TVA would provide the tools of opportunity: flood
control, malaria control, navigation on the river, low cost power, test demonstration farming to show how our soil could be returned to fertility. . . . He told
us the river would no longer defeat man but would become the servant of man.
"What you do with these tools," he said, "is up to you." Now that's where we
began.[89]

Certainly Lilienthal thought that A. E.'s utopianism was damaging to
TVA. In a talk to TVA Knoxville employees in 1936, Lilienthal asserted
that there was "no turning back from the machine" to a simpler romantic
time and handicraft economy. "I am against basketweaving and all that
it implies. . . . We cannot prepare for the second coming of Daniel
Boone."[90] This was a clear slap at A. E. Morgan. Lilienthal went on to
praise the balance of centralization of the generation of power by TVA
and the decentralization of its distribution through locally owned distributors and concluded:

I suppose it is clear enough that I have no confidence in progress that comes
from plans concocted by supermen and imposed upon the rest of the community for its own good. . . . I don't have much faith in uplift. I believe deeply in
the notion of progress . . . I have great confidence in the general good sense of
the average man and woman. I believe deeply in giving people freedom to make
their own choice.[91]

Lilienthal's realistic philosophy was most evident in his actions, and
therefore, having sketched the worldviews of these three men, I turn to
their creation of TVA as an institution.

THE STRUGGLE FOR CONTROL

The first meeting of the TVA board took place on July 16, 1933, in a
Washington, D.C., hotel room. Lilienthal recorded his impressions of the
meeting:

Dr. Arthur Morgan had on his lap a great stack of letters and perhaps memo-
randa, but mostly correspondence directed to him. . . . Most of these letters
inquired about employment opportunities, or key specific matters, one completely unrelated to the other. After several hours of this, of going through this
stack of disparate and unrelated subjects . . . I caught Dr. Harcourt Morgan's
eye and by common consent we got up. . . . We went over to one of the great
tall windows in the Willard Hotel and had what was probably a decisive conversation of a very few words but with a great deal of meaning. . . .

Harcourt Morgan was completely caught off base with this way of beginning a big enterprise, without . . . any proposals for organization, without any ideas about staffing or where we go from here, or where we have our offices, or who our general manager should be, as I was. . . . Harcourt Morgan . . . said in effect, "What do you make of this fellow? We can't go on like this."[92]

Lilienthal and H. A. respected A. E.'s reputation as an engineer, but they both had been warned by Antioch trustees that he was a terrible administrator. He was said to be full of idealism but had driven people at Antioch "half-crazy" by rushing in all directions at once without any unifying theme.[93] By July 30 H. A. and Lilienthal had moved to Knoxville, and A. E. Morgan began a board meeting that day with an outline of what he thought TVA should do. The first task was to begin to build the Cove Creek (later Norris) Dam and build transmission lines from Cove Creek to Muscle Shoals. The fertilizer operation at Muscle Shoals should be developed. TVA should apply to the president for authority to develop all the dam sites outlined in the Army Corps of Engineers report on the river system. These decisions were not controversial.

The second task was to develop plans for disposing of electric power and to provide technical assistance to farmers. A. E. recommended that TVA buy up the private power companies in the area of the Tennessee River drainage basin so that the authority would have a clear field to operate. It was agreed that the president and Senator Norris would be consulted on this question. H. A. Morgan was asked to present plans for an agricultural program, and A. E.'s memo suggested that "we do those things not being done by other agencies, and that we not see agriculture as an isolated activity, but as one phase of a designed social and economic order."

A third category encompassed social and economic planning, although the projects were unrelated. A plan for the social and economic work of TVA had to be developed. A training program for the work force at Cove Creek should be begun. A forestry program that did not duplicate the work of federal and state agencies should be planned "so as to fill the place that forests should fill in a well planned society." This was to include a "general forest program for public and private lands," and "new legislation, both national and state, will probably be required."

A. E.'s memo also called for setting up a commission to "study the proper function of real estate in an organized society and to formulate a policy with reference to real estate operation. We could then refuse to deal with real estate men who refuse to adopt that policy." Another less outlandish idea was to provide technical assistance with business methods for small industries that would be developed in the valley.[94]

A. E. felt that it was his place to present policy initiatives because FDR had assured him that he would be TVA's general manager as well as chairman. Finer summarizes what A. E. told him: "[H]e had not been appointed because of his expertness as an engineer but for his general vision, which was appropriate to the government of an experimental area for which a whole plan was being envisioned on a new, reformed social basis."[95] A. E. had also made several key staff appointments by himself, including a deputy chief engineer, director of personnel, comptroller, and director of planning.

H. A. moved that A. E. be the general manager, at A. E.'s suggestion, and it was agreed that H. A. would be vice-chairman and that Lilienthal would head the legal department. However, by late July it became apparent to H. A. and Lilienthal that A. E. was a visionary with a lot of power in his hands. They did not approve of his making appointments without board approval. A. E. seemed to be using appointments to impose his ideology on TVA. Finally, after one very exasperating board meeting, H. A. and Lilienthal met and agreed on H. A.'s idea that the direction of TVA be divided in three ways, with A. E. responsible for engineering, H. A. for agriculture and forestry, and Lilienthal for the power program and legal department. At the next meeting A. E. capitulated reluctantly to the memo describing the arrangement that H. A. and Lilienthal gave him. Lilienthal recalled years later that both he and H. A. knew the plan was unsound for the long run but were trying to save things in the short run.[96] The competing philosophies about TVA were thus reinforced by the system of tripartite governance, thus delaying the unifying of the new organization around a central credo.

The Troika

There were still controversies. A. E. wanted to build the new town of Norris not only to house construction workers and their families but in hopes that the same workers would use their leisure time to develop their own businesses and create new small industries in the valley. H. A. and Lilienthal were skeptical and, in fact, Norris never became anything but a bedroom town for TVA employees.[97] A. E. proposed that TVA confiscate the eroded land of farmers who had abused it, that script be used instead of money in some communities, and that TVA set about to reform the real-estate industry. His two colleagues said no.[98]

A. E. supported the idea of TVA developing a land-use plan for the region, but the other two did not agree. Earle S. Draper, head of regional planning, proposed to the board that his staff prepare a land-use plan for the valley that would bring people back to the land in new forms of settlement. For example, Norris would be only the first of many new towns. Draper envisioned the massive movement of people to the valley and saw this as a manifestation of the New Deal policy of creating subsistence homesteads in rural areas. TVA should identify the parts of the valley in which development should take place and develop plans for coordinated development to prevent duplication and waste. A. E. could have written the memo.[99]

Lilienthal was very critical of the idea: "So far as I know there is no instance in the experience of town and regional planners in which the economic and social policy of the region could be directly influenced [by a plan]. . . . this project is fundamentally different in kind from other American experiences in this field."[100] Neal Bass, H. A.'s assistant, said of Draper: "He was A. E.'s protege. Draper's idea was to do the planning and let the people carry it out. The regional planning office developed the idea of planning farms. This led to conflict with our department [agriculture] and they lost. The regional planning office diminished in stature within TVA."[101]

A. E. Morgan was not at all in favor of TVA delegating its programs of assistance to farmers to the agricultural colleges and county agents. But he deferred to H. A. because he respected him.[102] In August 1934, A. E. wrote a memo to H. A. urging more dramatic results from the program and a greater integration of agriculture with other TVA programs:

> The Agricultural program fits so closely with other phases of the program that delay in that element reacts in many other phases of the program. I am asking Mr. Draper to send you a copy of his suggestions on land purchase around the Norris lake. That program is closely associated with the agricultural program. So is Mr. Bennett's program of soil erosion. So is much of the work of Mr. Richard's department [forestry].

A. E. added that it was important that TVA produce results during FDR's term to demonstrate what FDR was driving at. "We are part of a national administration."[103] A. E. was trying to do what he thought FDR had expected and wanted him to do. TVA was an instrument for the New Deal effort to remake the face of America. H. A. and Lilienthal were not having any of this. They saw TVA as developing resources for people to use as they chose. And they therefore closely guarded their own organizational spheres from A. E.'s contamination which, of course, was what A. E. was complaining about to H. A. One result was the poor coordination of TVA programs across departments. H. A. did not want land taken from farming and put into parks around reservoirs. He did not want TVA foresters to plant trees that might reduce land available for farming.

The practical result of governance by a troika was that the separate empires proceeded apace under the leadership of each director. Dynamism was in the separate spheres. A. E. planned a superb system of dams for the river system. H. A. introduced farmers to phosphate fertilizer and encouraged them to convert from row crops to pasture and stock. And

Lilienthal created a transmission system of electric power. The vision of a new America in microcosm in the valley could never have taken root. In fact, A. E.'s speeches along this line alarmed many people. For example, Marvin McIntyre, a presidential assistant, sent a note to A. E. quoting a "friend of the administration" who had been shocked by one of A. E.'s speeches in which he had talked of reorganizing the economic life of the valley apart from the rest of the country with its own purchasing and distribution systems and its own currency.[104] McIntyre was one of many people who tried to warn A. E. of his critics. Such reports genuinely frightened H. A. and Lilienthal, and their protests made life more difficult for A. E. He told his secretary that he had mistakenly "thought that three intelligent men could work out things cooperatively."[105] A. E. told Finer that he had never worked with "equals" before and that his shortcomings depressed him.[106] Descriptions of board meetings show an aggressive Lilienthal, a silent H. A. Morgan, and a defensive A. E. Morgan.[107] Finer, who attended board meetings much later but saw the same kind of fighting, believed that the clashes were not only intellectual but personal. Each of the men saw himself as the only one who could avert catastrophe for TVA. A position on the board gave each director a national platform, and eventually A. E. and Lilienthal began to take advantage of the opportunity, sometimes criticizing each other as they competed for public support.[108] H. A. remained silent, so that a polarization developed between A. E. and Lilienthal. The most contentious point was the power program.

A. E. hoped to cooperate with the private utilities, but Lilienthal's Wisconsin experience warned him that the utilities would try to kill TVA.[109] An exchange of memos between the two men in 1933 illustrated the deep divide between them. A. E., in his memo, asserted that social and political conflict was "a great social and political waste" and that most issues could be resolved by an appeal to the facts. He therefore recommended that TVA choose a well-known economist who would certify that TVA was accurate in its reports on its power-program operations. The private utilities would be asked to find a comparable expert. The two experts would then find a third. And the panel would thereafter judge the truth of the facts about the relative merits of public and private power put out by TVA and its competitors. Thus, A. E. urged, it would be possible to get beyond propaganda to accurate evaluation.[110]

There is no record of H. A.'s and Lilienthal's response to the proposal. But two days later Lilienthal wrote a memo arguing against a premature delineation of a TVA electricity service area: "It is the worst kind of strategy to base one's policy . . . upon a premise contrary to all past experience. . . . The authority would violate its public duty if it based its whole program upon the desire of the utilities to cooperate in a program which is directly contrary to their private economic interests." Lilienthal went on to quote letters he had received from Senators Norris and LaFollete, Felix Frankfurter, and others in the field of public power stating that it would be a great error to trust the utilities.[111]

The exchange of memos illustrates that A. E. and Lilienthal had very different conceptions of politics. A.E. regarded all forms of conflict as "wasteful" and wanted morality and expertise to be the bases for social decisions. Lilienthal saw politics and conflict as not only inevitable but desirable. He was to carry the fight to the utilities in a way that A. E. could and would not do.

Running through all of these arguments were two conceptions of what TVA should be. A. E. Morgan wanted to transform society through experimentation and demonstrations. H. A. Morgan and Lilienthal wanted to use technology to improve the existing society. It is difficult to argue that A. E.'s vision was either practical or desirable. However, critics of TVA from that time to the present often invoke the spirit of A. E. Morgan in arguing that TVA has failed to live up to its ideals. And irony of ironies, Lilienthal was to appropriate A. E. Morgan's utopian cast of language in his own celebration of TVA as an example of democracy at the grass roots.

CHAPTER 3

Lilienthal's TVA:
The Politics of Leadership

DAVID LILIENTHAL and his vision of TVA triumphed over the romanticism of Arthur Morgan. The irony is that eventually Lilienthal added a romantic halo to TVA that was to inspire, confuse, and mislead his successors.

Joseph Swidler, Lilienthal's legal lieutenant in the power program and later general counsel for TVA, believed Lilienthal was the right man at the right time:

> [H]e has a lot of common sense, a streak of conservatism. I think it was probably helpful to him in the TVA that he was brought up in a small town in Indiana, and had taken his undergraduate work at a small school, Depauw University. He was, of course, articulate. He's a man of ideas, very intelligent, if not a brilliant person. He works very hard and knew his role. He tried to avoid getting involved in details, and had a set of priorities for himself, which involved spending a lot of time thinking and looking at broad policies and problems. . . .
>
> He didn't suffer fools gladly. He would withdraw. . . . He's a pretty good actor, and this helped a lot. He gives an image of friendliness. . . . He has a kind of impressive appearance. . . . I think he's an excellent showman in addition to his other talents.[1]

John Oliver, an assistant general manager at TVA during World War II, remembered that Lilienthal "could lift people and then they figured out practical solutions. Lilienthal's skill was to inspire confidence that the job could and should be done."[2] George Palo, TVA chief engineer in the 1960s, remembered Lilienthal as "one of the few men I have known who never failed to say something original."[3] A less flattering picture was presented by Bernard Frank, a TVA forester who told Finer in 1936 that Lilienthal's main quality was that he was a "driver." Finer's notes summarized Frank's thoughts: "He would rush anybody in his way. He would kick out anybody in forestry . . . if it were injurious to his authority. . . . He has a practical mind and long-run policy does not interest him. . . . He has periods of brilliance and an incessant desire to put his program into action. About the means necessary for his success, he is not over-scrupulous."[4]

Frank was describing the young Lilienthal who was engaged in fierce combat with A. E. Morgan. At the time Lilienthal was allied with H. A. Morgan, who, as head of the agricultural department, kept forestry under tight control. It is reasonable to think that Lilienthal would give the impression of a man who was interested in immediate victories rather than the long run because TVA was still in a precarious position. Lilienthal began to think long range about TVA in the next few years. However, Frank's portrait of the hard-driving man who would run over opposition is a commonly held view of Lilienthal, even by those who admired him. He manifested more than a healthy amount of egoism throughout his career. His journal itself indicated that he attached importance to his own career. He began to keep it in earnest in 1939 and continued for the rest of his life. Both Swidler and Oliver, both of whom later worked with Lilienthal in New York at the Development and Resources corporation, believed that Lilienthal gave significance to his life through his journal. His successive books, of which the book on TVA in 1944 was the first, presented its author as the prophet of a principle in human affairs, in the TVA case that of grass roots democracy. In this sense, Lilienthal was, like the Morgans, an inveterate theorizer.

Lilienthal's leadership style at TVA combined rhetoric and conflict. He used rhetoric to dramatize conflict. Writing in his journal in 1939, he asked why TVA water and agricultural programs had failed to capture the public imagination as electricity had:

> Isn't the answer that all the eloquence about land and water omits the factors almost essential to wide public interest of a lively kind, to wit, emphasis upon human beings and a fight? In my activities "crusading" on the power issue when we were surrounded by a "ring of steel" and the getting of a market, presented a problem, indeed I sensed the crucial importance of stressing the human factors, the concrete picture of men and women benefitting from low electricity rates, etc. . . . And of course the utility companies furnished the fight element.[5]

Lilienthal believed that the most effective leadership instrument was inspiration. In an essay on management written in the years after TVA, he praised the manager "who sees in human desires, loves, hates and inspirations, the materials from which to create something that did not exist before."[6]

He was always skeptical of experts, particularly planners and economists who relied on models or other techniques that obscured "the realities of human institutions and emotions" because "the driving force of development . . . is the aroused energy and imagination and motivation of the people."[7] He believed that TVA encountered a great reservoir of human talent in the Tennessee Valley and that this talent responded to the authority's programs in creative ways, drawing on "latent abilities." This was Lilienthal's interpretation of the Decatur, Alabama, story. He found a lack of self-confidence in the community's leadership, and his goal became "to change their thinking" and help them to help themselves.[8] These sentences reveal Lilienthal's understanding of grass roots democracy. TVA would place opportunities in people's hands, and people must seize and exploit them. Formal or procedural democracy in TVA's relations with its constituents was beside the point. TVA would do its technological job, and the people of the valley would shape the consequences of that technology as they wished. This was a utilitarian view of progress very different from that of either Morgan.

THE POWER FIGHT

The TVA Act defined the goal of the power program as the distribution of electric power to customers "within transmission distance," a vague phrase that depended on the number of dams built. Service preference was to be given to nonprofit municipal and rural cooperative customers, with maximum encouragement for introducing electricity for use on farms. There was a caution against duplicating power facilities of private utilities. The exact relationship of TVA with these utilities was open for discussion. A. E. Morgan hoped to work out agreement on a TVA territory in the valley with the utilities, but Lilienthal regarded that as negotiating from weakness. He believed that TVA must be up and going before it could successfully negotiate, and this required the creation of new, publicly owned distributorships. Lilienthal did begin to negotiate with Wendell Wilkie, chairman of the Commonwealth and Southern utility holding company which owned properties throughout the valley. Wilkie wanted TVA to sell electricity directly to C & S distributors, but Lilienthal saw that TVA would have little meaning to the people of the valley if it had to work through the utilities. People would not see the benefits of TVA, and there would be no yardstick for comparing of public and private power.[9] Lilienthal also believed that the utilities did not understand or accept his maxim that electrical usage would follow the lowering of its price.[10] Wilkie warned Lilienthal that TVA might not survive the New Deal unless it found an outlet for its electricity. Lilienthal's response was to sign an agreement with the publicly owned distributor in Tupelo, Mississippi, for Tupelo to get TVA power beginning in February 1934. At the same time, Lilienthal began to encourage municipalities to apply to the Public Works Administration for money to build their plants and distribution lines. In the face of these bargaining chips, Wilkie agreed to sell C & S properties in northeastern Mississippi, northern Alabama, and eastern Tennessee to new distributors.[11] But the deal fell through. The local com-

panies wanted more money for their properties than local power distributors could marshall. A group of preferred stockholders also filed suit in
federal court against the North Alabama Power Company and TVA, delaying the sale of any properties.[12] Lilienthal then turned the conflict into
a public drama. He encouraged the creation of distributorship and rural
cooperatives and polarized the fight as one between the people, represented by TVA, and the special interests, i.e., the utilities. And Lilienthal
became a salesman for the wonders of electricity. As one lieutenant remembered, Lilienthal was seen as "Prometheus bringing light to the valley."[13] Lilienthal thought up the idea of a consumer credit affiliate called
the Electric Home and Farm Authority, which gave low-interest loans to
farmers for the purchase of appliances. At the same time, he convinced
General Electric and other manufacturers to bring cheap appliances on
the market, such as a combination refrigerator and stove, that would appeal to valley farmers.[14] His boldness produced clear results. The combination of low rates and increased opportunities caused electrical usage to
soar in country and town. In Tupelo, average consumption went from 49
kilowatt hours to 178, and the price dropped from 7.40 cents to 1.58
cents. In the Alcorn, Mississippi, cooperative, usage increased in three
years from 49 kilowatt hours to 139, and the price dropped from 5.37
cents per kilowatt hour to 1.82 cents.[15] Lilienthal made sure that FDR
visited Tupelo in 1934, and FDR used the figures supplied him by Lilienthal to tell the people assembled how TVA was serving the purposes of
the New Deal: "The great outstanding thing for these past three days has
been the change in the looks on people's faces . . . today I see not only
hope but I see determination—knowledge that all is well with the country
and that we are coming back."[16]

By 1935 and 1936, newly constructed dams were generating increasing
amounts of electric power with too few market outlets, and Lilienthal
increasingly appealed to the valley public to create new distributorships.
A few pictures survive of the young Lilienthal speaking about the wonders of electricity from the courthouse steps of Corinth, Mississippi, and
other small towns to attentive audiences of farm families. He drew on his
experience and talents as a debater and felt that his small-town midwest-
ern background helped him understand the valley people. Swidler remembered that "he had enormous gifts of leadership. He was a carpet-
bagger who was adopted very warmly by the people of the valley. I don't
know of anyone else who could have brought the people of the valley to
accept TVA. . . . He had a good feeling for what they were interested in
and knew how to combine economic aspirations with expression of idealism so that following their economic interest would seem comfortable to
them."[17]

Lilienthal drew strength from the experience, as a 1935 entry in his journal about a series of speeches in Alabama makes clear: "The most gratifying thing about the whole trip is to see how meeting directly with people out in the field revitalizes you and makes you feel the program is worth carrying on." He knew that he was striking home. "There is somehow a magic about TVA kilowatts. We have really stirred public imagination about electricity."[18]

He deliberately tied TVA to the New Deal, particularly as the 1936 presidential election approached. Congress passed the Utility Holding Company Act in 1935, and the Rural Electrification Administration was established in the same year and strengthened in 1936. The supposedly nonpolitical TVA was a gem in the crown of the New Deal. Lilienthal did his bit, saying in a Memphis speech:

> We are proud to count among our leading enemies the whole Tory crowd concentrated in New York City and Chicago that always fights every move toward giving the average man and woman a better chance. The interests of this crew of reactionaries and your interests are diametrically opposed. There is a conflict here that cannot be reconciled. Either TVA has to be for you or it has to be for this other crowd. When that crowd begins to sing the praises of TVA it is time for you to throw us out.[19]

The fight continued, however, in the courts. Lilienthal built a strong legal department to fight the North Alabama utility shareholders' suit, used nationally prominent litigators, and asserted TVA's right to represent itself in the courts rather than rely on the Department of Justice. From that time on, TVA was to represent itself in legal fights.[20] In 1936, in the Ashwander case, the Supreme Court granted TVA the right to sell power at Wilson Dam.[21] But also in 1936, nineteen power companies initiated a suit against TVA charging that its power program was unconstitutional. Five months later, however, a federal court of appeals denied an injunction granted by a district court against TVA expansion. The Supreme Court let the denial stand.[22] These decisions cleared the way for TVA's power program to expand. Utility executives and shareholders now saw that the competition with TVA was unfavorable to them, and over the next year TVA was able to buy enough territory from potential competitors to match its need for markets. TVA's largest single purchase was the Tennessee Electric Power Company and portions of Alabama and Mississippi operations from Commonwealth and Southern. Wilkie had given up.[23]

Did Lilienthal make a difference in the power fight? The federal courts might have affirmed TVA's right to sell power even if he had not been there. He made no technical contributions to the formula of low rates and high usage. The idea had worked elsewhere, especially in Ontario, Canada. Lilienthal's unique contribution was to provide the public leadership that TVA needed to survive. Neither Morgan could have done so, although H. A. certainly contributed to Lilienthal's understanding of the need for support from the people of the valley for TVA programs. Lilienthal always acknowledged this debt. But he was the only one who could have simultaneously fought the utilities, engineered the creation of new distributorships, and taken the fight to the valley people. Many years later he recalled, "I'm a fighter. I enjoyed the controversy. I happen to think that conflict is about the only thing that really produces creativity."[24] Lilienthal was prepared for the challenge facing the infant TVA. His ambition and talents were well matched to the task as he understood it. His experience as a lawyer and a public-service commissioner had taught him the desirability of decentralizing utility holding companies, and H. A. Morgan's grass roots philosophy gave Lilienthal a fighting ideology to take to the people. His capacity for rhetoric permitted him to establish bonds of confidence with the plain people. And his aggressiveness and determination caused him to fight on every front and press every advantage. He also knew how to create support in Washington among important people, all the way up to FDR. A. E. Morgan could not even understand the need for such support, much less create it. TVA might never have gotten off the ground without Lilienthal's leadership. It might have become a captive of the utilities, and the popular demand for cheap electricity might have been stifled, but Lilienthal pressed the fight and won. His skill at mobilizing opinion and inventing popular programs enabled people to see and experience the value of TVA in the only way they could.

FDR and the Board

The balancing act with which FDR juggled A. E. Morgan and Lilienthal for four years gives a rich picture of FDR's executive style. Finer was critical that FDR did not convene the board and "tell them to act collectively and responsibly" as well as communicate his own goals for TVA. Instead FDR met with them as individuals and appeared to respond to each in turn, thus encouraging each director to think that FDR agreed with him.[25] This criticism described FDR's administrative style but, more importantly, also reflected his uncertainty about TVA objectives. Floyd Reeves, director of personnel for TVA, told Finer that FDR, with whom Reeves had recently talked, "is resting safely" because he had a divided board. He would keep the board as it was until he had made up his mind on power questions.[26] A. E. Morgan's secretary, Ruth Falck, remembered that A. E. had tremendous admiration for and belief in FDR, almost to the end of his tenure at TVA. They had long talks in the White House, and

A. E. thought he was carrying out FDR's ideas. However, Falck added that, in her presence Mrs. Roosevelt told A. E. that the president responded to the last person he talked with.[27]

FDR promised A. E. that he would not reappoint Lilienthal to the board when his short term expired in 1936. When the decision had to be made, however, FDR wrote A. E. that a failure to reappoint Lilienthal would be regarded in the country as turning against the principles of his administration, particularly in regard to public power, which FDR knew A. E. supported.[28] At the same time, FDR told Lilienthal that he would "sic" H. A. on A. E. to argue for Lilienthal's reappointment. And yet, FDR said, he wished to keep A. E. because his departure would "be bad for the whole idea of planning." A. E., FDR said, had a "great soul," but he did not understand the private-utility people.[29]

FDR presented different sides of himself to A. E. Morgan and Lilienthal, but in each case he spoke up for the other side. FDR did not at first see any fundamental incompatibility between the two men because he hoped to have TVA stand for all that they represented. The fundamental split between them about TVA's role in society was perhaps not apparent to FDR. One cannot know for sure what he saw. But whether confused or not, he understood his political needs, telling Lilienthal that his primary task was "to get myself reelected. . . . I can't take time now to straighten things out, nor take on any additional risks at this time."[30] After the election, however, FDR shifted to Lilienthal's side. A log of visits by TVA directors to the White House in 1936 and 1937, compiled by TVA's Washington office at Lilienthal's request, reveals that FDR saw more and more of Lilienthal and less and less of A. E. as the years gave way. For example, he saw A. E. only twice in 1936, once with Lilienthal, but he saw Lilienthal seven or eight times. In 1937 he saw Lilienthal alone seven times and did not see A. E. at all except with the other two, and he saw H. A. only once.[31]

It finally became apparent to FDR that A. E. Morgan was doing great harm to TVA. In 1937 A. E. began to criticize his two colleagues in magazine articles, making vague charges about their abusing TVA rules against political patronage in appointments and granting favors for political reasons. When Lilienthal and H. A. complained to FDR, he called all three to a White House meeting and asked A. E. to state specific charges. When A. E. refused to do so, FDR discharged him on the spot. A subsequent congressional investigation, requested by A. E., failed to substantiate any of his charges. H. A. Morgan became chairman, but Lilienthal took the public role of spokesperson for TVA, and his accession to the chairmanship in 1941 was only a formality. It is unlikely that FDR would have removed A. E. from the chairmanship and the board if A. E. had not forced his hand by making public accusations against his colleagues. FDR had no choice at that point. A. E.'s removal and Lilienthal's ascendancy set in motion a train of events that permitted Lilienthal, and his lieutenants, to fashion their own myth about what TVA was and should be. This myth was less about mission than about the organization itself.

The Creation of an Organizational Myth

In 1944 Lilienthal published *TVA: Democracy on the March*.[32] His thesis was that TVA embodied an innovative principle of public administration. He sought to reconcile the need for centralization of government in the face of the problems of modern society with the principle of decentralization of administration. In his view, policy decisions must be centralized in that the national government represents the whole nation. But the implementation of those decisions would fail if it too were centralized. TVA had proved, according to Lilienthal, that policy implementation could be decentralized at the grass roots so that government would act in close concert with the people it was serving. He cited the agricultural demonstration programs for farmers, the decentralized ownership of municipal and rural distribution systems for the transmission of electric power, and TVA agreements with other federal agencies and state and local governments for collaboration on a host of problems such as malaria eradication, forest improvement, and the development of schools and libraries at dam construction sites.

This book is the chief expression of the organizational myth of TVA. A myth is not a fiction but a set of missions and aspirations that guide an organization and give it legitimacy with the rest of society. Political support for bureaucratic programs cannot rest on achievement alone. Too few agencies would meet the test. There must be some accomplishment for support to exist at all, and the myth expresses the faith that achievements will increase. But there will always be a gap between achievement and reality. However, we do not abolish schools because they fail with some children or welfare bureaucracies because they do not overcome dependency. We simply try harder. Organizations particularly need myths at their founding and at times of change and adaptation to new conditions. Myths bind the members of an organization together, give them direction, and foster external support.[33] The TVA of the 1930s and 1940s had one of the strongest and most distinctive myths of any American public agency. Lilienthal had more to do with its development and articulation than anyone else. But he did not invent it out of whole cloth. The main ideas gradually emerged from TVA experience, and Lilienthal's achievement was to pull them together into a coherent doctrine.

THE FIGHT WITH ICKES

In 1939 Lilienthal spent much time in Washington trying to persuade Congress to authorize TVA purchase of the Tennessee properties of Commonwealth and Southern. Congressional hostility to the TVA meant that Lilienthal had to do considerable lobbying, at the same time that he was asking for increases in annual appropriations. His summer journal entries reflect restlessness and impatience. He asked himself whether he should resign because he was in a rut. Perhaps he had exhausted his usefulness to TVA? He hoped that he would not have to continue the seemingly endless negotiations required for the transfer of utility properties. He worried about the vitality of TVA as an organization. H. A. Morgan, the nominal chairman, was passive, and "there is a slowing down of new ideas for the very reason that we are catching our breath. . . . It is important that I somehow find time to do the thing that I am best at—to stimulate and prod and drive ahead. And that takes time—time to talk things over, time to visit the job and people in the Valley."[34]

Lilienthal found the opportunity he was seeking in the form of a fight. Combat was again to stimulate creativity. The Reorganization Act of 1939 authorized the president to issue executive orders placing independent agencies under the authority of departments. The act was a legal expression of the president's Committee of Reorganization, chaired by Louis Brownlow, which had concluded that too many new New Deal agencies were reporting directly to the president. The report recommended that most such agencies be swept under the umbrellas of departments which would, in some cases, be reconstituted around a central coherent theme.[35] A legal opinion prepared for Lilienthal by TVA's chief counsel in September 1939 suggested that TVA could be reorganized out of existence if the president chose. It could either be carved up with parts returning to departments, or it could be subsumed under one department.[36]

A clue to the eventual TVA response can be seen in a memo written in August of that year by Earl Draper, director of TVA regional planning, in anticipation of a visit to TVA by several congressional leaders. The task of persuasion, Draper told John Blandford, TVA's general manager, was not to present evidence of good work but to go further and

> convince them that other agencies to whom such work has previously been entrusted in the national programs could not be as effective as we are. I refer, of course, to the practical results of the regional approach in coordination of programs. If we can convince them that a better job of dam building can be accomplished by a regional agency then could be done by the same engineers employed by a national agency then I would say we have presented an un-

answerable argument for continuation of the regional approach to continuing problems. . . .

If we are successful in putting this viewpoint over, it would have to be by (1) convincing the parties that our relations with other federal, state and local agencies are most effective through our regional approach, and (2) that through a regional understanding of all of the factors involved we are able to consider aspects of every program that would ordinarily be overlooked in the normal approach to these problems.[37]

H. A. Morgan expressed these ideas in a September letter to FDR which was prompted by news from the Bureau of the Budget that Harold Ickes, secretary of the interior, was trying to persuade FDR to place TVA and future regional authorities under the authority of the Department of Interior. H. A.'s letter stated flatly that "if the Authority is to be required to report to the head of one agency having comparable interests, it may with equal justice be directed to review its decisions with several. Then the Tennessee Valley Authority as an independent corporate agency will be destroyed. The experiment will be ended."[38]

It is important to note that, in TVA's eyes, a decentralized organization was also a multidisciplinary one. Put back in Washington under one department, it would not only be recentralized but would lose its multipurpose character because programs in the purview of other departments would have to be coordinated with those departments in Washington. Thus, decentralization and multiple purposes went together.

H. A. listed TVA's accomplishments in his letter to FDR: the building of dams with its own labor force; the purchase of land and relocation of populations; the promotion of land conservation and crop experimentation; the pioneering in the construction of farm machinery; navigation and flood control; and the generation of electric power. Such achievements, he wrote, were testimony to the soundness of "a unified, decentralized approach." He concluded that there was no middle ground. Either TVA must continue as a decentralized regional agency, with the special privileges inherent in its form, or it would vanish. If TVA were placed in one federal agency, it would no longer be possible to make decisions at the grass roots. TVA would be one federal agency among several in the valley, and its coordinating role at the grass roots level would disappear.

By this time Lilienthal had joined the fight. He enlisted the support of Senator Norris, who wrote FDR of his opposition to Ickes's plan. The board members met with Harold Smith, director of the Bureau of the Budget, and won his support. Lilienthal met with Ickes to express his views.[39] FDR, who had been listening to Ickes, backed off.[40] Ickes's reach for control had been prompted by his belief that creating additional regional authorities in the Pacific Northwest, Missouri Valley, and other areas would require coordinating national policy about natural resources from Washington. He continued to press this claim, joining it to attacks on TVA.[41]

The dispute revived Lilienthal's leadership energies again. He found a role for himself as the articulator of the TVA gospel working at the grass roots. On November 12, 1939, he recorded his feelings in his journal:

> I am all excited these days, excited about TVA and the way it is working out, and by the fascinating place I have in it, the function of keeping it on its toes and on the qui vive.
>
> This is quite a contrast with my feeling of a few months ago. The change has been due to the wholly unexpected effort to put us into the Department of Interior. . . . That aroused my fighting impulses, and made it necessary for me to do some intensive thinking about a particular issue. . . .
>
> All of this has been exhilarating. It has been great to touch off other people, to argue and match ideas, especially if it involved a field of thinking which is relatively fresh, not only to me but to anyone.[42]

Lilienthal described in his journal the warm reception accorded to a speech he gave on November 10 to the Southern Political Science Association on the topic "The TVA: An Experiment in the Grass Roots Administration of Federal Functions." The speech was the result of thinking that he had been doing in the efforts to justify TVA autonomy and defeat Ickes. He added that the talk had stimulated internal morale and that he hoped it would "stir up controversy in Washington."[43] It was part of Lilienthal's uniqueness that he sought to derive ideas from conflict. He could realize his youthful ambition to be both a man of action and a writer. He saw the 1939 speech as an act of creativity, and it became the basis for his book on TVA. Of course, he added very little to the stock of ideas within TVA about the agency. The grass roots gospel was drawn from TVA practices as interpreted by H. A. Morgan's theory of action, which Lilienthal learned personally from the older man. He told a friend that the agricultural test demonstration program "brought H. A. and me together in a relationship which is the best thing I have gotten out of this job."[44]

Both men were realists about grass roots democracy. Lilienthal knew it was not a strong tradition in the south. In 1939 he wrote a friend about TVA's need to show tangible results early in its fight for existence so that local leaders would support it no matter what happened in Washington: "The support of as many middle-class small business and professional men as possible was essential, for organized labor in the South was at that time almost a negligible factor, and of course farm organization, while it has made great headway in the past five years, was almost nil."[45] One close associate remembered that by "grass roots" H. A. Morgan meant "the power structure, not ten farmers."[46] H. A.'s reliance on successful farmers for the test demonstration program was akin to Lilienthal's belief that the boards of municipal electric companies should consist of prominent local businesspeople.

There can be no question that Lilienthal genuinely believed that TVA's many cooperative endeavors were genuine grass roots actions. He praised the new strategies of farming, the introduction of electricity to rural areas, and TVA's assistance to local companies to get organized to deliver it. There were also innumerable cooperative projects with state and local governments. The gap between ideal and reality could not have seemed great to him.

The grass roots ideal became the standard TVA argument against encroachment from Washington. Lilienthal sent his 1939 talk to Harold Smith who made it required reading in the Bureau of the Budget.[47] The ideas were useful as propaganda. TVA had a strong public relations program from the beginning, and A. E. Morgan and Lilienthal had made frequent talks around the country and had written many magazine articles about the authority's work. The annual reports were often written by professional journalists. TVA made movies about taming the river and reclaiming the land. TVA photographers built an impressive archive of pictures of the authority at work that were featured in magazines and culminated in a TVA show at New York's Museum of Modern Art in 1942. There were TVA exhibits at world fairs and for high schools throughout the nation. Thousands of foreign visitors to Knoxville were given well-staged tours.[48] Visiting writers received special treatment. For example, Lilienthal cultivated the popular journalist Raymond Clapper, inviting him to tour TVA facilities. Clapper then wrote a series of columns that praised the grass roots ideal. Indeed, the grass roots theme ran though most TVA propaganda.

Lilienthal gave special attention to the grass roots theme in his public rhetoric. In a 1938 letter to Dr. Alvin Johnson of the New School for Social Research, Lilienthal responded to an invitation to speak about the grass roots idea: "There is a very important chapter in the work of the TVA, particularly as a demonstration in democratic method, that has never been told in any unified way, and that I am very keen to do, with the collaboration of some of our technical people."[49] After the Knoxville grass roots speech, he began a national campaign to spread the TVA idea, recording in his journal in late 1939 that "I have become excited over the prospect of thinking through the meaning of TVA. . . . and of trying to set it out so clearly and simply that everyone in the country can understand it."[50]

The campaign, which continued until Lilienthal left TVA in 1946, was carried on through speeches before all kinds of audiences across the nation as well as in the valley. He engaged in extensive correspondence with scholars and professional people. For example, his journal notes the enthusiasm of John Gaus, a prominent political scientist at the University of Wisconsin, and other "students of regionalism" for the grass roots speech.[51] After a speech at Columbia University in 1940, Lilienthal talked with the historian Charles Beard about the grass roots idea for three hours.[52] He explicitly sought to influence public thinking about the organization of new regional authorities. For example, in 1942 he asked the National Planning Association to revise a study of TVA that avoided the issue of how such authorities should be organized in relation to Washington, arguing that TVA should be the model. The changes were made.[53]

THE GRASS ROOTS MYTH EXAMINED

Philip Selznick's 1949 analysis of TVA challenged the accuracy of Lilienthal's descriptions of grass roots participation in TVA programs.[54] Selznick's primary focus was on the program of test demonstration farms which was managed by the land-grant colleges and county agents of the U.S. Department of Agriculture. In Selznick's view, TVA had given control of its farm program to the organized agricultural establishment of the valley. This was necessary, he argued, for TVA to win the support, in the valley and in Washington, of a politically strong constituency. But a price was paid in the skewing of the program toward service to the larger, more efficient farmers. Black farmers and the agricultural colleges that served them were largely shut out of the program. And the colleges and TVA waged a long war to keep the Soil Conservation Service out of the valley unless the SCS agreed to work through the system of technical assistance devised by TVA. This stance again helped large farmers.[55] Lilienthal had described the selection of test demonstration farms as being made by the farmers themselves through democratic processes.[56] Selznick thought this description overdid the democracy part and underplayed the degree to which county agents selected the test farms and managed the process.[57]

In a subordinate analysis, Selznick described TVA domination of municipal and rural distributors of electricity. Lilienthal had characterized the relationship as democratic, in the sense that distributors were governed by locally appointed boards and were responsible to the ratepayers for efficient service. TVA supplied electric power within a virtually uniform rate structure. Selznick saw TVA domination rather than democracy. TVA had been coopted by farm groups in the one program, but it had coopted the distributors in the power program. TVA set the rates through contracts, successfully resisted state regulation of rates or the creation of state regulatory bodies, and insisted that the distributors be made up of nonpolitical members. TVA officials feared that the presence of elected politicians on the locally appointed boards would pull TVA into politics and compromise its engineering integrity. This had the effect of denying the distributor boards political anchoring.[58]

Victor Hobday's careful analysis of the relation of the boards to TVA in the post–World War II years supports Selznick's analysis. The distributors were individually weak in relation to TVA. They were cut off from local governments. Citizen participation was nonexistent. The real feat of public administration was performed by TVA in welding 160 diverse distributors into a unified system for transmitting and selling power. Hobday saw the rhetoric of partnership as overblown and concluded that TVA's power program was not run by the TVA board but by TVA engineers backed by TVA lawyers.[59]

Hobday reported that TVA engineers originally wanted to create an organization to carry and sell electricity that would be managed by TVA but that Lilienthal refused because he thought the public lacked confidence in the utility industry because of its bigness and remoteness from control. But Hobday concluded that, despite its limitations, the partnership idea was sound because of TVA's need for local support for its programs, as seen in the popular support Lilienthal mobilized in the valley during the fight with the private utilities. According to Hobday, TVA might not have survived politically if it had assumed the distribution function and had not managed the creation of local distributorships.[60]

Selznick and Hobday saw institutional reality as more complex than Lilienthal's depiction. Whatever Lilienthal's private view, he certainly romanticized the reality of grass roots democracy in his rhetoric. But an analytical and critical focus on participation and cooptation also missed a reality that Lilienthal understood from his experience. He had created a genuine popular mobilization of opinion in the Tennessee Valley, and his preaching had been matched by the creation of new programs in agriculture, power and natural resource, and economic development. The Decatur story was the real one for Lilienthal. He had told the city leaders that TVA would give them opportunities which they must exploit. Formal notions about cooptation seemed academic when set next to the reality of increased mobilization of grass roots activity in the region in response to TVA programs.

Lilienthal also recognized that TVA could not be effective if it lacked popular support. His rhetoric helped create that support. For example, when TVA wanted to build the Douglas Dam in 1941, against the opposition of Tennessee senator Kenneth McKellar, delegations of Tennesseans organized and visited Washington to plead for it.[61] This was an instance of how TVA could manipulate public opinion against the politicians on its own behalf. But Lilienthal's strenuous and enthusiastic appeals to valley publics on several issues persuaded him that the grass roots idea was a reality. He was himself groping for an understanding of what he was doing. In 1947 he wrote: "It is a basic notion of mine that it is only when one deliberately puts himself out of a limb that he gets anything done. Thus, in TVA I took a public position on decentralization. . . . before I knew at all fully what this meant or how we would come through. By being on the spot, by my own voluntary and deliberate action, I had to come through—and pretty well did, both in act and in further statements of the philosophy."[62]

Lilienthal's achievement was to articulate a doctrine—the grass roots philosophy—which TVA was to use for its own benefit from that time on. As the fight with Ickes demonstrated, it was a good argument to use against attempts by Washington institutions to control TVA in ways that the authority saw as infringing on its charter. TVA would litigate with its own lawyers, not with Department of Justice attorneys. It would resist efforts of the General Accounting Office to tell it how to spend its money. The Soil Conservation Service would not be welcome in the valley unless it worked through TVA channels. Examples of this thirst for autonomy, justified by doctrine, will appear throughout this volume.[63]

The grass roots ideal also permeated the thinking and actions of TVA employees, especially the professionals. Everyone was inculcated with the doctrine on their entrance into the organization. TVA leaders continued to preach it just as Lilienthal had. The many cooperative programs with state and local governments were indeed cooperative and were clearly guided by H. A. Morgan's early dictums. Even though the power program was skewed in favor of TVA authority, and the agricultural program diluted that authority, both endeavors were sufficiently close to the grass roots ideal that they could be justified in those terms. The ideal was a reality in the minds of TVA people. The dramatic story of the Douglas Dam illustrates the kind of grass roots politics that developed out of TVA's fight to stay alive and prosper.

THE DOUGLAS DAM

The fight for Congress's permission to build the Douglas Dam in 1941 became a mythic event in the institutionalized memory of TVA. The chief articulator of the myth was Gordon Clapp, who told the story time and again in talks to TVA employees.[64] The proposal was to build a dam in Tennessee on the French Broad River, the Tennessee River's largest tributary. TVA engineers considered the chosen site the best possible one for responding to the defense emergency because it could be developed in one year, more quickly than any other site. The only sticking point was that ten to fifteen thousands acres of fertile bottomland would be flooded by the reservoir. TVA felt that it could rehabilitate less fertile land and minimize the loss.

Despite opposition from area farmers and from the president of the University of Tennessee, TVA persuaded FDR and the Bureau of the Budget to approve the proposal. The two Tennessee senators and the governor received detailed letters explaining the dam's merits. Unfortunately Lilienthal failed to talk with Senator Kenneth McKellar about the project. McKellar was highly irascible and angry at TVA for ignoring his patronage requests.[65] He permitted himself to be stimulated by local opposition to vent his spleen on TVA and openly opposed the site in favor of an alternative.[66] He probably would have prevailed had war not come in December 1941. But the dam was authorized in 1942 and built in record time.

This story illustrates the strategy TVA was to use again and again in subsequent years in the face of opposition to its projects, most dramatically in the Dixon-Yates proposal of the 1950s and the Tellico dam controversy of the 1970s. Whether the obstacle was the White House or Congress, the strategy was to mobilize popular support for TVA against the opposition. The irony was that at the same time it invoked grass roots support, TVA asserted its claim to nonpolitical, professional autonomy. Clapp, for example, cited the selection of the Douglas Dam site as a perfect example of the ascendancy of professional expertise over political considerations in TVA.[67] Lilienthal wrote in his journal about this fight: "The key issue is the freedom of the TVA from dictates on a political basis."[68] So it was, but this principle was somewhat in tension with the grass roots principle. H. A. Morgan held the Douglas Dam project up for a year within TVA because of his opposition to the loss of rich farmland to flooding, but the drive to make a contribution to war production was too strong.[69]

Lilienthal clearly saw the virtue of going directly to the people of the valley in such cases: "The members of Congress from Tennessee, who went into hiding before rather than brave the storm of McKellar's lash, have heard from home, and almost all of them have committed themselves publicly to Douglas. It will be the political issue in the state for some time to come."[70] After losing the fight over the Douglas Dam, McKellar attacked TVA with amendments to the act that would have denied TVA the discretion of reinvesting power revenues in the program. Lilienthal recorded his impression of the popular response, as whipped up by TVA:

Since the Senate committee's report was filed with these proposals in it, there has been a really amazing response from the grass roots. . . . My trips around the valley, plus a reading of the papers, editorials, resolutions, etc., . . . made it pretty clear that the overwhelming number of people who thought about these matters at all believed in TVA and were opposed to anything that we stated vigorously was harmful to the present way of running the job. . . .

It has been an attack that has more than repaid us in the educational value both for the TVA forces and more particularly for the people of the region. It is a ready-made and almost perfect vehicle for preaching the gospel of no politics in an important governmental enterprise.[71]

Lilienthal made many speeches in the valley against McKellar's proposal. He described the results of a talk he gave in Tupelo, Mississippi: "Following this talk the Mayor of the city of Tupelo, who had introduced me to the meeting, arose and made himself a little but rather excited and effective speech. Bear in mind that he is the Mayor and, as such, is active in politics and is elected by the vote of the people. . . . Said he, and I abbreviate, 'Wire your Senators and Congressmen to keep TVA out of politics.' "[72]

A public agency was urging the public to keep politics out of its affairs. The leaders of a nonpolitical organization were acting politically, in invoking public opinion, to protect themselves and their agency from politics. Lilienthal noted the freshness of this strategy: "There is something unique about the whole fight. I am not too coherent on it yet, but I think it may be something entirely new and certainly fresh about the situation it presents . . . the unusual picture of politicians urging the people to bring pressure to bear on other politicians to lay off a . . . publicly controlled institution. . . . except for educational institutions it seems like an original proposition."[73]

Lilienthal was describing an old American practice of an institution protecting itself politically by claiming nonpolitical status. The irony is that the practice may ultimately raise questions of the accountability of the institution to democratic politics. Lilienthal described in his journal a dinner in Nashville with the mayor and the board of the Nashville Electric Service at the time of the fight with McKellar. All those present argued that TVA should be kept out of politics. The mayor promised that he would never interfere with the administration of the Electric Service board, and the members, all prominent businesspeople, testified that they would stay out of politics.[74]

In more recent years, the people of the valley have found that the only means they have of holding TVA accountable is through politics, particularly through their representatives in Congress. So Lilienthal's strategy of a nonpolitical protective stance had an antidemocratic edge to it that was not apparent at first. In TVA's first decades, professional expertise and popular opinion were pretty much congruent. But that changed in time. Lilienthal was too caught up in the successful political leadership of a new, dynamic institution, which had wide popular approval, to reflect on such possibilities. He firmly believed that the fights with McKellar strengthened TVA's hold on the people of the valley and permitted TVA, as a regional agency, "to speak for the well-being of the entire region."[75]

New Departures

Lilienthal became increasingly concerned in the period after the fight with the utilities about whether TVA could keep its dynamic character as an organization. He loathed bureaucracy and its routines as he simultaneously praised TVA for not being bureaucratic. He did not see himself as an administrator and relied on Gordon Clapp as general manager for that. Lilienthal's role was to be a beacon and catalyst for the future. In 1939 he wrote: "I am now the central point of this enterprise and if I begin to show signs of weakening or losing courage, panic will spread throughout the whole organization. . . . I must keep driving ahead. I could never be happy working at ordinary routine . . . above all, I must do the thing that my nature compels me to do."[76]

Lilienthal appears to have believed that TVA's dynamism depended on him. However, he wished to transfer his "charisma" to the culture of the organization and worried about a slowing down. In 1939 he wrote the general manager asking how fresh ideas might come to the board from below: "[I]t is probably true that brand-new ideas with respect to the future course of TVA . . . find some difficulty in receiving board consideration. The board needs the stimulation of every suggestion [about] policy . . . that the members of the staff can possibly bring to it."[77] He worried that TVA was becoming complacent: "[T]here has been too much talk of 'peace'; too much 'peace' in a huge organization becomes lethargy, following the quiet paths of bureaucracy."[78] Even as TVA joined the war effort, Lilienthal found himself thinking about its postwar missions: "[T]he TVA program as a lesson for the whole country's thinking and action will become stale and dead unless it moves along with bold steps and does it damned quick."[79] He believed strongly that the future of government lay with regional organizations like TVA rather than with national bureaucracies in Washington. But TVA and its counterparts had to address relevant problems. He reached into his imagination for new missions for TVA, such as developing aluminum from clay, purchasing large areas of timber to demonstrate proper cultivation to farmers, establishing new labor-relations policies. National polices would have to follow regional initiatives, and TVA could lead the way.[80]

This ruminative search for new missions to keep TVA alive and vital was to be carried on by Lilienthal's successors. The unspoken premise was that TVA would not be true to itself if it were not a center for innovation in missions of regional development.

TVA GOES TO WAR

In 1939 Lilienthal sent a memo to FDR suggesting a TVA role in the "national emergency." Generating power for war production was a contribution TVA could make.[81] Less than a year later he wrote FDR about specific plans to manufacture nitrates at Muscle Shoals and to build six new dams so that by mid-1942 TVA generating capacity would increase by one third over the previous year.[82] The 1942–43 TVA annual report contained a portent: "The same factors which helped bring the TVA into quick effectiveness for national defense, hold a promise for the future, when the victory is won. The change to production for peace can come rapidly."[83] The 1944–45 annual report described the virtual completion of the major TVA flood-control and navigation facilities and cited TVA electric power as the main reason for the location of the Oak Ridge Laboratory. The next job, it said, was to "build a stronger and more fertile valley through the development of its basic resources of soil, forests and minerals."[84]

With the completion of Kentucky and Fontana dams, there were twenty-six TVA dams by 1945, sixteen of them built by TVA, five acquired, and five operated by the Aluminum Company of America and operated as part of the TVA system. TVA produced more electric power than any other single, integrated system in the country in 1945, close to 12 billion kilowatt hours, about three quarters of which went to war production, which was one tenth of the power generated for the war effort in the nation at large.[85] TVA rhetoric was moving from the language of raising up an underdeveloped region to commitments to full economic development of the region and its integration with the national economy.

Roland Kampmeier, an important figure in postwar TVA power planning, remembered that about 1940 a "sizable and well organized power planning group was set up to plan for the war so that it almost appeared to be the tail beginning to wag the dog."[86] Julius Krug, who headed the TVA power program in the early years of the war, did not believe that the power TVA needed for war production could all be gotten from hydropower. He thought it necessary to build steam plants. But there was an uncertainty about what Congress would say because TVA staff members outside the power program did not feel that steam plants fit with TVA's basic program: "We were developing water resources and the steam power plants had no role in that."[87] Krug remembered persuading Lilienthal that TVA could not meet wartime demands unless it went to Washington and persuaded the administration and Congress of the necessity to build. And, indeed, as a result the Watts Bar steam plant, the first one in the TVA system, was built. The same argument was advanced by Clapp and his successors after the war as a means of meeting the valley's expanding need for electricity. A subtle transformation of mission was underway.

A memo to Lilienthal from Clapp, then general manager, in early 1942 suggested points to be put in a memo to be given to FDR when Lilienthal met with him:

> The point of this memorandum would be to show that the Tennessee Valley Authority has become in fact the inner citadel of the nation's war production and stability of labor supply and efficiency and in citizen's concern for war preparation, high morale and unity. . . . In addition to this material the conference may provide an opportunity to present to him only: TVA was ready to accept these assignments and has been able to carry them out because it was a different kind of government agency. It has made repeated and successful efforts to remain different despite attempts to (1) swallow it into an executive department, (2) curtail its independence from the Comptroller General, Civil Service, Department of Justice, and (3) deprive it first hand of its revenues through the McKellar amendment. . . . The Authority has been able to overcome these efforts to destroy its unique character only by vigilance and the proof afforded by its accomplishments; it is important that TVA remain different if it is to continue to be the kind of agency the President, Senator Norris and others visualized at the time it was created.[88]

Clapp's memo is an early example of the belief, even insistence, of TVA leaders that the organization was unique and special and should continue to be so. An entry by Lilienthal in his journal during the war complained about the lack of imagination of TVA power staffs who were almost permitted to sell power to the city of Chattanooga, which in turn would turn around and sell it, at a profit, to a temporary army installation. This is what a private utility would do, he reflected: "We are in considerable danger of running the electricity program as if it were a private utility, a good, well organized, efficient private utility, but a utility nevertheless. . . . I have always conceived of this part of the undertaking as, to a considerable extent, a departure from the monetary standard enterprise."[89]

The refrain that TVA was not just a power company was to be expressed over and over again through the years.

CONCEPTIONS OF THE FUTURE

As TVA's war effort peaked, with victory in sight, Lilienthal began to think about postwar missions. He recorded in his journal that FDR had lost interest in TVA and that his own task was to create favorable public views of TVA without the president's help. The TVA ideal was to be held up as a model for the nation and the world: "[T]here is a job of leadership here that could change the course of the nation's life. I am sure the country is ready for the fresh, vigorous reality of the TVA idea."[90]

In September 1944, FDR sent a special message to Congress urging new TVAs after the war in the Missouri, Arkansas, and Columbia valleys, much to Lilienthal's delight. FDR had read Lilienthal's book on TVA and, the author felt, had been stimulated by it.[91] But in November 1944, FDR complained to Lilienthal that "people still don't understand, after all these years, that TVA isn't a power project."[92] The difficulty was that TVA was far more of a power project than it had been in 1940.

The tremendous buildup of hydroelectric capacity for the war naturally led to planning within TVA for building steam plants in the postwar period since the best hydro sites were gone.[93] John Ferris, who was in charge of industrial development for TVA in its first decade, believed that the mission of supplying power to the Oak Ridge Laboratory, one third as much power as the whole valley produced in 1933, threw the balance between TVA's power and nonpower missions out of kilter. As a result, TVA's power program "was no longer the byproduct of an ecologically balanced control of the water in the river system . . . it made the theory look a little phony. And people began to think more and more of power as a thing in itself. The relation with the river became a little bit tenuous and seemed to me a little less real. . . . Every steam plant they build exaggerates the problem. . . . It takes the TVA another step away from its basic ecological underpinning of philosophy and concept."[94] This was perhaps H. A. Morgan speaking because Ferris worked for H. A. and H. A. believed strongly that industrial development should not be so increased that the ecological balance of the valley would be upset. A paper without an author dated February 2, 1944, in H. A. Morgan's papers, argues that there was too much urban and industrial thinking inside and outside TVA and that more attention should be paid to the land as "the second source of renewable energy." The balance of water, soil, and forests must be heeded.[95]

But in 1944 Lilienthal was writing in his journal: "Now what? What next. How can the progress made be further developed? How can new avenues be opening to this [TVA] idea?"[96]

A certain drift seemed to set in at TVA in the absence of planning for the postwar period. Clapp wrote a memo to Lilienthal on postwar planning that recommended continuity with established programs but also advocated "resource development" in terms of the broad objectives of the TVA Act.[97] Earle Draper, who had directed TVA's regional planning staff from the beginning, left in 1940 because "my feet were on the desk." The original thinking had been done. TVA was now a power company, and "the scope of TVA's activities was getting into more or less a pattern and didn't enlarge."[98] Paul Ager, an assistant general manager, remembered that in a period of stocktaking and slowing down after the war, the emphasis within TVA shifted from engineering construction to recreation, forest resources, and conservation. But then came the tremendous demand for power from the Atomic Energy Commission plants in Oak Ridge and Paducah, Kentucky.[99] In fact, the Cold War and the Korean War came along in such rapid succession with strong demands for the expansion of TVA's capacity to generate power that the social and ecological programs were somewhat left behind.

Walter Crease, a planning scholar, is critical of this change because he adheres to H. A. Morgan's belief in the balance of man and nature: "The happier vision of a renewed arcadian landscape . . . was converted, under the auspices of Cold War psychology, into a single minded, routine exercise."[100] Crease also admits that TVA, like the National Recovery Administration, looked much bolder than it in fact could be. The reasons for TVA's turn toward becoming a power company were more complex than the advent of the Cold War. But it certainly was the case that the electricity requirements of the AEC installations gave TVA a powerful argument with Congress in its requests for appropriations to build steam plants. At the same time, however, as my story will make clear, the ideal of a multipurpose authority for regional development did not die but kept receiving new infusions of life.

Throughout TVA's history there has been a persistent radical refrain that the organization has sold out to the prevailing powers that be. Romantic critics such as Rexford Tugwell criticized the TVA of Lilienthal because it accommodated big farmers and made life more difficult for the marginal farmers supported by the Farm Security Administration. Tugwell charged that Lilienthal sold out to H. A. Morgan on the issue in order to have H. A.'s support for the power program. As a result, Tugwell felt, TVA sacrificed its birthright as an agent of fundamental change.[101] Tugwell did not believe that the problems of the Tennessee Valley could be resolved through power plants and existing agricultural agencies.[102] But the very kinds of "heroic" agencies with which Tugwell was identified in the New Deal did not survive that larger experiment because they could only be sustained from Washington and temporarily at that.[103] Tugwell and other romantic critics of the early TVA had no solution for the difficulties that plagued A. E. Morgan.

Latter-day critics have taken TVA to task for having seemingly abandoned its commitment to multipurpose regional development at the grass roots articulated by Lilienthal in favor of the values of a monolithic power company. I would be getting ahead of my story to explore these criticisms here. But it is important to point out that Lilienthal understood himself to be proclaiming a gospel, not just coming to terms with political reality. He hoped to go beyond accepted reality in the sense that he saw the TVA entity as an organizational form for the future. He was certainly a political realist who understood the need to match TVA to its political environment. But he also hoped to transcend that environment by using the TVA form to shape it. The myth that Lilienthal created was not a perfect match with reality. It was an interpretation of what TVA, at its best, could and should be. In this sense there was a certain tension between the myth and the environment which was perhaps not apparent in the early years but which became distressingly apparent in later years. The TVA myth was based on four values, each of which was part of a dichotomy: professional expertise supported by statutory missions versus grass roots democracy, and a multipurpose authority versus the power company. Lilienthal thought it very important to keep all four values in balance, and the importance of doing so was the legacy he left his successors. Most of his successors have taken that legacy seriously, even to the extent that more recent ones have become prisoners of myth.

CHAPTER 4

The Development of TVA Organizational Culture

THIS CHAPTER and the next describe the development of a governance system within TVA in the 1930s and 1940s as bureaucratization was required to overcome the deficiencies of tripartite leadership. The general-manager system was the antidote to failures of coordination of the areas of influence of the three directors. In that system, the board confined itself for the most part to policy decisions on the basis of recommendations from the operating divisions, with the general manager acting as conduit and coordinator. The general manager has never been an executive officer or manager of TVA operations. It has been a job for a diplomat rather than an executive.

This system of governance did not change, in essentials, until the discontinuities of the mid-1980s and the arrival of Marvin Runyon as board chairman in 1988. The structure, and the culture that sustained the division of labor etched by structure, were well matched for TVA's missions of the first two decades, i.e., vigorous action to alter the physical environment. Once the board decided what it wanted to do, it made sense to delegate the doing to skilled technicians below. It also made sense for the board to draw on the expertise of TVA staffs to assess the feasibility and desirability of particular plans and goals. There was not a great need, either perceived or actual, for analysis of the work of the operating divisions by staff experts in the office of a general manager who would report such analysis to the board. TVA was blessed with professionals of the highest competence; it could select from among the very best applicants during the Depression, and the war stimulated new, challenging work. The missions were clear, and the technology was reliable.

There was considerable interdepartmental collaboration, according to the TVA ideal and doctrine, when given missions required it. For example, the social and economic planning attendant on the construction of a dam required the relocation of people living in the area to be flooded by the reservoir and the cooperation of diverse professional staffs, from engineers to sociologists and land-use planners. But one also sees segmentation within the organization in which each operating division pursued its own goals quite independently of the others. By itself this was not a problem unless cooperation was required and was lacking. Even multiple and conflicting goals may comfortably coexist in one organization, in a loosely coupled fashion, as long as the external environment is hospitable to all such goals and provides the resources necessary to carry on the work. Organizational managers can act in serial fashion to carry out uncoordinated objectives without fear of conflict among them. This was certainly the case within TVA. When objectives did collide, TVA managers resolved conflict through bargaining and compromise at times, and at other times some divisions were simply more influential than others. In short, there was a balance among collaboration, separation, and bargaining. This integrated yet loosely coupled system was consistent with the ideal of action at the grass roots in cooperation with the constituents of each program yet permitted variations in interpretation of the grass roots ideal in different programs. It was the general manager's responsibility to orchestrate the whole.

DEVELOPMENT OF THE GENERAL-MANAGER SYSTEM

In the early days, A. E. Morgan was a de facto general manager, but his colleagues saw him as arbitrary and haphazard in his administrative style. Floyd Reeves, the first director of personnel, had observed A. E. at Antioch and knew him to be a poor administrator. He therefore called on Louis Brownlow, director of the Public Administration Clearing House in Chicago, and asked him to develop an organization scheme for the new TVA. Charles Ascher and Donald Stone, of Brownlow's staff, helped Reeves develop a plan.[1] The plan, which was submitted to the TVA board on June 16, 1933, by Reeves, called for a policy board and a general manager. Reeves also submitted the name of Alfred Scott as a potential general manager, and the board met with Scott, who, according to Reeves, was offered the job and refused. At that point the board decided to do without a general manager.[2]

The organization chart proposed by Reeves was adopted but later disregarded as tripartism developed.[3] A. E. did not believe in hobbling a new organization by charts. He wished simply to appoint good people and let organizational forms emerge out of experience.[4] According to John Blandford, who was the first coordinator and then the first general manager, Lilienthal had little practical experience with administration and did not like any organizational plan that might limit his freedom to act. H. A. Morgan understood organizational issues but was interested primarily in his own programs.[5] At the outset, therefore, none of the three directors wanted an organizational system that would limit their individual authority. It thus seemed better not to have a general manager.

TRIPARTITE CONFUSION

Many things had to be done quickly in the emergency atmosphere of the New Deal. The fight with the utilities had to be won. Norris Dam had to be built. Fertilizer development and testing on farms had to begin in a hurry. There had to be tangible signs of success across the board while the political mood of the country was behind the New Deal. But eventually all of this achievement would have to be organized in a coherent fashion.[6]

The board was not an effective body for policy making because the three directors often used their authority within their individual spheres to make administrative decisions with policy implications without consulting their colleagues. The first policy in regard to negotiation with the utilities was announced by A. E. Morgan and Lilienthal after a meeting with FDR but without consultation with H. A. Morgan. Lilienthal and his assistants set the first rates for electricity without asking for the board's consent.[7] It became clear that board members could not be both policy makers and administrators. Policy questions were neglected by or subsumed under administrative work. Conflict among the directors seeped down through the organization and intensified normal problems of coordination. People began to take sides behind their own director.[8]

Reeves kept pushing for a general manager and eventually proposed John Blandford, an assistant city manager in Cincinnati. There was no board support for a general manager, but Blandford was hired in October 1933 as a personal assistant to A. E. Morgan to perform coordinating assignments. He was officially named coordinator at a board meeting in January 1934. Blandford was not sure why this happened but remembered that all three directors favored the decision.[9] The coordinator's duties, however, were not defined. In the beginning Blandford helped develop management services for the departments and managed development of the budget. He was also responsible for planning services, which seemed to be a "no man's land." Eventually he and his small staff organized cross-departmental meetings on the construction of Norris and Wheeler dams.[10]

Blandford told Herman Finer that A. E. Morgan often blocked his efforts to coordinate the work of construction engineers with other departments. A. E. gave lip service to coordination, but if his engineers complained about delays and red tape because of the coordinator's actions, A. E. would be uncooperative with Blandford. Part of this was due to the engineers' desire to be left alone and part of it to A. E.'s distrust of his two board colleagues.[11]

Finer observed that Blandford, acting as coordinator, could not go against any of the directors on issues important to them. There was no formal mechanism for dispute resolution and very little central budgetary control over departmental programs. Both the board and the departments had plenty of money to spend. It was hard to extract teamwork from the departments even though a planning council, with six committees, was set up to facilitate cooperation. Lines of responsibility among the three spheres were often fuzzy, and friction resulted. The coordinator and his staff were seen as just another department without any special authority. The coordinator could play a broker role when one department complained about another. There was secretiveness and open conflict among departments. Land planning fought with forestry, and agriculture broke up grazing agreements with farmers established by forestry. The engineers fought with the legal and finance departments over dam construction. The engineers saw themselves as a group apart and became angry when they were charged with costs for adult education, construction workers and their children, TVA schools, and social and economic surveys about the effects of dam construction on people to be dislocated. Lilienthal would not relinquish one bit of control over electricity.[12]

Blandford and his assistants made up the agenda for board meetings, but Finer learned that board decisions were often taken without sufficient information. Each director protected his own operation and any effort to analyze it. Forest Allen, an assistant to Lilienthal, told Finer that too much was going on in TVA in the early years for one coordinator to be aware of all the frictions and obstructions that might develop. By the time something was understood, the situation would have changed. Each director had a personal assistant who worked with Blandford: Allen for Lilienthal, Carl Bock for A. E. Morgan, and Neal Bass for H. A. Morgan. Sometimes these assistants and Blandford would decide what the principal or principals would have done in a given situation, but most often the director had to be brought into operational issues. This need for the directors to deal with details detracted from their policy role at first, but it was also true that policy was in the details in the early years. This rapid flux began to level off by 1936, however, and there was a general desire for more orderly procedures.[13]

The story of the creation of a full general-manager system is important for this analysis insofar as it reveals characteristics of TVA organizational culture and structure that were to exist for a long time. What were perceived to be virtues in the founding years were often seen to be obstacles to adaptation to a changed environment in later years. On May 18, 1936, A. E. Morgan wrote FDR asking that he appoint a general manager to administer TVA, with A. E. making the nomination. A. E. also recommended the consolidation of the engineering and construction department with the power department, probably in anticipation of Lilienthal leaving the board in 1936.[14] A. E. was attempting to become the general manager in fact. Blandford learned of the request, and much discouraged by the feuding, tried to resign. Lilienthal and H. A. Morgan would not hear of it. A. E. asked Blandford to stay and help him become general manager. But the board met in June and appointed Blandford acting general manager. It was clear to Blandford that A. E. opposed this action. Blandford was also directed to write a report recommending an administrative system for managing TVA.[15]

Blandford went to work by consulting with forty staff members from all divisions. Life in the organization was very unsettled at that time because of the conflicts at the top and also because those conflicts had worn down the directors. A. E., feeling the nervous strain, was away for weeks at a time.[16] Lilienthal, also ill, was in Florida for several weeks. Blandford completed a first draft of his report in January 1937. Learning that FDR wanted to read it, Blandford finished it hastily.[17] In February FDR told Louis Brownlow that he would review the report with the help of a committee that he would appoint.[18] The members of that committee, when it was appointed in March, were Ernest G. Draper, an assistant secretary of commerce, who acted as spokesman; Admiral A. L. Parsons; and Herbert Emmerich, a colleague of Brownlow's. FDR saw it as an advisory group to help him, but TVA partisans saw it as a sounding board and court of appeal for them. The committee eventually played both roles in incomplete fashion.[19]

After appointing the committee, FDR told Emmerich that he was tired of all the fighting, that he valued both A. E. and Lilienthal, that he wasn't sure what the right course of action was, and that he hoped they would go to Knoxville, interview people, and find out what was going on. FDR added that he now knew it had been a mistake to have three directors.[20] A round of maneuver and comedy of errors ensued in which board members and Blandford rushed to Washington to see the committee, against the committee's wishes. The committee members wanted to interrogate TVA staff people in Knoxville and eventually did so, conducting several interviews. Emmerich told Finer that after some time of hearing charges and countercharges, the committee "didn't believe anybody" and "tried to find out who was lying to us most."[21]

The committee's written report to FDR made several strong recommendations.[22] It called for a strong general manager to be the link between the board and operations. The board should stay out of administrative detail and give its primary attention to planning and policy making. The committee was opposed to tripartite management and to the practice of individual directors negotiating with outside groups. It suggested the even more radical possibility of a fundamental change to a part-time board that would oversee the work of a strong general manager, who would be a presidential appointee.[23] The report was a dead letter before it reached FDR. The creation of a part-time board and chief-executive position would have required a change in the law, which always ran the risk of more fundamental changes in TVA. Emmerich also thought that FDR needed every senatorial vote he could get for the fight to enlarge the Supreme Court and that he was not about to risk losing support by a TVA sideshow.[24] When the Draper Committee eventually met with FDR, he gave them only a minute. Emmerich reproduced the conversation for Finer:

R. Did you enjoy yourselves?
C. Yes.
R. How were things down there?
C. It isn't possible to get the three directors together.
R. Too bad. A. E. was a good man, especially on regional and the social welfare side. Did you find any duplication down there?
C. Plenty of it.
Here the Secretary of State came in. Exit the committee.[25]

The committee finally concluded that Blandford and his report should be given a chance because at least Blandford had a three-year familiarity with the directors and the problems.[26] However, this was clearly second best for the committee. The idea of a part-time board and a single, strong executive has resurfaced at intervals in TVA history, usually when there is dissatisfaction with board leadership or policies. It is very much alive as this book is being written. The same political obstacle prevails as well; to open up the act runs the risk of a congressional attack upon it.

The testimony of TVA staff members to the committee reveals emerging patterns of organizational culture and structure. The recognition that a general manager was needed was balanced by the clear and widely held conviction that that person should not exercise executive authority over the departments. Rather, he should be a conduit to the board. For example, Harry A. Curtis, chief of the chemical engineering division and later a board member in the 1950s, reported that H. A. Morgan wanted to concentrate on policy rather than operations and that he, Curtis, favored a general manager if jurisdiction and independence were given to the technical men at the head of TVA activities.[27] C. A. Bock, the assistant chief engineer (A. E. being the chief), was critical of board requirements for cooperation among TVA programs, especially of efforts made by the coordinator and legal and personnel staffs to limit the freedom of engineers.[28] The only person to favor a centralized planning unit was Earle Draper, head of land planning and housing. He recommended that planning be divorced from the operating units and be located in a centralized planning board that would advise the general manager. There was no regional planning in TVA, he said. For example, the Guntersville, Alabama, dam was authorized without a thorough investigation of all the factors involved. Better planning would have led to better water control.[29] But Blandford told the committee that central planning was not workable at TVA. Planning done apart from operations would be ignored by the departments. Therefore, planning should be within each department for particular missions. The coordination of planning could be done in the general manager's office.[30]

Gordon Clapp, director of personnel and future general manager and board chairman, favored a general-manager position if details were not too centralized, adding: "Among the younger men, particularly, there is the feeling that they are participating in a new type of organization, but conflicts at the top tend to upset their confidence in the progress of the program."

Clapp added that the more the personnel division used its authority with the departments, the less effective it became. He was also opposed to the creation of a planning unit, with the general manager as a member reporting to the board. There was such a large variety of work that it was not possible to separate planning and execution. The board would use a planning unit to go directly into operations, which was the wrong direction to take.[31] The theme of orderly, structured decentralization of planning and operations was paramount. The board should set policy on the basis of analysis and recommendations coming from the departments. The general manager would help the board frame its choices and oversee coordination of implementation. The Draper Committee received several memos from consultant John Gaus, an eminent professor of public administration at the University of Wisconsin, who recommended a policy board with a general manager to oversee operations but with planning decentralized: "I have learned . . . from former students, and other friends employed by TVA (in confidence), that the actually effective planning has largely been done by indirection and as a by-product of the operating units."[32]

Gaus anticipated several major questions that were to emerge about the relation of TVA with federal, state, and local agencies. But the Draper Committee, FDR, and the TVA directors were far too concerned with issues in the short run to worry about such seemingly "academic" questions. For example, Gaus suggested that the board be asked to prepare a report for FDR on TVA joint activities, with other levels of government giving their judgment of the functions best carried out by a regional authority and those activities that it should avoid. Gaus was worried that TVA would appropriate too much for itself, causing wasteful duplication among levels of government. For example, he thought the National Resources Committee in Washington should oversee TVA regional planning. The NRC and the Soil Conservation Service should be able to do in the valley what TVA had done, he believed. TVA was established because of the accident of a wartime project, and before additional regional authorities were created, there was need for careful thought by the NRC:

> In my opinion, the authorities will have a tremendously difficult task for some time in getting a definite integration of the programs of the different levels of government in their area, all of which must be coordinated if wasteful and harmful expenditure is to be avoided. I need hardly add that unless the authorities are careful in the allocation of projects and costs, the national government will be left holding the bag for a great many enterprises, purely local in nature, many of which would not have been undertaken if the people in the area were to pay the cost directly themselves. . . . There should be every effort to avoid creating a new and complicated layer of government.

Gaus concluded that the regional authorities could and should "ginger up" state and local governments by focusing attention on the comprehensive character of regional problems. But the president should not approve projects by regional authorities unless he first knew how they would fit with other federal activities, the work of state and local governments, and longtime development programs for a given area.[33] Gaus also recommended that the Federal Power Commission oversee TVA planning for its system of electric power and fit it into a national power policy.[34] He was raising fundamental questions about the appropriate missions of regional authorities like TVA that might have been addressed had other such authorities been created. The fact that TVA continued to stand alone meant that there was no continuing debate about the missions of federal regional authorities within the structure of American federalism.

Emmerich was critical of TVA for not respecting the turf of federal departments in Washington. He told Herman Finer that "the TVA was simply centralized in Knoxville instead of in Washington" and was a "technical satrap" and a "newer and higher form of carpetbagging." And with insight into the distant future, he worried about the president's weak statutory authority over the internal organization of TVA. The fundamental weakness of TVA was, he felt, the absence of "real political control."[35]

The Blandford Report

The report accepted TVA as it was and recommended only that the position of general manager be strengthened to make that officer the conduit for all information that passed between the board members and the departments. Board members were to ask questions of the departments through the general manager, and department heads were to provide information to the board and make recommendations only through the general manager. The three board members would have only one staff assistant, and that was to be the general manager.[36]

Blandford told Finer that he felt that all the main theoretical questions about the shape of the organization had been settled and that therefore his role was only to articulate the practical application of accepted principles.[37] His reasoning followed from primary assumptions which were explicitly stated:

1. Orthodox public administration required grouping similar activities together under departments.

2. Coordination across divisions was the essence of organization. Central oversight of coordination was a necessary antidote to individuals conferring with other individuals "on the basis of their own technical interests and concerns without regard to the policy of the TVA as a whole."

3. Planning was foresight and all executives had to plan if they were to do their jobs properly. Those responsible for operations had to plan ahead.

4. The decentralization of decision-making authority to the departments was good on the assumption that each department head was a de facto "deputy general manager" with understanding of TVA purposes as a whole. Department heads could thus coordinate their work with each other without bringing every issue of disagreement to the board.[38]

5. TVA was a public corporation and the emphasis had to be on public service and public accountability. The prestige of public administration was to be a constant concern.

Blandford was not sure why he emphasized the TVA contribution to the prestige of public administration.[39] Lilienthal was later to dramatize the point.

6. TVA was a regional agency with responsibility for joining the resources of other federal agencies with state and local governments in developing programs for the region.

7. TVA was primarily a construction agency but it would increasingly shift to an operating role as the hydroelectric system neared completion. But TVA also had "unique responsibilities as a planning agency." Sections 22 and 23 of the TVA Act and the authority they gave to make studies and demonstrations were "potentially the seed of the future" for TVA.

Blandford told Finer that 22 and 23 were not merely "injunctions to study, but actually injunctions to govern," not in the direct exercise of power by TVA but in making recommendations to Congress and the state legislatures. As the public works aspect of TVA diminished in favor of larger social and economic work, TVA and other regional authorities might unite all departments of the federal government within their areas, thus reducing bureaucracy in Washington.[40]

> 8. TVA activities were one program, with unity of purpose, and it should be possible at all times to mobilize the entire resources of the organization for the solution of any given problem.

Blandford acknowledged the propensity of board members to divide TVA programs into autonomous parts because of their personal interests. But this overemphasized individual and professional contributions and raised particular lines of demarcation, producing mutual intolerance. He cited examples in which "professional conceit and blindness" had prevailed, such as the conflicts between forestry and agriculture and between engineering and social and economic planning. Blandford blamed the directors for this and soft-pedaled the particularism of bureaucracy itself. He made the implicit assumption that it was the responsibility of the board and the general manager to nurture unity within the organization. Finally, Finer reports that Blandford got many of his ideas for the report from Gordon Clapp, and this seems plausible since Clapp's primary contribution to TVA, as head of personnel, general manager, and chairman, was to preach the axioms of administration embodied in Blandford's report to new generations of TVA employees.[41]

THE GENERAL-MANAGER SYSTEM IN ACTION

Snapshots of the folkways of governance from 1939 to 1945 reveal the strengths and weaknesses of a policy board, a facilitating general manager, and strong operating divisions. Strength and weakness were necessarily joined in the logic of the TVA structure. A framework was created within which broad policies could be carried out in a decentralized manner by highly professional operating arms, guided and coordinated at points of overlap by an observant and tactile general manager's office. It was just the right form for an organization with concrete jobs to be done. The weakness of the system, which was evident in later years, was the pressure of centrifugal forces on the center to relinquish its authority. Each department sought to go its own way, and neither the board nor the general managers's office could control the departments without their full cooperation.

There was genuine cross-departmental collaboration in the planning of dams because of their multipurpose characteristics. Flood control, navigation, and power production had to be balanced. And the impact of construction on social and natural ecology had to be considered. Such collaboration was less necessary in the postwar period of steam-plant construction, when technology was divorced from ecology, until the 1970s when issues of air and water pollution arose. However, for the most part the loose mode of governance permitted each operating division to establish its own pattern of authority in relation to the constituents each served, all adhering to the grass roots ideal, which was consistent with the ideology of delegation of responsibility within TVA.

The general manager had a very small staff, principally a budget director, director of information, eventually two assistant general managers, and a Washington representative. Each of these positions had very small staffs attached to them.[42] The general manager's duties were set out in a board resolution. The general manager was to be the "chief administrative officer" of the TVA with four general duties: (1) prepare the agenda for board meetings and notify the administrative organization of board policies and decisions; (2) keep the board informed of the authority's activities, prepare special reports requested by the board, and make recommendations; (3) prepare and submit the annual budget estimate and assist in the presentation of the proposed budget to the Bureau of the Budget and the committees of Congress; (4) perform any additional duties appropriate to his task as requested by the board, including recommendations for further administrative revisions.[43]

Finer studied Blandford closely and perceived him to be staggering under a heavy workload. He seemed always to be rushed: "[T]here is an air of improvisation about the work of the authority . . . solutions are always just a little ahead of the man who realizes the necessity of finding them—cries of 'we haven't yet thought the matter out' but promises of 'we are about to do this.' "[44]

Finer also saw Blandford as too dependent on the board for his authority and lamented that the general manager was only a channel of communication, which for Finer posed the question "has the general manager, or has he not, the duty of being independently creative?"[45] Finer knew the answer, which was no. He wished the general manager to be a strong, independent force in his own right. But Finer was rejecting the logic of the organizational system as it had been established.

Board and General-manager Relations

The strengthening of the general manager's office gradually created confidence throughout the upper levels of the organization that the policy-making process would be an orderly one in which all views would be heard. The division of labor among the board, the general manager, and the departments became clearly established to everyone's satisfaction. There was increasing devolution of business to the departments as the directors gradually withdrew from administrative duties. The general manager became the manager of information up to the board and of implementation down through the departments.[46] But Finer's characterization of the board meetings, which he attended for a year, was of a somewhat haphazard process in which it was unclear who was presiding, people were late, the presentations by department heads were unclear, and issues were not joined. According to Finer, the general manager relied too much on the experts who were present to give requested information whether they were knowledgeable or not, questions were asked but not pursued, explanations were given and no one listened, much information was lacking when requested, two directors had often not seen background material in the area of a third director, files were read on the spot, and real discussion was infrequent.[47] The trisection of authority could still be seen, and the three directors did not appear to have become a fully collegial board.

Finer described a board meeting in which it was discovered that TVA officials had given different figures about the height of the Gilbertsville Dam and its storage capacity to congressional appropriation committees at two different times. The board had to testify on the basis of those figures. A letter of apology was sent to the committees, but the explanation given in the board meeting was that "we just tossed in the latest figures we had" for the first, incorrect estimate. Blandford admitted "there was a slip in checking," but Finer thought the incident showed how dependent the directors were on information coming up the pipeline through the general manager.[48] Finer captured the process in its early days, and in due course a more orderly process of sorting out issues and preparing analyses for the board appears to have developed, so that Lilienthal could write in 1941: "From an administrative point of view, we are so well organized and so admirably staffed that . . . TVA functions with little close administration direction from the board."[49]

The logic of the structure did not permit the board, or even the general manager, to have an expert staff to assist in the evaluation of analyses and recommendations coming from the departments. This has been the case throughout TVA history. From time to time, small analytic staffs have been created in the general manager's office, but they have been underutilized because the logic of the system, reinforced by the influence of the larger departments and divisions, has prevented the development of such alternative sources of information. Morris Leven, a Washington consultant, was brought by Floyd Reeves to advise on organization, and Leven suggested that the board employ an economist and an engineer who would draw on the expertise of the social and economic division and thus advise the board. Leven thought that the creation of an Office of General Manager made this a realistic possibility. But he found that there was no clear idea what the social and economic division should do beyond research and that even so there was little clarity about what kind of research should be done.[50]

GENERAL-MANAGER AND DEPARTMENT RELATIONS

The great discretion given to administrators to act according to their judgment, with an absence of detailed controls, set TVA apart from many government agencies, but there was still the question of accountability to the top for decisions taken elsewhere. Blandford did not believe that the answer was central administrative control. His answer was high professional standards. Finer summarized Blandford's ideas:

> It is important to get away from the idea of a continuous regimentation by the general manager. He wants every department head to be well up to standard and wishes to foster comprehensive vision together with the ability for self-coordination. Blandford's idea is that each department head should regard himself in the light of a Deputy General Manager. . . . The danger of too many parts is the danger of congestion of the Board of Directors. But if the department heads are self-coordinated the danger is minimized, and the direct inspiration of the administration by the Board, without refraction through the General Manager, can operate.[51]

By self-coordination, Blandford meant that department heads and their lieutenants would work out most cross-departmental disagreements without referring them to the general manager or the board. The general manager also had to insist that the departments do their homework so that the board would have good information. William Hayes, an assistant to Blandford, remembered that part of his job was "to shove stuff back on the departments, to let them do their homework rather than doing it for them or leading them by the hand too much."[52]

Finer saw only the first year of budgeting under the new management system and was not impressed. He described the budgetary process as the collection of submissions from departments, with little questioning or independent analysis by the general manager's staff. The general manager tried only to stay within the limits set by the Bureau of the Budget in Washington. Finer saw that Blandford and his staff had confidence that the engineers, who were spending $20 million out of a $40-million budget, knew what they were doing. Money for the other departments seemed to be allocated largely on faith. Board members did not appear to be serious about the budget as a whole and did not cross-examine recommendations in the areas of interest to the others.[53] The efficient and effective operation of such a decentralized management system relied heavily upon a shared conception of TVA and its mission as a whole. One can

thus understand why Lilienthal, and Clapp after him, gave such importance to the indoctrination of TVA employees. Clapp, as general manager
from 1940 to 1946, wrote memo after memo to his assistants and department heads in which he applied the broad principles of TVA organization
to specific practices. For example, on July 3, 1943, he sent the board a
copy of a note he had written to two of his assistants on the contribution
of budgeting and personnel services to general management. He also enclosed a talk that Paul Ager, chief budget officer, had given to the division
managers of the power department about the budget process as a process
of management.[54] Clapp's memo to his assistants stated the time-honored
theme:

> [T]he heads of the various TVA departments and principal offices and their
> immediate assistants have the authority and should be encouraged to make
> independently many important decisions in their assigned fields of responsibil-
> ity. Heavy reliance is placed on the judgement of these officials. It is assumed
> that their own discretion can be heavily relied upon to define the limits of their
> own independence among other departments, and the limits of their own au-
> thority in relation to the General Manager and the Board.

Ager's talk to the power managers was more specific. He asserted the
"basic principle of TVA management" to be the belief that each department knew its own budget better than the general manager did. The
budget was therefore a plan, put in money terms. Good budgeting was
good thinking in which every important factor had been explored and
considered. Most important, TVA budgeting assumed the high degree of
decentralization within TVA. Planning thus began in the departments:

> Our objective is to get the basic facts for budgeting from the persons who have
> the responsibility for administration. . . . We also place most of the responsibil-
> ity for budget control at the same point in the organization. The central staff
> engaged in budget review and preparation of budget reports of TVA consists of
> only a handful of people, and they devote only a part of their time to this
> work. . . .
>   In the review of departmental budgets we seldom, if ever, question the tech-
> nical judgement contained therein. Our major purpose is to identify and point
> up the choice of alternatives which need to be made if TVA is to have a unified
> program in any field of activity. . . . The biggest problem in TVA is the problem
> of communications—how to keep each other posted so decisions can be made
> in the light of all the facts.

The budget, he added, was a means for each department to inform the
rest of TVA of its plans. The board and general manager would finally
make a budget for "a unified program." Ager went on to hope for the day
in which TVA would have defined its programs and administrative rela-

tionships so that there would need to be only a "casual review of budgets to assess conformance with established programs, plans and policies." The task of the budget office, he said, was to identify important programs and policy problems, not solve them. The budget staff asks questions, "but other TVA people have a major role in working out the answers."

A concrete illustration of Clapp's and Ager's ideas can be seen in a memo written for the files in 1944 by Robert E. Sessions, an assistant in the general manager's office, after a conversation with Ager.[55] Sessions wrote the memo because it illustrated how the general manager's staff and the budget staff worked together. There were two problems to be resolved.

The first problem arose from Ager's dissatisfaction with a recommendation from the chemical engineering department about the price at which the department would sell ammonia for industrial uses. The recommendation was not supported by any analysis of the basis for fixing the price. Ager and Sessions agreed that the price should be set according to a TVA code for selling chemical products. But they did not want the analysis made by the budget office and sent the question back to the department. The task of the general manager and budget staff, they agreed, was to specify the relation of specific departmental recommendations to other TVA programs.

The second issue arose from the proposal of the same department for funds to build a pilot plant for the production of aluminum-silicon alloys. Ager and Sessions wanted to know whether industry would buy the product and whether negotiations had thrown light on that question. Again, the question was handed back.

Ager had written in his memo that

> departments tend to make their forecasts of necessary funds too much on the basis of a routine consideration of most recently approved estimates. What is lacking is a sufficient appreciation on the part of top departmental staff of the opportunity provided by the budgeting process to reevaluate program objectives, to identify the dynamic factors involved in its effectiveness and to project their program so that the forecast of dollars will reflect what they respectively wish to accomplish.

Sessions recorded the wish that he and Ager could do more "directional planning," by which he meant making sure that the departments were "fully aware of where the Board and the General Manager would like TVA to go, and conversely to make the General Manager and the Board more sensitive to the direction in which their approval of particular projects will cast the Authority's Programs." The pattern should be clear. Definitions of purpose came from the board through the general manager. Effectiveness relied on vision at the top and professional expertise throughout. Herman Pritchett's description of the workings of the general-manager system was consistent with Finer's. Pritchett had been Finer's research assistant but continued his own inquiry until 1943.[56] Unlike Finer, Pritchett thought the general-manager system a good one; for example, he approvingly quoted extemporaneous remarks by Clapp to a seminar of TVA employees in 1941:

> The role of general management . . . is certainly not to attempt to keep a close check on everything that is going on in the TVA as to deprive it of the drive, imagination and experience of its staff. . . . General management in the TVA . . . attempts to achieve the benefits of decentralization, to free the staff for collective achievement and general direction within a broad framework prescribed by policy. . . . and to see that the right minds, the right subject matters, come to bear in the right sequence to lead up to the best decisions. . . .
>
> The real function of general management . . . in the TVA is to bridge the gap between a staff that is organized clearly upon the basis of technical groupings and who think along terms of expertness and special subject matter, and the board of directors who bear the ultimate responsibility and who must, of necessity, think in terms of broad public effect. . . . There is a gap between these two levels of work. The role of the general management is to help interpret each of those levels one to the other and help create the kind of atmosphere that will make the compromises which spell good administration.[57]

Pritchett described the general manager as facing both ways. He formulated issues for board decisions. Policy alternatives were most often sharpened by informal meetings between the three board members and department heads. Final and formal decisions were taken in board meetings. The general manager then carried the decisions back to the departments and provided a loose oversight of the implementation of board policy. The general manager did not initiate policy. His broker role precluded a strong executive stance.[58] A premium was placed on collegiality up, down, and across the line. Collegiality was a point of pride among TVA professionals. George F. Gant, Clapp's successor as general manager, cited the importance of a lunch group that met at O'Neill's restaurant on Gay Street from 1935 to 1951 (Gant's years at TVA) which consisted of Lilienthal (until he left), H. A. Morgan, Harry Curtis, TVA lawyers, key people from the general manager's staff and personnel, and several engineers and program managers. Communication and coordination were enhanced in this informal gathering.[59] Gant emphasized that his office relied on the senior staffs of each department to coordinate issues across departments without appealing to the general manager for help. It is not surprising that Gant regarded Clapp as the spiritual father of the TVA management system. Blandford had relied heavily on Clapp's judgment, and it was Clapp, as head of personnel, who had provided the in-house indoctrination of TVA employees, as the talk cited earlier reveals.[60] John Oliver, Gant's successor, thought the management system worked wonderfully: "[T]he basic procedures . . . ways of doing things— were hammered out before I ever got to TVA [i.e., 1942]. They were developed until the organization ran like a swiss watch compared with other organizations that I had been familiar with. . . . The organizational pattern that was developed by 1942, I think still obtains to this day [i.e, 1962]."[61]

Such collegiality required people who understood the implicit premises of TVA's operational code. This fact may help explain why TVA, for most of its history, has developed its own staff members by advancement from within rather than by importing new people at all levels. Lilienthal noted this practice in his journal: "I followed the principle in TVA. I made Gordon Clapp personnel director from a junior post dealing with education; then promoted him, then a very young age, to be General Manager, then after looking outside for a new Chairman when I left, had Truman name him Chairman. Much the same story about Red Wagner, the present Chairman."[62]

However, the management system had weaknesses that were the obverse of its strengths. As early as 1939 Lilienthal wrote a memo of concern to the board and general manager:

> I wonder if there is not room for improvement in our administrative machinery in respect to the formulation of new policies or the drastic revision of existing policies. At the present time new policies . . . or departures into new fields, has come to the Board for discussion almost invariably as an incident to the effectuation of some existing activity. For example, the Department of Engineering raises the question as to the inclusion in the budget of items for the planning of future dams, and that leads to a policy on construction beyond the ten dam system. . . . it is probably true that brand new ideas with respect to the future course of TVA . . . find some difficulty in receiving Board consideration. . . . The purpose of this memorandum is to raise for discussion the question whether our administrative machinery can be improved so as to insure that ideas within the staff receive consideration.[63]

Lilienthal saw new ideas as appropriately emerging from the operating departments rather than from central staffs. Three years later he complained in his journal about rigidity within TVA ranks:

> One of the greatest sins that can grow up in an organization is the sin of infallibility. I suppose I have caused more headaches and used up more patience because of TVA staff members who have this failing than any one thing. Ordinarily this failing in a man is combined with a high order of ability, aggressiveness, self-confidence, and other invaluable traits. This means that you can't

take a chance with squelching methods because these are the very qualities you want in an outfit.

The sin of infallibility is simply this: that the other fellow, or the other department, etc., . . . are a bunch of dopes and that you or your department always have the answer. Now that looks at first blush like just plain conceit, but it is by no means as simple as that. In fact it often occurs where there is a very striking absence of personal conceit at least. A very strong sense of fraternity and enthusiasm within a group, say a department of the TVA, will produce this sort of sin by the head of the department although he himself may be a well-balanced and even humble sort of person.[64]

Lilienthal himself saw that valued talent and energy often carried "conceit." The tension between collegiality and discussion on the one hand, and operating virtuosity and action on the other, necessarily arises in the TVA system of management. Clapp identified the problem in the 1941 talk cited earlier:

I sometimes think that one of the greatest administrative problems of the TVA is to keep the center of the wheel sufficiently strong and sufficiently flexible so that it can rotate at full speed and still keep the spokes of the wheel attached to the rim so that the rim doesn't explode. This program is so far flung and reaches into so many things and it moves at such a rapid rate of speed that unless the channels of contact, information and confidence—and especially confidence—are kept clear and firm the organization could rapidly disintegrate and move off in a hundred different unrelated directions.

Clapp went on to say that the TVA of the future could not continue to achieve common purposes through a decentralized organizational form unless it continued to be a multipurpose agency for regional development. Otherwise its functions could be divided up among the federal departments:

That suggestion again goes back to the fundamental conception of what a regional agency is all about. . . . The whole idea of TVA is, if I understand it correctly, that if by drawing a string around some of the key problems of an area and pulling the string of the bundle up tight so that these problems are all related regionally before they go up to Washington we will be able to improve the result of public efforts to solve those problems. Now if, instead of that, we are going to visualize the segregation of engineering aspects of our planning, design and construction program for example, then our power job, our agricultural programs and other programs will develop into separate programs and run separate pipelines of control up to Washington. Then we will have lost the basic idea and value of a regional agency.

Clapp affirmed the multipurpose character of TVA as the key to its dynamism:

I think it is fair to say that the TVA has not yet had any experience of becoming inflexible or running in a rut. . . . The variety of subject matter . . . the variety of experiences . . . the wide variety and range of expertness . . . means that the process of each individual coming in contact with other individuals is bound to produce frictions between combinations of ideas which otherwise never would have been thought. . . . We are not permitted to become uniform in the TVA because our experiences run across so many fields and affect so many people who will not let us get by in a self-satisfied way. If we had a simple objective only, the chances of our becoming a dead outfit would be very real but the essence of a multiple purpose project generates enough conflict to create new problems which demand new solutions. . . . The best way to perpetuate our flexibility and make sure that we do not go to seed is to perpetuate the principles of a multiple-purpose project.[65]

These are very important insights for understanding why Clapp and his successors were so strongly committed to the multiple-purpose ideal. It was the key to organizational vitality and inventiveness. However, one can see a shift in TVA rhetoric toward the end of World War II. In earlier years the validity and clarity of the several missions had not been in doubt. But as these missions neared completion and TVA began to become more of an operating organization, the call for a dynamic organization seemed to become virtually an end in itself. TVA leaders searched for new missions largely to keep the organization on its toes. Of course, such rhetoric provided useful cover against attempts for control from Washington, but one also sees characterizations of an institution that gave meaning to careers and lives. The ideal had a dynamic of its own.

The oral histories of TVA professionals from the early years reveal the strong convictions and excitement that TVA was performing heroic assignments. The clear missions and high degree of professional autonomy were congruent. The pattern of internal governance matched the tasks of external work. Edward Falck, who helped Lilienthal develop the low electricity rates, remembered the great excitement of working at TVA. He thought it smart to put TVA in the valley: "so that it could develop its own autonomy and its own flexibility and its own individual personality. . . . TVA had the most exceptional, high quality and the most technical, most ethical and professional point of view of any organization I've ever been with."[66]

Harry Case, who joined TVA in 1937 and was the long-time head of personnel, succeeding Clapp, recalled:

[T]he thing that impressed me most as I came in was this indispensable dynamic quality about the organization. . . . One thing that was obvious to everyone was that we had a job to do. We knew what it was. . . . The program was visible and understandable, broad but simple. And the fact that we were building things, I think, was extremely important. An organization which is physically building things has a great advantage in morale over an organization . . . that is dealing with abstractions. . . . You don't feel the programs.[67]

John Oliver caught the excitement of the wartime TVA: "In the fall of 1942 Congress had just approved the construction of the Douglas dam and the authority was in the midst of a build-up for the tremendous construction program carried on during the war. So it looked like a very exciting place to work."[68]

We will hear abundant testimonials that this high morale continued as long as TVA was a building organization, up into the 1970s. It is now time to describe the clear and exciting missions of TVA in the first decade.

CHAPTER 5

The Organization in Action

IT IS TIME to lay out the actual work of TVA in the valley. The themes of governance—internal autonomy and collegiality—were consistent with belief in the partnership of TVA with public agencies and private groups in which the autonomy of all parties was combined with collaboration. We begin with regional planning because that was the most holistic endeavor within TVA, and its weaknesses illustrate the practical consequences of the victory of Lilienthal and H. A. Morgan over A. E. Morgan.

REGIONAL PLANNING

Sections 22 and 23 of the TVA Act authorized the president to initiate plans and recommend their implementation to Congress. FDR delegated that authority to the TVA board but reserved his authority to approve plans and studies before they were begun. The initial authors of section 22 were Frederick Gutheim, a land-use planner and student at the Brookings Institution, and John Nolen, Jr., a city planner who had worked with Earle Draper, TVA's first head of planning, in laying out Kingsport, Tennessee, as a model manufacturing town in 1915.[1] Gutheim explained to Herman Finer in 1937 how he and Nolen, both believers in regional planning, had taken their draft of what was to be section 22 to Frederic Delano, FDR's uncle and later head of the National Resources Committee, in hopes that FDR would see it. There was no word, so they took their idea to Senator Norris, urging that the river valley be considered in its development as a whole quite aside from the question of electric power. Norris accepted the idea, and it became part of the statute.[2]

Gutheim and Nolen knew that the federal government had no authority to plan for regions, but they hoped that TVA would lead states and communities in developing regional compacts in which TVA would receive the authority to plan for the region, but with continuous professional interchanges between TVA planners and their state and local counterparts. It is not clear from the record how section 23 was intended to work or who added it. But clearly, plans would have to be implemented by law, although the whole thing was a bit fuzzy.

Louis Brownlow told Finer that Norris gave the Gutheim-Nolen idea to Benjamin Cohen, a presidential aide, for drafting and that that was how the language got into the law.[3] A. E. Morgan claimed to be the parent of sections 22 and 23, and his TVA contemporaries describe him as initially wanting TVA to develop a plan for the valley region.[4] A memo from A. E. to FDR in September 1933 asked for and received approval to study rail and water transportation costs in the valley, the relation of agriculture to industry, and several social and economic aspects of the valley economy, as well as to do "a general study of possibilities of regional planning, with the aim of preparing programs of research, demonstration and development which can then be presented for consideration."[5]

In March 1934, Draper sent a memo to the board recommending that his department prepare a "coordinating plan" for the physical development of the Tennessee Valley. TVA and other federal agencies would in time stimulate extensive development, but there was no agency to check and guide such change. "The hopes of many for a planned economy and a better social and economic order may be centered in the Tennessee valley."[6] Draper recommended a classification of lands and resources and a coordinated plan for "long time development." The authority of the president and the New Deal were invoked on behalf of the principle of guiding development in the interest of the population rather than through "wholesale exploitation." The memo envisioned an analysis of the valley areas best suited for agriculture, development of minerals by industry, and other economic uses, to be done by the TVA planning staff in cooperation with the agriculture, forestry, and geological divisions. The development of the valley was to be understood in terms of a "single system." This was not to be a fixed plan but one that would develop as the TVA divisions did their work. The first purpose was to coordinate views within TVA about future land use.

A second purpose suggested by Draper was to unite TVA planning with that of other federal, state, and local governments, but he set this idea out in only the most general fashion. The subtitle of the paper was "Section of the National Plan," meaning that Draper expected that each region would develop its own development plan under the aegis of the National Planning Board in Washington, which was created in 1933 to oversee planning and development of the nation's natural resources. This idea was consistent with the hope for the creation of other regional authorities like TVA. Draper explicitly cited the NPB as the coordinator of regional plans in a 1935 talk he gave at Harvard.[7] FDR expressed the hope for regional planning in his message to Congress calling for the creation of the TVA: "If we are successful here we can march on, step by step, in a development of other great territorial units within our borders."

Creating several regional authorities would have required national planning for the protection and utilization of resources.[8] This was the context of Draper's paper. His vision was similar to that of Gutheim and

Nolen, for in his Harvard talk Draper stressed the importance of state involvement in developing regional plans and of the crucial state role in implementing plans. By the same token, he said, state plans failed to capture the necessary regional perspective. By region Draper meant something more than a river watershed. Economic activity was also to be included in a regional plan which would delineate clusters of economic interdependence within an area that would differentiate it from other areas.

Draper admitted in his Harvard talk that TVA was not a planning agency but a regional development authority "functioning through planning, and implemented by construction projects." TVA planning was thus necessarily project oriented, for example planning for the resettlement of people in areas to be flooded for reservoirs and for the use of shorelines. It was Draper's hope and intention that such project planning would be grounded in a larger body of planning knowledge about forests, soil, water, and alternative uses for these resources. TVA, he said, was exploring the feasibility of doing such planning studies.[9]

Draper remembered that initially H. A. Morgan and Lilienthal had seen planning as A. E. Morgan's bailiwick and were hostile to it for that reason.[10] And indeed, Lilienthal approved Draper's proposal for planning studies with reservations that he expressed in a memo to his board colleagues:

> So far as I know there is no instance in the experiences of town and regional planners in which the economic and social policy of the region could be directly influenced and perhaps even canalized; that being the case this project is fundamentally different in kind from other American experiences in this field. . . . This imposes a special responsibility on those in charge of this project, that their activities in preparing a physical plan shall continuously take into account the radically different character and many sided aspects of the Authority's programs.[11]

In a 1937 talk to the American City Planning Institute, Lilienthal commended practical planning for concrete objectives. Government and business planning, for example in the Homestead Act and the creation of the American Telephone and Telegraph Company, worked because the objectives were specific and feasible. By the same token, public planning had to be "realistic and pragmatic" and take account of the needs and views of the "average man." Without such knowledge of ordinary people, planning would fail, and therefore it should be democratic "from the ground up." Lilienthal illustrated his point by describing how TVA, working with other national and state agencies, could develop a plan to stop soil erosion in the valley. The plan would be technically sound because it would specify how to deploy land for its best use. But it could not be imposed on people. They would have to agree to work within it. Therefore, TVA attacked soil erosion by helping individual farmers learn how to protect their soil through crop rotation and the use of fertilizers. The county agent system was the vehicle for introducing new ideas to farmers. All of this effort would move the valley toward conservation of land.[12]

Lilienthal did not reject planning that was an inventory of a region's resources. He thought it important to have a plan for developing hydro-electric power on the river and to classify land for different uses. But his emphasis was on specific projects of TVA on which planners could influence specific action rather than the "sterile tasks" of "collecting data and making reports."[13] In fact, the contribution of Draper and his staff to TVA planning was in specific projects rather than regional planning. The projected regional studies never amounted to much nor had any effect on specific projects. Lilienthal kept pushing for TVA planning to be focused and practical, as two memos from Forest Allen, his assistant, to John Blandford in 1936 reveal. It would be fatal for TVA to "put planning off on the planners," Allen asserted. All divisions should be involved. And most important, "the big task, the educational work that will bring the people of the valley generally up to the plan, has not been touched beneath the surface."[14] In a second memo Allen practically shouted, "I have no faith in Master Plans," but he did support TVA planning for recreation, transportation, and electricity for the region as a whole.[15] Draper remembered that Clapp, as head of personnel and thus in charge of TVA organizational plans, objected to the classification of regional planning as a "division," as if it were the only group within TVA that planned. "Studies" were better.[16] This interchange between Draper and Clapp suggests that the regional planning studies department suffered the same fate as the original coordinator's office: it was just seen as one unit among several without any special authority to coordinate others. Planning was only effective within projects. Lawrence Durisch and Robert Lowry, analysts in the social and economic studies division of the regional planning department, later wrote an account of the demise of comprehensive planning: "In a series of actions beginning in 1935 . . . the TVA board discarded preparation of a regional plan as a major TVA function. Thereafter, the regional planning programs of TVA were folded into the physical development program."[17]

TVA planners did help their regional government counterparts develop their own plans. To Durisch and Lowry this was technical assistance of the kind advocated by H. A. Morgan, and it was a far cry from Draper's original proposal. Herman Pritchett reports that the early missionary ideas of TVA planning life in the valley vanished once the actual limited authority of TVA over the use of land was realized. Two clear planning policies then developed. TVA would work whenever possible through local governments to help strengthen their planning capacities.

And planning within TVA would be limited to those areas clearly within the authority's jurisdiction and competence, the most thorough example being planning to mitigate the disruptions following the building of dams. Communities were helped to plan and improve public health, sanitation, recreation, and navigation. New municipal planning commissions were stimulated. Fish hatcheries and wildlife refuges were built. Malaria-bearing mosquitos were attacked.[18]

Early planning efforts focused primarily on improving forests and promoting recreation.[19] The planners were therefore advocates of forestry and recreation programs within TVA. Better cultivation of forests and creation of recreation sites around reservoirs would stimulate economic development. This vision was compatible with the imaginative picture of a valley of new, small, self-supporting communities, of which Norris, Tennessee, was the prototype. Draper had helped develop Kingsport, Tennessee. Tracy Augur, a TVA planner, had worked on the famous new town of Radburn, New Jersey, and one of their colleagues, Benton Mac-Kaye, had conceived of the idea of the Appalachian Trail.[20]

This meant that TVA planners favored the authority acquiring large tracts of forest and open country around TVA lake reservoirs. But after A. E. Morgan left, the board began to cut back the amount of land TVA held, so that by 1938 the operational rules called for minimal retention of reservoir lands. More than 100,000 acres of land were sold or given away by TVA in this connection.[21] Years later Draper told Walter Crease the reason: "We had the complete hostility of the agricultural group in the authority who favored no purchase whatsoever of land other than what was actually needed for the waters of the reservoir, leaving the rest for private ownership in any use and any way desired."[22]

By 1938, Howard Odum, the University of North Carolina sociologist who was much interested in TVA as a regional development agency, had concluded that there could be a "possible overemphasis upon economic and material matter and upon engineering and technological processes as against human and cultural fundamentals."[23] Both Finer and Pritchett have described the weakness of regional and comprehensive planning at TVA. Pritchett approved of planning as a project activity and quotes Clapp with approval: "We have made a persistent effort in all phases of this program to couple administrative responsibility for execution with the function of formulating plans for action . . . to bring about the widest possible diffusion of competence and responsibility for both functions among all of the departments of our organization."[24]

Finer deplored the demise of regional planning as such because he took seriously the idea that a regional corporation would integrate separate functions into an overall plan. If this were not so, then the work might as well be done by separate departments in Washington.[25] Finer felt that the lack of symmetry within TVA programs, in which power and agriculture dominated, was due to the absence of a "comprehensive plan." As a result, the programs were not integrated. He thought TVA needed a chief economist with a staff who would be responsible to the board for planning. As it was, there were too many specialists in charge of separate activities with no "scientific integration."[26] Finer reproduced a long list of planning studies carried out by TVA in order to illustrate how piecemeal and unconnected with any broad purpose they were. Most were carried out after the relevant policy had been set and were to assist operations.[27] A report from the Office of the General Manager to the board in 1940 confirmed this picture: "As far as the record can be followed no complete, balanced and long range program of surveys, studies and experiments and demonstrations directed toward the purposes set out in Sections 22 and 23 have been achieved, and the Authority has too little to show for the two million dollars expended on Section 22 activities up to June 30, 1939."[28]

The main reason for the failure of regional planning to develop was that neither H. A. Morgan nor Lilienthal thought it either feasible or desirable. They believed that TVA should use its technology to develop natural resources that the valley people could then exploit as they wished. But does this mean that H. A., Lilienthal, and Clapp thought of TVA as simply a power, water, and fertilizer company? I think not. They believed that the separate functions were complementary and integrated. They also believed that they were properly carried out at the grass roots with the people of the valley. They rejected holistic planning *for* people but believed strongly that TVA had a mission to contribute to regional development, meaning economic development, in any way possible.

An even more important point to be made here is the insistence that "planning" be part of the line activity. Some parts of TVA were not to "plan" for other parts. This may have been a strength in a period of fulfillment of basic missions, but it proved to be a fatal weakness of the organizational culture in the 1970s and 1980s when the analysis of existing programs and their merits was deficient, perhaps absent.

We now turn to a description of what the strong operating arms of TVA actually did in the first creative decade.

INTERDEPARTMENTAL COOPERATION

In 1942 David Lilienthal wrote a letter to Frederic Delano, chairman of the National Resources Planning Board, responding to Delano's request for an assessment of a recent NRPB report recommending federal action for the development of the Arkansas Valley region.[29] Lilienthal criticized the report because it appeared to reject the TVA model of unified regional development accomplished by one organization. The report recommended that development activities be conducted by regional offices of federal departments, with coordination through interagency committees. Lilienthal saw this as "going back to the old way of doing things," before the creation of TVA had shown a better way. Lilienthal quoted FDR's message to Congress in which TVA was cited as the path to a "new way" of "unified regional development." What was important about TVA, Lilienthal added, was not what it was authorized to do but the way it did it. He also cited a National Planning Association report that praised TVA as the model for future regional authorities, but he did not tell Delano that he had prodded the authors of the report toward their conclusion. This is a marvelous example of Lilienthal as a subtle propagandist for the TVA idea. But what was the relation of rhetoric to reality?

A year earlier in a question-and-answer session with TVA employees, Gordon Clapp had sounded the same theme.[30] Clapp was responding to a question of whether it might not be better to have one federal engineering office to handle the engineering for all regional authorities. The questioner implied that the regional authorities would all be temporary. Clapp answered: "[T]hen our power job, our agricultural program and other functions will develop into separate programs and run separate pipelines of control up to Washington. Then we will have lost the basic idea and value of a regional agency." A unified organization, however, gave TVA the "opportunity to do the best job that has ever been done in any field we tackle."

A questioner then asked how the departments managed competing missions as, for example, when flood control competed with water use in reservoirs for electric power. Clapp's answer was that competing claims were adjusted by using the calendar, so that decisions about water levels in the reservoirs were made according to the season. Conflicts could disappear when the different claimants realized that their claims could be handled in a serial fashion. If compromise was required, so be it. The most difficult task, Clapp said, was to develop a "TVA language" that transcended the different specialist outlooks. Organizational cohesion was the antidote to fragmentation. Such cohesion had grown out of the reorganization of 1937 and led to "a rash of interdepartmental agreements" in which disputes were easily settled.

Clapp went on to praise the TVA personnel department as being unique in the federal government because it was separate from the civil service system. This autonomy enabled the department to be a resource for unifying the agency because it could develop TVA rules, matched to the TVA situation, and not have to import regulations invented in Washington. Clapp's view of the relation of personnel operations to organizational cohesion was seen in a letter he wrote in 1941, as general manager, to the head of personnel in which he commended the placement of personnel officers in each department to act on behalf of that department. But Clapp added the caveat that the unity of the organization as a whole depended upon personnel officers in the departments being "alive to the whole TVA scene in which any particular department does its job." If they became special pleaders for the department, then TVA would disintegrate.[31]

Clapp was describing reality as he perceived it. This was not rhetoric for outside consumption. Finer's interviews also describe this reality, including tensions among departments. There are numerous examples of the general manager or his assistants brokering agreements among units that appear to have led to discoveries of new ways of cooperating. For example, agreement between land-use planners and construction engineers on the "taking line" for the Pickwick Dam reservoir was reached after one of Blandford's assistants placed a call to the site and asked both groups to concentrate on the issue. Despite initial tension, the differences were worked out satisfactorily.[32]

One gets the impression from the interviews that a great deal of coordination of this kind became a regular matter. Forest Allen described an early dispute between the construction engineers and the power operators about the appropriate design of a voltage line from the Norris Dam to the Wheeler and Wilson dams. Blandford, then the coordinator, recommended employing consultants to meet with the two groups and then report to him. But after settlement of that dispute, subsequent issues of that kind were settled more easily by people on the ground without appeal to the general manager.[33]

Still, not all tensions were easily resolved. The regional planning studies department collected information about local populations that were to be displaced by dam construction, in order that TVA might assist them with employment possibilities and resettlement. Studies of the impact of construction on local schools, roads, and economies were also necessary.[34] However, Carl A. Bock, who was in charge of construction engineering, was negative about social and economic planning of this kind. They just asked the same questions at each site, he said. The training and education of construction workers appealed to him, but to keep down costs he had to resist the scope of training. In short, he did not want any extraneous activities, whether research or training, charged against his budget.[35] Reports of such tensions make one skeptical of Clapp's idealizing rhetoric, but there was collaboration among experts at the dam sites, perhaps because it could not be avoided.

As one goes farther away from the construction of large-scale projects, however, one finds stories about lapses and failures of cooperation. There was a persistent push for autonomy on the parts of the engineering, electricity, and agriculture departments, with a generally negative attitude in those divisions toward planning or research about their work if conducted by any group outside the department. Such attitudes are not surprising in a bureaucratic organization because they reflect the normal protection of professional and bureaucratic stakes. Forest Allen described the electricity department, which was headquartered in Chattanooga, as not sympathetic to any land planning or research that suggested it should place its rural transmission lines on any other basis than financial feasibility. It might be important to know whether population was increasing or decreasing in a given area or whether the land was of good or poor quality, but those factors could not be decisive for the electricity people. Lilienthal tried to get them to talk with planners. For example, an attempt was made by social and economic research to study city finances to see if municipal plants would be successful. Finer summarizes Allen's completion of the story: "It never jelled very well. The people working in the Electricity Department more or less felt that they were spending the money; they were responsible for seeing the thing paid out; they drew the contracts, negotiated the contracts, knew the people in the city or the cooperative; it was their responsibility to police the contract, once established. The work of research was too academic."[36]

The most long-standing and bitter conflict was between forestry and agriculture. The land planners were caught in between in their wish that TVA retain ownership of large amounts of land around dam reservoirs for forestry and other uses. Donald Hudson, a geographer, was asked by Draper to do a geographical mapping of the valley, whereas forestry would map the forest areas. The agriculturalists were to interview residents to find out how land and forest had been used in the past. John McAmis, head of the agricultural relations department, was strongly opposed to both planning and forestry studies on the grounds that neither professional group were agriculturalists. He insisted that his own people do the studies, and he told Hudson, "I won't have anything to do with it, and I will do everything to stop you from carrying this out." McAmis had the backing of H. A. Morgan, and Hudson's study was not even submitted to the board for approval.[37] A. J. Gray, a land-use planner, remembered how the TVA agriculturalists were opposed to land-use planners assessing the productivity of land, and got such efforts stopped by 1939. They had the Extension Service outlook that the only planning necessary was with the individual farmer.[38] Bernard Frank, the number-two forester, reported continuous tensions between agriculture and forestry. For example, there was a dispute about how to best help farmers with forests as a crop. The agriculturalists wanted to work with each individual farmer rather than develop general forestry programs. H. A. Morgan prevented the foresters from doing studies of production and marketing of wood, contending that such work should be done through the Extension Service. Morgan was prepared to give money to the Extension Service for this purpose. But E. C. M. Richards, the chief forester, was bitterly opposed, arguing that TVA should not grant money without controlling its use. Richards finally resigned after TVA began the policy of divesting itself of reservoir lands.[39] Frank remembered that Neal Bass, the chief conservation engineer and a close associate of H. A. Morgan, tried on more than one occasion to persuade Frank that TVA's work was educational and that Frank should take a kind view of working through the Extension Service. Frank had a very negative view of that strategy. His language, as summarized by Finer, is worth reproducing because it anticipated later critical analyses of TVA agricultural programs and of the organization as a bureaucracy:

> It begins to look as though it is no more than regional partisan politics, making use of the TVA for local purposes [meaning the local agricultural establishment]. There has, unfortunately, been a conspiracy of silence on the Tennessee Valley Authority, which, in the long run, will do it more harm than good. The liberals and radicals might have done it a better service to maintain constructive criticism. Under the circumstances, the TVA has set itself up as being above reproach, since there is no criticism from its friends, and the criticism from its enemies is so bitter as to make it ineffectual. During the summer he [Bernard Frank] was talking to some people in the West about TVA, and their greatest interest was centered in the problem of hydroelectric power. The liberals were willing to use any means and to sacrifice anything, even when they damaged the fundamental values of TVA, so long as cheap power could be obtained through its means.[40]

We see two themes here. The first is the fight over turf, the second the assertion that TVA's friends were so anxious to protect the authority that there was little critical oversight.

Neal Bass remembered that A. E. Morgan had wanted to oversee forestry but that H. A. had insisted that forestry was part of water control on the land and belonged with him.[41] Willis Baker, who succeeded Richards as chief forester in 1935, reports that he was required to work through the land-grant colleges and the Extension Service and that "gearing forestry to agriculture meant concentrating our efforts chiefly on projects of soil conservation and erosion control, but it neglected a great many problems and opportunities to develop the forest resources of land among other than farmers."[42] These interviews reveal both interdepartmental cooperation and conflict, both of which are to be expected. The three departments with strong statutory bases for their authority—engineering, electricity, and agriculture—were particularly bent on autonomy. Holistic visions of planning fell by the wayside. But this is not to say that TVA was not fulfilling the idea of "unified" regional development corporation celebrated by Lilienthal and Clapp. The work of engineering, electricity, and agriculture was complementary, and it was certainly regional development. There was surely more complementarity and cooperation than would have been the case had three separate federal departments been managing three separate programs.

Working at the Grass Roots

I now turn to the cooperative working relationships of TVA experts with state and local agencies and private groups. A host of technical assistance activities were carried out by TVA professionals—planners, foresters, public health specialists, navigation experts, public administration experts. This activity has been, from the very beginning, the spiritual home of the grass roots philosophy and method. Perhaps the most important memo written in TVA history was H. A. Morgan's statement of the grass roots doctrine for his board colleagues in October 1933.[43] H. A. drew a clear distinction between TVA statutory responsibilities and the vaguer charge to make studies and develop plans for the valley. TVA had the authority to act by itself in the first case, but H. A. insisted that if studies and plans were to be carried out, it should be with the cooperation of the states and localities: "[T]hese plans will be futile unless in their formulation the people of the Valley and their agencies have participated. For the Authority to proceed in the making of surveys and plans without such work being in collaboration and in harmony with the existing agencies, will necessarily breed antagonisms, distrust and a feeling that the years of work in this direction will be disregarded and cast aside."

Just as H. A. anticipated modern ecology in his idea of the "common mooring," he also had the contemporary idea of "ownership," in which it is believed that participation by the implementors in the development of ideas and programs is the key to their implementation. He believed that state and local governments would not let TVA plan for them. The organization of TVA's agricultural program followed logically from his assumption. The introduction of new fertilizers to farmers would be best accomplished by working through the county agent system, to which farmers were accustomed to turn for new ideas. Another logical conclusion was that TVA professional staffs in planning, forestry, agriculture, public health, and education should be kept small since their best way of working would be with state and local professionals. No separate organizations should be set up in TVA, he said, to do what existing governments were already doing.

H. A.'s ideas prevailed within the board and TVA largely because he and Lilienthal had the influence to prevent A. E. Morgan from setting up TVA demonstrations in various program areas as a model to other governments. Of course, the value lost in this approach was coherence in

TVA's approach to regional problems. TVA technical assistance was necessarily subordinated to the goals of the receiving and adapting agencies and their clientele. Durisch and Lowry saw these decisions as leading to a tradition of research and development agreements between TVA and many state agencies, in which continuing relationships were established for the encouragement of community planning; recreation; research on minerals, farm equipment, and food processing; forest-product industries; and much else. TVA's role in such programs was developmental in that it was eventually terminated as state agencies gained capacity. But the range of such programs necessarily reflected the variety of diverse projects rather than any comprehensive attack on the development of the valley.[44]

There was also considerable stimulation of private groups by TVA in which TVA took the initiative but relied on a constructive group response. For example, in 1940 John Ferris, director of TVA's commerce department, spoke to a group of Chattanooga businessmen about developing of river terminals for commercial traffic.[45] Ferris described the near completion of the 650 miles of the river as a water highway for barges and boats and a link to other waterways in the Mississippi Valley, and he gave statistics on the actual use of the river for commerce. He then turned to the purpose of the meeting which was to stimulate construction of public terminals at points along the river. The benefits of such terminals were stressed, but Ferris also warned of building beyond estimated traffic levels. Terminals did not thrive well if they stood alone, he said, and communities needed to get together to create an integrated system of river terminals. The TVA Act did not give TVA the power to build terminals or operate a water transportation system. The states were likely to have only a limited interest. Private companies lacked a comprehensive view. Ferris did not recommend a solution but asked his audience to give the matter thought. This was clearly an appeal by TVA to local leaders to get their communities to build terminals. In due course a private organization, the Tennessee Valley Waterway Conference, was formed. Working with TVA experts, the association planned a series of terminals linked to water, highways, and railroads. Eventually TVA got an appropriation for communities to build the terminals.[46] This was the Decatur, Alabama, pattern. TVA would help people who would help themselves.

TVA AND FEDERAL AGENCIES

The TVA idea, clearly stated in official rhetoric, was that one organization, located in the valley, would better be able to bring together federal, state, and local agencies in partnerships to overcome duplication and fragmentation of programs. Was TVA able to mobilize other federal agencies in this way? Herman Pritchett barely touched on this subject. He noted that the Republican minority report from the 1938 congressional investigation of TVA, in the wake of A. E. Morgan's dismissal, recommended dismantling TVA and returning its functions to the several federal agencies. Pritchett argued that this would have been a mistake because of the coordinating role that TVA could play. But he concluded that there would be no more regional authorities like TVA because the federal agencies were too strongly rooted in other regions and were on guard against the possibility.[47] He was correct.

TVA succeeded in coordinating the work of other federal agencies only when they saw it as in their interest. And it was not always in TVA's interest to cooperate with other agencies. TVA was hostile to competition within the valley and succeeded in keeping the Soil Conservation Service out. The crime of the SCS in TVA's eyes was that it would not agree to do its work through the TVA channel of delegation to county agents but wanted to use its own people. TVA argued, both selfishly and on principle, that it was the agency for coordinating federal services in the valley and that it should be accorded that role. It was clear that TVA saw any federal program parallel to its own as a threat to its existence.[48]

Lilienthal understood the severe limitation the government structure placed upon cooperation among federal agencies and said very little about it in his book. An entry in his journal in May 1942 explored the issue. He was feeling gloomy about the prospect of other TVAs and blamed the problem on the political power in the West of old-line federal agencies, especially the Forest Service, Bureau of Reclamation, and Army Corps of Engineers. Only TVA, he believed, could promote "the tying together of all these various activities that go to make up the development of a region into a single scheme."[49]

This had been done to a limited extent with state agencies, but rivalries among federal agencies were harder to subdue. TVA had too few incentives to offer its counterparts in Washington. A 1939 memo in Lilienthal's files had celebrated TVA's role in coordinating the work of federal and state agencies but had, at the same time, insisted that to play that role properly TVA must not be under the authority of any other federal agency.[50]

By the same token, TVA was wary of being pulled into any comprehensive scheme from Washington that might threaten its autonomy. It was no different from its rivals in turf protection. Finer describes a 1937 meeting in which the general manager announced that there would soon be a national scheme for flood control into which TVA's programs would be fitted: "This, of course, would very much affect the appropriations for the TVA and all the ancillary activities which are possible when these appropriations are large and relatively unallocated. There were some glum looks and it was suggested that many internal arrangements, many contracts, and even the construction of dams so far planned would be put into jeopardy."[51] TVA could not be autonomous while other agencies were not, unless TVA were given a special status as first among equals.

There were also examples of cooperation when bureaucratic incentives matched. TVA cooperated with the U.S. Forest Service, the Works Progress Administration, and state agencies in a survey of the forest resources of ten states under the leadership of the regional office of the National Resources Council in Atlanta. But the NRC was the coordinating body, not TVA.[52] TVA loaned personnel to the Agricultural Adjustment Administration to work on an aerial mapping program, offered to help the Forest Service fight fires in federal and state forests, borrowed an agricultural economist from the Bureau of Agricultural Economics in the Department of Agriculture, and received the help of an entomologist in its fight against malaria. Data and technical services were exchanged with the Bureaus of Agricultural Economics, Weather, Chemistry, and Soil; the Forest Service; and the Soil Conservation Service. There was joint research with the Bureaus of Biological Survey, Chemistry, Soil, and Plant Industry.[53] But these were examples of mutual help without sacrifice. It was far more difficult to persuade other agencies to change their habits and rules to accommodate TVA. A 1943 report to Gordon Clapp, then general manager, from George Gant, director of personnel, reported on a recent administrative conference in which "relationships with outside agencies" were discussed.[54] It was agreed in the conference that TVA should "work toward achieving its objectives by utilizing or stimulating the development of state and local organizations, agencies and institutions, rather than by conducting a direct action program." But it was also agreed, on the basis of experience, that TVA's "major problems lay in dealing with certain federal agencies which tend to work directly rather than through existing local agencies." The programs that required cooperation with federal, state, or local agencies were necessarily ad hoc and fragmented since TVA had no statutory authority to supersede such agencies. It was cooperation and mutual adjustment or nothing.

The more difficult questions would arise when the dams were built, the test demonstration program was reduced, and TVA became an operating organization heavily committed to generating electric energy. Would the organization's integrated multipurpose character be lost? Clapp addressed this question in a 1943 memo to the board, which he suggested might be useful in "explaining the regional idea to others outside TVA."[55] The memo asserted the cardinal belief that the only justification for TVA's existence was its claim to a unified, regional development role. As Clapp put it, "the significance of TVA is not primarily <u>what</u> TVA is doing, but rather, the <u>method</u> by which it is doing the regional development job." Clapp opened the door to activity beyond the river because of his claim that TVA was authorized to act outside the river watershed. But the more important point was that, in the postwar challenge, "the regional agency will not tend to build up a vested interest in any particular program or activity. Instead, its program is of an evolving nature." Clapp continued:

> [T]he TVA program has been characterized by a continuously shifting emphasis, an emphasis shifting in terms of considered examination of what would most effectively further regional development. Thus, emphasis has ranged from hydraulic surveys to design, to construction, to operation for multipurpose uses, from traffic surveys to terminal planning and operations, from fertilizer research to manufacture, to more research to the introduction of new processes. The influence of these characteristics on tempo and on imaginative leadership in the TVA are probably greater than is usually supposed. Many of the influences that lead to hardening of the administrative arteries or bureaucracy may be inevitable where a program is essentially static or where the influences are in a static direction.

Clapp was saying that TVA could and should retain its dynamic character only so long as it invented new tasks of regional development. And such development, whatever the particular activity, was the goal. An inversion of ends and means appeared in TVA internal communications at this time as it was realized that the first generation of missions would be completed in the postwar period. The task thereafter was to keep the organization dynamic regardless of what missions it developed. TVA as an institution became an end in itself. It was a bundle of solutions seeking problems.

The Agricultural Program

The program of assistance to farmers was the model for all TVA grass roots activities, but it was also unique. In most cases TVA provided the technical assistance of its own experts to help recipients. In the agricultural case, TVA delegated administration of the test demonstration program to the seven land-grant colleges and the county agent system. Of course, it was easy to do this because the county agent system, through which farmers received technical assistance, was well established. TVA's contribution was to create and provide the best fertilizers possible from the plants at Muscle Shoals.

H. A. Morgan was convinced from long experience that radical agricultural improvement was an impossibility. Change came slowly and only when the people who needed to change were convinced of the need and educated on how to do it. It would not have occurred to H. A. that

TVA create a new bureaucracy of its own to teach farmers about innovative uses of fertilizer. The county agent already had the farmer's confidence. Why not rely on him? John McAmis, who headed TVA's agricultural program, remembered how the idea for test demonstration farms developed from his initial discussions with Tennessee farmers. McAmis, who had worked in agricultural extension programs at the University of Tennessee, agreed with H. A. that southern farmers needed to use phosphate fertilizers to restore soil that had been ravaged by nitrates. With H. A.'s encouragement, McAmis attended an east Tennessee farmer's convention and learned, through informal conversation, that some farmers were interested in having their entire farms treated experimentally, just like the university farm was treated. Fertilizer experiments had never been done on an entire farm. H. A., working through others as usual, asked McAmis to ask Harry Curtis, head of Muscle Shoals fertilizer operations, if the phosphates could be made available. Curtis said yes, and McAmis wrote a plan for submission to the board to pay one county agent to set up one test farm. Blandford did not know what a county agent was, but H. A. and Lilienthal supported the proposal, with A. E. voting no. Eventually that one agent met with farmers in his area and won agreement to pick one farm as the experiment for all to study, and the program gradually widened from there.[56]

H. A. subsequently met with the deans of the seven colleges and with representatives from the college experiment stations and the county agent system. All agreed on the need for phosphates. It was decided that TVA would finance the extra county agents required and that the experiment stations would test out the fertilizers developed at Muscle Shoals. The larger test demonstration program grew out of these plans.[57] This particular program structure, or any structure, was not set by the TVA Act, which simply authorized the demonstration of fertilizer uses under conditions permitting the accurate measurement of their effects.[58] The agreement provided for the seven colleges to oversee several innovations to increase the acreage of soil-protecting crops such as legumes, small grains, and grasses; to reduce the amount of bare land and land devoted to tilled crops; to apply phosphate fertilizers to promote the growth of ground cover; and to reconcile soil management, through fertilizer, with high levels of farm income.[59] H. A. Morgan and McAmis were convinced that the shift from row crops to pasture and other uses more gentle to the soil would not only be productive but would protect the soil from erosion and keep the rivers cleaner.[60]

John Ferris remembered that H. A. used the support of the seven colleges as allies against the U.S. Department of Agriculture in Washington which wished to run the program.[61] It was clear to Lilienthal that H. A. did not want the bureaucratic hassle of trying to work directly with

Washington officials.[62] But H. A. also wished to avoid bureaucratic competition with the existing system of services to farmers in the valley. Therefore, he did not favor TVA having its own technical assistance staff. There is no evidence that H. A. was thinking politically about winning the support of the colleges and their deans and constituents, but Leland Allbaugh, McAmis's successor, believed that the program would not have survived and certainly could not have flourished without the support of the land-grant colleges. The colleges and the county agents had credibility with farmers.[63] By inference, the colleges could have caused political problems for TVA with governors and Congress if they had been left out of the program. In any event, by 1938 there were 6,500 test demonstration farms in the seven states covering 1,103,000 acres.[64]

Finer saw that the test demonstration program favored the larger, more progressive farmers with farms of 125 to 150 acres. They were best able to take tracts of land temporarily out of use for fertilizer application and still earn income from the rest of their crops. This meant that although marginal farmers might learn from the demonstrations, they were less able to apply the lessons.[65] Farm tenants were thus less active in the program, and many of these were black. Nor were black county agents and the black agricultural colleges included.[66]

A second limitation was the failure of county agents to insist that the test demonstration farmers keep good records of demonstration work. There was also poor aggregation of data across farms to assess general performance. This was not something county agents or farmers had ever done, and it was difficult for TVA to change them.[67] Even worse, McAmis and his staff, being essentially county agents themselves, did not understand the need for accurate records of test demonstration work.[68] TVA's agricultural staff admitted to Finer that good data was scarce because farmers did not collect it, and neither the extension service nor TVA gathered it. Their view was that TVA was trying to "enable" the farmer. Research findings could come later.[69] In short, farmers could learn by trial and error, but learning would not go much beyond personal experience. Finer did not think that TVA was doing anything with farmers that the Department of Agriculture could not do and was doing elsewhere in the country.[70] However, TVA had the Muscle Shoals plant, and that was unique. TVA gave research grants to the college experiment stations on practical questions such as sweet potato processing and the manufacture of sorghum, cotton seed, and wood products. TVA's lawyers were nervous that the act did not permit research, but Finer saw it as a wasteful duplication of work that industry was doing.[71]

Norman Wengert has identified a major flaw in the TVA agricultural program which is only one example of a problem that was to plague the entire organization. The decentralization of program operations within

TVA was so authoritative that the board and the general manager's office had great difficulty analyzing and correcting deficient administrative practices.[72] The original McAmis staff, many of whom came from the county agent system, were disciples of H. A. Morgan and his grass roots philosophy. They were confident that they knew the best ways to help farmers and felt little need for over-the-shoulder or after-the-fact analyses of the results. But this attitude fostered staff provincialism and introversion. It also made it difficult to uncover and deal with deficiencies and failures.[73]

The advent of the general-manager system in 1937 did not change this situation. H. A. Morgan still ran the department, often bypassing the general manager and chief conservation engineer, Neal Bass, who oversaw both agriculture and chemical work at Muscle Shoals. And the reorganization increased the autonomy of the departments because they alone provided the technical data by which the board assessed their programs.[74] Thorough appraisal and analysis of test demonstration results were thus lacking, almost as a matter of implicit policy. TVA gave up the research role to the seven agricultural colleges.[75] Wengert, who once worked in the agricultural division, reported that "greater reliance was placed upon inspiration than on management and policy clarification. Personal relationships, informal conferences, and loose generalizations were usually preferred to written instructions and concrete program plans."[76]

This belief, that TVA people working at the grass roots knew best how to carry out missions, was to plague TVA in later years. It was assumed that professionals would discover and correct their own shortcomings. Neither the board nor the general manager's office attempted thorough appraisals of the agricultural program. Decisions were made as the result of informal conferences between the board and staff members. And the operating divisions were adamantly against the creation of any kind of central staff that might second-guess their work.[77]

I do not deny the efficacy of the agricultural program. The physical evidence of the results of assistance to farmers was impressive. TVA helped move southern agriculture away from row crops that depleted the soil and toward pasture, stock, and crops that were less abusive to the land. My point is simply that it became a feature of organizational culture to rely on operators with too little analysis of operations.

THE POWER PROGRAM

The TVA Act states that the generation and distribution of electric power are to be by-products of the missions of navigation and flood control. The authors of the act were anxious to win the support of those opposed to public ownership of utilities and also anticipated tests in the courts about whether the federal government could distribute electric power. It was also assumed that TVA would produce only hydroelectric power. There was no mention of steam plants or other technologies.[78] The act gave TVA discretion to build high or low dams, and the board chose to build high dams in order to achieve all three purposes—navigation, flood control, and power generation—to the fullest possible extent.[79] Only high dams could completely develop the hydroelectric potential of the Tennessee River system. But the subsequent decision to become a monopoly source of electric power in the region meant that from then on TVA would have to meet all demands for electric power in the valley. The first decision, to build high dams, biased subsequent decisions to become the power company of the valley and led to postwar decisions to build steam plants. Navigation and flood control would eventually take a backseat within TVA as a power company. The board could have chosen to sell hydroelectric power to private utilities, and TVA's power program would have then been more like the agricultural program in working through established institutions on a limited range of problems. But this path was not taken.[80]

When the first steam plant was built at Watts Bar, Tennessee, in 1941, TVA officials were ambivalent. They realized that a coal-fired plant would be more expensive to operate than a dam. This was a portent that was only dimly perceived at the time. But the plant was needed for the war effort.[81] As far back as 1937, Floyd Reeves had warned Herman Finer that use of the river for power production might be given greater weight than navigation and flood control. The temptation to earn money by the sale of electricity by a TVA cramped for appropriations might be a temptation to sacrifice other purposes to the power program.[82] The TVA annual reports from 1938 through 1945 increasingly stressed the importance of growing generating capacity for the war effort. The 1942–43 report promised that the same speed with which TVA had prepared for national defense would permit "the change to production for peace to come rapidly."[83] The 1944–45 report, however, described the virtual completion of the major flood-control and navigation facilities and said that TVA's next job would be to build "a stronger and more fertile valley through the development of its basic resources of soil, forests and minerals."[84]

These quotations suggest that there was uncertainty at the end of the war about TVA's future as a power company in relation to its other purposes. Herman Pritchett, who was very close to TVA thinking, believed in 1943 that the construction phase was over and that TVA would soon become an operating organization.[85] And he clearly approved of this slowing down: "[A] failure to see the concern of the TVA as basically for the control and utilization of the water resources of the Tennessee Valley in a true multiple purpose program will result in completely missing the point of the TVA." He completed the point later: "A proper agricultural and forest cover can do much more toward preventing floods and evening stream flow by storing rainfall and slowing run off than can a whole system of dams."[86]

Pritchett was voicing the implicit belief that TVA programs should be in harmony and balance with each other and that no one program should outweigh the others in importance. TVA's purpose was to combine the uses of land and water in an integrated way. TVA as a power company was alien to this sense of harmony. However, this dream was to give way in the postwar period to an imbalance in favor of the power mission. John Ferris caught the shift as he described the shakeup at TVA during the war:

> [TVA was] getting ready to produce a tremendous amount of power for the atomic energy program at Oak Ridge and Paducah, KY. . . . that was one third as much as the whole valley. . . . Very large amounts of power resulted in this frantic expansion of the power program, not just from generation at dams, but also from steam plants. . . . There is no question about the fundamental fact that the atomic energy programs produced such an expansion of power in the TVA's program that the first thing you knew, power was no longer a byproduct of an ecologically balanced control of the water in the river system. Rather the additional power stacked on top of that made the whole thing top heavy in power. . . . It made this theory [multiple purpose] look a little bit phony. And people began to think more and more of power as a thing in itself. The relation with the river became a little bit tenuous and seemed to me a little less real. . . . Every steam plant they build exaggerates that problem . . . it takes the TVA another step away from its basic ecological underpinning of philosophy and concept.[87]

TVA engineers originally wanted to create an organization within the authority to carry electricity to industrial and residential users, but the board opposed the idea. Lilienthal believed that the public lack of confidence in the utility industry had been due to the bigness and remoteness from control of the utility-holding companies. The idea gradually emerged of TVA going into partnership with local, publicly owned distributors who would sell power to customers and also provide local support for TVA.[88] Electricity was sold directly to some industrial users by TVA, including the federal government, and to publicly owned municipal distributors and rural cooperatives. TVA persuaded state legislators to permit newly formed municipal distributors to issue bonds to create the necessary facilities.[89] The rural cooperatives were organized by TVA.

Consumers in rural areas lacked the capital necessary to construct facilities, and TVA organized rural membership associations which members joined for a fee. TVA constructed transmission lines, and the associations, with TVA help, operated the systems and paid their debt to TVA.[90] The Public Works Administration gave loans to municipal distributors for building transmission lines, and the Rural Electrification Administration did the same for the rural cooperatives. TVA arranged this help in both cases.[91] A vast grass roots network of electricity distributors was created which TVA would have to serve in the future as the demand for electric power grew, especially in the war and postwar years. The outlines of TVA as a power company were implicit in this structure.

TVA also used a hidden hand to stimulate community requests for electric power. For example, TVA's Memphis office was active during the 1934 referendum on creating a publicly owned distributorship. The local office received instructions from Knoxville about tactics, suggested lines of argument to the pro forces, and stayed in close contact with the mayor about negotiations with the private Memphis Power and Light Company. But TVA was required to deny publicly such activities for fear that it might suffer in continuing lawsuits in federal courts about the legality of its power program.[92]

The official TVA story, much told in public rhetoric, was that the relation of TVA to the distributors was a perfect example of grass roots democracy. But there were severe limits to this claim. In the first place, TVA set the uniform wholesale rates that distributors were charged for electricity. This was necessary if the strategy of stimulating use through low rates was to be tested. Secondly, contracts with distributors precluded any use of revenues from electricity sales for other municipal services. Again, TVA wanted the rates as low as possible. Finally, TVA insisted in its contracts that the membership of the boards of distributors not include any elected officials. This was justified by the claim that TVA was nonpolitical. Of course, it also denied local distributors the skills and incentives of local politicians who might have challenged TVA.[93]

TVA's power program was run by TVA electricity engineers and TVA lawyers, with limited discretion on the part of the distributors in regard to either product or price. But the decision to decentralize the distribution system was politically intelligent because it brought local communities directly into support of the TVA power program. In this sense the situation was not unlike that of agriculture. TVA needed the support of the local businesspeople who sat on the distributor boards just as it needed the support of the agricultural establishment in the valley.[94]

In due time the distributors network was to become the most important TVA constituency. From the beginning it was a valuable resource for making TVA's case in Washington, as Lilienthal confided to his journal in 1943:

> Last Tuesday I attended a meeting at Chattanooga of representatives of almost all the 134 municipal and cooperative distributors of TVA power. Their feeling of loyalty to TVA and what we are trying to do, and their commitment to the principle of integrity and freedom from partisan politics, was a heartwarming sight to see. Faced with the crisis that Senator McKellar's latest measure creates, together with his earlier revenue bill, they are certainly moving into action. And it is that response, those fruits of grass roots democracy, that will probably save the day for TVA.[95]

McKellar was on a tear against TVA, and Lilienthal was using the distributors as a weapon against him.

TVA has always set its electricity rates without regulation by either federal or state governments. Its status as a public corporation freed it from oversight by the Federal Power Commission.[96] It would have been intolerable for TVA to have been regulated by seven different state commissions. Therefore, TVA acted early in the day to persuade the states to exempt its rates from regulation and review, and it succeeded, in some cases with help from the federal courts.[97] Finer concluded that a strong case could be made that the FPC should regulate TVA. He saw TVA itself as a good regulatory body, at the time, which was working to improve local utility standards and operations. But this might change, he reasoned, and who would oversee TVA?[98]

TVA had strong precedents for freedom from regulation by the states. It had inherited federal water-resource policies that had, again and again, retained authority for the federal government over the hydroelectric sites. It was not a practical matter for TVA wholesale rates to vary from state to state depending upon the judgments of state commissions. Any coherent policy would have been upset. But why was TVA free from federal regulation? The very structure of a public corporation, which was supposed to combine the best of government and business, argued for autonomy. The TVA board reported directly to the president. The board had discretion to act, aside from final approval of its budget, as it wished, within the context of the act. Perhaps most important was the generally accepted idea, which Marguerite Owen, longtime head of the Washington office, expressed in her book about TVA, that a public corporation combined responsibility and accountability, and because it was deemed responsible, it was also charged with keeping itself accountable. In short, the best check on TVA was said to be TVA itself because of its sense of responsibility.[99]

Philip Selznick understood that TVA's agriculture and power programs were organized on antithetical lines, and he was just as critical of undue centralization in power as he was of undue delegation in agriculture.[100] He also pointed out that TVA often violated the principle of grass roots democracy by acting on its own. For example, he saw the 1942 fight to build the Douglas Dam, despite much opposition from farmers in the area, as TVA acting as a national agency on behalf of national goals, without listening to the grass roots.[101] Selznick was pointing to a fundamental tension in the TVA myth between the responsibility of TVA to act as a federal agency and the principle of grass roots partnership. Subsequent history would show TVA acting on its own, often in opposition to public opinion in the valley but secure in its statutory mandates. This is not to deny the many real partnerships that were formed and continued.

The myth of grass roots democracy took different forms in different TVA programs. But in each case there was resemblance to the core myth. TVA was working in concert with the people of the valley through given representatives. One must believe that TVA officials were not cynics. They believed the myth, too. A 1940 speech by Julius Krug, the chief power engineer, to a meeting of the Middle Tennessee Farm Institute invoked the balance required by a federal agency working at the grass roots:

The job of distribution . . . has been turned over to local agencies—the non-profit cooperative association. . . . We believe the electricity distribution service should be run by the chosen local representation of the electricity consumers. We don't want, and we know you don't want, your electric systems to be run from Washington or even Knoxville. . . . The authority must, of course, do its share. The authority makes certain that the low-cost power generated at the great water control projects gets to the customer at the lowest possible rate; that the distributing agency maintains accounting records which let the public know the results of operations; that the distributor accords equal treatment to all the customers of the same general class. But we can and should go no further. We can advise local officials and give them our help, but we should not try to dictate where or when they should build lines or spend their money. . . . Realizing that ultimate responsibility for management rests with the distributing agencies, the authority does not try to dictate rural electrification policy, but we do everything in our power to persuade the distributing agencies to make every extension which is within the range of economic feasibility. . . . You farm leaders throughout the state must take an interest in these local agencies. You must participate in their work and help to guide them.[102]

These are the words of an administrator with clear ideas about the finely meshed relation between TVA and its partners. The grass roots myth was not a sufficient guide to action alone, but its spirit permeated the details.

There are many mythic elements in the TVA story, some invented by

TVA leaders, some by laudatory outsiders. Pritchett captured some of the myths that arose from attribution. In 1938 the *New York Times* published a series of articles on TVA followed by an editorial entitled "TVA and the American Dream." Pritchett could not think of another federal agency that could have inspired such a phrase.[103] The picture of twenty-eight dams, all operating as a single system in a watershed of forty thousand square miles, symbolized human control of the environment for grand purposes. Electricity itself was a powerful symbol of progress that reminded Pritchett of Henry Adams's use of the dynamo as the symbol of modernity. This was especially true of hydroelectric dams. A steam plant was an installation and nothing more. "But the damming of a river creates an entire new physical environment."[104] The symbolic power of TVA was heightened by the simple yet grand design of its dams, with their sleek, functional lines, in which architecture and engineering were fused. To Pritchett this was "the architecture of public relations."[105] Finally, Pritchett regarded TVA as having contributed positive symbols of government: its corporate form as an agency for the development of a region, its enlightened personnel system which was free from the claims of patronage, and its proof that "planning can grow out of popular consensus." TVA gave Americans confidence that government could get the job done, in depression and war.[106] Such powerful symbols appealed to both the pragmatism and idealism of Americans. TVA was doing very concrete things for people, and the tangible results could be seen in the water and on the land. There was also appeal to the "myth of Arcadia." "The impulse to look down a valley in order to gain a new prospect, an aperture into the future, was as old as the opening, following on the American revolution, of new awareness of the national landscape."[107] The memory of Daniel Boone opening up the Cumberland Valley was refreshed in a new form. In a time of economic and spiritual depression, TVA promised the hope of renewal and tapped the romantic, utopian strain in American culture. The emotional power of these representations of TVA was used, by Lilienthal and others, to strengthen public credibility in TVA. The halo effect perhaps survives to the present day.

Luther Gulick, presidential adviser and prominent public administrator, described TVA in 1944 as "an integrated, decentralized, regional democratic agency for planning, executing and administering not only a great series of multipurpose, engineering works, but also for dealing with the social and economic problems which are involved within the framework of a system of free enterprise and free elections."[108] Gulick's praise is evidence that Lilienthal's claim of TVA's significance in terms of public administration found a responsive audience. Even though the grass roots myth was useful to defend autonomy from Washington and any other source of interference, TVA leaders believed in what they were doing. As Lilienthal was writing his book, he confided to his journal:

> I am trying now to point the book toward a statement of the TVA idea as it is exemplified in what we have done and the way we have done it; and its application to other situations. The more I ponder over it, the more fundamental the whole way of going about it seems. I am firmly persuaded that in years to come the deep basic lessons of the TVA will outweigh in the country's (perhaps the world's) thinking even the lessons it teaches on the mechanics of natural resource development, in much the same way as today people are coming to see quite commonly that the unified resource development of TVA completely out shadows the earlier persistent notion that it was simply a power enterprise.[109]

Lilienthal preached to the country, with an eye to the impact of his message on important people in Washington, especially the president. Clapp preached the TVA ideal to a generation of TVA professionals. There is abundant testimony from those who heard Clapp talk to TVA seminars that his words gave people a sense of meaning and purpose for their work.

Selznick regarded TVA as especially needing the security of a guiding ideology because it was an unprecedented kind of organization, set down in a region that did not ask for it and was suspicious of it, and with which it had to come to terms.[110] Myth for Selznick, then, helped TVA leaders mediate between the agency and its environment and provided internal cohesion and a sense of direction. It gave meaning to the lives of people who worked there, so that "to defend the organization is often to defend oneself."[111]

Selznick also understood that any such set of guiding ideas would be "diverse and unstable" in their sources and functions.[112] No organization could force a complete correspondence between idealization, which was myth, and reality. The core myth "may infuse the organization as a whole with a special outlook." But there would still necessarily be variations in response to practical realities.[113] The strength of the core myth permitted variations without any challenge to the central ideas. However, this could lead, Selznick thought, to organizational self-deception.

> The multiplication of the function it [myth] serves may strongly bolster the doctrine because of the ease with which it comes to hand as repetitive problems are faced. . . . The utility of an idea—not so much in inquiry as in smoothing over a predetermined course of action—may easily invest it with a specious cogency, drawing attention away from objective tests and evidence. . . . A formula, if it is sufficiently pat, may be a substitute for inquiry, a possibility which is strongly reinforced if the formula also promotes a resilient self-consciousness.[114]

Selznick predicted the future of TVA in these words better than he could have known at the time. The myth, as resource for action and protection, was to be become a source of unreality within TVA and among its friends, for the very reason that Selznick predicted. It became a substitute for inquiry.

The Past as Prologue

THE MOST important task for the leaders of a new organization is to create and manage an organizational culture consisting of two main elements, a sense of purpose and a method of work.[1] The creation of a culture solves two basic problems. The purposes of the organization are
made clear. And guidelines for internal governance and relations with the
external world are set. Even though the pattern of goals and relationships
that develops may be loosely coupled, an equilibrium is created which, if
it works to most people's satisfaction, acquires stability and is not easy to
change.

The myths that describe these patterns are not to be confused with
behavior itself, but they influence behavior.[2] Organizational culture need
not be uniform, but there must be some way of negotiating diversity, both
internally and externally. A loosely coupled organization may do this, as
TVA did to a great extent, by bargaining among divisions to give each the
autonomy it needs consistent with the needs of others.

The founding leaders of organizations must be teachers, and this is
exactly what the struggle between A. E. Morgan and his colleagues was
about. David Lilienthal, Gordon Clapp, and others invented a coherent
culture, and saw it as important to do so, because of the extraordinary
opposition TVA faced in its first years. The private utilities would have
killed TVA had they been able to do so. Many people in the valley were
unsure about it. The departments in Washington had their enthusiasm for
TVA under control. TVA faced a series of tough fights all at once, and it
had to be given an identity for which its people could fight. In addition to
fighting for its sheer survival, TVA was a hybrid that did not quite fit
within the structure of American federalism. A theory of justification had
to be invented.

Lilienthal's strong personal need to give general significance to his ambition and achievements was an important, and unique, factor in this
story. The fact that he kept a journal throughout his adult life, seven fat
volumes of which were published, only one posthumously, suggests a
person who gave some importance to his own career. Certainly this
strong personal need to be of significance, when combined with a genuine belief in the newness and creativity of the TVA idea and form, helps
explain the intensity and fervor that Lilienthal brought to the writing
of TVA: Democracy on the March.[3] Lilienthal was fortunate to have

Gordon Clapp as an alter ego, for although Lilienthal was a talented popularizer for external audiences, Clapp was highly self-conscious about the art of administration and continually taught as he managed. The combination of Lilienthal and Clapp meant that the first generation of TVA employees were very much influenced by their teaching. But such teaching was, in large part, consistent with the experience of the students.

Once the main contours of an organizational culture are shaped, then that culture is used to interpret new issues. Thus, choices made in an organization at one time in history may have special influence over subsequent decisions.[4] If past decisions are thought to have been valuable in achieving organizational goals, they are then seen as a good guide for the resolution of new problems.

Organizations also create their own environments in a perceptual sense.[5] The grass roots doctrine gave TVA a dynamic wedge into its own environment. For example, the use of valley constituencies to lobby Washington was seen as democracy at the grass roots. Fending off federal agencies such as the General Accounting Office or the Bureau of the Budget was understood as guardianship of TVA autonomy. TVA gave itself legitimacy to shape the environment to serve its requirements. There is a fine line here between genuine responsiveness to constituencies in the environment and their manipulation.

The stronger the organizational culture, the greater the risk that the culture will become dated and incongruent with changes in the environment. It is the task of leadership to make sure that this does not happen and that strategies of adaptation are formulated, articulated, and implemented. This may require the reinterpretation of myth. This task is at least as difficult as creating viable myths in the first place. Opposition is most likely to come from within those places in the organization and from constituent groups who most value myth in its original form. They are not as malleable as they were in the founding period. It may very well be that organizational culture can only be adapted to new missions but cannot be changed in fundamental ways. The mold is too strong.[6]

The capacity of an organization to tolerate ambiguity and even conflict among its several goals and ways of working requires continuous efforts by leaders to keep the diversity in balance. The very tensions among TVA missions drove TVA leaders to proclaim, over and over, the necessity for tolerance, balance, and coordination. This helps explain the intensity of mythic language. Unity had to be preached because it was always in jeopardy.

The ideological and political framework that future TVA leaders would accept and build on was solidly in place by 1945. The chapters in Part I have emphasized the strengths of this framework for the achievement of TVA missions. Latent weaknesses were apparent, but their importance only surfaced in later years. A policy board and weak general manager would have trouble getting the divisions to provide reliable information about their activities. Divisional autonomy would be pressed at the expense of coordination and cooperation. Some programs, especially electric power, would become so strong as to make the others appear negligible. As the myth became threatened, it was believed more firmly because to deny it was to deny TVA altogether.

All of these possibilities occurred in the post–World War II history of TVA, so one can truly say that the strengths of TVA, and its culture, were also its weaknesses.

PART II

Prisoners of Myth

CHAPTER 6

Consolidating Leadership:
Clapp and Vogel

SEVERAL UNRESOLVED problems were settled during the Clapp and Vogel years, from 1947 to 1962. TVA became the power company for the Tennessee Valley. The political opposition to congressional appropriations for the construction of steam plants was overcome by the passage in 1959 of the Bond Revenue Act which enabled TVA to finance its power program through the sale of bonds. The farm demonstration program reduced the scope of its mission, and the chemical division became the national center for testing new formulas for fertilizer. The ideal of multipurpose regional development took a new form in a program for the economic development of tributary watersheds. The Clapp and Vogel years created a strong institutional and political base upon which Aubrey Wagner was able to build new, innovative programs.

Clapp and Vogel had different professional backgrounds, opposing political sponsors, and never even met. Clapp was a professional public administrator and advocate of the TVA ideal who was appointed by President Truman. Vogel was an Army Corps of Engineers officer, appointed by President Eisenhower. But the continuity of policy across their administrations was considerable. Vogel resolved the political problem of financing the power program which Clapp could not solve. This was one of the last occasions for the responsiveness of TVA to the explicit wishes of a president because, as a result of the 1959 policy change, TVA achieved almost total independence from both the president and Congress in the financing and administration of its power program.

GORDON R. CLAPP

Clapp was a 1927 graduate of Lawrence College in Wisconsin, where he held several administrative posts until 1932–33 when he studied for an MA degree in educational administration at the University of Chicago. Floyd Reeves, who taught him at Chicago, persuaded him to join TVA in July 1933 as assistant director of personnel under Reeves. Clapp became director of personnel in 1936, general manager in 1939, and board chairman in 1947, serving until 1954.

Both Reeves and Clapp were originally in A. E. Morgan's camp because Reeves was a longtime associate of Morgan's. But as A. E. became more and more eccentric, Clapp joined with Lilienthal, thus forming the most important professional partnership of his career. They were a two-person team, with Lilienthal providing vision and public leadership and Clapp contributing great skill in managing an organization by teaching. Clapp was the custodian without peer of TVA organizational culture. As head of personnel, he helped John Blandford develop the nascent TVA management system. In this process, the personnel office became responsible for TVA's administrative rules and regulations which provided the skeleton for the management system. It was natural for Clapp to interpret the general manager's role as that of teacher of the canons of TVA organizational culture.

Clapp's primary talent as an administrator was in being able to steer people without directing them. He gave those below him a free hand, made occasional suggestions, and asked penetrating questions when ideas were presented to him. He often planted ideas in the organization, through suggestions, which would return to him as recommendations from the staff.[1] His executive style, both as general manager and chairman, was to convene staff members with diverse views and attempt to work out agreement through discussion.

John Oliver, as general manager, was very much an assistant to Clapp as chairman, who by 1946 had worked at TVA for thirteen years.[2] And it was perfectly clear to the heads of the TVA offices that Clapp *was* the board: "[B]elow the board, Gordon Clapp was primus inter pares. He was one of the geniuses, maybe the genius, of the organization," remembered Harry Case who succeeded Clapp as head of Personnel.[3] But Clapp continually encouraged ideas and discussion.[4] He relied on intelligent staff recommendations and urged staff members to resolve their differences before board meetings when a formal decision would be made. If they came to the board divided, he would send them back to resolve the disagreement, within policy guidelines set by the board.[5] He was not dependent on staff but valued their expertise, which he never hesitated to query.

John Oliver remembered the numerous self-correcting devices in TVA, which thirty years later he thought had been lost. One example was the action of Gabriel Wessenauer, the extremely influential head of the Office of Power, who after a dispute with other office heads, which he had won, stopped by Oliver's office to tell him that the other side had failed to make their strongest arguments. It was Oliver's view that Clapp instilled this ethic of collegiality and taught it by example.[6]

In a retrospective essay in the *Public Administration Review*, Harry Case described Clapp as "the administrative man," by which Case meant that "the administrator sees to it that the administrative environment is such that the expert has the maximum freedom to plan and carry out that part of the organization's total job that he, through specialized training, is equipped to execute. To do this the expert has to be fully aware of the organization's overall objectives and overall policies."[7] Case saw Clapp's artistry to be managing the union of organizational purpose and expertise.

One cannot measure the influence of Clapp on TVA organizational culture, but signs of his influence with TVA professionals crop up continuously. A 1989 interview with a retired TVA engineer evoked Clapp's name in response to a question about "idealism" in TVA when the engineer entered it in 1952: "There was idealism, a sense of purpose and integrity. It was the reason I stayed. It wasn't a job or career but a religious vocation." He particularly remembered a talk Clapp had given to a group of TVA engineers in 1954. Clapp was not going to be reappointed chairman, and political storm clouds were gathering in the form of the Dixon-Yates controversy. But Clapp talked of TVA achievements—twenty dams in twenty years, all built within 1 percent of estimated cost. He then told the story of the Douglas Dam in which TVA had resisted political pressure and ensured that the judgments of its engineers about the best site for the dam were respected: "There was a sense of idealism, a sense of respect and the understanding that the staff would make the technical engineering judgements and the board would do political activities."[8] The engineer had saved a copy of the talk, as if it were inspirational material. One sees in Clapp's words an appeal to the politics of the nonpolitical: "The Douglas Dam story illustrates beautifully the importance of integrity in engineering, integrity in management, the integrity of a Board that will not trim or hedge in the face of political pressure. . . . The Douglas Dam story certifies that the TVA knows and is willing to pay the price of making unpopular recommendations." Many efforts had been made, Clapp continued, to chip away at TVA's autonomy by bills in Congress, but "none of them passed because the people of this area and their representatives in the Congress rose up in protest to preserve the integrity of this organization."[9] Clapp was invoking nonpolitical politics as a resource for TVA, a nonpolitical organization governed by professional judgments. This is often the most effective kind of politics because it protects organizational autonomy.

Some of Clapp's associates at TVA thought he lacked a full range of political skills. Neal Bass did not think he worked with Congress as well as Lilienthal and remembered that H. A. Morgan often had to smooth over frictions between Clapp and TVA constituencies in the valley. Clapp, in fact, liked to keep his personal distance from such groups.[10] Harry Wiersma thought both Clapp and his disciple Wagner to be ideal "civil servants" who were not as good as Lilienthal at dealing with "big political problems."[11] Edward Falck, who regarded Clapp as a close friend, saw him as "honest and scholarly, unimaginative and unoriginal, an implementor and institutionalizer."[12] Clapp received no praise for having the personal skills of a politician. His personality was courteous and cordial but also reserved, even distant.[13] His virtues and deficiencies as an organizational leader, however, were two sides of the same coin. Lilienthal was a superb political leader and an indifferent manager, whereas Clapp was the ideal administrator who did not seek or relish tasks of political leadership. It was no surprise that when Lilienthal created the Development and Resources Corporation in 1955, to replicate his TVA achievements around the world, he called on Clapp to be his second in command. John Oliver, TVA general manager under Clapp, who also worked at D & R, remembered that the relationship of the two men at D & R was just as it had been at TVA.[14]

It would not be fair to attribute the failure of TVA to find a politically satisfactory solution to the problem of financing the power program to Clapp's limited political skills. In fact, Clapp was very effective in describing issues and problems to congressional committees because of his ability to state a position clearly and persuasively.[15] The political obstacles in the way of a self-financing program were too great. When Vogel, who was more skillful politically than Clapp, found a solution, the political context was also more favorable. Both Clapp and Vogel were very capable administrators who kept TVA programs moving forward.

THE SEARCH FOR MISSIONS

As the war neared an end, there was discussion within TVA about what possible future missions might keep the authority as dynamic as it had been. For a time it seemed that TVA would change from a building to an operating agency, as Clapp suggested in a 1943 memo to the board: "We are now well past the peak of heavy construction and find ourselves devoting more and more attention to operating problems. For a while at least we are going to find it difficult to make the transition from a growing agency with a lot of major jobs to an operating agency which continues to grow."[16]

It was too early to anticipate the great rush of postwar construction of steam plants for the power program. The prewar excitement seemed to have faded in the immediate period after the war. An unsigned memo of July 1945 from the TVA Washington office reported unhappiness with TVA postwar plans in the Bureau of the Budget:

A member of the Bureau staff told me that TVA's budget presentation for 1946 was disappointing. It was felt that coherent policy and program were lacking which was considered a serious threat to our independent status. Something of the nature of the programs suggested in our memo on problems and opportunities seems to be what is expected. Our more careful delineation of the objectives and methods of our development programs, on which we're now working, should be satisfactory.[17]

George Gant, the first general manager under Clapp, raised the question in the late 1940s of whether TVA should continue to exist at all. Perhaps, he asked, it should be seen as a temporary agency that would do its work and then fade away. Gant was responding to the decline in dam construction after the best sites were used. The development of the river for power, flood control, and navigation had been the clear focus that united the different parts of TVA, including agriculture. Once the dams were built, how were the separate missions to be linked?[18] But evidently this didn't get very far. William Hayes, an assistant general manager in the 1930s who left for the war and later returned, remembered:

[TVA] was running along pretty much as it had before, but at a slower tempo because the pressures and the volume of development programs, particularly construction programs . . . had slowed down. . . . And there was a bit of an effort to take stock of things and to really reach for some kind of post-war role for TVA that would be a substitute for the earlier glamour pressures. As an agency, there's always the question of what is the terminal point of some of these activities. And I know this is the first question I asked when I got back from the war, and it was damn near heresy.[19]

Hayes estimated when all the principal TVA programs might be terminated and found few to be long-lived, but "this was considered almost heresy in those days." He left TVA feeling that it lacked the dynamism of the prewar years.

Leland Allbaugh, who was John McAmis's successor as head of the agricultural program, remembered that H. A. Morgan was able to slow the development of the power program but that after he left the board in 1949, increasing attention was given to power. Still, "they were trying to keep power from overriding in 1952–53 and talked about it at board meetings."[20]

A strong search for new missions loyal to the multipurpose vision characterized the Clapp years, as one might expect from a Lilienthal lieutenant who had himself been influential in helping to articulate the TVA myth. This vision was consistent with the management system that Blandford and Clapp had created.

The management philosophy embodied in the Blandford report continued to be strong, in theory and practice. In a 1949 talk to TVA employees, general manager George Gant underlined the central principles of TVA management—the sole responsibility of the board for policy decision which exempted it from detailed oversight by Washington, the delegation of operations to the divisions, the commitment of all TVA staff members to the purposes of TVA, the need for compromise among the multiple purposes of TVA, and the importance of technical assistance to state and local governments on tasks of regional development.[21] In his talk, Gant divided TVA into two groups of programs: first, operating the huge physical resources of the dams, power-generating systems, and chemical plants; and second, working with state and local agencies and business groups. TVA had autonomy in regard to water, power, and fertilizer, he said, but "the very heart and spirit of TVA lie in this conception of strengthening local institutions as contrasted with centralized institutions."[22]

In a 1949 paper on management improvement, prepared at the request of the Bureau of the Budget, Gant described how TVA appraised the effectiveness of its programs—budget preparation, internal budget hearings, the formulation of work programs, the administrative release system in which specific units were made accountable to the general manager and board for accomplishing specific tasks, and employee-management conferences. This meant, he wrote, "on the spot" reviews of effectiveness rather than simple compliance with regulations laid down from the top.[23] It seems to have been assumed that practical people working together, at all levels of the organization, could determine how well programs were working without a formal process of evaluation.

Internal documents reveal a very strong commitment in the general manager's office to collaboration among programs and over all organizational cohesion. For example, in 1951 Gant asked Harry Case if it would not be a good idea to encourage each division head to distribute the TVA annual report and budget as the basis of staff discussions, because perhaps "we do not have enough general knowledge and understanding of current activities and emphases as might be desired."[24]

In May 1952, the new general manager, John Oliver, held a meeting of division heads to discuss hard questions about TVA management, such as the effectiveness of the general manager's office, how division heads might play a more effective role in general authority policy making and be brought to assume responsibility for the "total" TVA program, what plans existed for training people to assume major responsibilities, whether there was "real delegation" of responsibilities, and how the general manager might better help to foster responsibility below.[25] Such questions were presumably asked with a genuine desire for honest answers and a commitment to the ubiquitous canons of the TVA management system of collegiality, expertise, and delegation. Oliver's notes on the staff conference held on May 23 reveal a familiar mix of commitment to and uncertainty about how to achieve collegiality across divisions. Excerpts from his notes give the flavor: "Dam building program was cohesive, now gone. Case suggests more regionalization [of field offices]. Wessenauer says tributary watershed program could be it—harder to do. Coordination on most problems o.k. . . . Trouble is that on problems all in one field, others don't have a chance to contribute. . . . Agreed board meeting is not place for cross-fertilization."[26]

It was acknowledged in the meeting that program heads were not really interested in each other's programs. Joseph Swidler suggested that they meet regularly, perhaps once a week. The chief engineer thought that was too often, and the head of the power program said that he had no interest in discussing fertilizer chemistry. Oliver suggested that the regional studies unit should be of interest to everybody. It was finally suggested that each division head list four or five problems to be discussed at future meetings. This attempt at collegiality in a multipurpose authority reappears again and again.

Wessenauer described the management system at this time as one of strong division heads coordinated by Clapp and the general manager.[27] Leland Allbaugh, longtime head of agriculture, remembered the management system as working effectively: "I enjoyed working in TVA more than any other organization because we developed the ideas to go up to the board. You felt responsible for the programs when you got through. You knew you had the board behind you. That makes implementation work in contrast to having ideas handed down."[28]

Of course, Allbaugh was describing his responsibility for his own programs. He sent ideas up, and if they were accepted he felt secure in implementing them. It does not seem likely that there was much poaching by his colleagues. The system encouraged a mutual protection society among top managers. They did have to defend their recommendations at board-staff conferences when board members and the general manager and his assistants might ask hard questions. But the more important question was whether the board and general manager had sufficient control over policy alternatives and operations. Both the board and general manager had to trust TVA managers to a great extent. They had no independent basis for judgment. This perhaps explains the great emphasis placed by the board and general manager on collegiality and knowledge of the whole by the parts. Without such collegiality, the entire management system would be called into question.

POWER COMPANY OF THE VALLEY

The most dramatic and important story of the postwar TVA was the gradual emergence of the agency as the power company for the Tennessee Valley. This development was not anticipated by the TVA Act. The act was ambiguous about the reach of the electric power mission. Provision (j) of section 4 grants TVA power to build specific dams and reservoirs, create a nine-foot channel in the river, maintain a water supply, promote navigation, control flood waters, and adds that TVA "shall have power to acquire or construct power houses, power structures, transmission lines, navigation projects, and incidental works in the Tennessee river and its tributaries, and to unite the various power installations into one or more systems by transmission lines."[29] Power is not mentioned again until section 10 which authorizes TVA to sell surplus electric power not used in its other operations, giving preference to states, counties, municipalities, and cooperative organizations of citizens or farmers not organized for business or profit. The fullest possible use of electricity on farms is to be encouraged. Section 11 gives priority in service to domestic and rural consumers of power over corporations. Industrial sales are to be used primarily to secure a sufficiently high load and revenue return to permit domestic and rural use at the lowest possible rates or to increase domestic and rural use of electricity.

A paper written in the Office of Power in 1948 to be used as a pamphlet by the Office of Information stated that "TVA is directed to provide for the maximum generation of electricity consistent with the primary purposes of developing navigation and controlling floods." And power was to be provided "at the least possible cost and in such manner as to encourage increased domestic and rural use of electricity." The goal of low-cost power, especially for farmers and people in cities, was originally the prime objective.[30] This language fits the context of a backward region in 1933. Electric power development was presented as part of an integral program of water and land development. This is not the same thing as expecting TVA to become a monopoly power company for the Tennessee Valley.

The roots of the power company, however, were present in Lilienthal's policy to keep the utilities out of the TVA area. If there were no other providers, TVA would, by implication, have to meet the needs of all future power users in the region. These implications were not at first clear because the number of distributors was so small and the potential hydroelectric power seemed much greater than any potential demand. But Lilienthal's victory over A. E. Morgan ensured that TVA's electric power program would eventually be understood to be the best way that TVA could contribute to the economic development of the valley. A monopoly power company would have to keep pace with potential demand.

Neal Bass remembered some uncertainty within TVA about how the power capacity developed during the war years for defense production would be used after the war. Lilienthal would ask the board, "How will we use all this power?"[31] Yet in a February 1944 talk to TVA distributors in Chattanooga, Lilienthal used the line that was to be voiced by TVA until the early 1980s:

> Ten years ago there were some who said that there was already too much elec-tricity in this region—a "surplus" it was called. Therefore the building by TVA of additional power supply in large quantities was a waste of public funds—the argument ran. In reply we said that there could never be too much electricity provided its price were so adjusted as to encourage the almost limitless use for it. The record of the region supports that proposition. Looking into the post-war period I am willing to stand on that statement of ten years ago and to repeat it. There is no such thing as too much electrical energy. For electricity is a creator, a builder. Electrical energy creates its own market.[32]

Lilienthal had acted on this principle when he had created the Electric Home and Farm Authority to sell electrical appliances to farmers so they might increase their electrical usage. Decisions of this kind gradually led to the development of a TVA gospel that economic growth was depen-dent on the electricity supply and that the power supply should stay ahead of demand in order to create growth.

The decision to build steam plants, once the hydro sites had been fully developed, was a choice to develop coal-fired plants independent of the river. There is some indication from oral histories that H. A. Morgan was reluctant to see this happen for fear that the balance of land and water ecology would be upset in favor of excessive industrial development. But the logic of the monopoly of power was too strong. Both H. A. and Neal Bass regretted that the eventual dominance of the power program within TVA overshadowed the multipurpose fabric.[33]

It is not conceivable that either TVA or its congressional sponsors would have deliberately set limits to the growth of TVA's power program in the postwar years so that the generation of electricity would be limited to hydro sites. To do so would have been to invite the private utilities back into the valley and to require TVA to develop a new partnership with them. It is not realistic to think that an organization that had swollen during the war would be content to stop building and set limits to its growth. However, there was a prolonged partisan political struggle in Washington about the issue, which ended only in 1959 when TVA was empowered to issue bonds to finance its power program. The conflict was not about ecological balance, as H. A. Morgan might have posed it, but a rehash of the old public versus private power fight.

The first postwar request for a steam plant was for the New Johnson-ville facility in President Truman's 1946 budget. The TVA annual report for 1946–47 explained the need: "The seriousness of a shortage of power can hardly be over emphasized. It would, in effect, place a ceiling on the development of the entire region . . . which is still behind the nation."[34]

The expansion of the power program was to be justified from that day on as the key to the economic development of a still backward region. Thus Clapp told a House subcommittee in 1948 that "TVA is the sole supplier of electricity for this entire region that we serve. . . . We are the generating company, the transmitting company and the wholesaler. We have contracts over a period of 20 years from their initial dates. We are committed by terms of the contracts entered into under the policies established by law, to do our utmost to keep up with their load growth in supplying electricity."[35]

The private utilities were opposed to the new plants for fear of TVA expanding into their service areas. The Republican controlled House rejected the bill in 1948, but Truman's reelection and the return of a Democratic Congress led to approval in 1949.[36] A second steam plant was subsequently approved, and both plants were under construction by 1950. The annual report of 1949–50 explained how easy it was for TVA to adapt to building steam plants because TVA had its own engineers and construction teams ready to go to work. Such staffs could be quickly deployed from one project to another. The same argument was later made in the construction of nuclear plants.[37]

By 1954, 64 percent of TVA's power was from hydro operations, compared to 80 percent in 1945, and 36 percent was supplied by six steam-plant generating units at two plants, not counting the large Shawnee steam plant built near Paducah, Kentucky, to provide energy for a plant being built by the Atomic Energy Commission. A new plant at Kingston, Tennessee, was also under construction.[38] An additional justification for expanding the power program was the need to meet the increasing requirements of national defense at Oak Ridge and Paducah, especially after the Korean War began in 1950. In 1937 and 1938 TVA had signed two contracts which provided that priority would be given to the needs of the federal government over other customers should the federal government request it. In 1953 Clapp told a conference of TVA staff members and representatives of the Tennessee Municipal League that federal agencies "get priority on the power supply if needed, because the national defense requires it."[39] Permission from Congress to construct the Shawnee plant was given in 1951, after TVA had to buy power from outside the region for Oak Ridge because of the Korean War.[40]

As early as 1949, TVA director and former senator James Pope wrote President Truman, in Clapp's absence, that "if another defense emergency should arise, the existence of margins of power supply which can be immediately channeled by TVA into defense production will no doubt prove to be of the same incalculable value to the Nation as was the case in 1939 and 1940."[41] In 1951 Clapp wrote Senator McKellar of Tennessee about TVA's "large and expanding construction program" which had been approved by the House. It included five steam-generating plants, two hydroelectric dams, and the installation of several generating units at existing sites. TVA's generating capacity would be doubled, reaching 3 million kilowatts. Clapp's justification was national defense.[42]

During these years it became TVA doctrine that the supply of energy was the principle stimulus for demand and that therefore TVA must always stay ahead of existing demand in its building program in order to meet future needs. In his 1954 lectures at the University of Chicago, Clapp gave a litany about how the experts had consistently underestimated the need for electric power in the Tennessee Valley. The private utilities, he said, had waited until demand exceeded supply before building. They preferred to restrict expansion, limit demand, and keep costs high. The heavy capital requirements and lack of competition among private utilities meant that there would soon be too little electric power in the United States. Therefore, TVA and other public utilities must be bolder and respond to national needs by anticipating future demand. This could be done by keeping rates low in order to encourage use and permit expansion. Economic development would follow. And, of course, the requirements for national security would be met.[43] Aubrey Wagner and David Freeman were to make the same argument twenty-five years later.

Steam-generating plants use coal, and TVA eventually found itself to be one of the biggest coal customers in the nation. John Oliver told the Tennessee Valley Public Power Association, the network of distributors, in 1952 that TVA would soon require more than ten million tons of coal a year. He then added a point of great importance for later years. The TVA rate structure "would be endangered unless we bought coal at the lowest possible price."[44] The TVA axiom that power must be sold at the lowest possible cost was dependent upon the price of the energy source. Hydroelectric power was relatively cheap, as was coal in the early years. But not only did the cost of coal become greater in the energy shortages of the 1970s, but the cost of cleaning the air from pollution became a great burden for TVA and other utilities. This helps explain TVA's struggles with the Environmental Protection Agency in the 1970s. Cheap energy was the basis of TVA success. Ironically, Aubrey Wagner was persuaded in 1965 to move toward nuclear power because he thought it would be cheaper and cleaner, and therefore less controversial, than coal.[45]

TVA officials preached the gospel of cheap power as the key to the valley's industrial development. New jobs had to be created in order to reduce the departure of youth from the area. Therefore new electricity generating capacity had to be increased, in the words of a TVA staff economist, "in advance of the requirements of industry."[46] Political scientist Roscoe Martin noted in 1956 that TVA was still reluctant to claim the obvious, that power was now its dominant activity. The official claim, he said, was still that power was auxiliary to other purposes. Yet the production and sale of power had come to dominate TVA thinking:

> Here is where TVA takes its stand, here is where the battle lines are drawn in Congress, here is where attacks on the agency center. The process by which TVA evolved as a great electric power utility was a gradual one, with no one step calculated to produce the end result achieved. That result is an over-all program in which a secondary activity, the production and sale of surplus power, has come to overshadow other program goals, some say to the considerable disadvantage of the whole.[47]

These developments strengthened the influence inside TVA of the two strongest divisions, engineering and power. The engineers in both groups thought of TVA in technological terms rather than as a multipurpose agency. Louis Van Mol, general manager under Wagner, remembered that Clapp used to talk to the engineers about TVA as a whole but that the top engineering staff had little interest in broadening the views of their engineers.[48] Van Mol also remembered that the professionals in the Office of Power had little interest in such broadening lessons. In fact, he said, "power tried to operate pretty much on its own. It didn't pay much attention to other parts of TVA. Many, many efforts were made to encourage the power people to get curious about what TVA was doing elsewhere. Everything that TVA did had to do with some kind of resource development which ultimately would provide a market for TVA power. They didn't seize on that opportunity."[49]

Van Mol attributed this indifference to the rest of TVA to the fact that the Office of Power had the largest number of employees, expenditures, and revenues of any TVA division. Another reason was that the office had its headquarters in Chattanooga, physically separate from the rest of TVA. The office was a virtually self-contained unit. The functions of marketing, power production, and distribution were all under the manager of power. These developments in the late 1940s and early 1950s forecast the future shape of TVA and some of the problems it was to experience when the power genie was completely out of the bottle.

The Agricultural and Chemical Programs

These two programs were under the same administrative umbrella because the fertilizers developed at Muscle Shoals were supplied to farmers in the test demonstration program. The number of test demonstration farms increased in the immediate postwar years, but emphasis then shifted toward the development of new fertilizer for the industry with few test demonstration farms and those strictly for research on fertilizer. The

1951 annual report publicized the contracts that TVA had signed with seven private fertilizer manufacturers, each of which would undertake an educational program in behalf of new fertilizers developed at TVA. It was also reported that the state agricultural colleges had assumed the primary financial responsibility for the planning and supervision of 75 percent of all the test demonstration farms in the region, consistent with the TVA philosophy of shifting responsibility to local agencies.[50]

These policy changes in the direction of increasing TVA's technological capacities in fertilizer research and development occasioned a reorganization. The position of chief conservation engineer, held by Neal Bass, was abolished in 1951, and Bass became an assistant general manager. The next year a new Office of Chemical Engineering, directed by Harry Curtis, was created. The technological work at Muscle Shoals was thereby put on an equal level within the organization with engineering and power. Agriculture remained a division, comparable to divisions like regional studies, forestry, and reservoir properties. The dominant offices within TVA, as the former departments were now called, were the technological ones—construction engineering, power, and chemical engineering.

The agricultural relations program had received skeptical review from the top for some time. General manager Gant wrote the board in late 1947:

> There is no phase of TVA responsibility undergoing more scrutiny than that related to the production, distribution, and use of nitrogen and phosphatic materials. The TVA should be much better prepared for this review than it is and as it must be if it is to avoid compromises. This preparation calls for reappraisal of distribution and financial policies, more precise techniques for reporting on program status and progress toward stated objectives, and a strengthening at key points in the organization where there is too great reliance on too small a number of individuals. Mr. Bass and I have discussed these problems at length and in detail. Steps are being taken to correct this situation by the end of the fiscal year.[51]

Gant's memo was a not too oblique reference to dissatisfaction with McAmis and the agricultural relations division. Norman Wengert described the problem to which Gant referred as the reluctance of "old timers" to develop more systematic methods of testing fertilizer. They preferred the informal, personal relations with farmers that had prevailed to a more rigorous research and evaluation strategy.[52] TVA top managers began to see these problems in the agricultural relations division by 1940, and many conferences were held in the next few years to see what could be done. Efforts were made from the top to enrich the variety of expertise within the division by adding economists, agronomists, and other agricultural scientists, but they usually left in frustration from lack of an appreciative audience from the "old timers." The weakness of TVA's management system was that it assumed that subunits were willing and capable to discover and correct their own deficiencies. But the agricultural people did not regard the analysis of test demonstration results as inadequate. They relied on farmers learning from other farmers, through the county agent system, a practical and empirical method. The board, general manager, and chief conservation engineers were not going to substitute their judgments for those of the operators, despite their uneasiness. They wanted the group to appraise its own work.

Wengert understood these issues as symptoms of TVA's failure to develop a clear "review and analysis function" through a formally established staff in the general manager's office. The tradition of small, central staffs and reliance on the line for analysis and evaluation precluded this possibility. Wengert, who had worked in the agricultural relations division, believed that effective decentralization required the auditing of line functions by staff at the top. And, in addition, the integration of programs required the kinds of studies that only independent staffs, rather than the line divisions, could provide.[53] We see here the legacy of H. A. Morgan's and John McAmis's preoccupation with serving individual farmers to the exclusion of broader issues and missions. Wengert complained, for example, that questions such as the role of agricultural credit, the need for capital and markets, farm size, and rural employment opportunities were simply ignored by the division.[54]

The reader will remember how the role of forestry within TVA was limited by Morgan and McAmis. A 1944 memo to Neal Bass from Willis Baker, director of forestry relations, illustrates the point by arguing that a recent memo from the agricultural people had overemphasized "the importance of agriculture in a region where relatively large areas of land are so poorly adapted to cultivation." It would be better, he said, to emphasize a balanced economy.[55]

Leland Allbaugh, who became head of the agricultural division in 1952, succeeded in broadening the approach to fertilizer development and use. He remembered that the board had depended entirely upon McAmis. "He was the Wessenauer of his day."[56] This was a reference to the great authority within TVA exercised by Gabriel Wessenauer, longtime manager of power. Allbaugh remembered that he had had to fight McAmis and Harry Curtis, the latter being the former head of the chemical office who had joined the board and was a friend of McAmis's.[57] John Oliver, the general manager, was Allbaugh's chief ally in this fight. Oliver remembered "I began turning the screws on McAmis and had no hesitation about talking to Curtis. . . . McAmis was a stubborn old guy. The program needed a good reexamination, for example, the shift back to nitrogen began to occur while I was still there."[58] Allbaugh was highly critical of McAmis for trying to preserve even the smallest family farm, no matter how uneconomical. He was critical of the agricultural colleges for not examining larger questions about the economics of agriculture so that larger and more productive farms might be encouraged in the valley. He believed that his chief achievement had been in creating support for TVA fertilizer products in the commercial industry so that the Muscle Shoals research center became recognized as a world center for fertilizer research and production.[59]

The creation of the Office of Chemical Engineering, with agricultural relations a secondary unit within it, was a perhaps inevitable step toward a TVA of separate, largely autonomous offices, each of which was located in a different city. Construction engineering was in Knoxville, power in Chattanooga, and chemical engineering in Muscle Shoals. Each Office was virtually a world unto itself. When Aubrey Wagner became general manager in 1954, he initiated tours of TVA installations by groups of fifteen to eighteen division heads. Louis Van Mol, then assistant to Wagner and later general manager, was amazed to discover that some of these division heads had never met; they had done business by telephone. The tours improved the situation: "[I]n the earlier days the top people did know each other. . . . Maybe the wartime concentration on getting a job done just didn't provide enough time for these people to get together— and maybe this spilled over into the later years."[60]

NATURAL RESOURCE PROGRAMS

Within Clapp's TVA, the term *natural resource development* applied to most of the nonpower programs—agriculture, forestry, navigation, regional studies, and recreation on TVA reservoirs. Congressional appropriations paid for such programs, which have never been a large part of the TVA budget. Funding declined from $7.5 million in 1947 to $3.25 million in 1953, which was less than 2 percent of the total TVA budget.[61] Yet these programs were seen by Clapp and his general managers, in Roscoe Martin's words, as the basis to "the whole TVA idea." Without resource development activities, Martin wrote in his twenty-year retrospective volume on TVA, the authority would be only an engineering and public utility enterprise, which explained why TVA people referred to resource development as the "critical idea" behind the agency. Martin believed that TVA's character would be substantially changed if resource-development activities were further diminished or eliminated.[62]

Clapp certainly believed in this bundle of missions. His 1954 lectures described the idea of a single government corporation with multiple purposes as derived from the ideals of the conservation movement in which the resources of a region could be developed.[63] He encouraged a small number of economists in the general manager's office to think creatively about natural-resource issues. Steven Roback, who later joined the faculty of Columbia University, headed the staff; John Krutilla, later of Resources for the Future, thought about power questions; and Vernon Ruttan, later of the University of Minnesota, looked at agricultural questions. Their assignment was to produce fresh ideas for possible TVA activities. Krutilla recalled that Clapp was understood to believe that "the ideas don't bubble up" from below in the organization as they once did.[64] Clapp valued staff ideas, but Vogel tried to replace them with a management office reporting directly to him. Most of the staff left by 1955.[65] Richard Freeman, later a board member, was a young TVA lawyer in the 1950s, and he remembered the liveliness of the economic analysis staff and was himself a member of a luncheon group of young turks that included Vernon Ruttan and David Freeman, also then a young lawyer.[66] It is not far fetched to suggest that the two Freemans developed their commitment to TVA as a natural-resource development agency in the TVA of the 1950s. Clapp nurtured the effort because he believed in it. But he made limited use of the analysis. The tradition of relying on the line offices for analysis and advice was too strong.

Several attempts were made by Gant and Oliver to organize natural-resource programs in a coherent way. In 1948 a new Office of Reservoir and Community Relations was formed. It had within it divisions of regional studies, health and safety, and reservoir properties. As George Gant wrote to the board, the ostensible purpose was to encourage more "effective organizational association at levels below the Office of the General Manager."[67] John Ferris, who became the head of the new office, was less than enthusiastic about its prospects at the time. He later saw it as an effort to respond to the hostility of the Republican 80th Congress which identified resource development ideas with "planning." The new office seemed to do tangible and useful things. But Ferris saw no great benefit from the experience. No effort was made to strengthen any of the programs. The divisions had little work in common.[68] The new office was not long-lived. Regional studies was eventually brought into the general manager's office, and by 1953 the divisions of agriculture, forestry, health and safety, navigation and flood control, and reservoir properties were listed in the organization chart as a cluster of programs, apart from any office, titled "Unified Resource Development."[69]

The political temper of the time was not conducive to natural-resource development. In 1952 Roscoe Martin, a political scientist at Syracuse University, approached Clapp with the idea of convening several social scientists to write an independent book on TVA that would focus on the "social science aspects of the TVA program: on the social, economic, political and administrative phases of TVA operations, and upon the manifold effects of those operations on life and living in the Tennessee Valley."[70] Such an analysis would have had to examine the national-resource programs in their variety. Clapp and the board were agreeable, but the study was never begun. The book that was edited by Martin and published in 1956 contained essays, primarily by TVA staff members, that idealized TVA programs.[71] The original study was not begun because Clapp, who had supported the idea strongly, did not wish to give the new Republican administration any information about TVA programs that might be seen as "experimental or controversial," in Martin's words. In fact, the House of Representatives, dominated by Republicans, had attempted to eliminate all TVA resource-development programs, but the Senate had refused. Martin wrote the prospective authors that the timing for the study was bad.[72]

Even though unified resource-development programs were not flourishing in the post-war political climate, however, Clapp had an idea for work in the tributary watersheds of the Tennessee River that would strengthen the multipurpose mission. This vision was to be revived by Wagner and to lead to the Tellico Dam fiasco of the 1970s.

TRIBUTARY WATERSHEDS

In 1936 the TVA board submitted a report to Congress that called for the development of the best dam sites on the Tennessee River but also cited the need for smaller projects for water storage, flood control, and recreation on the river's tributaries.[73] The Elk and Duck rivers were singled out as particularly promising sites. At that time, TVA interest was in the watershed as a "hydrologic unit," with little thought to relating water and land.[74] Clapp, as general manager, set up a committee to examine problems of flooding in the Chestuee watershed in the late 1930s. He wanted a demonstration project of some kind as a basis for future plans, but the idea was postponed as war intervened.[75] Marguerite Owen credited herself with inventing the postwar idea of tributary development after taking one of her periodic tours of TVA installations in the valley at Clapp's request.[76] But George Gant, general manager under Clapp, also remembered helping to develop the small watershed program, which was "part of our rethinking of what TVA should do."[77]

TVA's first effort at watershed planning was as a laboratory for hydrologic research. A 1945 report on the Chestuee project called for complementary flood-control and land-management projects and urged the importance of local citizens participating in planning the work to be done. In 1951, teams for the Tennessee Extension Service and the state departments of education and health were brought together with TVA engineers to see what complementary projects might be developed. Unfortunately the state's interest in the project was limited, and local leadership and citizen involvement were low, so TVA let the idea languish.[78]

Clapp believed strongly that tributary watershed programs would not work unless the state governors made commitments to them. He wanted TVA to "touch with a light brush" by giving expert assistance to the initiatives of state and local groups.[79] Unfortunately the states had left such projects to federal agencies like the Bureau of Reclamation and the Army Corps of Engineers and had little interest in expanding their role.[80]

Nor was the idea that popular in TVA. The construction engineers were not enthusiastic about such small-scale projects. They thought in terms of dramatic high dams. It was unclear to the agriculturalists what their role was to be. In 1951, Harry Curtis, who had moved to the board, wrote a short paper that was critical of the Chestuee project.[81] The original plan, Curtis claimed, was that TVA would at long last make a determined effort to link the changes in land use accomplished in test demonstration farms with concomitant changes in water yield from a drainage basin. But the Chestuee project had become much more comprehensive, which raised serious doubts about the logic of selecting a watershed for the broader plan that had evolved. The project had turned into a demonstration of the creation of a community organization that would seek help from public agencies in solving agricultural, forest, hydraulic, social, and economic problems. The Chestuee project was to be a "little TVA" operating intensively in a watershed. Curtis urged that the project not be attempted in other watersheds until the lesson of Chestuee had been absorbed. Data should be gathered on the effects of changes of land use on water yield. According to Curtis, TVA's annual reports made exaggerated and unsubstantiated claims about the beneficial effects of intelligent soil management on water storage. It was believed, mistakenly, that soil management could prevent floods. But the truth was that "never in its 18 years of operation had the TVA actually measured the overall hydrologic effect of test demonstration farm practice in a single small watershed and . . . there had been no TVA project scientifically planned and executed that would relate specific single changes in land to water yield."

Curtis called for more research before a new program was launched. John Oliver answered Curtis's paper with a letter illustrating the perspective of an administrator compared to Curtis's scientific outlook. Oliver agreed that the Chestuee project was like "a little TVA operating intensively in a little watershed, which stood in relation to TVA as the authority stood to the federal government." In this sense the Chestuee project, "if developed energetically, offers the same latent threat to the TVA organizational structure that the TVA offers to the federal department structure."[82] Indeed, Oliver added, the project required that TVA achieve a higher degree of coordination and integration of technical skills than "we have ever achieved in the Valley as a whole." Curtis seemed to want to abandon this challenge, Oliver wrote. But to do so would be to set back current efforts to get different TVA divisions to work together on resource development. The enthusiasms that had developed should not be dampened. Curtis and Oliver were talking past each other, the one calling for good science and the other for imaginative administration.

Organizational difficulties within TVA also emerged. The Chestuee project was managed by a full-time coordinator who had difficulty securing cooperation from the operating divisions. He had the same problems that Blandford had as coordinator; his status in the organization was below that of the division heads he was supposed to coordinate. Eventually the director of forestry was placed in charge of all watershed coordination, but he had no staff for this purpose nor any leverage over his counterparts.[83] Natural-resource programs had very small budgets, and the tributary watershed program only limped along.[84]

Clapp saw working in the watersheds as an exploratory venture without any clear sense at the outset about what might be achieved. He devoted a section of a 1952 paper to the idea of TVA working with the states. It was time, he wrote, for TVA to "think more carefully of how we organize ourselves in relationship with the states" to strengthen their capacities.[85] He suggested that TVA might wish to create liaison officials who would work with the states on all TVA programs as representatives of the general manager and the board. Some answers might then emerge to the perennial questions that continued to plague TVA about how to relate itself to local governments and organizations. Such answers might "slow down the drive for centralization in local matters to which most other federal agencies are contributing their support and strength." If TVA could energize the states in resource-development tasks and be the contact point for state and local groups, decentralization of programs would be enhanced. Ever the public administrator, Clapp was always looking for ways that TVA might play its self-styled role as a coordinator of other government agencies at the grass roots. In the tributary watershed idea, he had a solution searching for problems to solve. He suggested the idea of valleywide conferences with state officials and community leaders in which TVA would be a catalyst for conversations about regional issues such as forestry, stream sanitation, public health, labor and management problems, agriculture, power supply, and industrial development. The catalyst role would serve an institutional purpose because, according to Clapp, "We need to find ways to make TVA continue to be conspicuously identified with economic development" and "to keep the TVA before the public in its proper role," even if the work "will be less dramatic."

Clapp was fearful that TVA might be ignored as states and local governments assumed more responsibility for economic development. TVA's role could be to "enunciate a regional objective" over and beyond its specific assignments in power, water, and agriculture. It was the only agency in the valley with that responsibility. TVA was especially well suited to lead in areas "in which regional and national interests merge." Clapp believed, as had A. E. Morgan and Lilienthal, that TVA should invent ways of doing things that could be applied elsewhere in the nation: "If we can devise methods whereby state responsibility in local flood control matters and in tributary watershed development programs takes on substance, we should be able to define a workable idea around which others may rally." This would continue to demonstrate "TVA's ability as a regional agency to contribute to fundamental national policy." And the method must be found to dramatize such a role. The nation must be told what TVA was doing for the national interest.

Wagner and Freeman both picked up this torch, each in his own way, as they struggled to invent new TVA missions in economic development. And they both tried and failed to overcome a warning that Clapp gave in his paper, which he did not surmount. TVA must choose, he wrote, between pursuing ad hoc economic development projects opportunistically, in which it competed for funds with other federal agencies, and more coherent "policies that have far-reaching significance for the art of government . . . the kinds of local, state, regional, national and international policies that will affect the lives of many people for many years to come."

Was this sound creative thinking or intellectual daydreaming? Clapp was a professional public administrator who believed that TVA had a unique contribution to make to the art of government. But was this any more than wishing? TVA had little claim or authority for leadership in the region beyond its statutory powers. There was no great recognition of a convener and catalyst role for TVA in the region.

POLITICS AND POLICY

Clapp's 1952 speculations about the public authority as a creative device in American government were conceived in a vacuum. The postwar political climate was moving in just the opposite direction. Regional public authorities could only have an impact on American government if there were a number of them and if new modes of public administration, in which TVA was a coordinator of national, state, and local agencies, were gradually developed. But this did not happen. FDR sent Congress a message in 1937 suggesting seven regional authorities and did so again in 1944.[86] Politicians from several regions were promoting TVAs in the Arkansas, Colorado, Columbia, Missouri, and St. Lawrence river valleys.

There were strong advocates for the idea in the Department of the Interior.[87] However, the federal agencies that TVA had displaced in the Tennessee Valley were hostile to the idea. The Army Corps of Engineers, U.S. Forest Service, and Soil Conservation Service were not about to hasten their own curtailment by the creation of more TVAs.[88]

President Truman introduced a bill for a Columbia River Authority in 1949, but it lacked sufficient political support to pass. The ideal of regional planning had been left behind in the 1930s. Truman's own staff, led by David Bell, a young economist, questioned whether regional authorities really contributed to economic development or national policy. New techniques of fiscal policy, derived from the theories of British economist John Maynard Keynes, might be more effective in promoting economic growth, Bell suggested. The question of accountability was also raised. A hard-pressed White House could not oversee several regional authorities, and the states would be precluded from doing so.[89]

TVA could not be a model of public administration for the nation if it was one of a kind, an orphan child from the New Deal. As a result, TVA was increasingly perceived in Washington and the valley as an institution unique to a time and place. The political fights about TVA in the 1950s were over the issue of whether the federal government should give any support at all to a uniquely regional body. This question could not be avoided as it became clear that federal appropriations for power plants would be required if TVA was to serve as the power company for the valley. Any ideas about innovativeness in public administration were completely buried beneath that more dramatic fight. From 1945 to 1947, annual residential electrical usage in the valley increased by 60 percent. From 1945 to 1948, generating capacity increased by only 2 percent, whereas average annual electrical usage, both in cities and countryside increased by almost 44 percent. TVA had to have new generating capacity and thus asked for funds to build the New Johnsonville steam plant in 1948. The Republican 80th Congress refused. This was the beginning of several years of uncertainty and struggle about the future of TVA's power program. The private utilities fought TVA expansion even in its own monopoly area, for fear it would expand further. The New Johnsonville plant was approved after Truman's 1948 election victory. And then, with the advent of the Korean War, and TVA's commitments to the Atomic Energy Commission, additional steam plants were built.[90]

TVA had been building new plants with its power revenues, which it was permitted to do, under a schedule of repayment to the Treasury.[91] Still, the Bureau of the Budget reduced TVA's power construction program by 25 percent in 1953. TVA officials were worried that they would not be able to meet their commitments to either the AEC or residential, rural, and industrial consumers.[92] The House Appropriations Committee and the full House cut all TVA natural-resource programs from the budget in 1953 as well. However, John Sherman Cooper, a Republican senator from Kentucky, saved the programs in the conference committee.[93] Lilienthal wrote Clapp a note about "the great news that the heart hasn't been cut out of TVA." Even though ideas of regionalism were at a low point, Lilienthal said that "the chance of continuation of the guts of what TVA is doing still lives."[94] The nonpower, natural-resource programs were seen by both Lilienthal and Clapp as the "heart" of TVA.

TVA officials knew they were engaged in a political fight for survival. The animosity between the White House and TVA can be sensed from a reply of Sherman Adams, an assistant to President Eisenhower, to a 1954 letter from Frank Clement, governor of Tennessee, complaining about cuts in the TVA budget:

> Dear Frank:
>
> Your recent letter to the President . . . has been received in the spirit in which it was intended. . . . The emphasis you place on a "partnership" with the federal government achieved by the democratic action of the people of the region, appears somewhat overdrawn where there is an entire dependence on the Government to provide funds from taxes levied on all the people of the nation for the initial capital outlay of a large and continuing expansion of a steam generated electric power system. This is particularly so when the active participation by local authorities or groups primarily has been directed to obtaining the use of Federal funds and capitalization to the maximum degree on the special advantages derived from their use.

Adams concluded by saying that TVA's estimates of future growth needs were perhaps inflated and that national defense needs could be met by other (private) sources.[95] It was perfectly clear that the administration was not going to permit TVA to grow any more.

The defeat of the effort of TVA partisans in Congress to restore a Memphis steam plant that had been cut from President Eisenhower's budget revived the idea of TVA financing its power program by taking bonds to the market like a private utility. Clapp was on record as opposed to self-financing of the power program because of his skepticism that Congress would give TVA "blank check authority" to issue bonds at its discretion like any private corporation. If Congress were to require its approval before bonds for particular plants could be issued, Clapp felt that it would be difficult to build ahead of demand and that TVA would thus fall behind. Congress could also influence TVA planning in ways that might weaken the returns to bond holders. Clapp also argued that the nation would eventually own TVA because TVA was paying off its debt for the power program to the U.S. Treasury every year. The cost of borrowing money would surely lead to higher rates, in addition to the payback requirements. Anything that harmed TVA's "ability to maintain low cost production" was bad for TVA and the ratepayers.[96]

George Gant remembered that Clapp spent hours discussing the issue with staffs.[97] Gabriel Wessenauer recalled that Clapp feared opening the act because of his concern that valley politicians would find ways to get leverage over TVA expenditures.[98] Clapp flirted with the idea of financing TVA through a seven-state compact, which would eliminate the need to go back to Congress every year, something he hated. But TVA lawyers believed this to be an unreliable vehicle for long-term financing.[99] Aubrey Wagner reported that Clapp understood that appropriations for power financing were going to dry up and that he set up a staff study of alternatives. But no fresh ideas emerged, and Clapp had to continue defending the existing system even though he saw the need for innovation. Clapp liked a factual basis for decisions, and the staff was unable to give him one.[100]

It is reasonable to conclude that Clapp would have favored a self-financing method that left TVA free to make its own financial plans quite independently of Washington. Vogel came close to this result in 1959, but Clapp was not the person to do it. He was too much a part of TVA orthodoxy and too little a politician to explore fresh alternatives with a Republican president and Congress. He really did believe that a public authority should be independent, once telling John Oliver that the TVA engineers were to decide in which state a new steam plant was to be built without telling him in advance. There were to be no politics of plant location in his TVA.[101]

Clapp worked with Congress under the direction of Marguerite Owen, who was TVA's Washington representative from 1933 until the early 1970s. She told the chairmen who to see in Washington and sometimes what to say. They seldom took initiatives with members of Congress independently of her advice. Her strategy was the quiet working of a few key friendships, with George Norris, Lister Hill, Kenneth McKellar, Jamie Whitten, and other friends of TVA from the valley delegation.[102] Owen was particularly close to Lister Hill, and because she was a very good writer, she often wrote speeches for him.[103] Although Owen nominally reported to the general manager, John Oliver remembered that "I reported to her."[104] Owen believed that the key to TVA's vitality was its continuous political insecurity: "There never was a time when political support for TVA was not precarious. This is the right way to live. No one is comfortable but you develop new ideas. Look at the Weather Bureau— no new ideas for years."[105]

Owen's thesis that precariousness spurred inventiveness could also be extended to include perennial defensiveness. There was a long-term absence of careful congressional oversight of TVA because TVA's friends in

Congress were so anxious to protect it from attack and decimation. The Time and time again, TVA called on its friends in Congress to restore appropriations, defeat bills that limited its autonomy or treated it like other federal agencies, or protect it from General Accounting Office controls. And, of course, members of the valley delegation sat on key committees that could help TVA. The correspondence between members of the TVA board and friends in Congress over many years deals largely with staving off threats to TVA. Very little of traditional pork-barrel politics appears, however. The principal TVA programs of power and agriculture were valleywide, and members of Congress appeared to see their interest to be in protecting TVA as a whole rather than in advancing particular claims. But this protective politics made it difficult to develop constructive, long-term solutions to the financing problem.

Grass roots political support for TVA among the people of the valley in the Lilienthal years had been widespread as Rotary clubs, chambers of commerce, mayors, and civic organizations of all kinds acted to support TVA in Washington. But this kind of support was latent most of the time, unless TVA was in some way threatened. TVA's most important constituency was organized in 1946 when the Tennessee Valley Public Power Association was created, representing the municipal distributors. The TVPPA became an important TVA advocate in the Dixon-Yates controversy, but in the first years it was simply a liaison organization between TVA and the distributors.

Clapp kept his personal distance from such groups to guard TVA independence.[106] He was very much a product of the TVA organization and its culture which he, more than any other person, had shaped. Despite his keen analytical mind, he never challenged the basic premises of TVA's management system, missions, or the politics that sustained it. Clapp believed strongly that TVA should go against public opinion if it was being faithful to the purposes of the act. His nonpolitical leadership style succeeded largely because of Lilienthal's political skill in laying a solid base of support for TVA in the valley and in Washington. Clapp was well suited to managing a TVA with strong political support and great autonomy. But he was not the leader to forge a new contract with Washington. That task had to be accomplished by his successor.

HERBERT VOGEL

Herbert Vogel was a brigadier general in the Army Corps of Engineers who was facing retirement when President Eisenhower asked him to become chairman of the TVA board in 1954. Vogel was never sure why he was chosen, but he did know that corp officials and several governors with whom he had worked had written Eisenhower asking that Vogel be exempted from mandatory retirement.[107] The support from governors indicates the political skill that Vogel had developed while working with state and local governments on corps projects. He understood the need for a technical organization to explain itself to publics and politicians. Paul Evans, longtime director of information for TVA, recalled that

> Vogel had the best sense of public relations of any director that I knew, next to Lilienthal. He had a gut feeling for it. . . . [He] used his adroitness to carry groups in the valley with him. He spoke to groups, for example the distributors, with the aim of winning them over. . . . He is a good speaker, took speech lessons when he was in the Corps. To run a Corps region and district you have to be more than a competent engineer but must have public relations skills.[108]

The general himself agreed that his corps experience had given him political antennae: "You always have to be listening to people."[109]

Unlike Clapp, Wagner, and Freeman, Vogel was not a product of the TVA organizational culture, and he never subscribed to or articulated any special sense of a TVA myth or mission. He brought the perspective of an Army Corps of Engineers officer to TVA, particularly in his great interest in flood control, navigation, and construction on the river.[110] As a corps man, he understood the multipurpose character of dams and thought of TVA as a vast series of water projects.[111] In later years, Vogel was quite clear in his own mind about his main achievements at TVA: "[T]here were three achievements from which I derive the greatest satisfaction. First, was working out its [TVA] financial future. Second, was bringing about harmony, not only in the valley, but with the private power interests around it. Third, was an attitude among the people of the valley that made them eager to help themselves with the guidance of TVA."[112]

It was Vogel who achieved, with much help, the passage of the Bond Revenue Act in 1959, which established the financial independence of the power program. The act also limited the distribution of TVA power to the existing service area. These were not measures on which tried and true TVA career people could have been expected to lead. In reference to his third point, about stimulating self-help in the valley, Vogel did not rush to embrace tributary area development and other nonpower projects in search of new TVA missions. He wanted the initiative to come from groups of people in the valley. He was most comfortable with TVA as a multipurpose river enterprise.

When Vogel arrived in Knoxville in 1954 as the appointee of a Republican president who had referred to TVA as "creeping socialism," many TVA people believed he had been directed by the White House to dismantle TVA. Vogel denied that he had ever received any such message. President Eisenhower had told him in their initial interview; "All I want is for you to use your heart, your brains, and facts as the basis for any recommendations you may bring me in the future."[113] Sherman Adams handled TVA matters for the White House, and Vogel told Paul Evans that Adams had told him that TVA was a "nest of socialists." After Vogel had been at TVA for some time, he showed Evans a letter he was going to send Adams telling him he had been mistaken. Evans advised him against sending the letter and did not think it was ever mailed.[114]

Vogel came to TVA in the midst of a fierce controversy about the Dixon-Yates plan. The Eisenhower administration was opposed to any further appropriations for TVA steam plants and had conceived a plan in which a private consortium of utilities, headed by two men named Dixon and Yates, would build a new plant to serve the needs of Memphis, thus freeing power in the TVA system to meet the increased demands of the AEC plant at Paducah, Kentucky. The plan became a partisan issue in which congressional Democrats attacked the administration as anti-TVA and anti-public power, and TVA itself mobilized grass roots groups in the valley to raise such a clamor that the idea would be abandoned. The controversy generated more heat than light, and much rhetorical excess on both sides, perhaps because neither side had a good idea of how to resolve the fundamental problem of financing TVA's power system for the long run. The Dixon-Yates plan was only a temporary expedient. President Eisenhower's thinking was clearly expressed in a note to Herbert Brownell, his attorney general:

> In the study and negotiations that finally resulted in the proposal for the Dixon-Yates contract, the initial factor was the allegation by the TVA that large quantities of additional power were required in the Tennessee Valley region in order to meet the needs of the near future. The rigid position of the TVA authorities was that the US government should build additional steam plants to meet these needs. . . . The TVA has a complete monopoly of production and distribution of power in the region: consequently, it would appear most necessary to have a considerable time for review and restudy of the whole matter without occasioning damage to the region and without building the additional steam facilities at Federal expense. To adopt the latter would mean that the nation's taxpayers would be forever committed to providing cheap power for the people in the TVA region. While some argument for this practice may have been valid so long as the development was confined to hydroelectric power, it does appear that when carried on indefinitely into steam plant facilities, justice to other regions requires some kind of adjustment.[115]

In July 1954, Eisenhower had received a letter from the president of the Tennessee Valley Public Power Association opposing the Dixon-Yates plan and making all the traditional arguments in behalf of an expanding

TVA. The plan would not meet future power needs. The cost of power would rise. Divided management and responsibility for power in the valley would give private utilities leverage over TVA, and of course, supply needed to precede demand: "We are also painfully aware of the grave effects on this region of further postponement of new power generating capacity. Instead of the capacity being provided in advance of load growth, as should always be done, the construction of new capacity is already being allowed for a second year to lag behind demand."[116]

Vogel thus stepped into a hornet's nest. Two board members, Harry Curtis and Raymond Paty, were openly hostile to the administration plan, and the top echelon of TVA staff were worried about Vogel's intentions and goals for TVA. Vogel had to represent the administration yet win the support of the organization. It is a tribute to his political skill that he eventually did both.

Vogel's immediate objective was to initiate conversations with the Atomic Energy Commission on the terms of the sale of the extra power as presumed by the Dixon-Yates plan. Curtis and Paty had refused to permit staff members to engage in such discussions with the AEC. For some time after Vogel's arrival at TVA, the TVA staff people who were called before congressional committees to testify about the Dixon-Yates matter were ordered by Curtis and Paty, speaking for a majority of two on the board, to present their views rather than those of Vogel. Neither Curtis nor Paty thought themselves articulate enough to press the case themselves.[117] There had been considerable discussion between TVA experts and the Bureau of the Budget about the terms of such an agreement, with TVA dragging its feet every step of the way.[118]

Vogel himself believed the Dixon-Yates plan to be a "bad arrangement" except as a stopgap measure. He believed that power services should be provided by monopolies. But he supported the plan in order to have time to work out a better long-run solution, which he had believed from the beginning had to be TVA self-financing.[119] He took it upon himself to meet with the general manager of the AEC, an old army friend, in Washington in the absence of the AEC chairman. The two men concurred that any agreement between TVA and the AEC would not impose extra costs on either party, but they accepted the need for detailed negotiation. Waiting reporters were told by Vogel that there had been "a meeting of the minds." This was impolitic on Vogel's part because it caused a firestorm back in Knoxville. His board colleagues would hardly speak to him. He was the target of anger from the governor of Tennessee, the newly created Citizens for TVA, and the American Public Power Association. However, in due course the negotiations began.[120] They dragged on into the fall of 1954, with Curtis and Paty still resisting an agreement.

Vogel was trying to steer a center course, telling a correspondent in November that

> TVA is basically doing a good honest job and . . . has accomplished a great deal of good in the region. The main problem now is to find means for future financing within the requirements imposed on it by law, to be "self-sustaining and self-liquidating." . . . I believe it is well to keep in mind that moderation is a wonderful thing. . . . We are trying to take a moderate course toward accomplishing those things which the laws of Congress have directed us to do.[121]

Vogel sent copies of this letter to Curtis, Paty and other top TVA officials.

The Dixon-Yates affair ended in 1955 when opponents of the proposal discovered that a consultant to the Bureau of the Budget on the plan was also connected to the private utilities involved. At the same time, the mayor of Memphis announced that the city would build its own steam plant, and once sure of this, the Eisenhower administration was happy to scrap the whole thing.[122] But the long-term issue of financing TVA's power program had not been resolved. Vogel put the staff to work on alternatives, after having obtained the blessing of Eisenhower and the Bureau of the Budget. Curtis left the board in 1957 and was replaced by A. R. Jones, an accountant and former Bureau of the Budget staff member who brought to the question the financial expertise that Vogel lacked.[123] The Dixon-Yates episode is important for our study as an illustration of Vogel's willingness to challenge the sacred cow of appropriations as the basis for TVA's power program. Vogel was an outsider, a prisoner of no myths, who was a moderate pragmatist seeking a solution to an unresolved problem.

The TVA staff members who worked closely with Vogel noticed a gradual recognition on his part of TVA's virtues. They attributed this to their own straightforwardness and honesty with him. They also gave Vogel credit for being a good engineer who recognized superb engineering when he saw it. Vogel once told Marguerite Owen that he thought in the beginning that he would have to fire both Aubrey Wagner, the new general manager, and herself. But he discovered they were "decent people."[124] John Oliver resigned as general manager upon Vogel's appointment so that Vogel might have a free choice of a general manager, but Curtis and Paty chose Wagner to succeed Oliver before Vogel arrived.[125] Wagner made a great effort to work closely with the new chairman, and in retrospect he believed that he and Owen had helped sell TVA to Vogel by being honest with him and educating him about TVA programs:

> He was an able man and a thoughtful person. You could convert him. For example, we made studies of the flood problems of small cities from rain. There

was no way to build dams. We recommended zoning. . . . he became an advocate of the local flood control program. Vogel would go to Miss Owen's office. He learned she was honest. She would tell him she would get in trouble and he would too [from a proposed action]. He hadn't been used to that in the Army. He came to trust that. That was one of the methods we used to handle him.[126]

Vogel told Owen that the Bureau of the Budget people had lied to him about TVA but that the TVA people had never lied to him. Owen gave principal credit to Wagner for educating Vogel.[127] This is deserved praise. Vogel was initially somewhat stiff and distant in his administrative style. He thought TVA was like an army installation and once asked the forestry division to deliver firewood to his house. But eventually he loosened up. In Paul Evans view, "the thing that saved TVA was Vogel's respect for competent engineering and Wagner's absolute integrity. Wagner always told it to him like it was."[128] But these accounts do not give enough credit to Vogel's own ways of learning about TVA:

> There was no teaching role [by Wagner and others]. I did all that myself, by going around and talking with people, leaving my door open. . . . The decision/management system is efficient if you make it so. I had to circulate, walk to [others'] offices and visited. I went to Chattanooga and Muscle Shoals. Pretty soon people loosen up and tell you what you need to know. If the board just sat at formal meetings it would never get anywhere.[129]

Harry Case confirmed Vogel's open-door policy, particularly in Vogel's willingness to hear individual grievances, which was contrary to TVA practice. But Vogel wanted to learn about the organization:

> And he knew it was a pretty tight organization, a very tight organization. . . . I think he . . . had special reasons why he wanted to see what people were saying in the organization. And for him to refuse to listen to disgruntled government employees . . . might have been, in his mind, to cut his own throat and not find out anything because the top management around him is just too doggone tight. And they are not going to point out faults in the organization to him. . . . But he did develop this confidence in the organization which, in the course of time, I think, was quite complete.[130]

Vogel made an initial attempt to create a management analysis staff that would assist him directly in assessing the management of TVA.[131] He put $100,000 in the budget for such a staff, reporting to him, but his two board colleagues told the Bureau of the Budget to take it out. The bureau put the funds in for one year as a "contingency item."[132] Vogel had presented Rowland Hughes, director of the Bureau of the Budget, with his reasons for wanting such a staff. His language came awfully close to requesting a change in the TVA charter to make the chairman the chief executive officer:

> The work of the Government Relations and Economics staff is of such an esoteric nature that it could properly be done by a management division as a side line to practical investigations designed to improve the efficiency of the entire TVA. Such a group could act as staff advisers to the Chairman of the Board, who in turn should have his responsibilities defined by law whereby he would become the executive head of the organization to dispatch details of business in accordance with broad general policies determined by the Board. This would parallel the method by which successful businesses are conducted. . . . The Chairman does not disagree with decentralization of operations in any organization. On the contrary he strongly favors decentralization as a general principle. He does feel, however, that top management cannot pass off its responsibilities to lower operating groups and rely on those groups to report upon their own efficiency of operations. Coordinated control is necessary at the top level to insure that policies are being carried out and that all operations are conducted with maximum efficiency. Moreover, every organization needs a directive head to take executive action as needed to see that Board policies are complied with. This should be the function of the chairman as executive head. Working with the General Manager, he could then dispatch the multitudinous details now requiring action by the Board.[133]

Vogel was certainly frustrated with his two recalcitrant board colleagues, but one can also assume that his military background caused him to want TVA to act. He saw the same problems in TVA's management system that the Draper Committee had seen in 1937 and that critics of TVA in the 1980's were to see. Too high a price may have to be paid for decentralized collegiality. However, once Dixon-Yates was past and new board members more congenial to him were appointed, Vogel learned to use the system for his own purposes.

Vogel was fearful of provincialism in TVA leadership. For example, he opposed the efforts of east Tennessee's Republican congressman Howard Baker, Sr., to be appointed to the board, because of Baker's extensive coal holdings. Vogel resigned a year before his term was due to expire in 1962 for fear that President Kennedy might appoint Buford Ellington, the sitting governor of Tennessee, to take his place, since Ellington's term ended at the same time as Vogel's.[134] Vogel believed that TVA directors should come from outside the valley, much as commanding officers in the Army Corps of Engineers were moved around, so they did not become too parochial. Vogel thus stood somewhat outside TVA as an institution even as he developed confidence in its people. He eventually came to see TVA as his agency, not unlike the corps in its high professionalism. Charles McCarthy, who succeeded Joseph Swidler as general counsel, saw the similarities: "In his mind TVA and the Corps of Engineers are kissing cousins. He always saw TVA as a water control and engineering project and saw TVA people as competent, like Corps people. He began to develop an affection for TVA. I am not sure that TVA concepts got through to him."[135]

ECONOMIC DEVELOPMENT PROGRAMS

The test demonstration farm program continued under Vogel, with increasing emphasis upon testing fertilizer rather than educating farmers. Forestry continued to emphasize technical assistance to the states and private citizens in planting, cultivating, and harvesting woodlands.[136] Vogel's principal interests were in navigation and flood control since this had been his life's work.[137] He liked the construction of new locks and engineering projects and let Harry Curtis run the agriculture and fertilizer programs.[138] Vogel did not have much interest in the power program for its own sake, apart from the self-financing issue.[139]

Vogel supported the tributary watershed development program under rules of thumb learned in the corps, in which local groups developed project ideas that could then be taken to the corps and subsequently sold to Congress as having public support. It was important to Vogel that local groups take the initiative. For this reason, he stimulated the formation of the Tennessee River and Tributaries Association: "The Corps had so much support by river associations. In the Tennessee Valley I saw a vacuum that could be filled by an organization that could politically speak for the people of the area."[140]

By the early 1960s, TVA's conception of watershed development had evolved to one of general economic development, in which TVA would have only one piece in the form of water projects or agricultural and forestry development. It was hoped that citizen associations would assume responsibility for developing other areas of a region's economy. Vogel had hoped that the Tennessee River and Tributaries Association would foster such local groups. This would then make it easier for TVA to approach Congress with requests for appropriations.[141] However, tension quickly developed between TVA and the TRTA because the TRTA wanted TVA to take the initiative and seek congressional appropriations for local construction projects. In 1959 Vogel told the Elk River Development Association that TVA engineers saw little economic feasibility in traditional water projects in the tributaries. New kinds of benefits would have to be identified. There had to be favorable cost-benefit ratios for dam construction in terms of flood control, navigation, or power, he said, before new projects could be undertaken. At that time TVA economists were using econometric methods to develop a unified approach to watershed development, but the technical problems resisted resolution.[142] In April 1961, the board established the Office of Tributary Area Development, largely at the behest of Aubrey Wagner, who was a new director. Other offices were told by the board to cooperate with OTAD, which was to coordinate their work. The work would be done by divisions in other offices.[143] After Wagner became chairman in 1962, he built up the work of OTAD, as the carrier of Clapp's legacy. Vogel was less enthusiastic because he saw a limited role for water projects in economic development in the tributaries. Wagner took a different view.[144]

A memo for the files in 1961 written by Richard Kilbourne, a forester and head of OTAD, described a meeting that Vogel and Wagner had with the TRTA board. TRTA officers complained that TVA was asking state and local governments, which were overburdened with taxes and debt, to do too much in tributary development. TVA had done a wonderful job of river development and should "complete the job on the tributaries." Vogel and Wagner both responded that conventional TVA water projects could only be part of economic development and that the communities should find other sources of funding as well. A TRTA representative urged that "TVA should itself should take action to capture land enhancement values from its water projects." This prophetic insight foresaw how TVA would seek to justify the Tellico Dam in later years. The TRTA people wanted TVA to spend $1.5 billion for the construction of new dams and to seek out such sites for new appropriations from Congress. TVA officials were not prepared to do this. They wanted grass roots initiatives.[145] It was only later, under Wagner's leadership, that TVA assumed central responsibility for economic development in the tributaries.

The high marks that Vogel received from TVA colleagues were not accompanied by public support until late in the day, after the Bond Revenue Act had passed. The organized TVA constituencies in the valley linked Vogel with the Eisenhower attempt to curb TVA. When Vogel told a reporter in 1955 that TVA management practices were not always the best, and that he could see an argument for enlarging the board and giving more authority to a general manager, the director of the Citizens for TVA, an anti-Dixon-Yates group, wrote Vogel and said that they would not stand in his way if he was thinking of resigning.[146] Later that year Tennessee governor Frank Clement called on Vogel to resign, saying Vogel he was trying to destroy TVA from within.[147] In 1956 the TVPPA, the Tennessee River Electric Cooperative Association, the Labor Council, the Municipal League, and the Alabama Power Distributors and Municipal Utilities, acting as a group, petitioned Congress for Vogel's removal.[148] Vogel's astuteness at public relations could not allay this anger. He got caught in the Dixon-Yates buzz saw and the politics of the defensive coalition originally put together by Lilienthal to support TVA. But Vogel read the long-term politics of Washington better than most TVA advocates and therefore served TVA better than they knew. He understood that a political solution for self-financing must be found.

Vogel also preached about TVA to the people of the valley, but it was a very different sermon from that of Lilienthal and Clapp. Vogel scaled down the grandiosity of the traditional rhetoric. He had a practical, down-to-earth sense of the TVA enterprise which might have served TVA better in later years. For example, Vogel said that the federal government should be a father and not a mother to TVA because a father puts a son on his own after he grows up.[149] In 1955 he argued that too much emphasis had been put on TVA as "an adventure in faith" and as "a way of life" and not enough as "a sound engineering project." It was better to look at TVA as engineering than "from the standpoint of social improvement and uplift."[150] The next month he said that TVA had been doing too many things for people that they ought to be doing for themselves. There was much greater need for local initiative.[151] He told the Kingston, Tennessee, Rotary Club in 1955 that TVA was doing for the southeast what the Army Corps of Engineers and the Department of Agriculture had done in the southwest, adding, "There's been a lot of frosting put on the cake—sometimes too much. The real job has been done by engineers, not by lawyers, sociologists or administrators."[152]

Vogel criticized excessive rhetoric about TVA, saying it did no good to be the object of either extreme praise or attack.[153] His language and actions were consistent with one another, and both were different from the TVA style. He used the same language in Washington, and it may have contributed to the eventual political settlement that was reached about self-financing, just because he was receptive to the views of TVA critics at the same time that he supported TVA missions. After four months on the job, Vogel wrote a letter to President Eisenhower giving his initial impressions of TVA. His two board colleagues insisted that it be made clear that the letter was personal rather than a report from the board.[154] He praised TVA employees as "capable, energetic, selfless and devoted to their jobs," although "perhaps more localized in their thinking than is proper for Federal employees to be. . . ." Then he added:

> It must be remembered that many, who are now key employees, took their jobs in the depression, have served continuously under one philosophy, and have become loyal and staunch supporters of it. While this has resulted in a laudable dedication to their work, it also has created some inflexibility in the acceptance of new ideas. There exists a basic premise on the part of many, though not all, that everything in TVA is right and any suggested change would be for the worse.

While it was understood from the beginning, Vogel wrote, that TVA would generate electric power, "it is doubtful, however, that even the most ardent supporters of the public power sections of the measure [TVA

Act] envisioned the rapid expansion which has taken place." The answer had to be self-financing of the power program, he told Eisenhower. The board had ordered a study and hoped to have it finished in time to get congressional action in 1955. Vogel underestimated the political opposition, especially from private utilities. But he did make clear that there was no desire within TVA to extend the territorial boundaries of the power program. This letter to Eisenhower set the tone of Vogel's subsequent leadership in the self-financing fight, that of a realist for TVA.

THE BOND REVENUE ACT

Vogel's great achievement was the passage of the Bond Revenue Act which permitted TVA to finance its electric-power program through bond issues. He did none of the technical work, but he provided the leadership necessary to steer between extremes in a way that matched President Eisenhower's inclinations.

In 1953 TVA's power program was 63 percent hydro and 36 percent steam plants. Six steam plants were under construction from past appropriations, but this was thought within TVA to be insufficient to meet the need for power in 1956.[155] The 1954 submission to the Bureau of the Budget requested no appropriations for new plants and promised a self-financing bill.[156] The TVA proposal for self-financing was sent to the Bureau of the Budget in 1955, modified in important respects, and then sent to Congress, but no action was taken. The next two annual reports emphasized the increasing demand for electric power in the valley, particularly from the AEC. New construction was needed by 1958 if there were not to be serious power shortages. However, TVA continued to build steam plants during the 1950s with funds authorized before 1953 and with new power revenues.[157] The initial plan developed by the Office of Power and the General Counsel, which never changed in its essentials, recommended that TVA be empowered by Congress to issue revenue bonds, to be secured and repaid by power revenues, to be sold to private investors or the U.S. Treasury. The bonds would not be guaranteed by the Treasury. TVA rates would be sufficient to cover operating expenses and payments on bonds, as well as long-standing repayments of past appropriations to the Treasury. The TVA board would report on the financing and operation of the power program to the president and Congress annually. By presumption, the federal government could deny new bond releases but would not be able to cut back facilities for which bonds had been sold.[158]

TVA was able to sell the distributors on the plan, through the work of the TVPPA, which offered political help in getting the bill passed.[159] The first sticking point was the Bureau of the Budget revision of the plan to ensure that the issuing of bonds would be subject to the same process of approval by the bureau as appropriations. The Bureau of the Budget also insisted that the secretary of the Treasury approve the sale of TVA bonds beforehand.[160] Vogel indicated that he could live with these changes, but his two colleagues did not like them any more than did TVA defenders in Congress.[161] In September 1955, Vogel informed Eisenhower of TVA opposition to a proposal by the Hoover Commission that TVA power rates be subject to the regulation of the Federal Power Commission. Such a policy, Vogel told Eisenhower, was inconsistent with the management autonomy required to balance revenues and costs in terms of commitment to the lowest possible costs.[162] This is an illustration of TVA's hope for maximum freedom in self-financing.

Congressional committees held hearings each year from 1955 through 1958 on the issue of self-financing, but agreement foundered on two main questions. The first was the fear of private utilities that TVA would expand its geographic service area if new funds were available for expansion. This issue was eventually settled by general agreement that TVA would stay within existing boundaries. The second question, about congressional and executive approval of bond issues, was harder to resolve.[163] The Bureau of the Budget was particularly adamant in arguing that it must scrutinize and approve all TVA expenditures, whatever the revenue source. TVA officials, in particular Joseph Swidler, general counsel, and Gabriel Wessenauer, manager of the Office of Power, disagreed in contending that the job of providing electricity in a region of rapidly growing demand required the assurance, by the producer, that needs would be met. To subject such assurances to annual review was to place controls on TVA that private utilities did not have. TVA's view was that such controls would keep the authority on the edge of power shortages all the time. But the Bureau of the Budget was unyielding, charging that TVA was "attempting to go too far in getting flexibility without regular budgetary control."[164] The Bureau of the Budget had not historically liked government corporations, of which TVA was only one, because their very independence freed them to some extent from the scrutiny the bureau could exercise over federal departments and agencies.

By the same token, TVA did not wish to be subject to annual congressional approval of its plans for new plants for which bonds might be issued. But as a compromise, it was willing to accept congressional veto of plans for new plants during a ninety-day period after the notification of both houses of Congress.[165] In 1959 both houses passed bills that eliminated Bureau of the Budget authority over TVA building plans to be financed by bond revenues but that empowered either house to veto TVA plans within a ninety-day period after notification. The president was left powerless in such instances, and the law explicitly said so. He was simply to send TVA proposals to Congress. Eisenhower announced that he would not sign the bill because it weakened the executive branch in relation to Congress by denying the Bureau of the Budget authority that Congress had given to itself.[166]

The TVA board was happy with the final compromise. They were looking forward to the authorization of expenditures of up to $750 million within five years with the opportunity to return at that time for a new authorization. Congress could veto new projects, but it had been able to do that under the old requirements for authorization and funding of new plants. In no sense did TVA see itself as "turned loose" under the bill. Rather, one memo to the board said that it would "be living in a gold fish bowl while operating under the bill."[167] Other examples of the legislative veto in statutes were cited in the memo.

Gerald Morgan, the White House counsel, told Vogel that Eisenhower would veto the bill and that there was no point in Vogel coming to Washington to try to talk him out of it. Vogel insisted on seeing Eisenhower and telegraphed him asking for an appointment, which was granted. The three board members, Gerald Morgan, and Eisenhower met in the Oval Office a few days later. Vogel reminded the president of his charge that Vogel use his heart and brains at TVA and then talked for thirty minutes about "how important this whole thing was to the future of the valley." Eisenhower broke in irritably to say that he wanted to sign and that the private utilities wanted him to do so. He said he was receiving calls from their presidents at night and that "they would give me a golf course in Georgia if I would sign it." But he could not do it because it weakened the presidency by giving Congress a veto over TVA plans while explicitly denying comparable authority to the president. Vogel described his next action:

> I reached into my pocket, took out my pencil and said with the appropriate gesture, "what do you say we strike out both paragraphs?" He said, "that's a good idea. Let's do that." At that point [Gerald] Morgan leaped from his chair in amazement saying that could not be done, but he failed to point out to the president that the bill had to be either vetoed or signed. It could not be amended once on his desk. Instead, he said the corporations control act would be violated. . . . By this time the president, anxious to get to his next appointment, stood up, came around his desk and said, "o.k., that's fine." He put his arm around my shoulder and said, "you boys go and work this out now."

Outside the Oval Office, Gerald Morgan erupted, shouting at Vogel, "What have you done?" But Vogel told him to work it out according to Eisenhower's instructions. When the Bureau of the Budget came up with nothing, Marguerite Owen called Senator Robert Kerr, chairman of the Public Works Committee and author of the Senate bill, who promised to introduce and carry a resolution saying that if the president signed the bill it would immediately be amended to strike out the offending language. Brooks Hays, then a TVA board member and former Democratic congressman from Arkansas, asked Sam Rayburn, Speaker of the House, to do the same, which he did, with help from the president to bring House Republicans in line. And the matter was resolved.[168]

Charles McCarthy, at that time TVA general counsel, reports that Vogel's suggestion that the bill be amended informally was not as spontaneous as it appeared:

> Vogel had the guts to insist on seeing the President when he had to. Neither Clapp nor Wagner would have had the guts. . . . No one else could have gotten self-financing through. He had an ungodly amount of guts. . . . Everyone in the White House was opposed to it. I saw him three or four times a day during that period. [Gerald] Morgan was telling him not to come up. Vogel would not take no for an answer. . . . The idea of an amendment was his own. He called me and asked about it, and said, "let's try it."[169]

The Vogel story at TVA illustrates that a presidential appointee can fashion agency programs in response to administration policy if that policy is clear and authoritative. Vogel was responsive to Eisenhower policy for TVA, the chief element of which was self-financing of the power program. Vogel was also prudent and cautious in his advocacy of TVA nonpower programs, limiting them to traditional TVA missions. But at the same time, Vogel protected TVA's long-term interests as they were understood in the agency, particularly in regard to autonomy and independence from Washington.

By 1961 the federal share of TVA's budget was only a few million dollars because of the Bond Revenue Act of 1959. TVA's nonpower programs were similar to those of agencies like the Army Corps of Engineers, Soil Conservation Service, and Bureau of Reclamation. TVA was doing in the valley what these other agencies were doing elsewhere in the country. With self-financing, TVA ceased to be a national institution. This is ironic because Vogel always insisted that TVA think of itself as a national institution. But his goal was to override sectional selfishness and shake people in the valley out of the idea that they were due special treatment. He thought of TVA as performing missions for much the same purposes as other federal natural-resource agencies. He identified no unique national role for TVA, nor was one available in his time. The yardstick theme of comparing public and private power had died with the New Deal. The ideal of several multipurpose regional authorities had died. TVA had become an enlightened power company for a seven-state region.

The receding of a national mission was furthered by self-financing. After that the Bureau of the Budget gave attention only to the small number of appropriated programs in TVA. Borrowing limits for bond issues had to be approved by Congress from time to time, but there was little oversight from the authorizing committees. By 1961 the political controversies that had continued from the New Deal era were dead. TVA had a power monopoly in its region, and the private utilities around it were safe. TVA had become a provincial institution protected by members of Congress from the seven states who sat in key seats on authorizing and appropriations committees.

It is important to note that Vogel attempted to demythologize TVA rhetoric by describing the agency as just one among several regional development entities. He valued TVA missions in their concreteness and specificity. I will suggest later that this modesty about TVA would have been valuable two decades later when TVA leadership pursued self-defeating heroic missions. Vogel was the only outsider to serve as chairman until Runyon. Vogel was never a prisoner of myth.

CHAPTER 7

Rise and Fall of the Dynamo

"AUBREY J. RED" WAGNER began to work for TVA in 1934 as a navigation engineer, not long after graduating from the University of Wisconsin. He worked his way up to be head of the navigation division, assistant general manager under Clapp, general manager under Vogel, member of the board in 1961, and chairman of the board from 1962 to 1978. He was surely the most important figure in TVA history after David Lilienthal.

Gordon Clapp was Wagner's mentor and his ideal. Wagner admired Clapp's nonpolitical posture, his insistence on professional expertise as the basis for decisions, and embraced the multipurpose regional development mission Clapp articulated. Wagner's conception of TVA was, in his own words, as a "resource development agency which integrated a lot of activities. . . . I got the grass roots idea pretty early . . . and I still have this conception. . . . But my conception of what TVA has to do has changed. Construction was the first job and agriculture had to be converted. We have painted with the big brush; now we have to do the fine print."[1] By fine print, Wagner meant the Tributary Area Development program, which he had fashioned from Clapp's initial ideas. Clapp, he remembered, "saw TVA as a catalyst to help people in the valley take charge of their own grass roots development. I see it that way too. Too bad we got diverted by the power program."[2]

Wagner was an enthusiast for the power program, even as he expressed ambivalence about it. He saw it as a blessing in giving TVA a sense of organizational accomplishment as the one program the authority operated by itself. It was a curse "because it is so big that it swallows up all the dollars." But, he believed, "TVA could never have survived in the region without the power program."[3] In 1961, as a new board member, he told a Senate subcommittee that the power program was the key to regional economic development. The formula was to keep rates low in order to stimulate increased usage. By 1961 the electric power program was certainly TVA's central activity and mission. The balance had shifted in three decades from water and land to the primacy of electricity.[4] Yet Wagner was torn between the competing TVA missions. He very much wished to enhance nonpower programs at the same time as he planned for a power system of seventeen nuclear reactors. His colleagues, in retrospect described different sides of him. Leland Allbaugh, manager of agriculture, saw Wagner as a waterway man who hoped that the Tributary Area Development program would keep power from overriding other programs.[5] Louis Nelson, Allbaugh's successor, believed that Wagner's emotional investment was in power and new problems of rising rates and pollution. He remembered that Wagner, as a midwesterner, had little respect for "red dirt" southern agriculture. Economic development would come with cheap power.[6] Wagner embodied the contradictions of TVA within himself and sought unity among them. Above all, however, he was a builder. He used the revenue from TVA bonds to build steam plants, the diverse TAD projects, the Tellico, Normandy, and Columbia dams and Browns Ferry and Sequoyah nuclear plants.[7]

Red Wagner and his senior colleagues, who directed the several offices, grew up together in TVA as the second generation of leaders after the founding generation. David Freeman, then a TVA lawyer, was assistant secretary to the board in 1957 and sat next to Wagner, the general manager, in board meetings. Freeman saw the senior professional people at work—Wagner, Joseph Swidler, Gabriel Wessenauer: "That top staff was brutally strong. They knew they were right. I don't mean to be critical of them. Red and Wes saved TVA from virtual extinction by their beliefs."[8]

Freeman meant that Wagner and his senior professional colleagues had saved TVA from the Republicans in the Dixon-Yates story and in their conversion of Vogel. One sees a key to Wagner's management style in this insight. He governed TVA on the basis of firm convictions about its rightness, convictions that were implicitly shared with other senior professionals. He was a strong, authoritative leader within the consensus shared by strong, authoritative office heads, whom he trusted and on whom he relied. Wagner's leadership model was Clapp, who encouraged full discussion among the board members and senior staff. That was one reason Wagner resisted open board meetings for so long. He thought they would inhibit internal discussion.[9] He ran meetings in an informal manner inspired by confidence. He was confident about himself, his senior colleagues, and TVA missions. He was sure of his own knowledge of the organization and could not be easily swayed by reports from below that were contrary to his experience. Yet he trusted his senior staff and seldom attempted to second-guess their recommendations or analyses. He was particularly close to Wessenauer. They owned adjacent summer cottages on Watts Bar lake and were both active in the Lutheran church. One gets the impression from talking with their contemporaries that many ideas about the power program were worked out through informal conversation on summer evenings at Watts Bar. And, indeed, this was how most policy making took place. The handful of senior people, most of whom had been with TVA for all of their careers, met regularly and informally and addressed issues within strong bonds of agreement about TVA and its purposes.[10]

Wagner never quite realized that he was no longer general manager after he became chairman. He thought of the general manager as the employee of the chairman, something Louis Van Mol resisted but with which Lynn Seeber was comfortable. Seeber was a good soldier who resigned when Wagner retired.[11]

David Freeman discovered how Wagner and Seeber ran board meetings when Freeman became a director in 1978. Seeber would only put items on the agenda that Wagner wanted there.[12] Wagner did not attempt to administer the organization but left that up to the general manager.[13] But he did approach office and division heads directly, and even when he seemed to be deferring to the general manager, he could "still be miles ahead of him," his personal knowledge was so great.[14]

In 1971 Phil Ericson, assistant to the general manager, persuaded Seeber that the board needed more formal policy planning.[15] One experienced observer felt that this was Seeber's way of prying Wagner loose from a too close reliance on longtime friends in senior management.[16] A small planning staff, headed by University of Tennessee economist David Patterson, was installed in the general manager's office. The staff could help programs that needed help making presentations to the Bureau of the Budget, like forestry and agriculture. But neither Wagner nor the managers of engineering and power saw any need for a separate planning staff.[17] Wagner was opposed to formal, written plans, feeling they might tie his hands for the future and become politically controversial. In fact, he wished to write down as little as possible about what TVA was planning to do.[18]

From Wagner's perspective, he and Wessenauer had the power program in hand, and the other 5 percent of TVA was in capital improvements, such as water projects, that he understood well. He saw little need for a separate planning organization.[19] But more importantly, a central planning staff violated TVA organizational norms. As Wagner remembered in regard to Patterson's staff, "I thought it was a mistake to have planners tell power people what to do, because they were not responsible for results. The group Seeber developed under Patterson did not amount to much."[20]

Some of Wagner's colleagues thought he relied too heavily on old friends among the senior staff. Paul Evans remembered that Wagner was "too confident that all TVA people would do the right things." He would defer to his senior colleagues too often, Evans thought.[21] However, Wessenauer felt that Wagner began to lack confidence in some of his senior staff toward the end.[22] Hugh Parris, manager of power for the Freeman and Dean boards, felt that Wagner had relied too much on

Wessenauer, who had been manager of power for twenty-five years. After Wessenauer retired in 1969, Wagner had to deal with the failure of the Office of Power to do any systematic planning. It had all been in Wessenauer's head. But Wagner would never have turned to a personal staff to help him with a problem like that.[23] Wagner became less collegial over the years, particularly as TVA was deluged with controversy in his second term. But overall he was Clapp's disciple, who wished to be a collegial leader, working hand in hand with senior staff, within a framework of shared assumptions about TVA missions and how decisions should be made.

Wagner certainly dominated his fellow board members and saw this as necessary and proper.[24] But he was careful to count noses before he would permit a potentially divisive issue to come to the board. He tried his best to bring the other board members around to his thinking and usually did so.[25] When William Jenkins was the only other board member for some time, Wagner would let nothing come to the board without knowing that he had Jenkins's vote.[26] Frank Smith, who had been a prominent Mississippi congressman before joining the TVA board, sometimes had to remind Wagner that his vote counted the same as the chairman's.[27] However, none of Wagner's colleagues were a match for him. He was an extremely formidable personality. Patterson remembered that "Red had a leadership quality that was almost irresistible. He could bring the staff around to his point of view even then they were deeply opposed."[28] The following descriptions by top TVA managers of Wagner and his effect on them reveal his great appeal: "He was knowledgeable, personable, had integrity. Watching him made me feel good about myself." "Wagner brought out the best in loyalty and morale. We would have fought for Red. He was on our side." "TVA was a family and Red was the father. He knew people by name, knew all the properties. People wanted to do what he wanted to do. Even if opposed, they went along with it, if he got the money." "Wagner was a prince of a gentleman, an excellent engineer, well disciplined and tough as nails. He had a strong sense of the worth of the individual and was a true egalitarian."[29] Wagner was like Clapp, his mentor. He lived and breathed TVA, and his faith was contagious. This was both a strength and a weakness.

PUBLIC LEADER

Wagner was also like Clapp in his insistence that TVA was a nonpolitical organization. Neither politics nor public opinion were to set TVA policy. In Wagner's understanding, TVA was different from a federal department, which was necessarily political and responsive to the president, Congress, and the public in a direct way: "The statute fixes responsibility on the board. The board has autonomy within the Act. That is the basis for accountability. So long as I stayed within the Act I was o.k." He found a credo in the Douglas Dam story: "The only thing that will save TVA is to hope you are right and be right, for example the Douglas dam. Gordon pressed our people to make sure they were right. The engineers were buoyed up because they knew he would not trim politically."[30]

Wagner believed in trying to persuade public opinion in the valley that TVA policies were correct, as Paul Evans put it, "to explain things. He saw people as rational and intelligent."[31] The tenor of Wagner's speeches was reasonable and rational, for example, trying to explain why TVA had to balance pollution control with the historic commitment to cheap electricity. Frank Smith thought that Wagner saw himself as acting in concert with majority opinion. He was trying to give people what he thought they wanted, which was electric power at the most reasonable cost.[32] But Wagner would not give in to the demands of particular publics. One former colleague remembered a public meeting in 1970 when TVA was considering banning houseboats built with oil drums on its lakes. Wagner told the audience, "We will listen and give consideration. But we have been threatened by experts and it hasn't worked."[33]

Wagner believed it was the chairman's task to persuade the public that TVA was doing the right thing. Even more important, he said, "you maintain credibility with the public by sticking to a position or changing it reasonably."[34] This comment was made in criticism of David Freeman, his successor, who Wagner thought had backed away from controversial projects like the Tellico Dam. However, some of Wagner's colleagues thought he was a poor public leader. His chief engineer remembered: "Wagner was never able to awake the assistance of the customers about costs. . . . Are we engineers poor at selling things to people? . . . Red's speeches fell flat."[35] Another remembered: "Red didn't have a sense of the public's power. He got into one mess after another with his engineering fixes. He lamented that the public didn't understand his objectives. They did and didn't want them."[36] In the 1970s Wagner and TVA went into a defensive mode, and much of Wagner's public rhetoric was defensive.[37] As Paul Evans put it, "The world had changed but Red wanted TVA to be what Clapp would have had."[38]

George Palo, the chief engineer, thought that Wagner had stayed too long. He fought a losing battle against environmental laws, and the organization began to make mistakes in its cost estimates of nuclear construction.[39] Wagner became a symbol of these problems. Red Wagner was a child of the TVA culture. He was apolitical and technocratic but always adhered to his conception of the public trust. He asserted TVA authority in major capital projects but was cautious in working out local partnerships in resource development. He thus embodied the contradictory fault line between top-down direction and grass roots participation that ran through the TVA organization.

Wagner was told that he could replace Vogel as TVA chairman after John Kennedy became president, but Wagner refused for fear that the job would seem political, changing when the president changed.[40] He was appointed to the board initially because Marguerite Owen, working through Senator Lister Hill, persuaded President Kennedy that he could show his support for TVA by appointing a career person to the board.[41] Wagner was reappointed by President Nixon in 1969, largely at the behest of Republican senator Howard Baker, who claimed that the action would affirm Nixon's friendliness to Tennessee and TVA.[42]

Wagner's approach to Congress was like his leadership of public opinion. He would state the facts and hope for support. According to Owen, he was good in this role, even though he did not particularly enjoy it.[43] He left the political strategies of helping TVA to members of the valley delegation. His job, as he saw it, "was to explain the situation to them and let them figure out how to get it done."[44] Just as he did not see TVA involved in the president's program, because of its autonomy, he wanted TVA to have the same independence of Congress: "Congress can overrule us but they can't make us say what we recommend is wrong. You undermine your credibility if you begin to trim your analysis for political reasons."[45] Frank Smith, who had hoped to be named TVA chairman instead of Wagner, was critical because Wagner did not work Congress in a more active way. But this was not Wagner's character.[46] His approach to Washington was guided by what he had learned from Clapp as symbolized in the Douglas Dam story. Do your duty and the rest will take care of itself.

Management and Purpose

Signs of organizational ossification appeared in several TVA studies done in the 1970s. The virtues of decentralized professionalism, which had unleashed energy for invention and construction in the early years, became detrimental. The several offices, especially the engineering-construction and power programs, were like juggernauts that bowled over everything in their way. But this is not to say that Red Wagner lost control. He was a product of the management system and knew how to make it work for his objectives, which were for the most part the same as those of his senior colleagues who directed the offices. The problem was not so much each man for himself as undue consensus. One sees here the seeds of the organizational crisis of 1985, when all five nuclear reactors were shut down. The board had finally lost control of the organization, and it was not even clear that the technocrats controlled their own machines. One can see the flaws of 1985 in earlier times in excessive reliance on seniority for promotion, reluctance to bring in outside experts to deal with new problems, and conflict between engineering and power, all to the detriment of careful construction and management of the steam and nuclear plants. Wagner's commitment to a dynamic and heroic TVA created an organizational momentum beneath which many of these flaws were concealed. All missions were expanding. And yet Wagner's idealism and ambition for TVA were his antidotes for organizational rigidity. For example, he hoped that the Tributary Area Development program would unite the power and nonpower sides of the organization in new multipurpose missions. In this sense Wagner and David Freeman were much alike. Each hoped to rejuvenate TVA through new missions, albeit different ones.

The 1960s and 1970s were years of building steam plants, to keep up with the valley's energy needs. But in 1965 a decision was made to build a nuclear plant, with three reactors, at Browns Ferry, Alabama, after a lengthy and thorough process of costing that alternative against coal-fired steam plants of equivalent magnitude. Nuclear power appeared to be less costly. This analysis was done each time a nuclear plant was planned. As a hedge against future needs for coal, however, TVA bought underground coal reserves in Kentucky, east Tennessee, and Illinois.

The first general increase in the wholesale rate of electricity took place in 1967. Two further increases followed in 1969 and 1970 and continued with greater frequency throughout the 1970s. The rising costs of energy, labor, and construction, following from an ambitious building program, were largely responsible.

The policy of limited TVA land acquisition around reservoir sites was reversed in 1960 with the Melton Hill Dam where considerable land was acquired with an eye to water-related industrial development. This policy came to full expression in the Tims Ford, Tellico, Normandy, and Columbia dams of the 1970s. The Tributary Area Development program was raised to office status in 1961, and TVA embarked on several multipurpose projects in partnerships with fifteen local watershed associations. Ammonium nitrate, manufactured at Muscle Shoals, became the most popular fertilizer in the United States. The education of farmers through demonstration projects gave way to techniques developed by commercial firms to sell fertilizer to consumers. TVA thus gained a valuable group of supporters in the fertilizer industry. The TVA Fertilizer Center became an important agency for worldwide transmission of fertilizer technology, and TVA became an adviser to the U.S. government in regard to its overseas agricultural development work. In 1974, striking twin office towers on an imposing hilltop site in downtown Knoxville were completed. One of the buildings was occupied by the board, general manager's office, and TVA support services; the other was completely filled by staff of the Office of Engineering Construction and Design, reflecting the massive building program.[47] However, a note of sadness is detected amidst all this activity. It appears in the memories of TVA professionals, and a few are sampled here. William Hayes, a former assistant general manager, told an interviewer in 1970:

> [There] still prevails in TVA—a kind of "hold-on" to the concept that it's a permanent agency, that it has a permanent job to do in terms of developing a region. Well, you run out of those things. I mean with the kind of intermediary agency that it is, you run out of those things that you can legitimately do . . . and if you don't watch yourself, why you'll get into some awful situations and really some leaf raking.[48]

A. J. "Flash" Gray, a longtime TVA regional planner, commented in 1974:

> [W]hen the initial program of decentralized administration developed, the TVA mission was clear-cut, and everybody knew and understood what it was. We had to develop the river. We had to relate the river to the region. . . . But after 1955, I did think TVA changed significantly because we had built the major components of the river system and the question that TVA faced was: what is our mission in the region? I do not think that TVA has solved that basic policy question and I would contend that the decentralized administration is one of the reasons it has never been able to do this because it has never been able to establish strong, centralized planning to provide the kind of guidelines. . . . that I think absolutely necessary in this kind of situation. . . . I do not think the great autonomy of the departments is appropriate under present situations, as it was in the pre-1955 situation.[49]

This note of sadness or uncertainty may very well have fed the dynamic activity of the several offices and divisions in their search for new missions. But bureaucracies age, and it can be seen in the reflections of TVA professionals. Chief engineer George Palo, who had come to TVA in 1934, felt it:

> I am very much in favor of the TVA system. It began to weaken in the mid sixties. So many of us were in the organization at the beginning and we knew what we were supposed to do. For example, the design division had five branches. Bob Monroe was chief design engineer, 1954–59, but he never held meetings of the five branches because all five of us knew each other personally and we made it work. It could not be done today [1981]. You need more direction and control today . . . you suddenly get people coming up who lack the experience and have not been taught the TVA way. . . . The problem is also due to greater organizational size in later years. For example, the design division had nine hundred employees and five people could speak for them. Today there are three thousand people in the division.[50]

Palo then practically committed heresy:

> I am not personally of the opinion that TVA can go back into the early stages of things. For example, Red Wagner wanted to develop TVA research on the electric car. The problem is probably too hard for TVA to do. A battery must first be developed and then TVA has a mission to use those batteries. TVA doesn't invent thermal and sun power cells but implements those ideas. . . . TVA cannot be the originator of anything.[51]

Hugh Parris, who became manager of the Office of Power in 1979, reported the lack of central control that was later to damage his own career in 1985:

> Back in the forties and fifties some pretty good planning went on. A lot of top management attention was given to it. After bond financing was settled, that relaxed a big constraint. We [Office of Power] turned in pro forma budgets to OMB [Office of Management and Budget] and the board. Our program planning went to pot. We did some good project planning. That was where the focus and the technical skill went. This went on through the early seventies. Wessenauer retired in 1969. He used the power budget as a control device. He didn't need any help—he was the manager of power for twenty one years. After he left the budget document was a paper exercise.[52]

Two separate but related problems surface in these comments. There is uncertainty about TVA's mission as a whole. And it is difficult to control the parts from the center. The problems are related in that separate divisions, hell-bent on achieving their own missions, will not contribute to a sense of the whole or be easily controllable from the top. The old-timers' laments reported here reflect nostalgia for an earlier TVA.

William Willis, executive vice-president under the Runyon board, general manager with Freeman and Dean, and a construction engineer in the Wagner years, described the decline and fall of a way of life

> It was a heroism period. We were killing dragons. Red emitted the idealism. . . . People sensed that in Red and followed him, committed their lives to him. . . . This began to erode in the mid seventies. Problems were occurring throughout TVA. The [organization's] size tripled because of nuclear programs. There was less dedication in the work force. It was hard to get things done, to get total commitment. The criticism of the TVA came and undedicated people were ill prepared to deal with that. . . . It was difficult for Red to accept the death of a concept.[53]

John Bynon saw the same trends:

> The organizational system of Blandford lasted until the early seventies. . . . There were strong requirements for self-coordination and a system of checks and balances, the chief engineer vs. the chief of power, agriculture vs. chemical

engineering. The board and general manager could smell collusion. The system began to fall apart because the TVA went from a large, complex organization with many programs to a nuclear program that overwhelmed everybody.[54]

Phil Ericson, assistant to the general manager under Wagner and Seeber, entered TVA in 1937 as a navigation engineer:

> I never met a guy that was not admirable in those early years. They were all fired up with what they were doing. I very rarely ran into a situation in which anyone lied. I could believe the answers I got. This was true of my peers and my immediate supervisors. . . . We all saw this as an important element in the atmosphere. A weakness that I have since come to see—didn't see it then—is that things were pretty much settled before they came to the board. Few options were given the board in the nineteen sixties and early seventies. I don't recall the board asking for options. They believed their managers. . . . They gave a man his head and believed him when he came back with a recommendation.[55]

These interviews provide some insight into bureaucratic problems within TVA in the later Wagner years. Empirical studies of the organization during the same period revealed general patterns consistent with the insights of individuals. In 1975–76, the International Institute for Applied Systems Analysis (IIASA) sent four study teams of several persons each to examine TVA's managerial structure and patterns of decision making. The study was one of several analyses of large-scale planning projects conducted by IIASA.[56]

The IIASA study teams wanted to understand how TVA sought to be a multipurpose, regional development organization. They first looked at the board/general-manager system and concluded that the board was too often presented with yes or no options by the bureaucracy, the alternatives having been screened by the operating divisions. For this reason, the board found it difficult to leave nonpolicy matters alone. Its three members had to dip down for information, but the board had no staff of its own to help it get systematic information. Its members relied on ad hoc informants throughout the organization. It was the IIASA team's perception that TVA goals and objectives were what they always had been, to promote regional development of natural resources. But they asserted this was not done effectively because each subdivision pursued its own concerns so much that there was no coherent strategy for improving the economy of the valley as a whole. And, in fact, the programs often clashed. For example, the Office of Power was opposed to introducing TVA requirements on strip miners to reclaim the land, for fear that the price of coal would be raised and affect TVA rates adversely. Power also objected to keeping water levels high in reservoirs to increase their appeal as recreation sites. The history of TVA, they said, had shown many efforts at regional development that had been abandoned because of conflicts among programs.[57] The team was struck by the fact that the public language of the board still claimed the multipurpose, regional-development role for TVA but that such claims led to internal tension: "One consequence of the discrepancy between formally stated objectives and the actual situation is the rather widespread concern about the TVA's future. Both internally and externally we heard comments about 'the lack of direction.'"[58]

There was great concern within TVA in all divisions except power that TVA would soon be only a power company. In the absence of a "regional development plan," TVA had lost its vitality: "As the enthusiastic sense of mission of TVA's founding generation is no longer available to provide a forward thrust, the absence of a clear sense of direction would seem likely to breed a loss of confidence, slow down the authority's momentum and lead to internal confusion and conflict."[59]

The solution, the IIASA team argued, was a "dynamic leader that keeps pushing new targets out in front of both the enterprise and its environment . . . in order to prevent the enterprise from being overwhelmed and coopted by the environment."[60] Red Wagner was trying to be such a leader in the mid-1070s with the Tellico Dam and the nuclear program, but the IIASA authors missed it. They saw sluggishness in TVA's bureaucracy but did not perceive what Wagner was doing to combat it.

The IIASA team advocated a greater planning role by the board and general manager, not in an authoritative sense but as a coordinator of "many agencies and individuals."[61] This was TVA doctrine, but it did not seem to be practice, according to the team, because "self-coordination" simply led to burying conflict below board level and there was almost no planning across separate offices and divisions. Thus the advantages of coordinated action were precluded. Conflict was avoided by giving freedom of action to each unit, and "the informal 'general review' of plans by senior management is defended on the grounds that greater emphasis could be destructive of TVA's decentralized organization."[62]

The IIASA study drew a picture of a relatively weak top hierarchy that permitted the parts of the TVA bureaucracy to adapt to their environments without direction from the top. Long-standing personal relationships often compensated for the lack of formal integrating mechanisms. But this led to a "relatively undisciplined management process" in which "there appears to be little inclination to take a strong minded approach to the review of capital expenditure proposals or annual plans. Likewise the control process and the relationships are characterized more by conflict avoidance than by conflict resolution."[63]

The report described the competition of operating divisions for influence within the appropriated budget without any kind of cost-benefit analysis at the top. Estimates of performance before the fact were "notoriously speculative," and as the environment was changing, this made any kind of planning unstable. Most written proposals sent to the board for approval were qualitative with little support in the form of figures. And the numbers presented often appeared to have been prepared on an "ad hoc basis." Interoffice conflicts were not explicitly faced, and the compromises that might be reached informally among the offices were not necessarily those favored by the general manager.[64]

The IIASA team understood that a strategic plan for the whole of TVA was not realistic. But they did advocate the practice of regular assessments of regional trends which might be used as a basis for the planning of the offices and divisions. The report recommended that the office of planning and budget within the general manager's office have a small number of "analytically trained problem solvers" who could work with their counterparts in each division.[65] This was exactly what Wagner rejected and Freeman later tried to develop.

The study team thought that TVA leadership had been handicapped by the decentralized management system in assessing the relative merits and trade-offs among programs. For example, the tension between cheap electric power and a clean environment might not be adequately addressed because there were no mechanisms at board or general-manager level to do so.[66] The study team may have been wrong here, in the sense that Wagner and his colleagues knew there was a trade-off between cheap electricity and clean air and water but simply decided in favor of the former. Would analysis have really made a difference? The authors of the IIASA study thought so and conducted two case studies to support their point.

The forestry division of almost four hundred people did its work by "traditional TVA demonstrational/educational methods," working with groups outside TVA. Success would be assessed by how well the foresters accurately perceived regional needs. The division was described as loosely organized, with considerable communication among branches. All employees were encouraged to suggest ideas in an open planning process, which also sought advice from outside constituencies. It was thus fairly easy for the division to adapt itself to the perceived needs of its environment. High levels of interaction and permeability made for high internal morale and commitment to shared objectives.[67]

The Office of Power implemented one technology that was not difficult to operate. Much of the work was routine and could be covered by rules. Individuals were seen to have little discretion in their decisions. The external environment was also relatively simple, changing levels of demand being assessable by simple models. Negative effects of electricity upon the physical environment, such as air pollution, were usually decided in favor of the Office of Power because of its great strength within TVA. The office of approximately one thousand people was organized into two branches for planning and transmission with limited lateral links between them. Staff members of each saw the world in terms of their own unit. Communication came down from the top rather than sideways or up from below. And there was very limited interaction with the external environment. The only interaction with other TVA units that seemed to work was the old relationship with water control in the operation of dams. Coordination on environmental issues was poor and could only be improved by intervention from above.[68]

On the basis of these two case studies, the authors of the IIASA report concluded that the forestry division was open and adaptable in relation to its environment and sensitive to questions about quality. The power program was said to be relatively closed and sealed off from its environment, and quality-of-life questions were minimized. The result, the authors contended, was weak monitoring of TVA's effects on the environment. A stopgap remedy of placing a coordinator of environmental policy in the general manager's office had not worked; the position was seen as weak and ineffective.[69]

A second study by Marc Roberts and Associates in the late 1970s revealed many of the same organizational characteristics as the IIASA study. The historical pattern of decentralization was found, not surprisingly, to have created strong group loyalties. People spent their careers in one division and saw little of people in other units. Vertical movement up in rank was slow and dependent on retirements, and promotion was tied to length of service. The expansion of the work of divisions thus created career opportunities. One consequence was that TVA tried to do as much work in-house as possible in order to maximize the number of internal opportunities. Consultants were seldom used, and each division did its own troubleshooting. These practices reinforced TVA's sense of its own technical competence. Red Wagner was quoted as saying: "We don't want to hire consultants who are the best experts. We want our staff to be the best experts available."[70]

According to Roberts and his coauthors, the great emphasis placed upon technical expertise meant that the general manager had difficulty assessing the work of the divisions and was only a coordinator. That meant, they concluded, that the board had only a limited capacity to set directions for TVA. The technical arguments of the division heads were usually accepted. Wagner told the authors: "You have to ask the right questions and sometimes go into matters in some detail in order to get the right answer. The board reads a great deal of material, including some very thick reports, and time doesn't always permit complete and careful reading."[71]

Lacking its own analytical staff, the board was not able to assess the options being recommended but could ask enough questions to make sure the division had done thorough program analyses. Nor could the board oversee implementation well because it was dependent on the divisions' reports. Roberts and his associates reported that division directors often worked out agreements with each other, quite independently of the general manager or the board. Of course, according to TVA norms they were supposed to do so. Such practice was also consistent with the strongly held belief that TVA work was technical and nonpolitical and that issues were best resolved by experts.[72]

The bargaining process among offices and divisions was said to favor strong personalities, particularly if the goals of their programs were very clear. This meant that Wessanauer and his successors in the Office of Power had been first among equals for some years. In order to be part of winning coalitions, other divisions would often defer to power. For example, the environmental planning division had developed practical methods of controlling sulfur-dioxide emissions that were consistent with power's opposition to low-sulfur coal or stack gas scrubbers. The Office of Engineering was expert in building very large steam plants, which took advantage of economies of scale, but in concert with power it may have "underdesigned" some units, which reduced costs but also increased risks because of imperfect construction. Forestry avoided taking a strong position on strip-mine reclamation in order to avoid antagonizing power.[73]

Wagner is not depicted in the Roberts study as a patsy for power and is properly credited with taking initiatives on behalf of environmental values in the face of opposition from power.[74] But the general picture of TVA professionals in the study is one of self-confident men with strong loyalties to their particular units and specialties, who had been at TVA a long time, and because of limited communication with outside ideas, were sometimes slow to adopt new techniques or technologies.[75] Top management was dependent upon the expertise of professional staffs, and therefore the rewards were high for those office and division heads who could make plausible technical arguments to the board and general manager and who appeared authoritative.[76] Such technical "decisiveness and authoritativeness" were valued and rewarded throughout TVA, but this sometimes led to experts claiming more than they knew in order to win with higher management.[77]

Roberts and his colleagues decided that TVA's policy consistency and energy were due, in part, to the "coordination from the middle" exercised by the Office of Power. The authority of middle managers over their staffs also contributed to stability, as did the "deeply internalized sense of their agency's mission" held by TVA professionals. Senior managers said very explicitly that dedication to the TVA mission was essential for promotion. Roberts concluded that it was not easy to change behavior in such an organization because it "involves converting the membership from one faith to another."[78] Top management lacked the leverage to change behavior below, and it would take much time and conflict to get new people in key posts.

Wagner's style of authority was consistent with these snapshots of TVA organizational culture. But Wagner was not a prisoner of the management system. He used it for his own purposes and was hostage to it only in the sense that he was limited by what it could or could not do for him. Major policy decisions during the Wagner years can best be understood by an analysis of Wagner's leadership style in the context of the TVA culture.

TRIBUTARY AREA DEVELOPMENT

This program is important to our story for three reasons. First, it illustrates Wagner's search for a new economic development mission. Second, it reveals how difficult it was to create cross-divisional programs within TVA. And third, it is the prelude to the story of the star-crossed Tellico Dam, which was Wagner's most dramatic attempt to revive TVA's multipurpose, regional development mission.

TVA had plans for developing the Tennessee River tributaries in the 1930s which were postponed by World War II and then revived by Gordon Clapp. The approach was to be one of cooperation with locally organized citizen development groups and state governments. By the late 1950s, ten tributary associations had been formed and were receiving help from TVA in planning for the development of their areas.[79] Wagner encouraged these developments as general manager, board member, and chairman. In a 1961 statement to the Senate Appropriations Subcommittee, made when he was a TVA director but not yet chairman, he grounded the tributary program in TVA's two initial goals, unified resource development and partnership with state and local government.[80] The TVA role, he said, was one of coordination and technical assistance, with state and local groups in the lead. Each project would be different, but each was organized on the principle of an integrated plan for the fullest possible development of the natural resources of given areas for economic development. He cited a chapter in Lilienthal's TVA book *Experts and the People* as a source of inspiration. TVA's direct contribution was to be the building of dams and attacking of soil erosion (e.g., through planting trees and working with farmers), but it would also give advice on industrial development, unemployment, transportation, etc. Wagner made it very clear that TVA would not stud the tributaries with dams just for the glory of it. Dams had to be justified by the plans developed by local groups. Coherence of plans therefore had to be provided by local sponsors.

Wagner was inspired by the vision of the industrial development of the tributary areas, which he saw as preferable to the continued growth of large cities.[81] He had been worried in the early 1950s that TVA agricultural people might capture tributary development, and he hoped to steer the program toward industrial development. So when the Office of Tributary Area Development was created in 1961, Wagner made sure that its head was Richard Kilbourne, a forester who worked on the development of forest products for industry.[82]

There was some excitement about the new program. Kilbourne remembered that "there was the idea floating around that TVA could come in and completely remake the community." The difficulty was that the Office of Power was not interested in such trivial work. And Wagner wanted the Office of Power on board.[83] However, after self-financing was established, some people in the Office of Power began to think they might benefit from additional appropriations for hydroelectric projects in the watersheds. The election of John Kennedy to the White House and the interest of the new administration in regional development, particularly in Appalachia, strengthened Wagner's case.[84] But TVA regional planners like "Flash" Gray were opposed to the new program. They thought economic development would come with industrial development in small cities and service sectors in large cities. As one of them put it, "They [Office of Tributary Area Development] wanted to start up little TVA's all over the valley . . . and that was taking the easy way out by trying to repeat TVA's successes, only on a much smaller scale."[85] TVA planners made fun of Wagner's idea of "factories in the fields."

The state of Tennessee did not do much to implement a 1954 agreement with TVA about assistance to local tributary associations, and the associations looked to TVA to solve their problems. This often took the form of lobbying members of the valley congressional delegation in behalf of appropriations for TVA projects in their areas. TVA's tradition of "engineering correctness" was hostile to this effort.[86] John Bynon remembered that "Red didn't create TAD to get an interest group that would go to Washington as they [the local associations] did. He accepted the political reality but didn't like it."[87] TVA has always resisted classic pork barrel both in theory and fact.

TVA hopes for comprehensive planning of watershed areas were also disappointed. Each area program was a bundle of separate projects, so that according to one student of the Tributary Area Development Program, "it is questionable whether any comprehensive plan has been more than partially implemented in any tributary, except where tributary dams have played a major role in the development of the tributary area."[88] The multiplication of ad hoc projects increased in 1965 when Congress passed legislation that would grant funds to the states for economic development. Each state was to create development districts, but those areas had no necessary links with the river. TVA requested complementary funds under section 22 of the act, but this led to ad hoc programs without much coherence.[89] As a TAD director told a friend in the agency, "I'm trying to come up with sellable programs until the big boys get their act together."[90]

TAD was never very popular within TVA. It had no program budgets of its own but had to rely on other offices to orient some of their programs for TAD purposes.[91] For example, the foresters wanted a total return on the dollars they spent, and TAD wished to use forestry solely for economic development.[92] TAD people were labeled by other TVA professionals as generalists in an organization of specialists.[93] Chief engineer George Palo felt that TAD failed to clear projects with others before it made commitments to local groups.[94] There were not enough engineering projects in TAD to satisfy those who preferred, as Bill Willis put it, "the old meat and potatoes work."[95] TVA had become a builder of giant projects, not only dams but the largest steam and nuclear plants in the world. It was a source of organizational pride. Tributary projects did not measure up.

THE TELLICO DAM

Wagner's strong desire to unify TVA around a new generation of multipurpose projects was most fully realized in the Tellico Dam. Although the dam was to be in the Little Tennessee, which is a tributary of the Tennessee River, the Tellico idea was a manifestation of the search in TAD for new economic development tasks. Although TVA did not want to be told to build dams where they were not justified, it was still true that a dam evoked more multipurpose activity than any other kind of TVA product, just as it had in the 1930s. The innovation in the Tellico story was the TVA justification of the dam, not by the traditional criteria of power, navigation, and flood control but by future economic development around the reservoir.

The Tellico drama lasted thirteen years from the first request to Congress for an appropriation in 1965 to the 1978 amendment that permitted the dam's gates to be shut by exempting it from the Endangered Species Act. It is an absorbing story which cannot be retold in its richness here. Our interest is in Wagner's use of Tellico as a vehicle for rejuvenating the nonpower, regional development mission. The story also illustrates the technocratic side of TVA, for it was the Douglas Dam story all over again, with TVA sticking to its expertise in the face of politically inspired opposition. But Tellico did great damage to TVA's public credibility even though it won the fight to build the dam. The Douglas Dam helped win the war. The Tellico Dam only revealed how the country had changed. TVA met opposition from farmers, conservationists, environmentalists, fishermen, Cherokee Indians, and the governor of Tennessee. The Tennessee congressmen and senators stood with TVA, as did the Tennessee Valley Public Power Association and local groups who might benefit from the dam, but the winning coalition was very weak. The development tasks of TVA were no longer pristine. They clashed with other values.

The dam was Wagner's brainchild. On February 5, 1959, he sent a memo to twenty-six top TVA professionals inviting them to a meeting for the purpose of "a brainstorming session" on how TVA might justify the building of new dams. The memo clearly states the ambition for a new mission:

> A few weeks ago the staff met with the Board and summarized our investigation of possible future dams and reservoir projects. It seemed clear from this discussion that if past methods for justifying and financing such projects are continued in the future, few, if any, more dams will be built in the Tennessee Valley. At the same time, it may be possible to demonstrate that added projects would contribute enough to further regional development to amply justify their construction. This could well be a field in which TVA could plow new ground. It may only depend on how ingenious and resourceful we can be in finding a basis for evaluating a project's usefulness and for financing its construction. . . . Come if you can and bring all the optimism you have.[96]

Some of TVA's most important professionals attended the meeting, including Gabriel Wessenauer, Richard Kilbourne, Leland Allbaugh, Paul Evans, and Lawrence Durisch. Wagner presided and made it clear that he wanted TVA to build more dams and reservoirs. He lamented that TVA had only built one multipurpose project, Melton Hill Dam, since 1951 because no proposed project could be justified according to the conventional criteria of power, navigation, and flood control. Ways and means had to be found "for pushing a water-resource development program, over the next hump, assuming that additional dams and reservoir projects will make a valuable contribution to the region."[97]

Wagner was evidently trying to bring the power and water people within TVA together in these water projects. William Wheeler and Michael McDonald found a tension between two different conceptions of TVA in their study of Tellico. The power people thought of TVA as a power company and, being geographically apart from Knoxville, showed little interest in the rest of TVA. The water people were a disparate cluster of navigation, flood control, recreation, forestry, and regional and economic studies. They thought of TVA in multipurpose terms.[98] But there were few multipurpose projects in 1959; the Tributary Area Development program was only an idea. Fertilizer people had little interest in such issues, but the agricultural division was not happy at the thought of more dams and reservoirs, which would cover farmland. But it was too weak politically within TVA to make a difference.[99] The construction engineers turned up their noses at small watershed projects, but the prospect of building a large dam appealed to them. The narrow constructionists had prevailed in TVA since the war because the emphasis of TVA's building program had been on steam plants. The days of hydro projects seemed to be over. An internal report in 1944 calling for a "small purchase" policy of land around reservoirs had become board policy.[100]

Two developments during the Eisenhower administration had favored the broad constructionists. Self-financing removed the yearly battles over appropriations to build steam plants and perhaps eased the way for appropriations for water projects. The Eisenhower administration had also articulated the "partnership principle" in which federal agencies were to seek collaboration with state and local governments and the private sector in projects of shared interest. Both developments encouraged the broad constructionists within TVA. There is also some indication that Wessanauer became more supportive of dams if he thought it possible that new power could be generated.[101]

Wagner was well suited to bring the broad and narrow constructionists together. He was a water man, having come up through navigation. But he was also an apostle of the power program who was personally close to Wessenauer. Both Wagner and Wessenauer saw TVA as a multipurpose agency.[102] In 1960 Wagner secured board reversal of the "small purchase" policy, paving the way for TAD. And just before that he had appointed a Future Dams and Reservoir Committee with the charge to find new ways of computing cost-benefit analyses of water projects.[103] The Tellico dam emerged as the project that was most likely to yield favorable cost-benefit ratios. As Wheeler and McDonald have described, Tellico became a unifying force within TVA:

[T]he Tellico project became the conjuncture of the agency's reversed land purchase policy, the intra-agency decline of the agriculturalists, the emphasis on industrial development, the devising of more imaginative methods of computing cost-benefit analysis, the use of citizen cooperation and support and the affirmation of the new mission of creating "little TVA's" in the tributary areas throughout the Valley.[104]

The initial difficulty was that a favorable cost-benefit ratio for Tellico could not be obtained if couched in conventional terms. The new committee, even with help from outside consultants, informed Wagner of the problem, but he would not heed, insisting in a memo that it was essential that they move ahead as rapidly as possible to apply to the Tellico project any new and different methods that could be devised for justification and financing.[105] The committee chair remembered that Wagner "would have preferred to dump benefit-cost ratios and just go ahead with the project."[106] But Marguerite Owen had made it clear that Congress would not appropriate funds for a project that lacked favorable benefit-cost ratios.[107] The committee identified three potential areas of benefit: land enhancement, recreation, and "general economic benefits." The first required TVA to buy land and later sell it at a profit, but how were future land values to be estimated? There was no agreement on how to measure recreation benefits. And it was very difficult to estimate future industrialization, job creation, and tax revenue. Wagner told the committee to keep working.[108]

The Kennedy presidency helped keep Tellico alive because the new administration favored public works to increase employment and regional economic development. But both Gabriel Wessenauer and George Palo told Wagner that the search for a favorable ratio for Tellico was not likely to be successful. Incipient opposition from farm groups was also on the horizon. There was opposition within TVA from the land-use planners, agriculture, fisheries, wildlife, and forestry, but most dissidents came around quickly when they saw how determined Wagner was. In 1963 the board approved the Tellico plan, even though favorable benefit-cost ratios had yet to be found.[109]

The plan called for TVA to purchase 38,000 acres of land with the reservoir covering only 16,500 acres. The rest was to be saved for development. TVA would promote industrial, commercial, and residential development in the area. It was estimated that about $10 million would be returned to the Treasury from land sales, to offset initial costs.[110] Wagner kept pushing for better benefit-cost analyses in terms of future returns from land use and was confident they would be found.

TVA's dams had historically drawn opposition only from people who had to be resettled, and not all of them. But the Tellico project was a hornet's nest. Fish and wildlife people opposed the damming of a free-flowing river, the Little Tennessee. The Tennessee State Planning Commission and the Fish and Game Commission favored preserving the Little Tennessee for recreation. Local farm bureaus and the Tennessee Farm Bureau Federation were strongly opposed.[111] There was solid public support for Tellico in the counties closest to the dam, which were economically depressed.[112] But more prosperous counties along the river did not favor the plan.[113] Wagner spoke at a public meeting in the area in 1964 at which strong opposition was expressed. TVA could not build even a local consensus for the project.[114] Eventually the Cherokee Indians attacked TVA for its plans to flood their ancestral burying grounds. Supreme Court Justice William O. Douglas fished on the Little Tennessee River and publicly criticized the idea of a dam. And the controversy continued to fester through 1965 when Representative Joe L. Evins, Democrat of Tennessee, who chaired the relevant Appropriations Subcommittee, won an appropriation for the Tims Ford Dam in his own district in preference to Tellico.[115] In addition, Senator Allen Ellender, Democrat of Louisiana and chairman of the Senate Appropriations Committee, was hostile to TVA and to Tellico and attacked TVA's speculative benefit-cost ratios by invoking a less sanguine Army Corps of Engineers analysis.[116]

The TVA benefit-cost studies made five assumptions which seem, on their face, to be highly optimistic:

1. The area would remain economically depressed without the project.
2. All economic programs after the project was completed could be properly attributed to it.
3. The predicted economic benefits of Tellico would occur.
4. No future economic benefits, unrelated to Tellico, would be reduced because of the dam.
5. The costs of the project would not rise faster than the annual rate of inflation, which was 3 to 4 percent in the early 1960s.[117]

To produce favorable benefit ratios, it was necessary to keep costs low and estimate a high return from benefits. Accuracy may have been stretched at both ends of the analysis. Agricultural analysts within the agency wrote two highly negative reports on the economic losses that would result from removing so much land from cultivation, but the board was not listening. H. A. Henderson, who wrote one of the reports, claimed that "TVA was victimized by sycophantic supporters who would not tell the board anything but what the board wanted to hear."[118]

Tennessee congressman Joe Evins became a Tellico sponsor and got a favorable vote for Tellico from the Appropriations Committee and the House in 1966. The vote then passed the Senate and was signed by President Johnson. Benefit-cost ratios were not really an issue in the legislative history.[119] Wagner had insisted in congressional testimony that construction begin as soon as possible because the people of the area wanted and needed the benefits. He simply ignored the opposition. Wheeler and McDonald contended that the belief in Tellico was so strong among its adherents within TVA that their minds were closed to any negative information. They had faith in themselves and in TVA and what it could do.[120]

So by 1966 it looked as if the dam would be built, but a comedy of errors intervened to slow construction and prevent completion until 1978. The National Environmental Protection Act was passed in 1969, and because of it, construction on the dam, which had begun in 1967, was halted. Tellico opponents argued that the new law required TVA to develop an Environmental Impact Statement on Tellico, but Wagner refused, saying the law did not apply to a previously authorized project. He wrote Congress to that effect, sounding more like an antigovernment businessman than a public servant.[121] But TVA lost in a federal court in 1971, which ordered TVA to meet the NEPA requirements.[122]

About the same time, Republican governor Winfield Dunn, of Tennessee, spoke out publicly against the project on environmental grounds. A former assistant to Governor Dunn remembered: "It was TVA's foregone conclusion that whatever is good for TVA is good for the state, and therefore it was a shock to Wagner and TVA that the state disagreed on Tellico and challenged TVA."[123]

In 1971 a group of University of Tennessee economists issued a study, known as the Phillips Report, that criticized TVA's economic assumptions about Tellico. The project director, Dr. Keith Phillips, later commented: "Tellico was not an investment without risk; TVA just started out with basic benefits and then doubled everything. According to TVA they account for every dollar generated in the valley, and it's simply not true."[124]

Despite such criticism, TVA attracted the interest of the Boeing Corporation in building the new town of Timberlake on the Tellico reservoir. A feasibility study was conducted in 1971, and Boeing became an ally in the fight. TVA also succeeded in winning approval of its Environmental Impact Statement by 1972, and it looked as if Tellico would be completed.[125]

Then in 1973 the tiny snail darter fish was discovered in the Little Tennessee River, and since the fish was legally protected by the recently passed Endangered Species Act, work on the dam stopped again. Groups opposed to the dam had a new legal hook with which to delay or defeat Tellico. Wagner insisted that moving the snail darter to a nearby river was sufficient, but the U.S. Fish and Wildlife Service did not agree, declaring the fish to be an endangered species in 1975. The issue went to court, with the Department of the Interior arguing for the fish and against TVA. Finally, in 1978, with the dam 90 percent completed, the U.S. Supreme Court decided that TVA was wrong and it was forbidden by law to close the gates of the dam, which was to be permanently halted. A commission of congressional members and administration officials, chaired by Secretary of the Interior Cecil Andrus, reported in 1979 that Tellico could not be justified on economic grounds, quite aside from the snail darter. Charles Schultz, chairman of President Carter's Council of Economic Advisers and a member of the Commission, said at the time: "Here is a project that is 95% complete and if one takes just the cost of finishing it against the benefits and does it properly it doesn't pay, which says something about the original design."[126]

However, Representative John Duncan, a Republican from east Tennessee, attached a rider to the Energy and Water Resources Appropriation Bill exempting Tellico from the act and won voice approval in a poorly attended House session. The amendment was deleted in the Senate version, but Duncan put it back in conference and it passed both houses and was signed by President Carter, even though Carter had publicly opposed the dam's completion. TVA closed the gates of the Tellico Dam with Red Wagner looking on.[127]

On balance one must conclude that even though the dam was completed, the long fight to do so represented a massive failure for TVA. It was not a repeat of the Douglas Dam story. TVA discovered the new regulatory state which pitted TVA habitual claims to autonomy against the new legal responsibilities of other federal agencies. TVA was depicted as an overbearing bully throughout the valley just at a time when electricity rates were skyrocketing and the authority was already very unpopular. A new economic development role was not discovered. In fact, the Tributary Area Development program was killed by the Freeman board in 1979. And in the long run, the existence of the dam did not contribute to the economic development of the area. Industries were not attracted to any degree, and eventually TVA withdrew from responsibility for developing the land.[128] But to be fair, the snail darter seemed happy in a new location.

Clean Air

Throughout its history, TVA had been successful in protecting its autonomy from the General Accounting Office, the Civil Service Commission, and other agencies in Washington that might have wished to control TVA's way of doing business. As a government corporation, TVA had legitimate claims to such autonomy. TVA lawyers also cut off potential state regulators every time they raised their heads. TVA controlled its organized constituencies, such as the Tennessee Valley Public Power Association, far more than it was controlled by such groups. This history ill prepared TVA for the Environmental Protection Act and other federal regulatory measures that would inevitably challenge its autonomy. The creation of the Environmental Protection Agency in 1970 gave TVA a potential antagonist and created an unprecedented situation for TVA in which it became subject to regulation by another federal agency.[129]

At the same time, TVA became more vulnerable to lawsuits than it had been in the past. A crucial case in this regard was *Hardin vs. Kentucky Utilities Company* in 1968, in which the U.S. Supreme Court decided that the TVA Act was reviewable by the courts, contrary to the claims of TVA lawyers. The particular question was a conflict over territory with a private utility, but the decision encouraged other parties, particularly environmentalists, to challenge TVA's interpretation of its own act in the courts.[130] Paul Evans remembered that no one in TVA thought that national environmental laws would restrict TVA actions until the first lawsuits appeared. The idea that policies of the Environmental Protection Agency, for example, could override decisions of the TVA board contradicted TVA's entire history.[131]

One irony of the story of the conflict with the EPA is that TVA was planning to reduce its reliance on air-polluting coal in favor of nuclear energy, which it was thought would be cheaper and cleaner. Wagner and others consistently argued that it was a mistake to put expensive antipollution devices on coal-fired plants that would soon be shut down. Thus, as we will see, the rush to get the EPA off its back may have contributed to TVA's eventual problems with the nuclear construction program and the deadly duel with the Nuclear Regulatory Commission.

In 1970 coal accounted for almost 80 percent of TVA's power, but it was hoped that the amount would be reduced to 35 percent by 1985. Thus TVA could claim that its contribution to air pollution was temporary and that new technology would greatly reduce the problem. However, the passage of the Clean Air Act in 1969 and the creation of the EPA in 1970 were direct challenges to the high levels of sulfur dioxide emissions from TVA steam plants, with consequent acid rain and effects on humans.[132]

There were many ambiguities at the outset. The EPA had delegated the implementation of the Clean Air Act to state agencies. The degree of emissions reduction required by the law was uncertain. William Ruckelshaus, the first EPA administrator, moved slowly on implementation, approving state regulatory plans in turn. But by 1972 TVA found that it was subject to several stringent state plans for the reduction of sulfur dioxide emissions in twelve plants.[133] The law permitted a variety of techniques to control emissions, such as the use of low-sulfur coal, technology to take sulfur dioxide out of coal, or the use of tall stacks to diffuse pollution in the atmosphere. TVA favored tall stacks because the eastern coal, which it used, was dirtier than western coal but also cheaper, and the cost of scrubbers would raise the costs of old plants that would eventually be closed. Wagner also thought that scrubber technology was very uncertain in its effectiveness. Tall stacks pushed the pollution high into the air and perhaps sent it out of the valley altogether. Wagner's attitudes toward the situation were never in doubt.

> We [TVA] ought not to pollute, but we ought to take into account clean-up costs as well. TVA saw sense in protecting [the environment] but we had other responsibilities—economic development, low-cost energy production for consumers. . . . We had an obligation to resist spending money until we could find

out if federal and state [sulfur dioxide] standards made sense. We were convinced that scrubber technology had not been proved to work effectively or efficiently at large power plants, and that low-sulfur coal supplies were not adequate to the supply demands that CCS techniques would require. [Moreover] TVA is an independent agency; if it has to take orders from any other federal agency, then it loses its independence.[134]

EPA regulators in Atlanta did not agree that tall stacks were an answer. They saw stacks as just creating more pollution. But Wagner stressed the uncertainty of technology in his letters to successive EPA directors, and even offered TVA "as a large laboratory" to work on such problems in conjunction with the EPA.[135] Then after both the states and the EPA began to bear down on TVA, Wagner shifted his argument to invoke the high rises in the price of energy because of the OPEC (Organization of Petroleum Exporting Countries) oil embargo of 1973. He asked for relief from stringent environmental regulation in light of the soaring costs caused by OPEC.[136] He also asked Congress to subsidize the cost of scrubber technology, if it should be imposed on TVA, by reducing the amount of money TVA had to return to the Treasury each year for the initial financing of the power program according to how much was spent on the new technology. Wagner was committed to low-cost power above all, and the costs of externalities were to be borne by others.[137] The key to his thinking was seen in a 1973 letter to Roy Ash, director of the Office of Management and Budget, in which Wagner appealed for help against the EPA regulation:

> In practical terms, EPA's restriction would probably require TVA to build sulfur dioxide scrubbers on all 63 of its coal fired generating units—at an original capital cost of over one billion dollars or an annual cost of about $200 million. At the same time there is no assurance (in fact we think it is unlikely at this stage of development) that they would function satisfactorily. So that in the end, the investment would be wasted. Such expenditures could increase TVA electric power rates by 30 per cent and would add over $40 million per year to the electricity bills of the Atomic Energy Agency Commission and other Federal agencies. . . . TVA is and always has been concerned with the total environmental picture. To us, jobs, economic and social well-being, preservation of scarce natural resources, and other aspects of the physical environment are also important. It is unfortunate but true that many environmental decisions result in trade-offs among several of these elements. However, the use of tall stacks . . . for controlling sulfur dioxide concentrations does not result in trade-offs; their use alone makes it possible to meet the ambient standards necessary to protect the public health and welfare. For this reason we cannot in our minds justify the hugh expenditures and resulting adverse environmental efforts which EPA's regulations will cause.[138]

Wagner made the same argument with Jamie Whitten, the Mississippi Democrat and chairman of the House Appropriations Committee, and other members of the valley congressional delegation.[139] Wagner continually invoked TVA's character as a multipurpose agency as an argument against any regulation of a single mission.

EPA administrators were not impressed with Wagner's figures on the costs of regulation. Russell Train, who succeeded Ruckelshaus at the EPA, sent an EPA analysis of Wagner's case to Representative Bob Jones of Alabama, one of TVA's protectors, which challenged the TVA argument. Alvin L. Alm, assistant administrator of the EPA, prepared the memo which concluded that an $800 million cost for air-pollution controls was negligible in light of the $8 billion that TVA would have to raise between 1973 and 1983 for its nuclear construction program. Alm also proved himself to be prophetic: "[A]ny potential financial problems that TVA may encounter will be due <u>primarily</u> to TVA's plans for doubling its generating capacity every ten years. Expenditures for environmental controls will not significantly affects TVA's ability to raise money."[140]

In 1976 the EPA issued its guidelines for tall stacks which put most of TVA's plants outside the acceptable range of EPA standards for reducing dirty air. The next year, after much resistance, TVA agreed to comply, but the method was still in dispute. In that year several citizens suits were brought against TVA, and the Department of Justice, representing the EPA, joined one of the suits, which also included the attorney generals of Alabama and Kentucky. TVA was being sued for refusing to comply with the Clean Air Act. The 1977 amendments to the act stipulated that tall stacks could not be used as a means of evading other emission controls, thus demolishing TVA's compliance strategy.[141]

Just as the door was closed on tall stacks, President Carter made it clear in a letter to Wagner that he wished TVA to provide leadership on environmental issues. The agency was to do more than produce cheap energy. The appointment of S. David Freeman to the board in 1977 was a clear sign of what Carter wanted. When Freeman traveled to Capitol Hill to make a courtesy call on Senator Edmund Muskie, Democrat of Maine and chairman of the Senate Environment and Public Works Committee, Muskie said to him, "[G]o down to TVA, grab those sons of bitches by the nape of the neck and drag them into compliance with *my* law."[142]

After a complicated series of negotiations, in which Freeman represented TVA, an agreement was reached in 1978 in which TVA promised to comply with EPA standards. However, neither William Jenkins, the third board member, nor Wagner would vote for it. Jenkins resigned from the board rather than do so, and Wagner retired with a public blast at the settlement and interference by the EPA in TVA's business. The agreement was not signed until Richard Freeman joined the board a year later.[143]

It would not be fair to Wagner to portray him as hostile to environmental values. He was far more responsive to the EPA on the issue of thermal pollution into the river from TVA's nuclear plants than he was on clean air because the technology was more certain, the nuclear plants were extremely important to TVA's future, and TVA had a long history of working for clean water.[144] But Wagner thought of the environment in economic and social, as well as physical, terms and was not willing to sacrifice TVA's economic development role for an absolutely clean environment. His credo was clearly stated in a 1972 speech to a Sierra Club conference:

> Every once in a while, particularly over the last two years, someone asks me, "Isn't this a hopeless conflict? How can you discharge your responsibilities as a conservation agency and at the same time operate your power system with all of the problems that it creates in the field of conservation?" I reply, "No, I think there is no conflict. Or if there is one, it's the same conflict that faces the whole nation. . . . We [TVA] try to solve the seeming conflict by placing our conservation responsibility first. Let me give you our definition of conservation. We borrow the definition Gifford Pinchot used when he defined conservation as 'the use of the earth for the good of man.' In all of our decisions, whether they are in the fields of agriculture, or forestry or river control or power production, we try, first of all, to determine the human impact and to maximize the overall benefit to man."[145]

Pinchot was a conservationist who wished to maintain forests to serve human needs for wood. He was not a wilderness advocate, to speak in contemporary terms. Wagner stood in Pinchot's tradition. He was unable to agree with those in the environmental movement who sought clean air or water above all other values.[146] His own conservation philosophy, whatever its origins, was completely consistent with his conception of TVA as a multipurpose entity and not simply as an agency for conservation. He defended TVA's right to autonomy as a government corporation, and this had usually been effective against federal controls in the past, but it no longer protected TVA on an issue of overriding national policy like the Clean Air Act. Wagner perhaps never realized this, or at least never accepted it.

ORGANIZATIONAL DYNAMICS AND ENVIRONMENTAL DECISION MAKING

The International Institute for Applied Systems Analysis (IIASA) study of TVA organization in the mid-1970s inquired about the integration of environmental planning into the design and management of the TVA power program. In particular, it asked if the environmental position had a seat at the table as part of the management system.[147] The IIASA interviews found the environmental management system to be in a "state of flux" because of all the turmoil with the EPA. The reader will notice the strong parallels between management for environmental values and management for safety in the construction of nuclear plants, described in Chapter 9. Both efforts confronted the difficulty of getting strong offices to respond to externally imposed goals that would limit their primary objectives. And in both cases, the TVA organizational structures for environmental quality and safety were an unwieldy combination of central staff, in the general manager's office, and quality control divisions down in the line that were administratively and politically weak in relation to the strong offices. The result, in both cases, was a failure to fully integrate quality controls into the management system.

The board's first response after passage of the Environmental Protection Act in 1969 was to delegate the responsibility to perform the environmental impact analysis required by the act to the Division of Health and Environmental Affairs. This did not work well because the criteria for assessing impact were unclear and there was much internal disagreement. One division could not manage an environmental program for the entire authority. Therefore, in 1972 the old division was reorganized into a new Division of Environmental Planning (DEP), and the position of assistant to the general manager for environmental affairs was created. That assistant was to use the resources of the new division to bring environmental issues to the top of the organization. The general manager was to coordinate the TVA-wide environmental programs.[148]

The new DEP was the expert body within TVA on environmental law and regulations. Along with TVA lawyers, it advised the board, through the general manager, and helped work out implementation strategies once the board had set policy.[149] The IIASA case study of environmental management seems applicable to the clean air issue since it coincided in time with it. The IIASA team's conclusion was that TVA had not succeeded in gaining an equal voice for the environment in management decisions because "the majority of personnel and funds are delegated to power considerations."[150]

Assigning a coordinating role to one division "disrupted the compartmentalized system," which was fine with the study team, but the DEP was not able to convince the Office of Power that environmental considerations were integral to its operation. In fact, the DEP staff did not see their role as changing the Office of Power so much as that of an independent unit doing research on environmental issues. The reorganization and new name changed nothing. The new assistant general manager for environmental affairs helped the board keep abreast of compliance requirements but was not able to secure the integration of the environmental perspective throughout all operations.[151] Coordination from the general manager's office had not worked very well from the beginning.

Marc Roberts and his colleagues looked at the same issues within TVA in the late 1970s and came to much the same conclusions. They found flexibility in the TVA Act for balancing environmental and energy requirements. The act required that power rates be high enough to cover costs but urged that rates be as low as possible. However, TVA was also charged with agricultural development, and electricity rates could be raised to pay for pollution controls to protect agricultural vegetation. But the strong Office of Power had stressed the "legal obligation" to keep electricity rates as low as possible for the good of regional economic development.[152] This position was reinforced by the increasing costs of producing power after the 1973 energy crisis. Nor was there any regional movement or demand for environmental values before the mid-1970s. Most valley communities welcomed new steam plants and industries.[153]

The Roberts study also found that the general manager's office was more a mediator than source of authority in behalf of the environment. To a great extent, office and division heads worked out agreements among themselves without involving the general manager or the board, and of course this was the time-honored TVA practice of "self-coordination." But the Office of Power was the dominant partner in such bargaining.[154] However, the Roberts study gave credit to Wagner for the continuous strengthening of environmental units within TVA. Wagner wanted an independent advocate, as an "internal policeman." And he followed the DEP advice that tall, thin stacks were more effective and less costly than scrubbers.[155] The problem of lagging TVA policy was not the organization of environmental expertise and coordination but the strong commitments in the organization, from the top down, to cheap power as the chief means to economic development.

However, there were organizational problems, and they appear to have been some of the same ones that later appeared in the construction and operation of nuclear plants. The Office of Engineering Design and Construction (OEDC), whose chief customer as well as rival was the Office of Power, was under continuous pressure from Chattanooga to minimize construction costs. The OEDC design group therefore issued performance specifications that were perhaps not sufficiently rigorous. Units were bought from the lowest bidder, an incentive for suppliers to underdesign equipment, and TVA did not seek outside help for its lack of expertise in antipollution technology. The Office of Power wanted to install the new equipment in the least possible time in order to get plants back in service, and the installation job was sometimes shoddy. As a result, the new devices often worked poorly.[156] The very same pattern, and relationship between the two offices, appeared later in the construction of nuclear plants.

Another characteristic of TVA construction that the Roberts study uncovered was the great pride, throughout the agency, in TVA's ability to build and operate the largest power plants in the world. But this hubris may have exacted a price. Operational problems resulted from simple designs on a grand scale; the complexity was too great. The paradox was that lowering the reliability of the plants required a larger number of them in order to meet power commitments.[157]

The Roberts study compared several public and private utilities in regard to their responsiveness to environmental values and regulation. They found the greater responsiveness in those organizations whose constituents, particularly publics, supported regulation for a clean environment. These organizations, especially Ontario Hydro (public) and Pacific Gas and Electric (private), sought to anticipate future problems and prevent them. TVA, in its resistance to external regulation, was the worst in responsiveness. But its public was also the least demanding, except for wanting the low electricity rates that TVA had promoted for a generation. Of course, the fact of air pollution was more readily acknowledged in Toronto or Los Angeles than in the Tennessee Valley. The affluence of Ontarians and Californians, compared to valley residents, may have also permitted greater concern for cleaning up the environment.[158] TVA was also less subject to regulation than the others, and one thus has a chicken-or-egg question. The EPA could not directly regulate TVA but had to sue it in the courts, a cumbersome process at best. TVA was the most committed to keeping rates low as a matter of principle, whereas other utilities gave a higher priority to avoiding bad public relations and regulatory problems, perhaps as a result of less historical autonomy.[159]

Organizational structure seems to have influenced the choices made in TVA. The crucial issue was whether top executives could successfully impose their goals on the organization. The Roberts study concluded that "a deep control system" in which the management could directly control the incentives of middle managers, for example through rewards and promotions, was more effective in securing compliance with environmental goals than the decentralization of control as in TVA. A more centralized organization could offer the possibility to middle managers that they might rise to the very top of the organization. An organization with very strong divisions, a small hierarchy of executives at the top, and limited opportunities to advance had little control over the incentives of managers. There were only a few jobs in the general manager's office of TVA, and it was therefore difficult to build an executive team across the top of the organization. A small central group had to bargain with strong office hierarchies. The absence of diagonal mobility, in which people might work in different divisions in their careers, also encouraged fiefdoms in TVA.[160]

The comparison suggested some things that managers could do to develop responsiveness to policies in their organizations, the most important being strong leadership at the top that encouraged discussion and dissent. This would keep the organization open to the external world and sensitive to the need for adaptation.[161] If dissent was not encouraged from the top, the organization might persist in faulty policies until disaster struck. For example, the fundamental principle of cheap power at TVA was unchallenged for years, with bad consequences for environmental policy. For this reason, the Roberts study suggested that analysis of choices should be institutionalized in a strategic planning process.[162] David Freeman was attempting such an innovation just as Roberts and his colleagues were studying TVA.

The Roberts study discovered that public managers had fewer management tools than those in private companies. There were fewer general management jobs, control systems were weak, and organizational ideologies were strong. Perhaps fear of too much power at the top in public bureaucracies serves to increase the influence of middle managers, making them difficult to control. Public organizations may also be more difficult to lead than private companies because they are more likely to have multiple, and even conflicting, missions.[163] A strong ideology in public agencies provides organizational cohesion but can easily be used for defense by senior executives who have spent their entire careers in one agency. Such agencies are not easily changed.[164]

The public companies also had more engineers in their top leadership than the private utilities. The Roberts study suggested that engineers are likely to see decision making as technical and nonpolitical. There are correct answers to questions. But such a mode of thought could lead to dismissing the importance of external political criticism, which might be justified.[165] Such comparisons of effective management of utilities will be seen to be relevant not only for environmental policy but for the management of the TVA program of nuclear construction.

NUCLEAR POWER

In 1966 the TVA board decided to build TVA's first nuclear plant at Browns Ferry, Alabama. Subsequent decisions were taken to build eight plants with seventeen nuclear reactors by 1985. It was projected that by that year nuclear power would account for over half of the power generated by TVA, whereas steam plants would be down to 20 percent and hydro would make up the rest.[166]

Gabriel Wessenauer, director of the Office of Power from 1944 until he retired in 1969, took the first nuclear steps by assigning a small number of engineers to the Oak Ridge Laboratory to learn about nuclear power. TVA therefore had the competence to estimate the relative costs of its first nuclear plant compared to a new steam plant. An internal study showed that it would be cheaper to build and operate the first two Browns Ferry nuclear rectors than to build a steam plant that would generate comparable energy. The Browns Ferry plant was begun in 1967, and it was not long before increasing demands for power from the Atomic Energy Commission and the pressures of the Vietnam War led to decisions to build a third reactor at Browns Ferry and a new plant with two reactors at Sequoyah, Tennessee.[167]

Wagner was an enthusiastic proponent of nuclear power. It promised TVA a continuing source of power at lower cost than coal and with less harm to the environment.[168] TVA had been concerned for some time about the rigidities of the coal market. There were too few firms, and pricing was insufficiently competitive. TVA had bought coal reserves of its own, but they were not enough for the future. The 1965 internal report that recommended moving in a nuclear direction was optimistic about both costs and the feasibility of operating nuclear facilities. It was a time of great optimism about nuclear energy, in the AEC and throughout the country.[169] There was very little criticism of the decision to build the first nuclear plant. Tennessee citizens were accustomed to living with the gigantic installation at Oak Ridge. Private utilities were moving in the same direction. Congressional committees were told by Wagner that nuclear power would be cheaper and cleaner. Only the coal industry and a few anti-TVA newspapers raised questions. When TVA came to Congress in 1966 and asked to have its debt limit increased from $750 million to $1.75 billion in order to build nuclear plants, few questions were asked.[170] The autonomy given TVA by self-financing made it easier to decide to build Browns Ferry than if appropriations had been required. By the same token, Congress had less incentive to look closely at the decision.[171] But nuclear was bullish at the time.

Wagner used time-honored arguments to justify the increase in the debt ceiling. TVA would have to add 1.5 million kilowatts a year, at a cost of $2 billion in new plants if the region was to "grow and prosper." An increase in the debt ceiling would provide that assurance for six or seven more years, he said.[172] TVA officials saw themselves as moving carefully and incrementally. As Wagner remembered, "We did not realize we were making such a big decision on nuclear power. We made the decision on the Browns Ferry plant alone. After that we considered coal as an alternative for each nuclear decision. We did not make a nuclear policy per se. If I had not done this, we would have failed in our mission . . . would have had to buy power from the outside and the people of the valley would have been mad."[173]

Even if the move into nuclear power was gradual and taken one plant at a time, as both Wagner and Wessenauer claimed, the policy was informed by a broader view that a steady power source was needed beyond hydro and coal. The decisions of the Clapp board to move into steam plants had been exactly the same. TVA had to expand if the valley was to grow. Once this assumption was made, technology became simply a means to an end. The assumption made it possible to accept the increasing costs of the nuclear building program because the energy crises of the 1970s had also increased the costs of steam power.

The size of TVA's power program kept increasing, from 17.2 million kilowatts in 1966 to 19.4 million in 1970. TVA committed itself to an 8.3-million-kilowatt increase, of which 5.7 million would be from nuclear power. This was almost half the size of TVA's total generating capacity in 1966. The plants were also very large. The Browns Ferry units were the largest nuclear reactors in the world. TVA made a bigger commitment to nuclear power between 1966 and 1969 than any other utility in the world.[174]

The initial problems of construction were manageable. AEC licensing requirements could lead to delays, and unanticipated problems of thermal pollution were encountered. TVA installed cooling towers at nuclear plants, at great cost, to deal with thermal pollution.[175] A. R. Jones, who left the board in 1966, was the only TVA official to predict that TVA would face increased costs from the expanding power program. He was an accountant who had played an important role in the self-financing story. Wessenauer and Wagner disagreed with him that the nuclear decision was a quantum leap and saw TVA as taking the less costly option each time it decided to build a nuclear facility.[176] However, TVA's first rate increase for residential customers came in 1967. It had been possible to actually decrease rates in earlier times by using economies of scale in construction. But the inflation of the Vietnam era had taken hold. Even though TVA residential rates were half the national average, electrical usage in the valley was twice that average, so the increases were visible and painful.[177] Congress did not challenge the increase at first. One observer described the members of the Public Works subcommittees as "apathetic and uninformed" about TVA nuclear power.[178] Wagner was easily reappointed to a second term in 1969. Larry Calvert, who had become head of the Washington office in 1973 after Marguerite Owen retired, remembered: "Members of Congress had enormous respect for Wagner. If he told a member something, they believed him. He could lay things out clearly. His credibility record was good. He was good at testimony—knew what he was talking about. He projected his expectation of trust to his audience."[179] Wagner's compelling persuasive powers within the TVA bureaucracy have already been described. One suspects that they were equally effective with members of Congress from the valley.

In 1970 Congress raised the TVA debt limit from $1.75 billion to $3.5 billion, and then again, in 1976, to $15 billion. The hearings were pro forma, consisting largely of statements on TVA's behalf by members of the valley congressional delegation. Congress as a whole was not interested in TVA.[180] During the 1970–77 period, TVA committed itself to adding twelve nuclear reactors at five plants. This was a dramatic shift to nuclear power as the dominant source of TVA energy. Yet Congress asked few questions. It was only as rates increased that Congress raised its head, but there was no initial link between the nuclear program and rate increases. TVA officials blamed the energy crisis of 1973.

Citizen groups began to voice opposition to the TVA nuclear program on grounds of health and safety in 1974. But they were not taken seriously by TVA officials, who called them enemies of the industrial development of the valley. These groups had no spokespeople in Congress. A near disaster occurred in 1976 at Browns Ferry when a fire got badly out of control. The plant was shut down for several months. There was a brief congressional inquiry and temporary national publicity. The Nuclear Regulatory Commission, which had succeeded the AEC, criticized TVA for lax quality-control procedures which contributed to the fire. But the incident received nothing like the attention given to the Three Mile Island event a few years later.[181] When William Jenkins was nominated to the TVA board in 1972, there were no questions from the Senate Committee on Environment and Public Works about the TVA nuclear program.[182] Cost overruns on the nuclear construction program were discussed in congressional hearings in the mid-1970s but TVA's growing commitment to nuclear power was not challenged.[183] Criticism of TVA by Congress in those years was responsive to criticism at home about strip mining, air pollution, and controversial dams. Little attention was given to the expanding nuclear program. Wagner linked the nuclear program to jobs, an appealing theme to members of Congress: "Based on population trends in recent years, it now appears that the Tennessee Valley region will need to provide about 70,000 new jobs annually over the next several years to assure that no young person will have to leave the region for lack of opportunity. Manufacturing alone would probably provide between 20,000 and 25,000 of those jobs."[184]

It followed, as night follows day, that TVA had to build just to stay even. Senator Howard Baker of Tennessee asked Wagner a rhetorical question in which the cost overruns from building nuclear reactors were described not as overruns but as "reappraisal" because of inflation and design changes required by the Nuclear Regulatory Commission. Wagner agreed and went on to say, in response to further friendly prodding, that nuclear power was still cheaper than fossil fuel and that there were "no insuperable problems" in operating nuclear plants.[185]

However, the cost overruns increased. By 1977 the actual cost of Browns Ferry and Sequoyah had tripled over the original estimates, and the costs of the new Watts Bar and Bellefonte plants had doubled. The newest plant at Hartsville, Tennessee, had increased in costs over the original estimate by more than one third. The first two plants were unfinished in 1992, and Hartsville was canceled in 1982. There was no effort by the board or the Office of Power to reevaluate the ambitious building program in the light of possible reductions in demand for energy as a result of the energy crises of the 1970s. It was still assumed that an increase in supply was necessary to meet ever increasing demand. William Willis, general manager under Freeman and Dean and executive vice-president under the Runyon board, had a historical perspective on things in 1990:

> Red's tenure was guided by expansionist theory which served TVA well into the late sixties. It kept moving TVA without a good understanding of economic changes. The idea was—build load and everything will come up to it. After the late sixties the technology had been pushed as far as it could go. We exceeded economies of scale. Energy economics turned around. Every new product increased the average cost of power at a penalty to the current rate payer. TVA didn't realize it until the late seventies. But a lot of commitments had been made. We thought linear growth would return. Red had a hard time accepting such changes. He was opposed to the cancellation of nuclear plants. His response to the economic studies was "I would have gotten another economist."[186]

The cancellation of the ambitious nuclear construction program comes later in this narrative. It is not possible to establish that Wagner and his lieutenants should have been more cautious. Only experts in nuclear power financing could address that question, and they might not agree. The point for this study is that Wagner was pursuing the TVA mission as he understood it, and there was no congressional or executive branch questioning that mission. Certainly there were enough signs of trouble that oversight should have been exercised.

NUCLEAR CONSTRUCTION

There is one study of nuclear construction in this period that illuminates organizational culture. The IIASA team examined the planning and early construction of the Hartsville plant. A TVA study team chose nuclear energy over coal by a process that "appears somewhat informal and unstructured. There appeared to be no plan that determined what information was needed and why. It was difficult to separate what constituted information in that process and what was evaluation, prescreening, or recommendations."[187] The Office of Power dominated the selection of the site in terms of its estimates of need, with secondary attention to engineering feasibility. The site was chosen before environmental concerns were expressed, and therefore few were considered. Once planning for the facility itself had begun, the IIASA group looked for the decision process to be one of "checking and balancing" among TVA divisions. This was how TVA managers described it. Decisions were made on the basis of diverse information and perspectives. But TVA managers did not live up to their rhetoric:

> [T]he planning process looks rather loose and informal. [There was] the lack of well defined goals and operationalized objectives. . . . No precise format was given either for the collection of information or for the evaluation. No formal rules for collecting and aggregating information and no analytical tools for the evaluation of the alternatives were applied. The results of the information collection process were thick, unreadable reports, usually accompanied by strong recommendations on the basis of one value aspect. These reports, together with their short and abstracted summaries, constituted the basis for the General Manager's and Board's evaluation and decisions. Checking and balancing in the form postulated by TVA management may have taken place during that process . . . but certainly not in any well defined and integrated fashion.[188]

It appears that decisions at each stage unduly influenced decisions at the next stage, and so on. In addition, the "reports often reduce doubt and complexity by stating certainties where in reality none exist." For example, demand and capacity estimates, and time and cost estimates, were often stated roughly. In regard to reactor safety, for example, "the reports simply discount the enormous consequences of disasters . . . on account of the small probability of their occurrence."[189]

In short, TVA's planning, from the perspective of these outside analysts, was "characterized by a loosely structured, highly sequential and deterministic strategy." The analysts concluded that the only possible benefit of such an informal approach to planning was the burial of conflict. The Offices of Power and Engineering dominated all stages of planning, and secondary objectives, like the environment or safety, were so muffled that the "uncertainties and consequences of alternative courses of action" were also neglected. Nuclear reactor safety was one example of this situation, and "uncertain costs or construction completion dates" were others.[190]

This impressionistic case study reveals remarkable similarities to what is known of planning and decision making in regard to the Tellico Dam and the air-pollution controversies. We will see it again in postmortems on the nuclear debacle of 1985. An organizational culture is being described.

PUBLIC UNHAPPINESS

Wagner's second term as chairman was one of rising public controversy and anger at TVA. Paul Evans, the longtime director of public information, was very close to the shift in public moods:

> TVA was a very popular organization. . . . The people were confident that it was competent in its field. When TVA made a decision it would make an honest decision. . . . Well this changed in later years. . . . it came with the new environmental movement. . . . we lost friends . . . [and] the new environmentalists . . . were a different generation than the generation that was running TVA. . . the effort to communicate between the two groups was extremely difficult. The new environmentalists had never known a major depression. . . . They weren't even sure these dams should have been built. . . . There was TVA's preoccupation with power—electrical energy—as being the one element which encompassed everything and which touched on everybody's life. . . . We opted for the low cost of electrical energy. . . .
>
> [T]here was one other factor that should be mentioned . . . it doesn't seem to make much difference to the power consumer in the Tennessee Valley that he is still getting electricity at below the national average. The fact remains that he is paying three times what he paid for [it] at one time and he is unhappy about that. So he is disenchanted with TVA. . . . TVA's strong public supports disappeared when this power rate increase took place. . . .
>
> I think that some fair case can be made that as TVA grew older it became more difficult for it to adjust to changes in circumstances . . . organizations are like people. . . . TVA did become slow. . . . A. R. Jones was the first administrator in TVA to say "Hey, if you look at these figures on our power program, we are going to have to increase rates. We can no longer meet our costs. . . ." Nobody would listen to him. . . . I think that the rate increase impact—this is hindsight—would have been easier for TVA . . . if we had taken smaller bites earlier . . . the power people . . . who resisted . . . had always been able to come up with a few rabbits out of a hat like bigger units, lower unit costs. They would always manage to hold those costs down. . . . coal prices held down and so forth, but all those dogs jumped out from under the porch and started biting them at the same time.[191]

Evans worked for Wagner and was very sympathetic to him. He regarded him as a victim of the changing environment: "In his second term Wagner felt more on the defensive. He was not uncomfortable because people didn't agree with him. The Lord was on his side—as a good

Lutheran. . . . The world had changed but Red wanted the TVA to be what Clapp would have had. Red dealt with public criticism by explaining things. He believed that people were rational and intelligent. . . . He is a real democrat."[192] Evans told the story of Wagner at a public hearing in a crowded, hot room, at which "he had tried to explain, been rational. He took off his coat. Some woman took after him. Finally he sat down. She shouted for him to stand up. He would go anywhere and make a speech."[193]

Wagner's speeches and public statements in the 1970s repeated the same themes over and over. TVA *was* environmentally sensitive, but that value had to be balanced against the cost of energy and the economy of the valley, which also affected human well-being. TVA had an obligation to provide electric power to meet the needs of a growing economy, and the nuclear program was the best solution. The Tellico Dam was a good project, and only extremists opposed it. The rates had to go up because of increased energy costs, but they were still the lowest in the nation. He expressed these thoughts over and over again to all kinds of audiences.

However, the rising volume of criticism continued, primarily because of rate increases. For example, in 1976 the Tennessee House of Representatives passed a resolution calling for an inquiry into TVA rate-setting policies. Wagner immediately wrote the Speaker and offered to cooperate.[194] An index to the state of public distress can be seen in a letter Charles Dean sent to TVA in 1974. Dean, who was to be appointed chairman of TVA himself in 1981, was writing as general manager of the Knoxville Utility Board. TVA had sent a press release about a rate increase to the distributors: "We are returning your press release with a suggestion that the TVA issue its own press release explaining once more that the rate increase was initiated by the TVA, at a time of TVA's choice, and for the financial benefit of TVA exclusively. I have been cussed, TV'd, interviewed and accused of lying, stealing and gross mismanagement by enough people to ride me out of town on a rail should they become sufficiently organized."[195]

Despite all the furor, the valley delegation in Congress stood with Wagner. They raised questions about rate increases but took his word about the necessity for such action in hard times. The habit of encircling the wagons to protect TVA died hard. However, the valley delegates were more brutal with Wagner's successor, David Freeman, who did not have Wagner's credibility with them. The Tennessee Valley Public Power Association and the distributors stayed with TVA during these difficult years, despite their concern about rate increases. They placed their faith in the future nuclear program and therefore lobbied in Washington for higher debt ceilings for TVA. To them Wagner was a symbol of past achievements and future hope.[196]

CONCLUSION

Red Wagner did his duty as he saw it. The Tributary Area Development program and Tellico Dam were consistent with the TVA mission of regional development. Nuclear expansion was necessary if TVA was to fulfill its obligation to be the power company of the valley. The grass roots and technocracy were brought together in a grand multipurpose design.

But Wagner faced new circumstances that neither David Lilienthal nor Gordon Clapp had had to confront. The environmental movement had law on its side. Unprecedented constraints were placed on TVA as the federal government attempted to regulate itself. Energy shortages in the 1970s not only drove up costs and rates but violated the TVA credo of cheap power for the people. The reform issues of the period conflicted with TVA's two most successful strategies for defending its autonomy. Political issues were not so easily transformed into technical ones, as had been the case in the Douglas Dam story. And the courts could no longer be relied upon to protect TVA autonomy from other federal agencies.[197]

TVA's political insulation was a handicap in its efforts to adapt to new challenges. The first generation of leaders had created the strong image that TVA was free of politics, to protect the authority from requests for patronage. The engineers' credo that decisions were guided by expertise, rather than politics, strengthened the emphasis upon autonomy. The TVA Washington office, and the board, developed a way of working that preserved this nonpolitical stance. Lilienthal had relied on Senator Norris and FDR to protect TVA from its enemies. Marguerite Owen subsequently built a network of protectors such as Lister Hill, Robert Kerr, and Jamie Whitten to make sure that TVA was insulated from attack. After Lilienthal, the board chairmen were not political strategists, with the possible exception of Vogel. The need to protect TVA, as it was perceived on Capitol Hill and in Knoxville, left little room for oversight from Washington about what TVA was actually doing. The defensive politics of the Dixon-Yates story continued long after the episode itself. After self-financing was begun, Congress and even the valley delegation had little political incentive to look at the TVA power program. And the relatively small appropriated programs became part of the national network of pork-barrel programs perpetuated by Congress.

TVA also kept its valley constituencies at arm's length. It blessed the formation of the TVPPA and was glad to receive its help in Washington but only as a cheering section. TVA told the distributors what to do. The eventual political effect of self-financing was that TVA became a solely regional institution without pretention to a national mission. The chief constituency became the people of the valley who were electricity consumers. Eventually they were to turn on TVA.

Wagner was no better equipped than Clapp to cope with these changing times. The kind of professional, nonpolitical leadership they provided is most effective when missions are generally agreed upon and the external environment is stable and supportive. When new demands, which require fresh thinking, rise up in the environment, more imaginative and original leadership is required. Red Wagner's personal and professional integrity and his strong belief in TVA's missions were his undoing. It would have been possible to be more accommodating about strip mining and air pollution and still have kept power rates reasonably low. Wagner adhered too fiercely to the credo of cheap power above all else. The Tellico Dam was an expression of the credo of regional development, but a more skeptical turn of mind might have been more careful at the outset when the difficulties of establishing benefits to justify costs appeared. The Tellico project was not a repeat of the Douglas Dam story.

In Wagner's last years, after Marguerite Owen retired, TVA's grip on the valley delegation began to slip away. The seeds of trouble that Wagner planted became trouble for his successor, David Freeman, as members of Congress began to respond to public unhappiness with TVA in the valley. When Governor Winfield Dunn of Tennessee openly opposed Tellico, it was a great shock to Wagner. TVA, which had encouraged the valley states to develop conservation departments, state parks, and forestry programs, saw itself attacked by its own children and could not believe it.[198]

The TVA organization was not as supple by the 1970s as it had been in earlier years, and some of the virtues of decentralization had become vices. Means had become ends, and TVA's survival was too easily equated with the public welfare. Red Wagner's TVA was engaged in a self-defeating escalation of commitment in both the power and nonpower missions. But given his premises about TVA's purposes, Wagner could not do other than he did. He had grown up in TVA in the heroic period of depression and war. He and his friends had saved TVA from its foes in the 1950s. Self-financing gave him the resources with which to build. Wagner's TVA was a logical culmination of all that had gone before.

CHAPTER 8

The Politics of Organizational Renewal

S. DAVID FREEMAN was nominated by President Carter for appointment to the TVA board in July 1977. It was assumed in news stories that Carter would name Freeman chairman when Wagner retired in 1978, and Freeman did become chairman in May of that year. He was removed as chairman in mid-1981 by President Reagan, on the advice of Senator Howard Baker, and served as a director until mid-1984.

A Chattanooga native, Freeman had been an engineer and lawyer with TVA from 1948 to 1961. He later worked as an assistant to former TVA chief counsel Joseph Swidler, who was chairman of the Federal Power Commission, and served in the president's Office of Science and Technology from 1967 until 1971, with special attention to energy policy. From 1971 to 1974 Freeman was director of the Ford Foundation's Energy Policy Project which produced a report entitled *Energy: The New Era* in 1974.[1] The report recommended national policies for energy conservation. Freeman served on the staff of the Senate Commerce Committee until joining the Carter campaign in 1976. After the inauguration, he worked in the White House, helping James Schlesinger, Secretary designate of the new Department of Energy, design and organize the department.

Freeman, who was fifty-two years old in 1977, was an energetic, imaginative, and combative person. His verbal style was one of slash and burn. He would attack, and attack again after a counterattack, hoping that new ideas would be tested or even developed from adversarial discussion. By all reports he did not take disagreement with him personally, often goading others to disagree. But his aggressive style could inhibit people with a distaste for conflict or ridicule directed against themselves.

Freeman's leadership strategy at TVA was to use a new policy-planning process to invent missions that would, he hoped, revitalize the TVA bureaucracy, which he believed to be tired and sluggish. He was a true believer in TVA as a multipurpose agency and attempted to integrate its power and nonpower sides in complementary economic development missions. His primary initiatives, however, were to force TVA to accept the claims of environmental policy, in which he was successful, and to proclaim TVA to be the "energy laboratory" of the nation, in which he was far less successful despite several imaginative pilot programs. Freeman initially accepted the nuclear power program, waxing hot and cold on it depending upon external politics, but after his demotion he and his board colleague Richard Freeman made hard decisions to cut back the number of nuclear plants that TVA would build. This step was taken only after the evidence became overwhelming that the market demand for future power was not as great as had been anticipated.

Freeman was similar to Aubrey Wagner in his intention to keep TVA programs dynamic and integrated. The two men had different values and read politics differently. Wagner practiced the politics of growth, and Freeman advocated the politics of conservation. They sought different balances among TVA missions, but each sought balance and coherence and was strongly resistant to the idea that TVA should become a single purpose organization.

Schlesinger wrote President Carter in February 1977 to report that Freeman wished to fill the vacancy on the board.[2] About the same time, the new president received a memo on TVA from two staff members of the Senate Committee on Public Works and Environment.[3] The authors told the president that TVA's high reputation had declined and that people in the region were highly critical of TVA because it was not responsive to them. The central issues were TVA rate increases, failure to control pollution and to push for strip-mining reclamation, and excessive reliance on nuclear energy. The memo recommended that TVA find ways to reconcile energy production and environmental values and explore new approaches to regional economic development. The most important immediate objective was to nominate someone to the board who could revitalize the agency and point it toward contemporary problems.

A few days later Hamilton Jordan, an assistant to Carter, received a memo from Carter's science adviser, Frank Press, about TVA.[4] Press cited recent troubles with air pollution, the resistance of the Wagner board to open meetings, the fire at the Browns Ferry nuclear plant in 1976, and the overexpansion of nuclear facilities. Press was critical of TVA but urged that it could be "once again an exciting demonstrational arm of the Federal government" for energy conservation, a sound energy "mix," and new technology.

In March Freeman wrote a brief memo to Carter about the future of TVA in which he made the now familiar points about organizational backwardness and the need for revitalization of the agency.[5] As a result of all this information, Carter asked Freeman to write a letter to Wagner asking what TVA could do for innovative energy policy. New programs were suggested for home weatherization, rate design for conservation of electricity, coal-cleaning and coal-mining technology, solar power, fluidized bed boilers, flue gas desulfurization, and increased public participation, all causes Freeman took up after he joined the board.[6]

These memos were surely appealing to Carter because of his commitment to energy conservation and his interest in technology. He wanted an energy expert in the job, saying publicly before the nomination that the nominee should be a "technical person and the choice free of politics."[7] According to Freeman, he was told indirectly that he would be the chairman of TVA when Wagner retired. He was filling an open vacancy on the board, and Wagner's seat would have to be filled in 1978. Freeman was told that the position would go to John Gibbons, a University of Tennessee physicist and director of the UT Environment Center, who later became director of the congressional Office of Technology Assessment and President Clinton's science adviser in 1993.[8] But Gibbons was not chosen, and Freeman was later told that it was thought he was too much like Freeman himself.[9] This tells something about the politics of energy conservation and the environment, and the something surfaced during Freeman's confirmation. When Freeman told Senator Robert Stafford of Vermont, the ranking Republican on the committee, of his intention to improve air quality, Stafford asked him, "Have you checked that out with Howard [Baker]?" There was evidently some concern that Freeman was too much of an environmentalist, for Senator John Stennis of Mississippi put a hold on his confirmation. When Schlesinger asked the reason, Stennis told him that a Mississippi newspaper publisher had doubts about Freeman, and Stennis asked if Freeman could meet with the man, who was important to Stennis because "he puts a newspaper on every doorstep each day." Actually, Freeman and the doubter had a "love in" because, according to Freeman, the other man was a New Deal Democrat who was worried that Freeman was an environmental elitist who didn't care about poor people.[10] Stennis took the hold off but asked Freeman, "You're not an environmental radical are you?"—to which the nominee answered no. TVA supporters in Congress knew that things had to change. Jamie Whitten, the Mississippi Democrat who was chairman of the House Appropriations Committee, lectured Freeman about the evil of "scrubbers" on TVA smoke stacks but told him that he was what TVA needed.[11]

In his confirmation hearings, Freeman depicted the TVA of the future as the agent of President Carter's hope for energy efficiency. TVA, as an energy laboratory, would promote efficient and safe energy sources through learning how to clean coal, making nuclear energy work, and developing alternative sources such as solar power. Freeman was less clear about what should be done on the nonpower side of TVA but deplored the "imbalance" between the power program and the rest of the authority. He described TVA as a "decentralized, grass roots agency" and quoted David Lilienthal in the cause of "participatory democracy" as

TVA had practiced it. His confirmation hearing was a good guide to his actions as TVA chairman.[12] Before he was sworn in as a TVA director, he found time to tell reporters that the Tellico Dam was "relatively unimportant" in relation to other TVA objectives and that he thought TVA was "dragging its feet" in coming to terms with the Environmental Protection Agency about clean air.[13]

Freeman spent his first weeks traveling around the valley gathering impressions of TVA from both public and private meetings. At the same time, he was trying to gauge support for his own ideas.[14] During a meeting with TVA employees, he made it very clear that "TVA does have a social conscience. . . . We are not just another utility. . . . We were created to try to help people. We are not here just to supply electricity."[15]

When a speaker from the floor told Freeman that the spirit of TVA was "somewhat dampened" because of "inefficient and incompetent management," Freeman responded by urging people in the organization to "say what they think" because "the true friend of somebody at the top is a person who will tell you what's wrong down the line and give you some insight into what you need to do." He made clear that he was not nostalgic for the TVA of the 1930s and 1940s. In fact, his listening sessions around the valley had convinced him that TVA was a "mystery" to many people and that it was thought to be "stubborn" and "bureaucratic" and out of touch with the people. He described himself as a "very firm believer in institutional democracy" who wanted to hear more opinions than those of the general manager or program director. He promised to "confront top management" with dissenting opinions in the organization.[16]

From his first day in Knoxville, Freeman began to pepper Lynn Seeber with what came to be called *Dave-o-grams*, in which Freeman asked for information and ideas about what TVA was doing, not doing, and perhaps should be doing. All such memos were supposed to go through the general manager. The restlessness and impatience behind these queries reveal Freeman's style:

> I'm impressed with the tremendous pay-off from money invested as a catalyst for starting small industrial parks, etc., to create jobs in sparsely [sic] areas such as Lenowisco territory, Hancock County, etc. . . . I'd be interested in staff ideas for a very major expansion of such efforts as an alternative to building dams in the future.[17]

> There was a sentiment expressed [in meeting with Elk River Association] which was repeated at every place in the 3-day tour—that TVA needs to strengthen its forces in the field that are working with these regional groups on a daily basis. Their most valuable contact is the TAD [Tributary Area Development] person who lives with them and these folks are spread too thin at the moment. Please comment.[18]

I'm evaluating TVA current positions on controversial issues. I'm handicapped by the absence of a formal opinion explaining why actions were taken. . . . I'd like your reaction to a policy of preparing and publicizing opinions on significant actions by the TVA Board so as to state the reasons for such actions.[19]

Some employees at a listening session felt that facts are distorted and opinions suppressed in reports going to the Board in the interest of a single recommendation. . . . I would like to be sure that differences of opinion among the divisions are presented to the Board and that dissenting views within the division are presented.[20]

Freeman was continually probing for new missions. After a conversation with officials in the U.S. Department of Agriculture, he wrote Seeber: "I would like staff to develop a list of possible projects that we could discuss [with the USDA]. One project that interests me is the production of alcohol to supplement gasoline as transportation."[21] And then soon after: "I'd like TVA to include a demonstration program on garbage to energy in its overall programs. . . . I'd like the staff to suggest a positive program and then we'll address the issue of financing."[22]

Of course, Seeber had to return with answers, and his irritation was sometimes obvious, especially when Freeman approached the staff directly: "Attached is the result of your conversations with several members of the . . . staff, in which you asked them to produce some sort of 'concept/scope' paper to make Norris a model energy village. This has not been coordinated among other offices and divisions. Since my office was not involved in the matter, we are simply passing it on to you without any attempt to assess its merits."[23]

Freeman persisted in sending his notes because, as he said four years later, he found TVA, as an organization, to be "dead in the water." Wagner called him into a meeting with Seeber and asked him to stop sending the Dave-o-grams because they were unsettling to the staff. Wagner said that Freeman abrasively expressed displeasure when the answers to his memos were inadequate and that he was traveling and listening to TVA critics too much. This had created morale problems among TVA people, Wagner told him.[24] But Freeman kept sending the notes.

President Carter's request for an energy conservation program from chairman Wagner, which Freeman had written in April, led to a sixty-five-page report to the president from Wagner in August, in which it was proposed that TVA mount demonstrations and experiments for designing electricity rates, low-interest loans for insulation, and the use of wood stoves. The report also urged Carter to support TVA research on the process for trapping coal pollutants at the combustion stage in power plants.[25] Freeman's thinking was even more ambitious. The manager of the Office of Power reported to Seeber that the new director had asked for "solar co-ops, a bio-mass program, wood alcohol to replace gasoline, railroad electrification," and a "massive electric vehicle program" which would "bring Detroit to the Valley" by ordering electric cars for TVA itself as well as for all TVA distributors and other federal agencies.[26]

The tension between Freeman and a bureaucracy unaccustomed to his way of doing business was very clear. He was asking comfortable people to feel uncomfortable about what TVA was doing and not doing. This is an irritant in an organization that has long grown accustomed to established procedures. For example, Herbert Sanger, the general counsel, advised against Freeman's idea of written explanations of board decisions for fear of legal complications.[27] Seeber also rejected the idea, writing Freeman that the preparation of such documents would slow up a slow organization even more.[28] Freeman was not satisfied:

> I appreciate Herb's point and yours as well but the "court" I'm interested in satisfying is the court of public opinion and the public is entitled to know our rationale when we take action. Logical explanations later when we're on the defensive in court or elsewhere aren't good enough. . . . We've got to know why we're doing things and there's no substitute for putting it in writing so everyone knows. Having said all that, I'll punt on this one for the time being.[29]

Aubrey Wagner, as a board member, received copies of all the Dave-o-grams and the responses back from Seeber. On some occasions he could not contain himself. When Freeman suggested that certain recreation programs be paid for by power revenues, Wagner responded to Seeber, "I disagree!! The principle is wrong—the precedent is dangerous."[30] When Freeman objected to the closing of an unused field office in West Virginia, Wagner responded: "It seems to me the Charleston Office question is an operating matter which should not require Board involvement. I would expect the staff to proceed in the manner that is most efficient."[31] And when Freeman suggested that every industry in the valley be required to purchase interruptible power from TVA as a conservation measure, Wagner commented: "If industry wants to and can use interruptible power, fine—but we should not force it on them."[32]

Freeman proposed that any land purchased for the controversial Columbia Dam, which might not be completed, revert to the owner if the land were not used for the dam. Seeber strongly argued against the idea, calling it "an administrative nightmare," adding that if another board member would join Freeman in "this suicide pact," he would comply.[33] And finally, when Freeman wrote a note setting out ways in which TVA might save gasoline in its operation, he received little help. He suggested more efficient cars and trucks, electric vehicles, fuel from wood and grain, closed-circuit TV for meetings, reducing travel, and using bicycles more, adding in regard to bicycles, "don't laugh." Seeber replied in part, "Re item 6 [bicycles] on your note. . . . May the Lord forgive me—I laughed."[34]

The friction between Freeman on one side and Wagner and the third board member, William Jenkins, on the other was apparent in board meetings. For example, the *New York Times* described a May 1978 meeting in which Freeman publicly clashed with his two colleagues over contract terms about pollution controls for large industrial customers who bought power directly from TVA. Finally Wagner remarked with exasperation, "I wasn't going to say this, but it is one thing to be an observer and another to participate in management."[35] The story noted that although Wagner, Jenkins, and "generally the TVA bureaucracy" gave general support to Freeman's "enthusiasms," the difference in emphasis was great. The older guard supported monitored studies and small-scale demonstration projects of alternative energy sources. But Freeman was impatient. "School's out," said Mr. Freeman, almost rising out of his office chair. "Some of these things have been studied to death. My view is that a lot of things are ready to go."

The story described how Wagner and Freeman disagreed about a pilot study of 220 residential customers in Knoxville to see if they would wash clothes in off-peak hours in order to reduce their rates. Wagner was skeptical that an inexpensive metering system could be developed. Freeman wanted to turn the demonstration into TVA policy immediately. Likewise, Freeman wanted to install hot-water heaters in 100,000 homes within four or five years, a goal that Wagner saw as impractical.

The *New York Times* story described Wagner and Jenkins's TVA as an engine for economic growth because it could provide cheap electricity for power-hungry industries like aluminum and smelting. Freeman's TVA would forsake power intensive industries and pursue the growth of high-technology companies because the latter would permit the maintenance of a nice environment in the valley. TVA, Freeman was quoted as saying, "must not be just another power company. . . . We need to go back to the Rooseveltian vision of TVA as a great innovator, a place where things are tested out and proven—a living laboratory and the first place where national energy policy becomes a reality."

Freeman was very frustrated as a new board member. He felt that the board had lost contact with the program divisions and didn't know what was going on. Wagner was tired, and Seeber was running things. No controversies came to the board because Seeber settled everything beforehand. It was considered "bad form" for a board member to talk to office heads without Seeber being present.[36]

William Jenkins was more attuned to Wagner than Freeman, but Jenkins understood that TVA had unresolved problems. A Rogersville, Tennessee, attorney and state commissioner for conservation before his appointment to the board in 1972, Jenkins regarded himself as a "conservationist" but not an "environmentalist." He felt that TVA had gone overboard on water projects like the Tellico, Columbia, and Normandy dams because good farmland was flooded unnecessarily. And he also chafed at Wagner's dominance of the board and the organization. When Jenkins had arrived at TVA, he had asked for some personal staff people who would report to him, but Wagner had refused, saying that all staff work was done through the general manager, a system which Jenkins saw that Wagner could dominate. Jenkins saw that Seeber managed conflict below the board level and understood that inaction was often a result of the inability of the offices and divisions to agree. Jenkins resisted, and was frustrated by, the admonition, often given to him, that board members should stick to policy and avoid management. He had a strong suspicion that neither the board nor the managers of the Office of Power were in control of power operations. However, Jenkins sided with Wagner against Freeman in the dispute with the Environmental Protection Agency. Jenkins did not believe that TVA was seriously polluting the air. The coal-fired plants were all in rural areas, tall stacks were sufficient, and scrubber technology was not perfected. And the EPA demands would seriously increase TVA's debt. Jenkins believed that Freeman had negotiated a settlement with the EPA on his own but acting for the board, without knowledge about how the ratepayers felt. Wagner retired without signing the agreement, and Jenkins took the occasion as a reason for his unexpected resignation in May 1978, as Wagner left. Jenkins saw that he would be an outvoted minority member. He did not approve of the leadership that Freeman subsequently gave the organization: "We both saw the outfit as hidebound. We differed on what changes to make especially as to people. My replacements would have been different from his. I would have looked for people from the valley and with more conventional and conservative attitudes. I would have turned to universities, industries and the political life of the valley."[37]

Jenkins is an interesting figure because he, or someone like him, might have been able to lead TVA in new directions without igniting the political firestorm that later engulfed Freeman. However, Jenkins might not have challenged the bureaucracy enough. It is a point for speculation.

Wagner fought Freeman to the last day. On the day of Wagner's retirement, TVA employees crowded the plaza between the two buildings and cheered him as he walked to his last board meeting. As he got in his car to go home, Wagner's last words to a veteran TVA manager were "Keep your head down John."[38] Seeber left with Wagner. Everyone knew a new era had begun.

A May 1978 story in Nashville's *The Tennessean* by Nat Caldwell, a veteran TVA watcher, captured the uncertainty of many people in the valley about Freeman as TVA chairman. Caldwell reported that many distributors were uneasy about Freeman's rhetoric. Talk about energy conservation and environmental values appeared in their eyes to be antigrowth. Several distributors had expressed their feelings to their congressional representatives. As one put it: "We can only travel so far with the environmentalists. . . . Where we must draw the line against them is where living up to the rules means unreasonable rate increases for our consumers."[39]

Freeman did not intend to send out an antigrowth message, but his language was unfamiliar to many TVA constituents, especially the power distributors. In his first talk to the annual meeting of the Tennessee Valley Public Power Association, he stressed the growing cost of coal and nuclear power and called for a hard look at solar power, conservation, load management, flexible rate structures, and shared generation of power. He made clear that his goal was "a reduction of one million kilowatts of commercial and industrial load over ten years—equal to building a billion dollar nuclear unit." The various methods to achieve this goal, such as home insulation loans, solar hot-water heaters, load management, and so on, were laid out. The valley's needs for economical power would be met, he said, but he concluded his talk with an impolitic phrase for an audience of power distributors: "If we ever fall into the mold of being 'just another power company,' we're not living up to our basic reason for being in business."[40]

Freeman's problem was that the power distributors and their political friends were much stronger than a nascent constituency of environmentalists. It is also likely that the former were in far better touch with general public opinion because TVA was seen by the public, for the most part, as a power company. The lieutenant governor of Tennessee, John Wilder, a veteran Democratic politician, was probably a good barometer for public opinion when he opposed the final consent decree between TVA and the EPA which was finally settled in March and signed in June 1979. Wilder wrote Jack Watson, an assistant to President Carter for federal-state relations, that the settlement was a "260 million dollar overkill" and that the "people in Tennessee are very much upset about this . . . penalty." Watson replied that "the President believes it is a reasonable resolution to a very difficult problem."[41] Carter even called Wilder on the telephone and asked him to stop opposing the agreement.[42] Carter had won the presidency with the votes of environmentalists, and his appointments reflected that fact. Both Freeman, and Marvin B. Durning, a Seattle environmental lawyer and new deputy administrator of the EPA for enforcement, believed that they were executing Carter's mandate in the agreement between their two agencies.[43]

After the final agreement was signed in June 1979, twenty-two municipal and rural cooperative distributors sued TVA in federal court for negotiating unfair terms for TVA.[44] Even though the judge sustained the agreement, the political atmosphere in the valley had been darkened. Wagner had personally gone to Washington and told members of the valley delegation that Freeman did not know what he was doing in the EPA agreement. However, Senator Baker and Representative Albert Gore, both of Tennessee, encouraged Freeman to go ahead.[45] Indeed, the Tennessee Valley Public Power Authority board of directors had endorsed the terms of the settlement in September 1978. The TVPPA usually followed as much as it influenced TVA since the TVPPA was dependent upon TVA for its information.[46]

David Freeman was the only TVA director from May until October in 1978, but he proceeded to innovate through administrative action while reserving important policy decisions for a full board. He set up a Citizens Action Office to respond to public concerns, with its director reporting directly to the board. A toll-free information hot line was created for citizen calls to the new office.[47] In lieu of board meetings, Freeman held weekly executive sessions open to the public in which important issues were discussed. He encouraged TVA officials to attend and solicited questions from the public for them.[48]

Freeman was bold verbally. He told the *Washington Post* in May 1978 that "the President is very much aware of what's going on down here. . . . He knows he's got two crucial appointments to make. And he wants very much to turn TVA into what it historically has been—a laboratory for the nation. We're going to get back in the limelight where we belong."[49]

The chairman's office files during the transition period contain memo after memo in which Freeman told the White House what he was doing and asked for support for particular plans: a consumer solar-energy cooperative; production of gas, oil, and charcoal from wood chips; reclamation of abandoned strip mines; removal of communities from flood plains; a TVA lawsuit against the international uranium cartel.[50] As will be evident later, the White House was supportive with minor appropriations but never underwrote the energy laboratory concept and was more concerned with balanced federal budgets than with expenditures on TVA.

Freeman also tried to talk sense, from his perspective, to the distributors. In a July speech to the Tennessee Municipal Electric Power Association, he invited them to join a partnership with TVA in giving the valley "quality growth." Rate increases, although necessary, would be kept to a minimum, and the best way to keep down costs was to encourage consumer conservation of energy. He defended the EPA settlement as inevitable and as preventing large costs in the adverse health effects of air pollution. Rate increases from the settlement would be gradual and spread over several years, raising costs only 9 percent by 1983 and then declining to 4 percent by the end of the 1980s. Pollution was an impediment to growth, and conserving energy was not inimical to growth. In fact, TVA would have surplus power to sell to other regions short on power in the future. Finally, he called for TVA to resume its intended role as "part of the people's lives in a special way" and quoted David Lilienthal, who said that the "physical job will be done. . . . But if the people aren't an active part in this great task, then they may be poor or they may be rich, but they will not be free."[51] Freeman was trying as best he could to foster new constituencies behind energy conservation and a clean environment and, at the same time, tell the core TVA constituency of distributors that it was in their enlightened self-interest to go along.

The chief order of business for the White House was to appoint two more board members. In May 1978, Carter received a memo from two assistants reviewing a list of candidates. The memo recommended that the nominees have experience in business management, be well versed in the economics of utility rate regulation, understand the administration's energy objectives, and be compatible with David Freeman.[52] Carter first nominated Richard Freeman, a Chicago lawyer who had also been a railroad executive. He was a friend of David Freeman's who had worked in TVA in the 1950s. His work had kept him close to Gordon Clapp and a group of young turks in the general managers's office, and he had imbibed Clapp's idealism about TVA.[53]

There was some uncertainty in the valley about the appointment. The TVPPA board sent a delegation to interview Richard Freeman and returned satisfied.[54] But Tennessee's lieutenant governor, John Wilder, was uneasy. In August, he wrote Senator Sam Nunn of Georgia that Richard Freeman must be "totally committed to production." It was important to keep down rates for the consumer. Electricity must be produced "efficiently and abundantly."[55] Tennessee's governor, Lamar Alexander, a Republican, opposed Richard Freeman's appointment. He was an "outsider," Alexander wrote Senators Baker and Sasser, and the board should consist of people who had lived in the valley. Alexander added that he had learned how unpopular high taxes and high electric rates were in his campaign for governor.[56]

In September, Frank Moore, head of White House congressional relations, wrote President Carter that Senator John Stennis would not act on Richard Freeman's nomination until he knew who the third nominee would be. Furthermore, it had to be someone from the valley.[57] Moore had informed Carter in May that Stennis had acquiesced in David Freeman's nomination. But because of "philosophical differences" with David Freeman, Stennis had preferred other candidates.[58] It is clear that politicians in the valley wanted TVA to produce cheap electricity in abundance because that was what their constituents wanted. The idealism of President Carter and the two Freemans was disquieting if it seemed to threaten cheap power. One does not know what assurances Stennis received. Richard Freeman was confirmed in October, and the third board member did not arrive until August 1979. At the suggestion of Tennessee Democratic senator Jim Sasser, Robert Clement was nominated. He was the son of a former governor, a member of the state's Public Service Commission, and an aspiring politician. As a board member for three years, he was to keep his distance from the Freemans, publicly oppose rate increases, and act as a fairly accurate barometer of public and congressional opinion. The Freemans regarded him as a nuisance.[59]

The skills and interests of the two Freemans were complementary, and they regarded themselves as equal partners in an adventure. David Freeman was an idea man who intended to galvanize the TVA bureaucracy around exciting new missions. Richard Freeman was a manager who concentrated on intelligent and vigorous administration of programs. David presented policy initiatives and received more publicity, but he relied heavily on Richard's judgment about internal matters and made sure they always agreed on controversial issues that might come before the board. According to TVA professionals who observed them closely, David would often defer to Richard when Richard felt strongly about an issue. This study focuses on David Freeman, but it should be understood that Richard Freeman was atypical among TVA board members in his great influence over policy throughout both the Freeman and Dean boards. In fact, the partnership of the two Freemans permitted them to dominate the Dean board until David left in 1984, and then Richard virtually ran things through sheer force of personality until his resignation in 1985.

REORGANIZATION AND REGIONAL DEVELOPMENT

In early 1979 the two Freemans, working with staff, reorganized TVA to strengthen the executive authority of the board, reduce the influence of the general manager, and emphasize more focused missions in economic and natural-resource development. Four new offices were created, but the number of offices was reduced from fourteen to seven. A new Office of Community Development subsumed the old Tributary Area Development program, as well as the division of navigation, development, and regional studies. The emphasis was to be upon community and economic development. The head of the new office was Sharlene Hirsch, who had a background in education, job training, aging, and human-resource development and had been most recently on the Carter transition team. The new Office of Natural Resources, under Tom Ripley, a forester who had directed forestry, fisheries, and wildlife development, now included not only those activities but water resources, land and forest resources, and the Land Between the Lakes, a nature-preservation project in eastern Tennessee and Kentucky. A new Office of Management Services, headed by William Willis, included personnel, management systems, property and services, finance, purchasing, health and safety, and environmental compliance. Finally, the general counsel was now to head an office rather than a division, and the Offices of Power, Engineering, and Agricultural and Chemical Development were unchanged.

The new general manager, succeeding Lynn Seeber, was Leon Ring, who came from the private sector of air space and technology. His office retained the planning and budget staffs and the Washington office. The Freemans felt that Seeber and other general managers had held too much authority to stifle controversy within TVA so that it did not reach the board, and they were determined to avoid that by playing a strong role in management themselves. When Ring discovered that fact in the summer of 1979, he left TVA, and Bill Willis moved into the general manager's job. John Bynon, a longtime deputy director of personnel and organizational troubleshooter, helped the Freemans with the reorganization, a central objective of which was to clarify and focus the two missions of community economic development and natural-resource conservation and development. David Freeman believed that the Carter White House and Congress would be receptive to such focused missions in preference to the welter of splintered programs and divisions of the past. He was well connected with both White House and congressional staffs and hoped to use those connections to revive the nonpower side of TVA.[60] General manager Ring described these focused missions in a February 1979 report to the board about the reorganization. The Office of Natural Resources was to manage TVA land and water resources, conduct environmental research and demonstrations, and provide technical assistance to state and local agencies in implementing environmental protection laws. A more general objective was to promote "the unified development of the natural resources of the Tennessee Valley region," especially for "the multiple benefits of land use planning for quality growth management." There was a gap between such goals and the specific tasks of the office, as in the past. The Office of Community Development was to work with federal, state, and local agencies and with private organizations to provide technical assistance for community and economic development projects. A variety of tasks were implied—education and skill development, transportation planning, including navigation and flood-plain management, solid waste management, and community financial planning and administration. Again, the specific tasks were rebundled assignments from the past with a new cover but an ad hoc character.[61]

The Freemans intended the reorganization to become the institutional platform for a new strategic planning process, orchestrated by a new planning staff, which would formulate imaginative TVA missions, with special attention to regional development responsibilities shared by two or more offices. They wanted ideas and controversy to bubble up as they had in an earlier TVA, in a bureaucracy that they saw as set in its ways and unresponsive to the board. In this sense the traditional but idealized TVA organizational culture was affirmed. This was seen in a memo from the Freemans to all management staffs:

> It is natural that differences of opinion exist among the offices (and within each office) on matters of policy and execution of policy. In the past we gather it has been the practice by and large to resolve issues on the basis of consensus or nonresolution (and thus resolution by inaction). We certainly do not wish to discourage consultation and cooperation among interested staff. Indeed, we wish to encourage interaction among members of the staff. However, we wish to stress that a decisionmaking process exists in the General Manager's Office and with the Board for deciding issues promptly. We do not want anyone to feel that they need "to go along in order to get along"; or fear to rock the boat. We want issues and differences of opinion brought to the attention of the General Manager and the Board promptly. Resolution of genuine issues, of difficult and important questions should be one of the roles of the Board.[62]

In June 1979, the board held a retreat at Fairfield Glade, Tennessee, for top staff members with the goal of formulating policy statements that could be discussed and developed into a strategic plan by the end of the year. A group of policy experts had been invited to undertake what was called a "Summer Study" of TVA programs and to make recommendations for new departures. The task of the retreat was to provide ideas for that group as a point of departure. The transcript of the meeting provides an interesting window on TVA at a time of transition.[63] The general manager began by asking those present to think of TVA in terms of a fifteen-year future horizon in which organizational capacities could be matched to social trends favoring those capacities. He then called for reports from office heads on fresh thinking in their shops. Although all gave lip service to new, crosscutting regional development missions, the ideas presented were primarily an extension of what their divisions were already doing.

Tom Ripley, head of Natural Resources, described several ways in which his office could assist in strip-mining reclamation, the management of private timber lands, and the fish and wildlife work of the states. Such projects, however, fell short, in his estimation, of the need for land-use planning throughout the valley to save air and water quality and develop land intelligently. He suggested that TVA create land banks that would demonstrate multiple uses of TVA land. But, he added, TVA could not and should not prescribe the uses of private land. That would be too controversial. TVA could best help landowners achieve their own goals; it could help others but it could not plan for them.

Sharlene Hirsch, the new office director who was to resign later that summer, was less specific in her goals for community development. She cited several problems in the valley, such as low job skills and issues of working women and old people, but her presentation developed no general theme.

David Freeman then asked about possible links between the power program and community development in ways consistent with a clean environment. Hugh Parris, the newly appointed head of the Office of Power, began his presentation by responding that he felt uncomfortable with the idea of using power for economic and regional resource development in any way beyond generating electrical energy. He did raise the possibility that TVA could become more of an energy company in which new technology could be demonstrated as a yardstick for other utilities. The efficient use of waste heat and the development of gas from coal were cited as possibilities.

George Kimmons, head of engineering design and construction, predicted that the valley would be an "energy oasis" by the mid-1980s and that TVA would lead the nation in energy production. He called for a strong TVA role in helping state and local governments plan the future uses of energy in the region.

Louis Nelson, head of the Office of Agricultural and Chemical Development (OACD), reported on the relative backwardness of valley agriculture, in which the net income of farmers was low, the farming population was aging, and half of the 115,000 farmers had other jobs. TVA was helping these farmers be as productive as possible, but Nelson had no plans to reverse the retreat from agriculture as a livelihood. The exciting work of OACD was in fertilizer research and development, in which TVA led the world and provided an essential service for the fertilizer industry. In response to a query from David Freeman about how to integrate agriculture into the overall TVA mission, Nelson replied that he had not envisioned doing that at this meeting.

Bill Willis presented a plan for improving management services but expressed his belief that environmental compliance, occupational health and safety, and nuclear safety, all responsibilities of his office, be incorporated into the everyday work of the bureaucracy in order to "place more responsibility on the operating divisions." Then, and later as general manager, he emphasized the importance of line responsibility for implementing policy.

Herbert Sanger, the general counsel, and Ken Gray, head of the Washington office, both stressed the burden of environmental and social regulations imposed by Congress. Gray urged his colleagues to "think Washington" and gave examples of TVA announcing plans without thought for the possible effect on Washington constituents, particularly members of Congress. TVA had ignored Washington to a great extent, he said, but sunset-law requirements for the reauthorization of programs would change that. David Freeman struck a positive note by suggesting that Congress would be responsive to TVA as a "laboratory" for program innovation.

At the conclusion of the weekend meeting, David Freeman summed up many ideas that had emerged—land-use planning, coal gasification, power as a means to quality growth, raising educational levels, providing data for social and community planning. He preached the sermon that "we have a desperate need to think TVA, act TVA, and develop a team spirit." He had said earlier that it was "just terribly important that we get a program going so people [inside TVA] knew that they are a part of something larger than what they are doing. . . . We have literally become a giant bureaucracy." Freeman exhorted all those present to participate in the strategic planning process that would be developed by a new policy planning staff and asked each office to designate one person to represent the office to that staff. The real work in identifying and choosing new missions had yet to be done. It had originally been assumed, he said, that the Summer Study would focus on natural resources and community development, but now they "had to think overall TVA."

THE SUMMER STUDY

In April 1978, David Freeman had received a letter from A. J. "Flash" Gray, a retired TVA planner who had begun his work on the original regional planning staff.[64] Gray told Freeman that TVA's initial missions, to build a power network and improve the river and to link those two assignments to regional development by the states, had been completed by 1955 and that after that time "TVA's purpose in the region was no longer clear cut." The valley was urbanized and had joined the mainstream of the American economy. Lacking a clear-cut central purpose, "the regional program was unable to adjust and became a piecemeal, technical assistance effort and an expedient response to the solution of a few widely scattered Valley problems." To make things worse, since that time the president, and Congress had treated TVA as if it were a regional power company rather than a "regional development agency."

Gray urged Freeman to define a TVA regional mission for the president and Congress, using a "strong central planning staff." The objective should be to develop "national demonstrations to help carry out or determine national policy." Such a staff had not been necessary, he wrote, when TVA's purposes were clear in the years before 1955. "Decentralization of planning and management was both possible and desirable in order to detail and carry out regional plans." But after the regional development mission became unclear, decentralization protected many unconnected activities and one-shot solutions to complex problems. Gray thought the main obstacle to central planning was "the strong and cohesive power coalition formed by the general manager and the department heads—a coalition that the Board could neither control or penetrate." He recommended that the board establish its own office which would include the general manager and planning and budget staffs. Such an office would develop policy for TVA as a whole. Gray also expressed the view that TVA planning for the region could only be effective if done in cooperation with the seven states. TVA planners could set standards and goals in land use, transportation, and urban development. For example, TVA and the states could develop a consensus on energy policy, which could be applied to urban transportation and natural-resource development.

David Freeman sent the letter to all of TVA's top staff members and asked the acting general manager to develop a plan for implementing Gray's ideas. Later in 1978, Freeman talked with the planning staff about holding a national symposium on "Alternative Futures for TVA." Nationally known experts would assess the possibilities.[65] Nothing came of this idea as such, but the Summer Study in 1979 may have been the alternative chosen. The invited experts were to meet with the board and TVA staffs and write papers on possible TVA regional development missions. A group of eleven academics and policy analysts were assembled under the chairmanship of Vernon W. Ruttan, a University of Minnesota economist and former TVA colleague of David and Ricahrd Freeman. The group met in July and August 1979 in Knoxville and in October presented tentative assessments in a meeting with the board and office heads at Guntersville, Alabama.[66] The Summer Study is important for our story because it illustrates the Freemans' desires to rejuvenate TVA as something more than a power company and indicates the difficulty of the assignment.

Three members of the TVA planning staff prepared a background paper for the Summer Study panel that identified policy issues in regional development.[67] The paper set only two boundaries to the imagination, the language of the TVA Act and the assumption that TVA programs paid for by appropriated funds would not exceed $200 million in any year. All issues of interest solely to single offices were excluded. The goal was said to be crosscutting regional development programs. The paper posed questions rather than answers. How could TVA best influence regional development? Should there be a regional development plan? How could TVA cooperate with federal, state, and local agencies and yet maintain a distinct identity? How was "quality growth" to be defined? What role should citizens of the valley play in planning, and in particular how could TVA's grass roots policy be defined in the 1980s? How could TVA win congressional approval for a TVA role in implementing "national policy"? Several tensions were posed, such as between economic development and environmental preservation; between purchasing supplies at the lowest cost and using purchasing to promote social goals, for example by favoring minority suppliers. Specific policy areas were cited with questions about what TVA might do about transportation, human services, education and vocational training, urban and rural poverty, natural-resource development, environmental protection, and regional planning. It was an ambitious agenda but lacked form and focus.

The Summer Study advisers first met with the TVA board and other top officials on June 16 and 17, 1979, for a day and a half of general discussion.[68] The highlight of the first day was David Freeman, who presented a possible vision of TVA as a regional government that could integrate the work of all federal agencies in the region. Could the decline of popular confidence in the federal government be overcome by such regional government, closer to the people? To what extent should TVA, as a regional government, attempt "grand experiments" that would help all the people of the nation? Should TVA therefore take A. E. Morgan's rhetoric about TVA as a model for the nation seriously, and could that mission be combined with David Lilienthal's specific statutory "tools" of exploiting power, land, and water? Freeman did not answer his own questions and admitted their utopian quality. He even suggested that all such ideas might be rejected in favor of TVA as an "energy company" and energy laboratory for the nation, which would create a yardstick of standards for energy generation and use. He quoted President Carter on this possibility and cited the recent congressional appropriation for a TVA plant to demonstrate how coal might be turned into gas. He saw the theme of the energy laboratory for the nation as also congenial to A. E. Morgan's vision of TVA.

The office heads' presentations at the June 16 and 17 meeting were similar to those they had given at the Fairfield Glade retreat, and the same dilemmas were posed. A new note was a discussion of what a strategic planning process would look like. LeRoy Rogers, coordinator of the Summer Study, and John Barron, head of the planning and budget staff, described a plan for a central planning staff that would work closely with planners in the offices and other government agencies to develop shared programs. The budget process had theretofore been the only vehicle for planning within TVA, and it had been used primarily for the persuasion of the Office of Management and Budget rather than for analysis of internal choices. But the Freemans had made clear that they wanted the budget to be a management tool closely linked to strategic planning.

David Freeman made it very clear that TVA was going out of the dam-building business and was shifting to industrial development, land-use planning and demonstrations, and strategies of economic development. It was therefore very important, in his mind, that TVA find out what people in the valley were worried about and then, if missions to meet those concerns could be devised, to ask the president and Congress to support those missions. By the same token, TVA could be a demonstration laboratory for the nation, certainly in energy but also in economic development. Freeman had not found any creative ideas in the TVA bureaucracy but hoped that the strategic planning process would pull up fresh thinking. The office heads had been asked to bring their problems to the board for discussion of how problems might be turned into opportunities. The general manager was to be only a facilitator of this process. Freeman recognized that there would be conflicts within TVA about objectives, but he reported that he had found great agreement on fundamentals like a clean environment and quality growth. Freeman felt that the board had lost touch with the program divisions. When he and Richard Freeman asked the office heads to dream their best dreams, they were told that no one had asked them such a question for ten years.[69]

Richard Freeman was very hard-nosed about the importance of managing TVA intelligently. He wanted to establish an "analytic" capability at board level, where it had seldom existed. He remembered clearly that Gordon Clapp, who liked analytic thinking, had relied on the bureaucracy for new ideas. But Richard Freeman felt that the bureaucracy had become so stodgy that a strong hand from the center was badly needed. The two main tasks were to get a handle on power and construction operations and to develop new ideas for regional development programs. He said that from then on program budgeting would be conducted within a strategic plan as a framework of assessment for office proposals. However, his experience as a businessman had convinced him that central planning was effective only if the line organization participated in it as an equal partner.

Richard Freeman was very critical of the TVA organizational culture for becoming too much like a regular federal department in valuing procedures over substance. Private corporations did not have that luxury but had to be profitable to survive. Unfortunately the TVA had become defensive in the Wagner years. David Freeman, who had been a staff person, emphasized ideas. But Richard Freeman, who had been not only a lawyer but a railroad executive, stressed the importance of good management.[70]

The office heads did not think the Freemans were seriously interested in a strategic planning process as much as they were looking for fresh ideas. Certainly there was ambivalence in these quarters about central planning. The directors of the three programs that lived by federal appropriations—natural resources, community development, and agricultural and chemical development—were receptive to analysis at the center if it enhanced their appeal to the Office of Management and Budget and the congressional appropriations committees. Hugh Parris, director of the Office of Power, favored strategic planning for shared programs but was skeptical about using the Office of Power for any purposes other than generating energy. He was also quite clear that the office could and should plan for its own programs and operations. And he did not he see how public opinion could be brought to bear on power programs. His constituents were the distributors. It was the board's business to understand public opinion.[71]

The handful of analysts in the planning and budget office described a TVA under Wagner in which powerful offices had used the general manager to protect their autonomy. But there had been more conflict avoidance than disagreement. It was understood that planning could not work unless the offices cooperated with it. Unfortunately these few people felt that the TVA branch chiefs still saw themselves as next to God. The standard mode of thought was that of the engineer—"Let's do it"—so that social or economic analysis of what was to be or had been done was anathema. The analysts thought it would be tough to introduce analysis and planning into the TVA culture.[72]

The Summer Study group explored possibilities of TVA roles in rural and urban economic development, community development, quality growth management, the contribution of procurement for regional development, and cooperation of TVA with federal agencies and the states and localities. The August 1979 meeting with the board and top TVA staff saw a great deal of beating around the bush but little in the way of fresh ideas. One reason was that the Summer Study advisers lacked understanding of what TVA could really do, given its limited statutory powers. Discussion of urban, rural, and community development reproduced Tributary Area Development-like ideas of discrete projects. Suggestions for using the power program for regional development, through pricing and purchasing policies and plant location, violated the principle of producing electricity as cheaply as possible. Additional homework enabled the consultants to write draft papers for an October 1979 meeting of the board, now filled out with Robert Clement's presence, and top staff, including the office heads, general counsel, and head of the Washington office, at a Guntersville, Alabama, state park lodge. A new participant was John Stewart, a political scientist who had left Senator Edward Kennedy's staff to become the new head of the TVA planning and budget staff.

The two-day meeting at Guntersville went over the now familiar themes. A strong argument was made for TVA developing a regional plan for land, water, and energy use. TVA would convene state governments and federal agencies and act as the overseer and harmonizer for the development of such a plan. However, the incentives for other governments to cooperate in such planning were not specified, nor were the obvious disincentives taken seriously by the planning advocates. David Freeman was skeptical of such comprehensive planning. He preferred the alternative strategy of TVA working with local communities, especially counties, in grass roots development projects. However, this reminded people of the "projectitis" of the TAD program, of which Freeman had been critical. The two consultants on rural and urban development concluded that TVA's talents and capacities were in rural development and that cities presented altogether different problems. It was suggested that TVA target poor areas for development action, but the economists felt that this was a losing strategy. Rather, TVA ought to build on strength, where development was already burgeoning.

Suggestions were made that TVA should work with federal agencies on projects of common interest, such as reclaiming orphan mines or abating soil erosion. But TVA officials voiced a lack of confidence in "old-line" federal bureaucrats, especially in the Departments of Interior and Agriculture. Hugh Parris had very limited enthusiasm for the idea of using electricity rates to induce the location of industry in backward areas. He thought energy conservation was a better development strategy. Ken Gray, head of the Washington office, warned of the political peril of playing with electricity rates in ways that might ignite congressional charges of favoritism to some areas.

The final issue discussed was the strategic planning system. A structure was proposed that would seek balance between central planners and analysts in the offices in an effort to adapt the organizational culture rather than reject it. Ideas for new programs and for cooperation across offices would come initially from the central planners, but they would draw on thoughts and experience in the operating divisions and be subject to the reality checks that experienced staff in the operating programs could provide. Everyone agreed that an adversarial system in which central analysts were pitted against managers would flounder in conflict. The managers somehow had to be seduced by the planners, who would show how they could help stimulate fresh thinking. George Kimmons, head of the Office of Organizational Design and Construction, grew red in the face as he realized that a suggestion was being made that planners at the top were to assess his programs. Such an idea clashed with everything he believed about TVA, and he did not like it. John Stewart believed that the organization should be tilted firmly in the direction of central strategic planning, which meant curbing the offices' autonomy. However, it was well understood that even if new ideas emerged out of the planning process, the board would have to decide which were the most promising and act accordingly.[73] The planning process itself was not enough.

The papers that emerged from the Summer Study were published by TVA in March 1981.[74] Neither John Stewart nor Bill Willis felt that the papers had done any more than stir around ideas.[75] No bold initiatives had emerged. However, the discussion about the form of a strategic planning process had perhaps clarified agreement that such a process must be consistent with TVA organizational culture. Willis proposed a planning process at the Guntersville meeting that was eventually put in place. Board-staff meetings, perhaps at annual retreats, would send ideas to Stewart's planning and budget staff, which would develop program options for further discussion and eventual board decision. Planning was to address only those subjects in which there was overlap and cooperation among offices. Stewart's staff was not to pry into the programs unique to each office. There was general agreement that planning was to be a catalyst within the existing management system.

Vernon Ruttan's introduction to the Summer Study book pointed out that none of the three major program areas—power, construction, and fertilizer—were addressed by the study, nor was much said about water resource programs. Management of the river for power, navigation, flood control, public health, and recreation was discussed only at the margins, and Ruttan recommended that TVA conduct a review of water programs. He then made two telling points about TVA that had been only obliquely addressed by the Summer Study.

His first point was that, in the absence of markets, it was difficult for TVA to know which of its services to valley governments, communities, firms, and individuals provided what people actually wanted from TVA. Local, state, and federal politics were too diffuse to send clear signals. Informal power structures, in government, firms, and the media, had direct access to TVA staff and management but did not necessarily speak for the larger community. Organized interest groups were concerned with specific stakes, many of which were conflicting. Ruttan concluded that if TVA were to try to become "a regional development agency rather than simply an enlightened power company," it needed to develop a broad-based constituency, organized at the local level, which could resolve conflicts among groups and interpret local and regional needs in a more coherent way than state and local governments. He did not suggest how such a constituency might be created.

His second point was that TVA had been most successful in those areas in which it had exclusive responsibility for the development and execution of its own programs: electric power, navigation and flood control, recreation on TVA lakes, and the scientific development of fertilizer. Other very specific contributions had been made in technical fields such as forestry. TVA had been least successful, he argued, in those areas that required cooperation with others, like the rural and community development programs. Assistance to farmers had been delegated to the extension service and land-grant colleges, and TVA had really given up control of that activity.[76]

Ruttan did not draw the logical conclusion that TVA should stick to its statutory assignments and avoid regional development missions for which it had little legal or organizational leverage. He urged TVA to consider challenges in developing the valley's natural resources to overcome pockets of poverty and develop human resources. But this was only a general exhortation.

Strategic Planning

General manager Bill Willis initiated a planning process in October 1979. The board chose seven issues out of a list of eleven as topics for option papers.[77] Responsibility for preparing the papers was parceled out to teams of staff analysts from John Stewart's group and from the offices. Each group was charged with sharpening the objectives in one area, for example, how best to target regional resource development activities? Should TVA focus and concentrate its efforts or continue with a wide range of diverse tasks?[78] The other charges echoed themes from the Guntersville meeting, about the use of the power program to achieve regional goals, intergovernmental cooperation, development of social and economic data about the valley, the wisdom of a high-tech energy industry option, and how the strategic planning process should work.

In early January 1980, John Stewart drew on the option papers to write a brief statement of policy goals for the board to consider and release to the press. He predicted that the new decade would be "the most challenging and productive period for TVA and the people of the Tennessee Valley since the agency's first decade in the 1930's." The goals set out were to build the country's largest and safest nuclear power system, demonstrate new technologies for the efficient and clean use of coal, develop and use renewable energy technologies, foster quality economic growth through high-tech industry, and achieve "full income parity" with U. S. levels for valley residents.[79]

Stewart wrote in a separate paper that "serious planning" was just beginning. The most important message was to transmit to all parts of the agency "the Board's intention to change radically the organizational and operational behavior." Barriers to agencywide communication and collaboration were no longer to be tolerated. Operations across office boundaries were the new order of the day. Strategic planning, budgeting, and the evaluation of programs would be joined in TVA for the first time. Stewart's analysis of the option papers themselves was more cautious. For example, cooperation with other agencies first required a clear idea of how cooperation would enhance TVA's mission. Regional resource development was said to be dispersed because there were no agency-wide goals for regional development. In short, the papers spelled out only "intriguing possibilities."[80] Both Freemans responded to the paper by urging that a more specific definition of TVA goals be prepared as soon as possible.[81]

In June 1980, a Core Policy Analysis Group, under Stewart's leadership, sent a paper to the board with specific recommendations.[82] The five proposals were fashioned to meet the most critical problems in economic and human resource development, growth management, and community services:

1. TVA would create Development Centers of public/private consortia to develop and commercialize industries using energy-related technology, such as electric vehicles, alternate fuels from coal, and energy from biomass materials.
2. TVA economic development officers would work to establish firms in the region that would benefit from the work of the Development Centers.
3. TVA would establish a Valley Land Institute that would carry out demonstrations of growth management in communities wishing to develop economically. Demonstrations of alternative ways to protect the environment might also be staged.
4. TVA district administrators would assist small communities with expert advice in the areas of education, housing, health care, solid-waste management, and water supply. The focus would be on interagency cooperation in the communities themselves.
5. TVA would inaugurate a program of economic, social, and environmental research that would contribute to strategies for quality growth.

The Core Policy Analysis Group had finally crystalized ideas that had been incubating in the slow planning process that had begun at Fairfield Glade the previous year. Most of the ideas had been articulated by David Freeman at one time or another. The goal was to use an energy base for tasks of economic development. However, this program never left the paper on which it was written because the Reagan administration was not interested. The TVA budget request was cut from $100 million to $34 million. Congress restored much of the original amount, but little money was available for new initiatives. The work of Stewart and his staff for the next eight years was to save existing TVA appropriated programs, not create new ones.[83]

The board focused its subsequent initiatives on demonstrations for producing energy in cleaner and more efficient ways, and the general economic development task, which had been the work of the now abolished Tributary Area Development program, made very little progress. It continued to be a collection of small items of technical assistance to communities, much like TAD. Billy Bond, who headed the Office of Community Development for four years during this period, did not feel that the planning process was ever very effective in his area. It was seldom possible to make a definitive judgment that new ideas would be better than current programs, he said, adding, "We never had a consensus on what the economic development programs ought to be." TVA's programs were small compared to those of the states and were susceptible to pressures from congressional members from the valley, especially those who controlled appropriations. So "Congress was running the programs but not on a comprehensive basis." According to Bond, the economic development mission was vulnerable because it was so eclectic, just many small projects. The fertilizer and water-control programs could keep their autonomy because they offered little in the way of direct constituency benefits.[84]

Stewart and his staff felt that they made modest progress over the years on small but worthwhile objectives such as reservoir management, the uses of Land Between the Lakes, and especially in helping those offices that required appropriations to make their case with the Office of Management and Budget and congressional committees.[85] Bill Willis felt that the strategic planning staff's chief contribution was to make the bureaucracy more responsive to external voices. There was less "arrogance" in internal decision making and greater awareness of what constituencies in the valley and Washington felt about TVA. Willis also contended that the annual planning process helped move TVA away from the notion that it was just a utility because of the commitment to an integrated resource-management approach. TVA was reconciled with the environmental movement, as seen in the higher priorities given to clean air and water and quality growth. In Willis's view, if the Freemans had not moved TVA in that direction, the political backlash would have been very strong. The trends of the Wagner years had to be moderated.[86]

However, it is not clear that the offices warmly embraced efforts to direct and integrate their work with their counterparts. Everyone agreed that the strategic planning staff never succeeded in penetrating either the Office of Power or of Engineering Design and Construction. Allan Pulsipher, the chief economist who came in 1980, remembered that people in those offices often complained to him about the attempts of staff analysts in Willis's office to use analysis to second-guess office recommendations. The complainers saw this as "immoral." Pulsipher was not sure why morality was invoked except that centralized planning challenged the formal organization chart and the way things had always been done.[87] David Freeman felt, in retrospect, that John Stewart's operation "was helpful but not devastatingly so." Stewart was personally a "spark plug," but an overall pattern of themes for nonpower programs never emerged. "We were demonstrating some good projects, e.g., good forestry management, but it never got beyond the demonstration stage."[88] Craven Crowell, director of public information for TVA during the Freeman and Dean years, recalled that the nonpower programs were designed "to please everybody. They did a lot of things that were important but there was no one theme. We were just trying to keep the budget up in Congress."[89] Tennessee senator Jim Sasser suggested that neither he nor other valley congressional members got much political benefit out of TVA nonpower programs. There was no overall theme to them.[90]

Yet David Freeman believed that TVA would not be true to its basic mission without nonpower programs. The responsible officials in the Carter Office of Management and Budget tried to get Freeman to cut out such programs altogether, but Freeman told them he would give up energy programs first and would also take the issue to the president. He later successfully made the same appeal to Tennessee senator Howard Baker against David Stockman and the Reagan, Office of Management and Budget.[91] Freeman shared A. E. Morgan's original beliefs that the main justification for TVA's existence, and for the federal funding behind it, was to demonstrate projects for the nation, in both energy and other areas: "FDR added the larger vision. It has been like a neon sign; it comes and goes. Maybe TVA should be just a power program. I told Dick [Freeman] that and he disagreed. But I doubt that it will return again to a broader conception."[92]

Freeman wanted TVA to be a demonstration agency in energy use and not simply a utility, but his hope that energy and economic development programs could somehow be related in innovative ways was not fulfilled, in part because neither the Carter nor Reagan administrations supported such ideas, but also because Freeman's own policy planners and managers had difficulty inventing viable policy themes for regional development. The most innovative actions of the Freeman board were in energy conservation and demonstrations of alternative sources of energy.

Energy Conservation and Demonstration Programs

Most of the ideas came from David Freeman and had been articulated by him in his first years at TVA. It was his bold conception that TVA be an "energy laboratory" for the nation, and this was where he committed his talent and energy.

The energy-conservation measures were financed by revenues from the power program. This was justified as being in the interest of the valley people because of the high costs of energy. The board directed the Office of Power to create these programs, working through a new division of energy conservation. TVA offered free home-insulation audits to home-owners, and consumers and industrial customers were given interest-free loans to correct insulation deficiencies. Low-interest loans were also made available to consumers to install solar hot-water heaters, with the hopes of reducing monthly electric bills. Another loan program was begun to permit homeowners, especially in rural areas, to buy wood stoves as a source of energy. There were also programs promoting the use of heat pumps and heat-pump water heaters. TVA built an office building in Chattanooga for the Office of Power that used solar energy for much of its heat.[93] By the mid-1980s these programs had accomplished much. By 1986 there were 559,130 home-weatherization projects, and 43,311 heat pumps and 1,017 heat-pump water heaters had been installed. TVA had introduced 7,068 solar water heaters and 13,179 wood heaters. About a sixth of the residential homes in the valley had received some sort of energy-conservation service from TVA. This was not a negligible figure.[94]

None of these programs, valuable as they were, attained a magnitude sufficient to catch national attention. David Freeman wrote President Carter in 1979 pledging his solar energy program as a "man on the moon" type national commitment to solar-energy.[95] But the reality did not match the rhetoric. Nor were the TVA distributors happy. Jerry Campbell, director of the Tennessee Valley Public Power Association, explains why: " [Freeman] wanted TVA to be a living laboratory, e.g. solar heat. But there was not enough sunlight and he would use the rate payers money to benefit the world. This was at a time when our people were facing angry rate payers because of rate increases. It was a bad time to experiment."[96]

Campbell remembered a meeting between the board and the TVPPA executive council. The board wanted to change TVA policy to require residential and industrial consumers to pay higher rates as they used more energy. This was a conservation measure but also a reversal of TVA's historic policy of linking amount of use to reduced cost. The discussion became so heated that Richard Freeman, who had a temper, stalked out of the meeting. Campbell felt that the problem was that "TVA had not sold us on conservation as the way to go . . . Dave could be divisive. He didn't take time to persuade people. Another problem was the lack of education. The distributors don't like actions taken about their rate payers without their knowing it first. Dave didn't seem to care how the distributors felt."[97]

Energy demonstrations were a better example of TVA acting as an energy lab for the nation. The problem here was that the Carter administration was trying to balance the budget and, as its energy program developed, looked to new agencies, other than TVA, for this work. David

Freeman's rhetoric about electric cars was bold. In a 1978 profile, Freeman said: "Detroit hasn't had a good record. . . . It took laws to get safety belts, pollution controls, and economy cars. . . . We are going to show them that the Tennessee Valley can lead in making the use of electric cars and electric trains possible. . . . I hope we can, in this valley, do with the electric car the same thing that was done decades ago with the Model-T Ford. I know it is possible."[98] This profile reported that many TVA staff members were skeptical of Freeman's innovations, adding, "They think the price of power is going to continue to rise and that Freeman's words will backfire on him. They fear his preaching and hearing the prayers of the TVA faithful will raise false hopes of salvation."[99]

The actual TVA effort with electric cars was modest. TVA worked with the Department of Energy and the Electric Power Research Institute of the utility industry to demonstrate the uses and problems of electric cars on a very small scale in a special facility. The results were mixed. Such cars could not carry heavy loads, had to be recharged frequently, and were expensive. But it was recognized that TVA would save costs greatly if whole fleets of electric cars were available.[100] The most ambitious energy demonstration was the construction of a plant in Murphy Hill, Alabama, to create a synthetic fuel by turning coal into synthetic gas. This was one example of TVA's commitment to the emergence of high-tech industry in the valley.[101] The plant was to be paid for entirely out of appropriations. David Freeman persuaded Representative Tom Bevill, an Alabama Democrat and chairman of the appropriations subcommittee that oversaw TVA, to put $5 million in planning money in the 1980 budget. The plant was to be in Bevill's district.[102] Ken Gray, head of TVA's Washington Office, saw the request as part of a strategy to win Bevill's support for budgetary requests.[103] But such a political strategy was consistent with the board's vision of TVA as a national "energy lab."

The Carter administration had turned down TVA's request for $5 million, but Bevill added it and Carter signed the bill. The Office of Management and Budget opposed all subsequent TVA budget requests for Murphy Hill, but Congress kept adding to the project, up to about $200 million in 1980 and 1981. The administration went so far as to tell Congress that the plant would cost more than $3 billion, which was more than twice the original estimate. It also argued that the technology had already been proven and that no demonstration was necessary. In addition, the high cost of the product would make it too expensive to sell, and TVA had no outlets for any such product nor a pipeline to transmit it.[104] After the creation of the Synthetic Fuels Corporation in 1979, the Carter administration appeared to have decided that TVA was not the appropriate place for a demonstration project in synthetic fuels.

TVA was forced to admit that there were no apparent customers for the gas from Murphy Hill, but this was not particularly important because it was a demonstration project. Freeman told Bevill's subcommittee that "TVA's history proves that what we do in the [Tennessee] Valley can have national and even international applications."[105] However, the fall in the world price of oil eventually killed Murphy Hill, and neither the Reagan administration nor Congress would stay with it. It could not be justified as a cheaper alternative to gasoline.

Federal appropriations paid for more modest exploratory programs that were extensions of TVA's existing capacities. There was work on fluidized bed combustion of coal, a process designed to allow TVA to burn high-sulfur coal without violating air-pollution standards. A project for burning garbage to produce electricity and steam, and efforts to develop fuel cells from coal-derived fuels that could be converted directly into electrical energy, were also attempted. Projects of this kind were extensions of work already being done at the Muscle Shoals facilities.[106]

NUCLEAR ENERGY

David Freeman's commitment to a clean environment and interest in alternative sources of energy typed him, in some people's minds, as necessarily opposing nuclear power. But Freeman was ambitious for TVA, and after he became chairman he said publicly that TVA would be dependant on nuclear power for almost half of its generating capacity for years to come. Solar power, as an alternative, was not yet technologically feasible.[107] He embraced TVA plans to build the largest nuclear power system in the world, arguing that, unlike other utilities, TVA would have surplus power to sell to other regions of the country.[108] Admitting that the costs of construction were driving up rates, he stressed the importance of getting the plants on line as a means of stabilizing costs and rates.

Freeman had initially thought it possible for TVA to complete the construction of nuclear reactors through 1986 within the $15 billion debt limit set by Congress.[109] But in 1979 the TVA board went to Washington with a request to double the debt limit because of the escalating costs of construction. The increase was granted, and Ken Gray remembered that there was practically no scrutiny by Congress of the justifications for the increase. Howard Baker managed the issue with help from other members of the valley delegation. In retrospect, Gray thought that Congress should have asked some questions: "It was an optimistic, unintentional misrepresentation that turned out to be a lie. That gave the nuclear program another five years before the right questions were asked."[110]

In a letter to Jim Frey, a Carter White House assistant for congressional relations, Freeman stressed that the importance of raising the debt limit could not be underestimated. It was a necessity if TVA was to provide sufficient electric power for the region, especially for consumers.[111] Freeman continued to publicly defend the nuclear construction program in

1980 and 1981, despite soaring construction costs and public unhappiness with rate increases. In October 1980, he wrote Alabama senator Howell Heflin that the valley would be in a better position than many regions of the country because it would have enough power, adding, "My personal view is that the Valley will be in the catbird's seat once nuclear plants under construction begin producing revenues. TVA rates will still be among the lowest in the nation as they are today, and this region will be blessed with ample and reliable supplies of electric power."[112]

However Freeman was privately concerned that TVA might be building beyond the valley's future energy needs. In May 1979, the board decided to defer construction of four nuclear reactors at three plant sites in Tennessee and Mississippi indefinitely.[113] The decision was prompted by a decline in TVA power sales. The authority sold 118 million kilowatt hours of power in 1978, four million less than in 1977. Conservation measures and a decline in demand were both at work. However, Freeman continued to stress that TVA would have plenty of power for future needs. After Tennessee governor Lamar Alexander had met with the board in April 1980, he wrote Freeman: "One point which you discussed is absolutely crucial to our ability to attract better jobs to Tennessee: the reliability and the availability of electric power during the late 1980's and 1990's in Tennessee as compared with other regions of the country."[114]

Freeman's reply assured the governor that TVA would have enough power and added an optimistic note: "[T]his extra expense [cost of construction] will pay large dividends in the 1990's. . . . By the late 1980's we expect the impact of our construction programs on rates to begin leveling off. At that time TVA's nuclear power program will start to look like a very good investment indeed and our rates will become more and more attractive on a comparative basis."[115]

These estimates were way off the mark, as the two Freemans gradually realized, for they found themselves caught between two irreconcilable points of view. Critics argued that TVA was overbuilding. A General Accounting Office report in 1979 took TVA to task for not making more accurate estimates of future demand and suggested that additional plants be canceled.[116] The board decision to defer four reactors followed soon after the GAO report. The opposing view was publicly voiced by Aubrey Wagner in January 1981 when he charged that David Freeman had ordered TVA staff people to reduce load-estimate figures in order to justify the deferral decision.[117] Wagner blamed the 23.8 percent rate increases in 1980 and an anticipated 13 percent increase for April 1981 on the slowdown in the construction program. Wagner also charged Freeman with having changed his position to be more favorable to nuclear power as Carter was succeeded by Reagan and called him a "political opportunist."

These were difficult shoals to navigate, particularly as the Reagan administration, which was friendly to nuclear power, entered the picture. But the board had to promise the valley that it would have power yet respond to declining demand. This was something new for TVA, which had always preached that supply produced demand. It was ironic that the TVA power distributors, who were keen on nuclear building, attacked the high rates without admitting that construction costs were largely to blame. Instead of blaming the nuclear program for increasing rates, they attacked conservation programs and Freeman himself. He defended himself by trying to combine the best of both arguments. He told a Knoxville television interviewer in January 1981 that "TVA today has a stern and lean management that is running the agency. . . . We did cut back on four of our 17 nuclear power plants . . . and we now have nine more that we're going to finish." He added that he knew that the key to popularity for TVA was to "keep the lakes up and the rates down." But low rainfall and inflation had driven the rates up. However:

> [T]hese nuclear plants will provide us with economical power. They're going to be the salvation of this area and the source of prosperity over the next ten or twenty years. . . . It is our judgement that the units we're building are needed for maximum economic growth here in the valley. . . . If we don't build those . . . plants, we're not going to have the energy. We know for sure our growth will be lower. TVA will be putting the ceiling on the future of this valley. . . . We are looking at a range because we know we are not smart enough to know exactly what the demand is going to be. And we're building toward the higher end of the range because the risk there is very, very small, and if we have a surplus we can exchange it and make money on it. If we build for the lower end of the range, that's what this valley's growth is going to be—low.

Freeman had tilted toward nuclear power with the election of Reagan. He was counting on Senator Howard Baker to win support for TVA from the new president: "I expect to have good working relations with the Reagan Administration because we are pushing ahead on nuclear power. . . . TVA has probably got the strongest nuclear program in the country. . . . The principal source of advice to President Reagan on TVA is going to be Howard Baker."[118]

And yet the nuclear program was becoming more expensive all the time. One third of TVA's revenue from the sale of power went to pay for interest on the $10.8-billion debt, more than $7 billion of it for nuclear power. The original seven plant/seventeen reactor system was originally estimated to cost $7 billion, but estimates in late 1980 came closer to $17 billion. The story in the Nashville *Tennessean*, which reported these facts, also pointed out that because TVA electric rates were set by TVA with no regulatory requirement or overview, and because the debt limit had been raised to $30 billion, TVA could keep building and raising rates until it hit the debt limit.[119]

The board request for an increase in the debt limit was opposed by environmental groups such as the Sierra Club and the Tennessee Energy Coalition primarily because they believed that construction was the cause of escalating costs. However, the Tennessee Valley Public Power Association strongly supported doubling the debt limit. Freeman had to disagree with his friends and rely on his sometime antagonists here.[120] The well-timed deferral of construction on four nuclear reactors appeared to deflect any congressional criticism of the building program. Senator Jim Sasser had raised questions about the ambitious building program in the debt-limit hearings, citing the GAO report that TVA was overbuilding, but as the measure passed the Senate in June, he said that TVA officials had promised that the increased debt authority would not be used unless "absolutely necessary."[121] But by the time the House had approved the increase in borrowing authority in October, it was clear that TVA would need to raise its spending and debt in order to complete the nuclear program. Six nuclear plants were either under construction or in the planning stage. The current TVA debt was $10 billion and was expected to rise to $21 billion by 1986–87. TVA's cost projections had greatly increased beyond the original estimates. For example, the first five nuclear plants were originally estimated to cost $3.3 billion, but the estimated figure in 1979 was $8 billion.[122]

Despite its public bravado, the board was worried about controlling the costs of nuclear construction. It continually probed the Office of Engineering Design and Construction about its effectiveness in holding down costs. For example, in April 1980 OEDC was asked to give the board a report on the construction schedule and estimated costs. The agenda for the meeting in which the report was to be discussed, which Bill Willis prepared, indicates that the board and general manager did not believe that they were getting good information from OEDC:

Key points.
  – continued increases in overall cost forecast with no clear explanation of causes in the report.
  – OEDC forecast information supplied to Office of Power for recent study is not current. . . .
  – current practices do not provide a way to clearly quantify estimate increases by cause, e.g. scope change, estimate changes, escalation, etc.[123]

The board was committed to the nuclear program but at the same time was worried about rising construction costs. And frustration with OEDC was very high in the board and the general manager's office.[124] In April 1980, a *Christian Science Monitor* story provided a good synthesis of the dilemmas the board confronted. TVA was described as committed to completing seventeen reactors at seven plants, and David Freeman was quoted as saying that additional safety measures, taken after the Three Mile Island incident, would ensure safe operation of all the plants. Charles Komanoff, an expert on nuclear energy, was quoted to the effect that the cost of nuclear safety measures was pushing the cost of nuclear construction up so fast that coal-fired plants might be cheaper to build and run. The Sierra Club had made the same point in opposing an increase in the debt limit. However, James Cross, TVA's assistant power manager, was quoted as saying that the price of antipollution scrubbers for fossil-fuel plants had so increased that they were equivalent to the cost of building nuclear plants. He added that all the energy-conservation projects at work in TVA were not sufficient to eliminate the need for even one nuclear reactor. The story went on to point out that unsettled safety questions had begun to surface in the nuclear program. The Nuclear Regulatory Commission had presented a list of "unresolved" safety problems at the Sequoyah plant to TVA. And there had been no explanation for why the Browns Ferry plant had stopped operating without warning three times between February 10 and February 15, 1980.[125]

This was a difficult bundle of problems. The increase in the debt limit was to be quickly absorbed by unanticipated costs of nuclear construction. There was pressure to get the plants up and working as soon as possible in order to limit costs from the stretched-out construction program. But this pressure was in implicit conflict with the need for making sure that the plants were built in accordance with the safety requirements for operation. It is understandable that the board members did not feel that they were fully in control of all these elements. The remainder of David Freeman's chairmanship, and the three more years he spent on the board, were years of continuing tension between a commitment to the nuclear plan and escalating costs. Freeman and the board were juggling balls in the air.

Their biggest political problem was that it was necessary to keep increasing electricity rates. The TVA Act required TVA to pay for all electricity as it was generated out of current income. As costs went up, rates had to go up. Public opinion in the valley, which had been told for a generation that TVA would provide cheap energy, was not prepared for the high rate increases during Freeman's tenure. When TVA sponsored public meetings around the valley about the possibility of rate increases, the response was uniformly one of anger.[126] When voters got angry, politicians took notice. By the end of 1979, politicians were openly criticizing TVA. Tennessee lieutenant governor John Wilder chaired a special legislative committee that criticized the negative effects of TVA rate increases on industrial growth. If industry did not grow, then homeowners would have to pick up the load. Wilder particularly attacked the settlement with the EPA. His committee also pointed out to TVA officials that TVA's rates for industrial users were higher than the comparable rates of twelve southeastern utilities.[127] At public hearings in Muscle Shoals, Alabama, in February 1980, both consumer and industry spokespeople attacked TVA. A businessman charged that valley industries were "at the mercy of TVA." Others threatened that industry would leave the valley. Individual citizens asked that industrial rates be higher and their rates lower. Nuclear construction costs were blamed by some. Rural customers claimed that TVA rates were higher for them than for city dwellers. No one was happy.[128]

TVA was required by the act to give preferential rates to home residents over industry, and this caused a drumbeat of criticism from industries that TVA was antibusiness. In early 1980, a group of the thirty largest industries in the TVA region produced a study which showed that of the twenty-seven power companies in the south, seventeen charged lower industrial rates than TVA. One spokesman said that industry feared that the "populist philosophy" of David Freeman would be reflected in TVA's rate-making standards, with industry paying even more.[129] Hugh Parris understood this criticism and worried about it: "TVA preferential rates for residencies over industry could slow regional development and industrial growth. The industrial community is giving me hell because of our power rates. I try to convey this to the board. . . . The industrial people are scared to death of Dave [Freeman] and will locate industries outside of the region because of his philosophy, not on sheer economic grounds."[130]

Robert Clement, who had come on the board in the fall of 1979, soon began to attack rate increases and call for cuts in TVA spending. Time after time he voted against increases that his two colleagues insisted were necessary. Taking a leaf from David Freeman's book, Clement urged that "TVA has got to be more available and accessible to the public."[131] Clement was a professional politician with ambitions for higher office, and the two Freemans might have done well to listen to him more carefully. However, they simply dismissed Clement as grandstanding for his own purposes. But he was more in touch with public opinion than either of the Freemans.

The Freemans' general response to these criticisms was that the valley would be an "oasis" of energy by 1990 whereas the rest of the nation would experience electricity shortages. David Freeman made this argument in a meeting with the Tennessee governor and other state officials in April. A 10-percent rate increase was needed to finance nuclear construction, Freeman said. But that would add 13 million kilowatts to TVA's power capacity by 1990, he claimed. Public Service Commissions in other states and regions had denied such increases to utilities, he reported, thus stifling growth. The fact that TVA rate decisions were not regulated was therefore a good thing.[132]

By May 1980, David Freeman was saying publicly that rates were certain to jump 15 to 20 percent in October, if not sooner, despite the 10.8-percent April increase. This was because TVA's operating costs would increase by $600 million during the year, including a $150 million jump in the cost of coal and a $200 million increase in interest payments on loans used to finance nuclear construction. Clement spoke at the same public meeting in Huntsville, Alabama, urging that TVA cut costs instead of increasing rates. He said he was trying to "alarm the public" because he was alarmed. He cited the number of expenditures he had voted against at board meetings, such as spending $100 thousand to microfilm a history of TVA employees. Distributor representatives who were present at the meeting attacked Freeman for living in "an ivory tower," saying they were on the receiving end of public criticism of TVA actions.[133] Freeman defended TVA's energy-conservation programs, which were under attack at the meeting, on the grounds that without conservation, rates would be even higher. But he had to admit that inflation had outpaced conservation.

In September 1980, the board raised rates by 13 percent in an open meeting. The two Freemans defended the decision, which they said would provide $401 million of the projected $508-million operating deficit for the 1980 fiscal year, ending in October. Clement dissented, asserting that TVA had too many employees and too much bureaucratic fat. This angered both Freemans, who charged Clement with making simplistic statements and voting against increases that staff analyses had concluded were unavoidable. When Richard Freeman accused Clement of missing two key meetings with staff on efficiency issues, Clement replied that he didn't "need to be in the ivory tower all the time."[134] However, Clement did not advocate any reduction in the nuclear program but urged its quick completion. Nuclear cutbacks were political hot potatoes because of the loss of construction jobs in the affected communities, and Clement was not about to tackle that issue.

The furor over rate increases finally began to get the attention of congressional politicians. Senator Jim Sasser held a press conference to accuse TVA of overbuilding and promised to hold hearings after the November elections. He cited the 1979 General Accounting Office report that said that TVA forecasts of power needs were too high by 18 to 40 percent and reminded TVA that even though they had challenged the GAO report's correctness, four reactors had been deferred soon after. He also agreed with a questioner who charged that TVA was "becoming arrogant to the point where it can't be controlled." Sasser said that his travels in Tennessee had convinced him that many people believed TVA was insensitive to the human suffering caused by rate increases and that public confidence in TVA was steadily eroding. David Freeman had discovered the same low credibility in 1977. The news story on the press conference also referred to a coolness between David Freeman and Sasser and pointed out that Clement had been Sasser's candidate for appointment to the board, over David Freeman's objection.[135] Also in September, Senator Howard Baker asked the Senate Environment and Public Works Committee to conduct oversight hearings on the TVA rate increases in early 1981.[136]

In October, the Electric Power Board of Chattanooga, the local distributor of TVA power, unanimously blasted new rate standards that TVA was considering instituting. The EPB's statement was based on a TVA staff report that had been some months in the making. The EPB was opposed to a continuation of lower-priced power to residential customers, time-of-day rates for both residential and commercial users, across-the-board adoption of seasonal rates, and a mandatory hookup charge for insufficiently insulated new buildings and homes. Their statement said that time-of-day rates were not cost-effective. Overall bills might be lower, but higher usage would also be encouraged. The idea of a $2,000 charge for hooking up power to any new home or building not insulated by TVA standards was, the EPB, said, "an exercise in police power" that would reduce the supply of affordable housing. The EPB manager, John McQueen, charged that "this is nothing but a reflection of Dave Freeman's opinion. The [TVA] board gave the rate branch the answers and told them to justify it."[137]

Despite widespread public criticism of TVA in the valley, residential electric rates were still the fourth lowest among twenty-eight southeastern utilities in early 1981. However, TVA industrial rates had slipped to twelfth place, whereas a decade earlier they had been the cheapest in the south.[138] In February 1981, the Tennessee Valley Industrial Committee, representing TVA's thirty-one largest industrial customers, made a formal request to the region's congressmen for help in convincing TVA to delay by sixty days a decision to raise rates in April by at least 13 percent. There had been 13-percent and 10.8-percent increases in 1980. Were more increases justified, they asked? David Freeman responded by writing valley congressmen that TVA was required by law to set rates sufficient to cover its expenses in each fiscal year. The Industrial Committee had plenty of time to study the need for an increase, Freeman said, because the necessity for a hike had been known since the previous August.[139] The board did increase rates by 9.3 percent, with Clement again dissenting. Hugh Parris told the board that the worst drought in ninety-one years and record interest rates on TVA borrowing, neither of which had been anticipated, made the increase necessary.[140]

The next day David Freeman said publicly that "the worst is over" because a new nuclear plant would soon open and the price of electricity would thus be a bargain by 1990. TVA should aim for the high growth end projections, he said, in order to have enough power for a booming economy. Surplus power could easily be sold to other utilities. Any further cutbacks in nuclear construction would be "sentencing the valley to low growth." He added that cuts could only be made in 20 percent of TVA's budget. Forty-one cents of every dollar of revenue were spent on fuel. Interest payments on the debt accounted for 25 percent of the budget. Only 20 percent was discretionary, and it had been cut to the bone.[141]

This was the political context for the congressional hearings that were held in late 1980 and early 1981 which preceded David Freeman's demotion from the chairmanship. Before we look at those events, it is important to understand TVA's relationships with its primary constituency, the power distributors, who are represented by the Tennessee Valley Public Power Association.

TVA and the Distributors

The distributors, for the most part, never really liked David Freeman. Bill Willis summed it up:

> Dave came across as arrogant. He wouldn't take the time to bring people along. He had great ideas but took no time to sell them. It did backfire on him. He never got the support he properly deserved in the valley, for example the distributors didn't like being told they were neanderthals. He should have spent two years in selling his concepts. . . . The TVPPA was important for Dave's demise in 1981. They talked to economic leaders in the valley and asked for a change. They felt Dave was carrying them too far. . . . The nuclear cancellation was seen as anti-business.[142]

The municipal distributors were independent TVA customers who were very dependent upon TVA, which set the price they had to pay for electricity. There was continuous consultation between TVA and the TVPPA board, but the client depended entirely upon TVA for information about the cost of energy and the value of given technology. The TVPPA had no independent sources of information. Indeed, the relationship had historically been very close because TVA had helped create the municipal distributorships in the early years. They were part of the TVA dream. Trust was therefore extremely important to a good working relationship. Jerry Campbell, executive director of the TVPPA, described its importance in the support that Wagner received: "TVPPA stayed with Red. We didn't have a lot of experts and have always depended upon what TVA told us. If Red said something the distributors were on his side. If no complaints, no problems. Red was responsible for the nuclear program. We assumed he made decisions on the best facts available. Red was a strong personality."[143]

The reader will remember that TVA employees felt much the same awe for Wagner. He radiated authority and would stand up for them and the things they believed in. Therefore, they would follow him. The distributors seem to have felt much the same way. Wagner invoked the symbols that were important to them, particularly the old credo of the supply of energy creating demand, and thus the need for continuous growth in capacity. Campbell describes how trust deteriorated with Freeman:

> Dave was likable, down to earth, but totally different than any personalities in this region. He was funny and would let his hair down but his philosophy was not at all like that of people here—very liberal. Our biggest problem was that he wanted TVA to be a living laboratory and use the ratepayers' money to benefit the world. But it was our money. This was at a time when our people were facing angry ratepayers because of rate increases. It was a bad time to experiment.

There had been trouble from the beginning. In early 1978, the TVPPA board of directors adopted a resolution that sent a clear message to Freeman. The following excerpt gives the flavor:

> Whereas the purpose of electric distributors is to generate revenue to meet expenses and to maintain reliable systems, and not to engage in programs other than those required to serve their area for the distribution and use of electric power, and, whereas the implementation and administration of social welfare programs is properly in departments of the federal, state and local governments designed to meet such needs, . . . this committee opposes having the Tennessee Valley Public Power Association distributors conduct any form of financial subsidy to any class of consumers.[144]

In June 1978, John McQueen, general manager of the Chattanooga Electric Power Board, criticized David Freeman's interest in solar energy. TVA should stick to generating electricity, McQueen said, asking if "TVA has become so involved in the pursuit of imagemaking and social and environmental experiments that it has abandoned sound basic management?"[145]

The TVPPA board did approve a resolution endorsing TVA's agreement on air-quality standards with the EPA, even though, as a TVPPA officer wrote the head of the Office of Power, "while the Board is solidly behind the resolution, there is still some sensitivity among the distributors and they do not plan to make a lot of publicity about the resolution."[146]

By early 1979, the TVPPA board was extremely restless about TVA policies. A TVA summary of issues discussed in a joint meeting of the two boards described TVPPA concerns:

> A general feeling of uncertainty, fear and distrust seems to prevail among most of the distributors about TVA's future direction. . . . There is a concern that TVA will concentrate less, in the future, on building nuclear plants for future generation, in favor of uncertain so-called "soft-path" energy sources—and too much emphasis will be placed on energy conservation, co-generation, etc. Will TVA use rate design to curtail electric energy use and will it become a "social agency" by providing lower rates to the handicapped, poor and elderly at the expense of other ratepayers.[147]

Freeman understood his problem:

> The distributors were a problem. They loved Red and I wasn't Red. I was talking conservation and they saw the EPA settlement as done with their money. . . . I was taking a neutral position on Tellico and angered everyone in East Tennessee. . . . I was hostile to the breeder reactor, which the distributors were all for. . . . The environmentalists were a weak constituency. I had a strong national constituency but the region is not an environmentally sensitive place.[148]

Note the contrast with David Lilienthal, who used the TVA experiment as a beacon with which to build a national constituency for the authority. Freeman was trying to invoke values that were strong in the nation as a missionary to the valley and to TVA itself. This was a much more difficult task than the one Lilienthal faced.

In 1980 David Freeman, in an interview with the Nashville *Banner*, criticized the distributors, saying they "have lost sight that they are part of something bigger than them. They see their programs as an end in themselves, but it was never intended that way. The power program, it's part of something larger. They don't understand we're interested in the environment. They have forgotten TVA's heritage and the breadth of our responsibilities."[149]

A *Washington Post* story in June 1980 reported that David Freeman had problems communicating with local people in the valley, including the distributors, who were among his constant critics. Part of the fault was said to be Freeman's. A top TVA staff member was quoted as saying, "He has about the patience of a two-year old. . . . He just refuses to get into the good-old-boy backslapping that can really be useful around here in getting things done."

Robert Hemphill, director of energy conservation and rates at TVA, told the reporter that the distributors "hated me" when he first arrived and "tried to get me fired." He added that things were better but that his programs were still not popular with the distributors.[150]

The Freeman board was enlightened, progressive, and understood the need for changes in policy far more than the distributors. But neither Freeman had much sense of the difficult political snares in which they were caught. Jerry Campbell summed it up: "Clement used to tell us that TVA employees had to be reduced. He provided a service in standing against the Freemans. He had a better political sense than they did. They didn't care."[151]

DENOUEMENT

We have finally come to the story of David Freeman's demotion from the chairmanship in 1981. He remained a board member until 1984, and he and Richard Freeman continued to exercise great influence over TVA policy, but that story is better told in the next chapter.

TVA's Washington office had declined in importance after Marguerite Owen retired in 1970. Representative Jamie Whitten of Mississippi, longtime chairman of the House Appropriations Committee, said in 1983 that "Marguerite Owen had the best knowledge of how to deal with Congress of anyone I have ever known."[152] The difficulty with verifying such a proposition is that Owen worked quietly and privately with a few key members, and very little of her work was described in writing. She evidently used the telephone in her conversations with TVA chairmen over the years, but no knowledgeable person who knew her doubts her great importance in guiding the directors on how to work with Congress.

The Freemans had a different idea. They wished to expand the work of the Washington office and make it visible, not only to the members of the valley delegation but to others in Congress as well. They chose Ken Gray to head the office. Gray was a political scientist with longtime service as a congressional staffer. His constant message to TVA people in Knoxville was to "think Washington" when they made decisions. He hired and deployed staff members to take the TVA word throughout Congress but eventually confessed disappointment. David Freeman's view of TVA as a national institution was not shared in Congress. Only the members of the valley delegation cared, and not all of them cared that much.[153]

Gray was critical of the failure of members of the valley delegation to see TVA as a national resource. Instead they took a parochial view. The habitual stance of TVA allies in Congress had been to protect it from its enemies, from 1933 all the way up to Dixon-Yates and Tellico. This meant that protection was favored over oversight of what TVA was actually doing. But as TVA became a more parochial institution, whose appropriations were protected by two or three well-placed members of the appropriations committees, it appears that many members of the valley delegation paid little attention to it. For example, Senator Jim Sasser, who did try to exercise oversight of TVA, reported that since the real threats to TVA had declined, he and other members looked at the authority "out of one eye." It was no longer a subject of constant attention.[154]

Gray felt that the "Wagner experience was at the heart of what went wrong at TVA . . . no American institution should enjoy such autonomy."[155] He was critical of the failure of Congress to ask hard questions about the TVA nuclear program in 1979 when the board asked to have the debt limit doubled. But there were no evident problems at the time, and Congress was not going to dig into an incredibly complex issue unless something was clearly wrong. Besides, the nuclear program seemed to be accepted at home. Why raise questions about it? Certainly the Freemans did not encourage Congress to do this.

The Freeman board relied heavily on Howard Baker as a defender and protector. Although the three board members went to Washington regularly and met with members of the valley delegation, they relied on Baker, Whitten, Tom Bevill of Alabama, and a few others, like Senator John Stennis of Mississippi and Ed Jones of Tennessee, all Democrats except for Baker. However, by mid-1980 public unhappiness with TVA had percolated up to members of Congress from the valley, and the board was increasingly asked to explain itself. In August, Representative Albert Gore Jr., of Tennessee cited a worrisome problem to Nashville's *The Tennessean*: "I am convinced of the need to increase TVA's accountability to the people it serves. . . . I'm not at all satisfied the public currently has enough of a say in TVA's decision-making process."[156]

Representatives of the distributors were quoted in the story as being concerned about the lack of congressional oversight of TVA. One representative of the rural electrical cooperatives was quoted as saying that TVA had begun to evade accountability after the self-financing act. The basic political problem for members of Congress was that the nuclear construction program was driving up rates with the potential benefits far off in the future. Sasser regularly reminded the TVA board of the 1979 General Accounting Office report that TVA was building beyond need or demand. Representative Gore took the lead in establishing a formal caucus of the valley delegation to discuss TVA's problems. An account of a long meeting in Washington of the TVA board with Senator Sasser and fifteen House members revealed the great difficulty of exercising oversight. It was described as a friendly meeting, with all the politicians expressing support for TVA. The topic was whether rate increases could be justified by the nuclear program. Several members wondered aloud about the wisdom of an ambitious construction program that would only pay off much later. The board argued that it was worth it, but they were urged by the politicians to hold down costs and rates as much as they possibly could and to explain to the public why rate increases were necessary. But no one called for any kind of drastic action.[157]

Sasser was a new senator, having been elected in 1976, and he felt perfectly free to criticize TVA publicly in defense of his constituents. He had not been party to the old-fashioned, comfortable arrangements of previous years. He held hearings in December 1980 with himself presiding and David Freeman testifying. In his remarks, Freeman placed a much greater emphasis upon TVA as the power company of the valley than he had ever done before. It appeared that he was trying to mollify the distributors and other critics by reaffirming the familiar litany that supply precedes and evokes demand. He told Sasser that TVA had to choose between estimating high or low future economic growth and that either answer was a self-fulfilling prophecy. Building for low growth would guarantee it, but building for high growth would permit the valley to take advantage of the available energy and grow faster than other, less fortunate, regions. TVA could always sell surplus power to others. But in either case the Tennessee Valley would "be in the catbird seat."[158]

Sasser was not impressed. He told the press that he feared that TVA was "overbuilding" and cited GAO testimony before his subcommittee that TVA should defer four, or even six, nuclear units and hold down expenditures. The GAO official testified that whereas most utilities were planning reserve power margins of 15 to 25 percent, TVA's reserve margin could reach 95 percent by the year 2000 if current economic trends continued and the agency's nuclear construction program were not cut back. Sasser pressed Freeman to say whether the nuclear program had reached a point of no return so that it was better to continue to build and hope for more growth in the future. Freeman replied, "That's not the situation we face . . . if I thought we were building for overcapacity I would defer four more units." Sasser was not satisfied. TVA was not taking account of the "continual cost overruns in nuclear construction."[159]

It did not help matters that the Reagan transition team recommended that two more nuclear reactors be deferred and the TVA Act be amended to expand the board to seven members. Leadership would be provided by a strong president of the board, and the other board members would be vice-presidents in charge of operations divisions. The post of general manager was obsolete and should be abolished. Vice-presidents for finance, power operations, natural resource programs, and procurement were particularly needed. The report was highly critical of the 100 percent increase in industrial rates since 1977 and the 50 percent increases to residential customers in the same period. The transition team criticized

David Freeman, saying that TVA's image had been damaged from top to bottom: "We found across the Valley broad-scale disenchantment and serious morale problems. The Valley residents and industries are concerned because of the rapidly escalating rates of TVA power." The team was critical of TVA for attempting to become a "mini" department of energy; it had taken on too many nonessential projects which had directed attention from the main task, which was responsibility to TVA ratepayers.[160]

David Freeman was quoted in the story as saying that transition-team reports were not important. In a later interview he said that Reagan would surely favor the TVA nuclear program and that, in any event, the new president would take his advice on TVA from Senator Howard Baker rather than from any transition-team report.[161] In an informal discussion with a few Vanderbilt University faculty members in late February 1981, David Freeman attributed his and TVA's unpopularity in the valley to the high rate increases, which had averaged about 15 percent for each of the previous seven years. The rates would have gone up, he said, even if there were no nuclear building program. Energy inflation was a fact of life. TVA was especially unpopular because it had always preached the gospel of cheap power. TVA had been almost a religion in the valley, and people were disillusioned when it acted to hurt them. He also felt that neither the people nor the politicians in the valley were future oriented, telling of one congressman from east Tennessee who told him that "a lot of my constituents are on social security. They won't live to see the new power plants."

Freeman said that the two key politicians for the future of TVA were Governor Lamar Alexander and Senator Howard Baker, both Tennessee Republicans. They wanted to help TVA but also did not want to damage their careers. All politicians, even Albert Gore, Jr., who was most friendly, were fearful of standing up for TVA because it was so unpopular. Freeman believed that the March hearings of the Senate Environment and Public Works Committee, which Baker had scheduled, would provide a safety valve, and Freeman indicated that he would try to slow down the escalation of rates. If he had to, Freeman said, Baker would take some action to persuade the public that something had been done to set TVA on the right course. For example, Baker opposed enlarging the board but might agree to it if political pressures were intense. Finally, Freeman said, he did not wish to meet with the new president but would rely on Baker to handle him.[162] Freeman was more right than he knew about what Baker would do to quiet the controversy.

David Freeman's testimony in the March hearings echoed familiar themes. Inflation was the primary cause of rate increases. The debt from nuclear building was a problem, but the valley needed the power if it was to grow. If TVA planned for low economic growth, things would be worse.[163] Bill Willis testified that TVA had begun a review of its management practices in 1978 and had created an effective corporate planning process that was able to set priorities and direct the organization's activities. There was sufficient strength in the general manager's office to ensure that board policies were clearly articulated to the implementing office. Cost controls over TVA's construction and power programs were much tighter than in the past. There was increased cooperation among the nonpower programs. Finally, Willis reported, there was increased sensitivity at TVA to the positive relationship among economic growth, energy, and conservation of natural resources.[164]

Willis was summing up what the two Freemans regarded as their principal achievements. But no one in the hearings lauded those innovations or even mentioned them. The participants, on both sides of the table, were interested in highly specific issues like rates and cost overruns. Howard Baker did the best he could by suggesting that rate problems could not be solved as long as inflation was so high. Doug McCullough, deputy director for energy and materials of the General Accounting Office, testified that future rate increases were unavoidable but that greater management scrutiny of power operations could reduce the increases. The central problem, he said, was that TVA's power program was not regulated by anyone. He suggested that congressional oversight and appropriations committees play that role and offered the GAO's expertise in assistance.[165]

Senator Sasser alternately criticized and defended TVA in a dialogue with Robert Sansom, head of the Reagan transition team on TVA. Sasser agreed with Sanson that TVA rate increases had been much higher than the rate of inflation. From 1967 to 1981, the inflation rate was 275 percent, but TVA's rate increases measured 580 percent. However, Sasser also argued against opening up the TVA Act for any purpose such as enlarging the board to produce better management, as the transition-team report had suggested. Opening the act to amendment might lead to redefining the service area or the relation of TVA to private utilities.[166] Sansom replied:

> I cannot judge whether that is worth opening up, but I think institutionally TVA was an accident waiting to happen in that you do not have the checks and balances. You do not have the alternative viewpoints. You do not pack the board with business expertise and consumer concerns of outside groups that other organizations have. It's possible to bring these views to bear without expanding the Board, sure. There are other ways to do it.[167]

William D. Towers, president of the Tennessee Valley Public Power Association, illustrated the balancing act that TVA constituencies had to perform. He was critical of TVA but not so much that the legitimacy of its mission would be challenged. He saw no need to enlarge the board or restructure the organization. The solution, he said, was to follow through with the plan to build nine nuclear units. Four such units had already been delayed, and others should not be stopped. Canceling units would drive up rates.[168] So even though the TVPPA was critical of the Freemans and their rate increases, it did not call for fundamental change in the way TVA was managed.

The Senate Environment and Public Works Committee published recommendations along with the hearings and left their implementation to the TVA board, asking for a report on steps taken after six months. TVA was asked to reassess its estimates of future demand and adjust its building plans to match the actual need for power. The committee report recognized how inflation and Nuclear Regulatory Commission regulations had driven up costs but asked TVA to keep costs down as much as possible. Greater time should be allowed for consumers to comment on possible rate increases. But the greatest problem, the committee report said, was TVA's lack of credibility within the valley region because of rate increases. TVA programs were being undermined by this declining credibility. The committee called for a comprehensive audit by a private firm to ensure that TVA programs were well managed and to serve as the basis for appropriate changes.[169] Congress is too far removed from the administration of programs to do more than criticize and exhort. It can ventilate problems and frighten agencies, but it cannot run them. And oversight is especially difficult when the political patrons of an agency in Congress must protect even as they criticize.

On March 18, 1981, just one day after the hearings were completed, Senator Baker said he believed David Freeman to be "perfectly capable of continuing to serve as chairman of TVA."[170] He did not say that Freeman should continue in that position, and indeed, on April 28 Baker asked President Reagan to remove Freeman from the chairmanship and replace him with Charles "Chili" Dean, manager of the Knoxville Utility Board.[171] Baker gave as his reason that Dean was familiar with the problems in the valley and that someone was urgently needed on the board who would represent the viewpoint of both the consumers and the distributors. An Annapolis graduate, Dean was a civil engineer, a director of the American Public Power Association, and a former president of the TVPPA. He was in no sense a national figure like David Freeman. The decision to appoint him suggests that Baker saw TVA as an institution of the valley and nothing more. One observer suggested that Baker wanted the new chairman to be from one of five big distributorships—Memphis, Nashville, Knoxville, Chattanooga, or Huntsville—and that all were Democrats except Dean, who was known to be a Republican.[172]

Senator Sasser felt that Freeman's impression that Baker would protect him was easy to understand because it was Howard Baker's business to make people like him. However, Freeman could be politically naive at times. In fact, Howard Baker saw Freeman as a liberal Democrat, and Baker was nothing of the kind.[173] Sasser remembered the negative messages that the distributors sent to members of Congress about Freeman, but they would not openly oppose him. They were too dependent upon TVA. David Freeman understood what Baker was doing: "He [Baker] needed to get the Republicans off my back. There was a lot of unhappiness with the nuclear program. Howard Baker called me in Chicago and told me he would name Dean. But he asked Dick and me to stay. That was a break for me. Chili took the heat from the Republicans and we were able to get on with shutting 'nukes' down and the conservation program."[174]

Ken Gray did not blame the distributors for Freeman's demotion: "I don't remember that the distributors did Dave in. I looked on it as a natural development. I was not surprised nor was Dave. The appointment of Chili put out all those fires. Howard Baker saw Chili's appointment as important symbolically. To save TVA, you had to quiet the fires. . . . The valley delegation didn't feel strongly. They thought Dave was a competent person who had taken on issues that had to be resolved."[175]

CONCLUSION

The Freemans succeeded in moving TVA in directions that it simply had to go if it were to adapt to the energy crisis and the need for conservation and to the environmental movement and the need to limit pollution. They saw these needs far more clearly than did most TVA constituencies in the valley or Washington. But they did not know how to win the support of those constituencies. They also seemed to have created something of a double bind for themselves as they tried to lead the organization. Their challenges to TVA professionals created more fear than inspiration. In 1980 David Freeman was quoted in a news story as saying that "people in the TVA organization have been the most insulated, isolated of any organization I know of."[176] A few months earlier, a top TVA manager was quoted as having said that "people are afraid to make waves, afraid to let Mr. Freeman know what is going on because they are afraid he will take a closer look at them too."[177]

In 1980 David Freeman acknowledged the difficulty of managing TVA: "The hardest job in the world is to take on an agency that's moving in one direction and turn it in another direction. It's like getting on a battleship. If you give it a hard right rudder, you don't feel any movement at first. It's got too much steam going in the other direction."[178]

In 1992 he admitted that mistakes were made but was not sure that he had any alternative but to press hard for change:

> I didn't appreciate how important it was to get the whole organization behind you. I underestimated the strength of resistance behavior and did not foresee the importance of institutionalizing [change]. This was my first big job. I assumed I would be greeted as a home boy and I wasn't. I did not have a well thought-out game plan of winning over the TVA organization. . . .
>
> Maybe I was too hard on TVA staff but if I had been less aggressive, I might have faded into the woodwork.[179]

In fact, the Freeman board was able to create innovative energy-conservation programs and to establish a policy-planning process that permitted crosscutting issues to be discussed and new initiatives to be taken. The most serious constraints on the Freemans' leadership of TVA came from outside, not inside, the organization. There was no clear mission for economic development programs aside from the power program. The distributors did not like energy-conservation programs and were opposed to TVA as an energy laboratory. Despite David Freeman's invocations of the president's support, Carter's Office of Management and Budget never supported the energy laboratory idea. In the final analysis, the Freemans failed politically because their interests in conservation and innovation did not directly face the problem of rising costs and rates that most people were worried about. Part of that problem was the escalating cost of nuclear construction, which will be considered in full in the next chapter. The Freemans' energy went into programmatic innovation in order to keep TVA alive and vital as a national institution. What they appear not to have fully realized was that most TVA constituents saw TVA as an institution for and of the valley. This was a political failure on the Freemans' part. Less visionary leadership, more attuned to the politics of the valley and of Washington, might have been more realistic. But this was not the Freemans' conception of TVA. They were in the heroic mold of Lilienthal and Wagner.

CHAPTER 9

Denouement

IN 1985 HUGH PARRIS, manager of nuclear power for TVA, shut down the three nuclear reactors at the Browns Ferry plant and the two reactors at the Sequoyah plant for fear that TVA would not be able to meet the safety requirements of the Nuclear Regulatory Commission. The virtues of decentralization for efficient operations, which had been a hallmark since 1932, suddenly appeared to be a major problem for it was apparent that the TVA board did not have managerial control over the implementation of the nuclear program. The safety problems themselves, within the Offices of Power and Engineering Design and Construction, revealed many characteristics of the professional cultures of these divisions—promotion by seniority, limited use of outside experts, belief that TVA professionals could do anything, dislike of oversight from the board in the form of safety and quality assurance inspection. The very characteristics that had been strengths in building dams, and even steam plants, now became severe weaknesses. The nuclear debacle of 1985 was the genie let out of the bottle.

A severe shock may have been required to free TVA leadership from the hubris of the past and invoke fresh thinking and action. In 1986 the board virtually surrendered the management of nuclear matters to Admiral Steven White, and in 1988 President Reagan, on the advice of Senator Howard Baker, demoted Charles Dean from the chairmanship and appointed Marvin Runyon, the president of Nissan-USA, to that position. Runyon stayed until 1992 when he became U.S. postmaster general. His concerted attempts to change the organizational culture of TVA would be another book and are only described in the epilogue to Part II. A Runyon was only possible after the shock of 1985.

DEAN AND THE FREEMANS

Charles Dean was fifty-five years old in 1981. He had been general manager of the Knoxville Utility Board, the valley's third largest utility, since 1971. Howard Baker hoped that Dean's appointment would pacify the distributors, and Dean himself said he was "going to be relying awfully heavily on the distributors for input. They've been in this business for a long time and they know what works and what doesn't."[1]

The two Freemans publicly welcomed Dean to the board and said they foresaw no problems working with him, and he reciprocated. But in fact David Freeman often said informally, "I can count," suggesting that he and Richard Freeman could outvote Dean if necessary. It soon became apparent that Dean's management style was very different from the Freemans'.

In a retrospective account of the difficulties of managing TVA, Dean reported that "I tended to depend upon the system to inform me. I didn't bring in an outside group of my own and that was a mistake. I got it later—a source of unbiased advice on the nuclear program."[2] He was referring to Admiral Steven White as his source of unbiased advice. But Dean learned belatedly what the Freemans had known from the beginning, that it was not easy to get good information out of the TVA bureaucracy.

Dean recognized that he had been chosen by Baker to smooth TVA's relations with the distributors. He remembered that David Freeman did not care what the distributors thought, once telling Dean that TVA and the distributors were "natural enemies."[3] Dean's purpose was clear: "I tried to create some stability out of instability all the time I was there."[4]

Although Dean and the Freemans agreed on most issues, it was the general perception of top TVA staff members that the two Freemans dominated the board from 1981 until 1984 when David Freeman left the board to be replaced by a friend and former law partner of Howard Baker, John Waters, an east Tennessean.[5] Herbert Sanger, TVA's general counsel, did not feel that Dean had been prepared for the chairmanship by his utility experience because distributor managers faced few complex, technological problems.[6] The chief economist, who attended board briefings, recalled that Dean did not press the office managers for information because he seemed unnecessarily intimidated by their expertise. In board briefings, Dean would often precede a question of a staff member with the apology that "someone may ask me this."[7]

William Willis was the peacemaker who sought to smooth over disagreements among board members. He remembered that when he took the general manager's job in 1979, "it was a zero job" because the Freemans ran everything. But by the time David Freeman left in 1984, "we were up to a 75% general manager's job." But after 1984 Willis felt his position was stronger because "board members came to me to persuade other board members to accept their ideas."[8]

William Mason, a TVA lawyer who attended board meetings, remembered that Dean "needed more of a general managership than Dick or Dave wanted." But Willis deferred to the Freemans on this score.[9] The general picture of Dean as an executive that emerges without contradiction is that of one who was not aggressive in probing or questioning, had no agenda of his own, and believed in the TVA management system of a policy board that relied on operating staffs for expertise and advice. Dean's style matched the organizational culture with which the Freeman's were at war.

NUCLEAR DEFERRALS AND CANCELLATIONS

A good bit of the tranquility of the early Dean chairmanship was due to the successful, but controversial, board decisions to reduce the nuclear construction program. This permitted a diminution in rate increases, which was certainly popular. In 1979 the board had deferred the construction of four nuclear reactors because of decreased demand as well as construction costs. In March 1982, two more reactors were deferred, and then in August the board canceled four reactors at previously deferred sites. Finally, in 1984 the board canceled four more reactors, which left TVA with five working reactors at Browns Ferry and Sequoyah and four reactors under construction at the Watts Bar and Bellefonte plants. These decisions took a good deal of political courage on the board's part because about half of TVA's employees worked in nuclear construction and the negative impact on the Tennessee economy was great. This was a complete turnabout from the traditional TVA argument that supply creates its own demand. It was slow in coming. John Stewart acknowledged this in a memo to Willis in 1981: "If TVA, at the time of the Baker hearings, had consciously opted for a low growth strategy aimed at trying to realize its low forecast rather than ensuring that it could meet its high forecast . . . I think it would have been too radical a change for either its managers or employees or for its constituents—congressmen and otherwise—to digest."[10]

These cutback actions were taken on the basis of analyses of staff in the Office of Power that demand for electricity would decrease greatly in the near future. David Freeman knew the handwriting was on the wall:

> I was skeptical of load projections but I didn't tell them [Office of Power] they were wrong. I asked probing questions and gradually their projections reflected the reality that the load wasn't growing. . . . But frankly the political constraints were strong. We had to educate people. . . . We went to the newspapers. The League of Women Voters sponsored forums. Shutting those eight plants down was the toughest economic and political action that we took.[11]

In the spring of 1982, board members traveled around the valley to participate in forums to discuss their options, which were to continue with the nuclear program, at high cost, and sell surplus power to other regions, or to scale back the program and rely on rehabilitated fossil plants. When the time for the first vote came, both Freemans supported cutbacks, saying that their objective was to reduce construction and borrowing costs.[12] Dean dissented but eventually joined his colleagues for the subsequent cancellation votes. He was concerned about angering the distributors and the valley congressional delegation because the nuclear program was popular with them. David Freeman wrote a newspaper editor that the March decision was based on staff studies of the reduced need for power. Several factors were involved. The Department of Energy had cut its requirements for power with which to enrich uranium. The economy would grow more slowly, and less electricity would be needed. The increased cost of building nuclear plants could be diverted to building new, more economical coal-fired units. As a result of the boards decision, TVA would have to increase rates only 10 percent a year for the next several years.[13]

In July, Hugh Parris recommended canceling four of the deferred units in order to save $265 million over the next ten years and $546 million over the next twenty years.[14] The board supported this recommendation unanimously. It could be that once the Freemans did not have to create political cover for TVA, because Dean was chairman, they felt free to vote their convictions. But the evidence of the need for retrenchment was very strong. A May *New York Times* story reported that TVA officials were feeling good about the agency's future: "Several of the higher-ranking officials in the agency say privately that political interferences and overwhelming public sentiment led to such debacles as the Tellico and Columbia dams projects and that construction megalomania, and previous management battles with coal producers, led to widespread over building of nuclear power plants. . . . They say the agency has demonstrated its ability to move in a difficult direction."[15]

David Freeman had no doubt that moving slowly was the only way to move: "Had that decision come earlier I would have been thrown off the board. Not a single public official in the valley supported us at the time."[16] Charles Dean later reported that the Freemans apparently knew by 1980 that some plants would have to be canceled. The Office of Power studies were telling them that. However, they were reluctant to fire large numbers of construction workers for both political and economic reasons. During the spring 1981 Senate committee hearings, Hugh Parris, in Dean's words, "begged Dave not to come on so strong" about how TVA would have surplus power because the need to cancel plants was clear to him.[17] James Robert Durall, who was Parris's deputy, recalled that weaknesses in demand for power began to be apparent by 1977 or 1978. However, the board feared negative economic impacts of cutbacks on areas around the plants. David Freeman also resisted abrupt action to cancel plants because he was thought to be antinuclear. There was also concern about the congressional reaction to any such decision. In 1982 Durall was sent to Washington to talk with Jamie Whitten, the Mississippian who was chairman of the House Appropriations Committee, who asked, "Why don't you just make a load estimate that says you do need the plants?"[18]

David Freeman discussed the political difficulties and opportunities in retrospect in 1989:

> The one issue on which we were unable to do what most people wanted was the rate increases. But, if we had, we would have gone broke. The plain truth of the matter is that our expenses went up and we had to raise the rates to cover them, but we also heard that anger about rate increases and that was the driving force that persuaded us to stop the overbuilding of the plants. It took awhile, but that lesson hammered home. I think that the last five or six years have demonstrated in a very forceful way the power of public input and the fact that this Board is responsive, if you have people on the Board who will listen.[19]

Freeman was sanguine about TVA's future as he left the board in 1984: "TVA is going to look better compared with the private power companies every year for the indefinite future because we have got our overbuilding stopped. We are achieving economies by a very strenuous cost study program under the direction of Hugh Parris, whose management strengths grow with each year."

Freeman predicted that TVA's power system would be "in terrific shape" by the 1990s, with nine large nuclear reactors operating. And he took credit for it:

> [T]his has not all happened through happenstance or automatically. We have worked hard the last five or six years to bring this power system under control and get it in line with realities of the '80's. . . . We are fine tuning the organization to the further strengthening of the nuclear organization. We have new management there that is going to do the job. We are going to really turn the corner on nuclear safety. We are not satisfied with our performance at Brown's Ferry, but we are going to do better. We are taking some tough action in the next few weeks to shake up the organization.

Freeman evoked the Douglas Dam story and a story about chairman Vogel refusing to locate a power plant in Kentucky, in spite of a White House request that he do so, as evidence that "TVA over its history has had a reputation of standing behind the cost effective best answer and not caving in to short term political pressure."[20] Freeman's optimism about the safety of the nuclear program was not justified, but neither he nor anyone else knew it at the time.

NUCLEAR SAFETY

The record reveals a pattern of infractions of nuclear safety from 1979 to 1985 in the construction and operation of TVA's nuclear plants. Top TVA managers attacked these problems vigorously but did not bring them fully under control, primarily because of severe flaws in the organizational culture.

In March 1975, the Browns Ferry plant in Alabama had been temporarily shut down because of a fire caused by two workmen who were trying to plug up air leaks in a cable. During the ensuing crisis, all telephone communications between the plant and the chief of the nuclear generation branch were recorded. The following conversation between J. R. Calhoun, chief of the branch, and H. J. Green, manager of the plant, indicates something of the culture that underlay practical problems:

> GREEN: I got a call that Sullivan, Little and some other NRC [Nuclear Regulatory Commission] inspectors are traveling tonight so all our problems will be over.
> CALHOUN: (Laughs) They will square you away I am sure.
> GREEN: We probably have a violation. We've kept very poor logs.
> CALHOUN: (Laughs) No doubt!"[21]

That brief conversation illustrates a casual approach to external regulation. A. E. Morgan had encouraged engineers to adapt dam designs during construction to meet unanticipated problems. The tradition appears to have stayed alive in TVA. But undocumented discretion, which was very common in the construction of the nuclear plants, clashed with the regulatory demands of the NRC, which wanted every step accounted for in a written record. Inability to tell the difference between a procedural violation and a substantive error could have severe consequences.

In the aftermath, TVA officials said that there were no fatal problems at Browns Ferry.[22] But after the mishap at the Three Mile Island nuclear plant in Pennsylvania in early 1979, David Freeman established new safety procedures at TVA. The purpose, he said, was to provide "a good yardstick that people around the country can hold other utilities up to."[23] At the same time, Freeman refused an invitation for TVA to join a nuclear safety study commission organized by the Edison Electric Institute, the association of privately owned utilities, saying that the study would be regarded as a "defensive measure."[24] TVA was going to lead the nation.

Freeman created a Nuclear Safety Review Staff, housed in the Office of Health and Safety and independent of the Office of Power but with a direct line to the board. The NSRS was to be the watchdog for the board.[25] Freeman understood that "any organization in middle age has problems of bureaucracy and of hardening of the arteries" and commented that "the pressure from the top . . . has been intense," but he didn't know whether "it has really taken effect yet."[26] The same story quoted "sources within the agency" to the effect that serious infractions of safety were "covered up by middle management—withheld even from the directors—for fear of self-incrimination." It was also reported that two in-house studies had revealed that hurried construction of TVA steam plants had resulted in engineering failures for as long as fifteen years after completion of the plants. Freeman accepted the validity of the reports: "We bought at the lowest possible price, we skimped on reliability and maintenance. . . . TVA was pioneering in those days and the units we were building were the most efficient and the largest at the time. It also led to being blind to the amount of air pollution being produced."[27] TVA nuclear experts were quoted as saying that modern technology, with engineering designs tested by computers, would eliminate the construction flaws of the 1950s in nuclear plants. But Freeman had the last word: "I think there has been a tendency in the past for the organization to pretend that it cannot be wrong."[28]

A limited insight into TVA organizational culture is seen in a letter sent to the three board members through Robert Clement by a TVA electrician in October 1979, which complained that criticisms were stifled by pressures for conformity. A few excerpts give the flavor:

> Why, in view of the recent catastrophe [Three Mile Island], does TVA tolerate a policy penalizing any workman who reports anything that might lead to another Three Mile Island OR worse? This I CAN PROVE in two cases by letters written by the electrical Superintendent with his usual attempt at a cover-up by ambiguous wording of these LETTERS. . . . Only when a letter addressed to the NRC was brought to their attention was this condition corrected. It took over a year and a half to correct. Yet I got a LETTER threatening me with discharge and blaming me for the bad workmanship. I CAN PROVE all of this. . . . the general feeling among electricians now is "I wouldn't report anything now, no matter how bad or I would get a letter." This seems to me to be counterproductive to a safe and sane nuclear plant.[29]

Clement also received an undated and unsigned memo from an official in the Office of Health and Safety which complained that the Offices of Power and Engineering had too much influence over workplant safety. A few sentences give the argument:

> To soften Occupational Safety and Health's approach to accident investigations, all reports are now reviewed by the affected organization prior to their release . . . all conflicting opinions must be resolved during the review. I agree with this approach, but it tends to weaken Occupational Health and Safety's

position through compromise. . . . Even though I am the Director of the Office of Health and Safety . . . I must now go through Bonine and Bynon [assistant general managers] on most issues. My views are then secondhanded or third-handed to the general manager. I am not sure what is passed on and what isn't, or in what context it is presented. . . . At present POWER and OMS [Office of Management Services] approve Occupational Health and Safety's staffing and budget for health and safety monitoring, inspection and compliance work; a very convenient way to control the work performed.

As a result, the writer added, the office had too few inspectors and had to limit its work accordingly.[30]

In December 1979, the nuclear power industry, acting through associated organizations, created the Institute of Nuclear Power Operations (INPO) as an information broker among utilities about abnormalities at nuclear plants. David Freeman took no role and publicly questioned whether the step was a defensive reaction by the industry rather than a serious effort. Again, he wanted TVA to be out front.[31] The irony is that INPO played an important role in detecting the flaws in TVA's nuclear organization that led to the 1985 debacle. But in early 1980, David Freeman was confident that TVA was on top of the problem. In March he told a "Today" show audience that the very size of the projected TVA nuclear system permitted TVA to have a comprehensive safety program, in contrast to utilities with one or two nuclear plants.[32]

However, there were warning signs before 1980. The Nuclear Regulatory Commission had uncovered an increasing number of mistakes. The board was sufficiently concerned that it commissioned Theodore Barry and Associates, a Los Angeles consulting firm, to look carefully at the Office of Engineering Design and Construction (OEDC) to assess the efficiency and effectiveness of nuclear construction. The report said many good things about the office, especially the virtue of having its own construction staff. The two principle criticisms were that costs were not taken seriously enough and that there was poor coordination between design and construction engineers. TVA financial planning was said not to be on a level with other utilities because the money came too easily.[33] Another problem was that the vendors of nuclear plants underestimated construction costs and TVA lacked the experience to know that.[34] The report concluded that OEDC did not sufficiently address cost issues because it was not regulated.[35] TVA top management were blamed for using the annual budget primarily to satisfy the Office of Management and Budget rather than as a means of management control, an old complaint that went back to the 1930s.[36] Employees were said to see cost estimates as part of the budget process but not really related to their actual work.[37]

While praising the professional talent in OEDC, the report suggested that talent could also nurture failure:

> OEDC's principal strength is its experienced management, composed of dedicated, technically competent engineers who have pioneered in a number of engineering design and construction areas and in several innovative construction methods. But this strong experience could become a liability manifesting itself in resistance to making needed changes—for example, OEDC's reluctance to test organizational changes, such as stronger central project management to try and improve coordination between its EN, DES and CONST units [engineering, design, and construction]. OEDC is operating in a very dynamic environment where its flexibility and willingness to change will be severely tested.[38]

The report made very clear that the problems were not unique to TVA because it was much harder to build nuclear reactors than fossil plants. TVA's special problem was that there was an absence, within OEDC, of accountability for cost and schedule performance. Top OEDC management could not readily find out who was responsible for large projects because final responsibility was obscured. There should be a single manager instead of the separation and poor cooperation between engineering, design, and construction. There had been no organizational change in this respect for forty-five years, and this was too long because a new generation of problems had developed. It usually took four years to design and build a steam plant. But nuclear plants could take ten years because of the greater complexity of the process in which procurement, internal quality assurance, and external regulation made for a longer process.[39] The main problem was that no one was in charge.[40]

TVA announced that it would implement the report's recommendations. But nothing was done initially to increase accountability at the plant site. Changes did come later, in 1984, to abolish OEDC and move design and construction engineers into a new Office of Nuclear Power. But this was only possible after four nuclear plants were canceled. Construction workers were not needed in such numbers. The board members were concentrating on the scope and costs of the nuclear program, with perhaps less attention to its actual management.

The sparring matches between TVA and the Nuclear Regulatory Commission continued. In early 1981, an NRC report criticized TVA as an "excessively bureaucratic organization" which at times did not take NRC requirements seriously. The language was harsh: "Analysis of noncompliance and deficiencies identified . . . indicates that an underlying cause of their occurrence is an attitude that procedures and specifications are guides rather than requirements." The TVA quality assurance program, in which nuclear plants were inspected by independent staffs to see if

NRC safety standards had been met, were not working, according to the report: "The quality assurance organization does not have the respect of other line and staff organizations within TVA. . . . The quality organization and application of quality assurance appear to be fragmented in that no one individual has responsibility for the overall quality assurance."[41]

In July 1981, H. N. Culver, director of TVA's Nuclear Safety Review Staff, reported the findings of an NRC inspection of the Watts Bar nuclear plant to the effect that "there is inadequate Quality Assurance feedback within the TVA organization. This results in a lack of assurance that the plant is being built to requirements" and "communications between groups was very poor. This was particularly true between the site and Knoxville but also existed between organizations on site."[42] In early 1982, the NRC announced that safety devices designed to shut down the Brown's Ferry plant during emergencies might not work under real accident conditions.[43] A January report from Culver to the general manager and board about a series of violations and fires at Browns Ferry, was not optimistic:

> A large number of the problems that NRC has identified have related to failure to follow procedures. . . . Our records show that TVA performance from July 1 through December 31 of this year has not shown significant improvement . . . there is ample reason to be concerned about the control at both Browns Ferry and Sequoyah Nuclear Plants. We believe that there will not be significant improvement until there is a firm commitment at all levels within the TVA organization. The performance record tends to indicate that actions taken to date have not improved control at the plants to the level desired by either the Office of Power management or the Board.[44]

Hugh Parris wrote two memos in response, saying that his staff had "more extensive data" than the Nuclear Safety Review Staff, the latter of which showed "a great improvement in performance." The problem, Parris said, was that NRC citations rose in response to frequent power outages at Browns Ferry but that the two reactors had just completed continuous "runs" of over a hundred days so that "reliability and safety go hand in hand."[45] Marginal notations by board members on both of Parris's memos show that Culver's fears were allayed in their minds by Parris's report.

In March 1982, TVA delayed full loading of nuclear fuel at the Watts Bar plant because of a defect in the steam-generator system. Loading was delayed for at least a year.[46] During the same period, General Accounting Office report said that TVA had spent nearly five times more than original estimates on nine projects in 1981, including four nuclear plants, for cost overruns of $20 billion, the second worst record of all federal agencies, after the Appalachian Regional Commission.[47]

David Freeman knew that the problems were fundamental and difficult to correct. In a talk at Harvard University in May, he said that cost over-runs were partly due to the need to rebuild the plants while TVA was constructing them because of "legitimate safety concerns" on the part of the NRC. The problem was that the nuclear industry had not developed a good standardized prototype nuclear plant that could be easily built to specification. He was quite honest: "[I]t is time to confess that we went too far too fast in deploying a reactor we knew too little about. It's also fairly clear that we moved too quickly to capture the economies of scale." A lack of standardization of plant design made regulation an uncertain ad hoc process, and a better product simply had to be developed. However, Freeman concluded, TVA would be able to operate its reactors safely.[48]

Hugh Parris felt hard-pressed and complained in May to general manager Willis under the heading "Fish Bowl Syndrome" that "reporting of every operational incident to the press, NRC, and State Agencies lowers self-esteem and creates an atmosphere of uncertainty. Conversely, no recognition is given for consistent quality performance." There were, he said, so many edicts from the NRC that "priorities cannot be established, creating an atmosphere that every job is a crisis." Then he came to the heart of the matter:

> We understand that oversight organizations within TVA have responsibilities that require audits and evaluations of the operating division. However, the oversight organizations and operating personnel must recognize that our respective roles are directed toward a common goal. Mutual respect is essential for achieving this goal. This respect can be improved by reports that assist in improving operations, rather than condemning those operations.[49]

In mid-1983 the NRC reported that there were eighty-two regulation violations in an eighteen-month period at Browns Ferry. The plant was given the worst possible rating in five of ten categories.[50] David Freeman was publicly defensive, denouncing a report critical of Browns Ferry by Ralph Nader's consumer advocacy organization.[51] But it was later announced that the repair bill to correct mishaps at Browns Ferry would be $122 million.[52] In March 1984, the three board members told the Senate Appropriations Subcommittee on energy and water development that the violations at Browns Ferry were technical and had been solved for the most part.[53]

It appears that the board and top nuclear managers were worried, for in April hundreds of nuclear managers and engineers were moved from Chattanooga and Knoxville to the four nuclear plants in an effort to improve safety and avoid violations. In a reorganization, worked out with NRC agreement, each plant would be under the authority of a site director who would have responsibility for the plants' operations. Hugh Parris said that the purpose of the change was to get more control over the plants, adding, "We did feel we were in a mode where it wasn't all that clear who had the decision-making authority—who had control of resources."[54] The feeling did not go away.

THE 1985 NUCLEAR DEBACLE

In March 1985 TVA shut down the Browns Ferry plant for an indefinite period until the board could be satisfied that it could be operated safely. The recommendation to stop the three reactors was made by Hugh Parris. Parris was fearful that TVA would not be able to meet future Nuclear Regulatory Commission safety requirements without a thorough overhauling of the plant. Dean announced that Browns Ferry would be resurrected only in stages. The board was responsive to Parris, Dean said, who felt "that the problems that we've had at Browns Ferry are so complex, that we're going to have to tackle them . . . a little bit at a time."[55]

John Waters, the new board member, was a former chairman of the Appalachian Regional Commission and a friend of Senator Howard Baker. Waters's comment on the Browns Ferry incident was that although the facility was the largest and oldest nuclear plant in the country, the main problem was that its personnel were used to following procedures their own way and could not accept new rules imposed by the NRC. The board was trying to find a way to say to them, "You've got to operate this way or you don't operate." Richard Freeman agreed, saying that the "mind-sets" of Browns Ferry workers were not sensitive to the problems of nuclear power as the public saw them.[56] Jim Coffey, the Browns Ferry site director and former head of the division of nuclear power, was quoted as saying that TVA should stop complaining about NRC inspectors and face up to the real problems, for which there was no excuse.[57] In July the NRC southeastern regional administrator, Dr. J. Nelson Grace, said that TVA lacked a "strong line organization" and relied on outmoded, ineffective, and expensive management techniques. He drew a harsh conclusion: "In my opinion if TVA cannot fix the problem they should not be operating nuclear plants."[58]

Charles Dean said that there was nothing in the NRC critique with which he disagreed. In fact, the NRC could help TVA persuade Congress that it needed to be able to pay high salaries to key nuclear staff members because TVA had lost several good people to higher-paying utilities. Congress had rebuffed every effort by the TVA board to pay higher salaries.[59] Still, Dean seemed mystified by the problem: "How'd we get in this kind of shape? I'm not sure. The loss of key people, and all this shifting around of people, is not really conducive to continuity—to running a good ship."[60]

The board had named Hugh Parris as director of a new Office of Nuclear Power in 1984, and he appeared to have the board's confidence. But in August, Parris made a second decision, to shut down Sequoyah, because an independent review had pointed to safety problems that were not easily correctable. NRC officials supported the decision but said that they had not required it.[61] Shortly thereafter, 1600 construction workers at Watts Bar were laid off after an NRC inspection discovered inaccurate and inadequate welder certification records.[62] A September news analysis asked how TVA had managed to put $14 billion into a grandiose scheme to build seventeen nuclear reactors and wind up with none in operation at a cost to ratepayers of $1 million a day? Why was a once supposedly model program piling up four times the violations of the average nuclear plant in the nation? The answers, as gleaned from NRC hearings, according to the writer, were: poor employee attitudes, inattention to safety concerns and paperwork, a dedication to "mediocrity," an arrogant belief that the TVA way was the right way, and a failure of management and leadership. Chairman Dean was singled out by an NRC official who said that Dean had a policy of not intervening in management questions unless a problem was reported to him. Congressional sources were quoted as saying that Dean leaned heavily on Richard Freeman. Dean defended the board's methods, saying that two lawyers and one engineer were not qualified to say how a nuclear plant should be run.[63]

In September the Nuclear Regulatory Commission sent a detailed report about TVA's problems to the TVA board. The covering letter to Dean said outright that TVA "has demonstrated ineffective management of its nuclear program" and that the "underlying causes" represented "significant programmatic and management deficiencies."[64] The language of the enclosed report spoke for itself:

> The SALP [Systematic Assessment of Licensee Performance] Board's review of the overall performance concluded that there were fundamental, Corporate problems that are continually not acted upon and therefore uncorrected. These are believed to be the major factor on the marginal performance of the utility. The Board concluded that the root cause of the lack of improvement is the lack of effective management both at the Corporate and site levels. . . .
>
> There has been a continued lack of Corporate attention to the control of operating activities. This is evidenced by the decline and continued low SALP ratings in the functional area of maintenance at both operating sites, and of the numerous, repeated violations at the construction sites which indicates untimely or ineffective corrective actions. The Board further noted that there is a lack of feedback of operating experience to each site of those events that occur at both TVA and other nuclear industry sites. . . .
>
> The perception of the SALP Board is that the TVA organization is comprised of four separate companies, with little central direction. This perception results

from the documented facts that a lesson learned at one facility is not timely related to other facilities. . . .

There is an apparent lack of attention and control by Corporate headquarters of those activities that support both the construction and operating sites. . . . The Board also believed that the headquarters lacks the leadership essential to providing timely and controlled technical support by its centrally, specialized support staff. . . .

The above examples indicated a management failure to determine the root cause of these problems and take meaningful corrective action to prevent recurrence. TVA management recently established specific procedures to promptly resolve problems identified during QA [quality assurance] audits. Although some progress has been achieved for problem resolution between the Division of Quality Assurance and other TVA organizational elements, significant issues have remained unresolved. Such problems have persisted even though TVA has reorganized several times and has implemented a regulatory improvement program in order to provide more prompt and meaningful corrective action on previously identified problems. . . .

TVA senior managers have been directly involved in new initiatives to assure that line organizations understand their responsibility to achieving quality. These efforts are beginning to show improvement, but improvement at the working level has been painfully slow. . . .

TVA employees have expressed fear of reprisals from their management if they raised concerns.[65]

In October, Senators Sasser and Gore proposed a three-point program for the improvement of TVA: (1) hire a nuclear "czar" from outside TVA to advise the board; (2) appoint an inspector general to study internal mishaps and report directly to the board; and (3) ask the General Accounting Office to watch the two new positions to make sure they were independent of the TVA bureaucracy.[66]

In the same month, Dean was quoted as saying that he was "shocked" to learn that TVA workers had been concerned about safety problems in the nuclear plants. Senator Sasser said about the same time that TVA's middle managers had failed to tell the board about such concerns.[67] In due course, the board created an inspector general, responsible to the board with investigatory powers.[68] Sasser asked the GAO to keep a close watch on the new inspector general to make sure he was independent.

THE DYNAMICS OF ORGANIZATIONAL FAILURE:
QUALITY ASSURANCE AND SAFETY

TVA managers had never been comfortable with analysis of their work by a central staff or independent experts. Authority for evaluation had always been in the hands of those to be evaluated. The agriculture people had no interest in economic analysis. Engineers had no use for environmental analysts. Quality assurance for nuclear safety was no different. Quality assurance staff were seen as "whistle-blowers" to be harassed and penalized if they blew their whistles. Sandra Seeley, a Department of Labor investigator who had worked on several whistle-blower cases, drew on her experience as a graduate student in European history to describe TVA: "I was lying in bed one night and I thought of Hannah Arendt's *Origins of Totalitarianism*. This described TVA. The system was controlling the managers, the lawyers, and the board. They were reflecting the organizational system. Nuclear power is more than people can cope with."[69]

The Nuclear Safety Review Staff's assignment was to inspect construction and operations to ensure that TVA complied with safety standards.[70] There were also quality assurance units within the Office of Engineering Design and Construction and the Office of Power which reported to division heads and lacked a direct line to the board. The NSRS staff was to work with them, but there was uneasiness at board level about whether the quality assurance units could cope with the pressure on them from line operations to be good soldiers. Certainly the office heads were opposed to completely independent quality assurance activities, as George Kimmons wrote Bill Willis in 1980:

> Our position is that such an independent organization dilutes responsibilities and increases organizational interfaces which result in inefficiencies and ineffectiveness. . . . Delegation of responsibility to the responsible division with policy overview by each office gives more flexibility to tailor a program to needs and objectives and places responsibility and accountability for quality where it belongs. . . . Quality must be the responsibility of organizations and persons doing the work. Control of quality by means of checking, reviewing, inspecting, and testing must have independence, but it should not be so far removed that it loses intimate knowledge of the diverse operations and that it prevents rapid correction of deficient work. . . . We feel that each division should be responsible for its own quality assurance programs, with the Office providing necessary overall policy guidance and surveillance to ensure an integrated and effective program.[71]

Kimmons's memo was stimulated by a question from board member Robert Clement as to whether all TVA quality assurance work should be put in one independent division. And Clement's question was evidently spurred by a conversation with a TVA employee who gave him a paper written in 1978 by a quality assurance engineer.[72] The 1978 paper was critical of the decentralized structure of quality assurance and cited a 1977 study by a management team that reported lack of coordination among separate quality assurance units and the weakness of such units in relation to line operators. The 1977 report was quoted as saying that "there is overwhelming and unrelenting pressure in all divisions to meet schedule requirements. This pressure often results in confrontations between line requirements and quality assurance requirements. . . . Within the TVA organization the line traditionally has a powerful operating base, hence a tendency for line decisions to overweigh quality decisions."[73]

The 1977 paper had proposed that the separate QA units be organized into a division reporting to the general manager. This was important, the report asserted, because "it would mean that for the first time he [the general manager] would have unbiased information regarding quality problems within the agency."[74]

A report from Culver to Willis in 1981 suggested that little had changed since 1977. The staff study on which the report was based described quality assurance work as subordinate to line management. For example, the QA staff within each nuclear plant reported to the plant superintendent so that QA work came very close to being a line function and therefore less relevant for external audiences. By the same token, QA units at the management level in both the Office of Engineering Design and Construction and the Office of Power reported to operating managers who were responsible for relations with the Nuclear Regulatory Commission.[75] The study found little communication between plant construction sites about generic safety problems and concluded that there was not a clear-cut distinction between the responsibilities and functions of quality assurance and line managers in either office.[76] This was just the way line managers wanted it, not as a way to downgrade safety but, in the TVA tradition, to make the line responsible for all work.

The Nuclear Safety Review Staff's study reported that of the thirty-two utilities it had surveyed, twenty-two had put QA activities under one QA manager. These comparisons suggest that the traditional TVA organization norm, in which initiatives for program development and evaluation resided in the line, was inimical to the exercise of independent staff analysis of any kind, including nuclear safety. The NSRS report discussed the possibility of pulling all of TVA's QA activities into one central organization headed by a QA manager: "The primary driving force for this consideration has been the excessive violation of NRC requirements at TVA nuclear plants under construction and in operation, the concerns by NRC that there is no single manager within TVA that is responsible for QA at the nuclear plants, and the overriding concern that TVA's QA program is not getting any better."[77] The report concluded that QA activities had developed in a haphazard way in TVA without much thought, so that "the lack of overall TVA planning resulted in organizations that served the purpose of individual organizational units rather than TVA. In addition, Quality Assurance also appears to represent a repository for individuals that did not fit into other organizational units."[78] This was euphemistic language for mediocrity.

The only way to convince the NRC to inspect less, Culver told Willis, was to convince them that quality assurance was alive and well within the individual plants. The failures were due to "line deficiencies," but QA groups had been unable "to identify the root problems or to bring about sufficient corrective action to effect and maintain a viable program."[79] There was said to be a belief in the organization that top TVA management regarded quality assurance as a defensive device against the NRC and had not given serious support to grounding QA functions in the organizational culture.[80] Certainly this was the way line staffs had seen John Stewart's planning staff, as useful as a defense against the Office of Management and Budget but without leverage over their own work.

Despite this analysis and the seemingly obvious conclusion that quality assurance should be organized independently of the line, Culver's report to Willis rejected the idea on the grounds that a QA manager for all of TVA would not be able to change habits but would simply be in a state of continuous war with the bureaucracy, at all levels.[81] The solution was for line managers to become more responsive to quality assurance. Centralization and consolidation of quality assurance would not work unless line managers changed their habits. Top management was to further that goal by pressing hard for respect for quality assurance in the line.[82] The effectiveness of staff analysis within TVA was once more dependent upon the willingness of managers to cooperate.

Later in 1981, Culver wrote a memo to Willis describing a meeting TVA people had had with NRC officials in Atlanta. The NRC staff had said that they did not believe that TVA had sufficiently centralized quality assurance and that the number of inspections would therefore be increased. David Freeman wrote on his copy of the memo: "We need an early meeting on this subject no later than early January. Until we settle the QA organizational issue we can't expect maximum progress."[83]

As a result of these concerns, the board created a QA staff in the general manager's office. It was headed by George Dilworth, who as an assistant general manager had written a paper advocating the change.[84] Dilworth's paper was a logical extension of the earlier Nuclear Safety Review Staff report and the NRC criticisms of TVA. He argued that "assuring" functions should be independent of "performing" functions. The former should be carried out by a new quality QA unit in the general manager's office. Quality assurance units in the Office of Engineering Design and Construction and the Office of Power should report directly to the new unit in the general manager's office. The NSRS would be a troubleshooting staff that would work on specific problems. The QA staff would monitor overall compliance with safety requirements.

Dilworth and his staff spent much of their time in wrangles with plant managers who did not want a former OEDC engineer looking over their shoulders. Dilworth remembered what one power official, who oversaw all modifications of nuclear plants, told his staff: "Look at the manuals of NRC procedures here. But you do what I tell you." This particular official told Dilworth's deputy that "it's my purpose that you should fail."[85] In 1984, on George Kimmons's retirement, OEDC was abolished and its engineers were moved to the new Office of Nuclear Power, headed by Hugh Parris. The board decided that it made sense to put QA responsibility under Parris, so again quality assurance was denied full independence.

A former OEDC electrical engineer who could never establish a working relationship with power officials was Dan De Ford, the most prominent whistle-blower. De Ford was a combative person whose great-grandfather had died at the Alamo and whose mother had worked in terrible conditions in a hosiery mill. He was a fighter, and when TVA tried to push him aside, he fought back.[86] He was highly critical of TVA organizational culture, in both the Office of Engineering Design and Construction and the Office of Power. No one ever assessed anyone else's work. The organization was a "toothpick society," a house of sticks. If one stick collapsed, the whole house would fall. But group pressures kept everyone in line. TVA managers were nice people individually, but it had been his experience that they would collectively lie about their work with ease. The culture was based on the search for security. The pay was modest, but job security was high and less adventurous people were therefore attracted to TVA. Lies were the result of a subtle system of mutual protection. David Freeman, who symbolized change, was a threat to everyone.

De Ford, like Dilworth, knew that the Office of Power staffs were hostile to him because he had an Office of Engineering Design and Construction background. But he was equally critical of OEDC. His open conflict with TVA developed in 1980 when he reported serious infractions about Sequoyah to the NRC after his internal reports drew no response. One NRC staff member, who had once worked for Kimmons at TVA, identified De Ford as the "whistle-blower" to TVA and, after De Ford was removed from his job and given no new duties, he sued TVA and won his case finally in 1985 in the Sixth Circuit Court of Appeals. He returned to work at TVA to do electric communications and engineering oversight work but did not receive very good assignments.

De Ford readily admitted that many of the infractions that disturbed the NRC were due to a failure to follow prescribed procedures and were not necessarily unsafe. This was the predominant view in TVA. However, in De Ford's view, nuclear reactors were so complex that slipshod procedures could make it difficult to later correct a potential problem if the documentation was weak. He was also highly critical of TVA lawyers, whom he saw simply as hired guns. But eventually the lawyers woke up. Herbert Sanger, who was the general counsel for many years, told how "the Freeman board believed in people reporting on problems. Some of that message did not go down throughout the organization. I got conned on it myself. Our engineers lied to me about the [De Ford] case. We lost it and we should have lost it. I called an engineer after the decision and told him how the court saw the facts and asked him to tell me the facts. He admitted it wasn't the whole story. The engineers got his ass."[87]

William Mason, a deputy to Sanger who worked on most of the whistle-blower cases, remembered that he and his colleagues were hostile to the whistle-blowers at first but that as they lost case after case, their outlook changed. Lawyers don't like to lose cases, and the adverse publicity was hurting them and TVA. After the loss of the De Ford case in 1985, TVA lawyers began to investigate the merits of complaints themselves and began to understand that there were serious management problems. There was too wide a span of control and weak oversight and control in both the Office of Engineering Design and Construction and the Office of Power on safety questions. Mason came to believe that the board was managing the externals of safety, such as scrutinizing every communication that went to the NRC, but had little control over the bureaucracy. He was not surprised, for he found hostility, even to TVA lawyers, in the line organizations. They were seen as "outsiders." Mason read Sandra Seeley's report on the TVA organization and came to believe that her description of TVA organizational culture was accurate, even though she was on the opposite side of him in several cases.[88]

Seeley's understanding of TVA was influenced by De Ford and the other whistle-blower cases on which she worked. She did not feel that the Nuclear Safety Review Staff had been effective, because they tried to minimize their findings in order to keep some influence with line managers with whom they had terrible fights. She believed that the board saw the NSRS as a means of protection from the NRC more than as a management tool. She was critical of Willis because he hewed to the traditional TVA thesis that responsibility for evaluation should be in the line rather than in any staff. Yet she found no respect for Nuclear Regulatory Commission requirements among either OEDC or OP engineers and operators.[89] The central problem, in her eyes, was that the QA units in the two Offices had no authority figure to protect them from line managers. The NSRS had no staff in the offices and even had difficulty getting into plants to make inspections.

John Bynon, a knowledgeable TVA veteran and longtime deputy director of personnel, was asked by Willis in 1981 to assess TVA's labor relations. He visited many plants, talking with workers and managers and, in the process learned a great deal about nuclear construction and operations. The problems of quality assurance were apparent to him: "If the main line of growth is production that is where the careers are. There was no reward for looking at production [quality assurance]. The less able people got pushed into that group. . . . The production managers would not let the watchers watch. After a while the watchers felt unloved and resolved to show the bastards how important they were."[90]

One project manager made Bynon pledge to tell Willis about the QA problems, and even though it was not Bynon's assignment, he did so and reported Willis's response: "Willis said [in 1981] we turned the corner about six months ago. A strong statement by the GM [general manager] might have resolved a lot of these concerns. You leave with the impression that they don't want to hear."[91]

Unresolved issues of quality assurance were compounded by the long-standing rivalry between the Office of Engineering Design and Construction and the Office of Power. The OEDC construction engineers had always been the top dogs in TVA, and the chief engineer had always been the most prestigious professional. These engineers symbolized TVA as a building organization. The engineer on site, who creates an architectural shape out of raw matter, is a romantic figure, whether the product be dams, steam plants, or nuclear reactors. Bynon described the conflict between the OEDC and OP engineers: "The engineering [OEDC] mentality said 'We know best. They are our plants. We'll call you to operate them under our surveillance.' The operators said, 'You give us plants we can't operate and we have to modify them.' They were all engineers. Two sets of engineers developed."[92] OP developed its own engineering capability in part because OEDC resources were overextended on new nuclear-plant construction and could not adequately support operating plants. But when the board began to cut back the nuclear construction endeavor, the tension between the two offices became intense because by that time OP had a competing organization to OEDC.

Larry Edwards, who had been an OEDC engineer and had moved to the planning and budget staff in 1980, had an overview of the problem:

[T]he very qualities that made OEDC successful led to its downfall in the nuclear era. Dams and steam plants were built in a hurry. "I am building it with your drawings or mine, if you are not ready." We used to brag that we would begin to dig the power house site before we saw the design plan of where it would go. A. E. Morgan's encouraging of engineers to make changes at the dam site was part of that culture and it worked for dams and steam plants.

Nuclear plants were seen as the same kind of job. We saw no need for documentation. We assumed, from past performance, that we knew how to build these things. . . . But in nuclear plants people start asking, "who welded that pipe and was it certified?" New rules built up. The best organization of can-do engineers was in collision with the NRC. This old mind set that led to success led to all the problems we have had. The rivalry between OEDC and OP compounded the situation. The power plant operators were accustomed to altering plans, just as the engineers had. The organizational issues of who would do what became very confusing. These issues were not understood at the top at the time it was happening. I cannot tell you why it was not perceived.[93]

Bill Willis understood this problem, and that was one reason he wished to place all nuclear construction under Hugh Parris in 1984. Even though Willis himself was a product of OEDC, he believed that it was essential to stop the TVA "obsession with building."[94]

Both Dilworth and De Ford believed that the tensions between OEDC and OP engineers were the root cause of the nuclear safety problem. And this became worse after OEDC was folded into OP, as De Ford described: "The merger . . . accelerated the downfall of TVA. They started dismantling engineering because they didn't want them in control again. Hugh Parris was bent on wiping OEDC out. . . . If we had had organizational leadership in TVA in 1984 that could have controlled Parris's desire to wipe out OEDC, he could have been a good manager. He was not inclined to shoot the messenger."[95]

De Ford thought that the OP owner-operator principle, in which the superintendent of a nuclear plant oversaw all work in that plant, was a mistake because it prevented comparison of problems across plants. TVA was in a catch-22 situation. The owner-operator concept was intended to focus responsibility, as suggested by the 1978 Barry and Associates report. But such decentralization contributed to the weak position of overall quality assurance within the organization. There appears to have been plenty of fault to go around, and most important, the board had an imperfect grasp of the organizational turmoil beneath them. Willis described the growing realization that fundamental change was required: "We knew in 1983–84 that we had to make a major change in the organization—it was too chopped up—and put nuclear power in one group. The end of the building period required a stronger role in the organization for operation and maintenance . . . with Power in the lead."[96]

However, the board had to first decide to reduce the size of the nuclear plan before it could boldly address the question of what to do with the surplus of construction engineers and workers. But Willis also realized that merging OEDC and OP was not easy. It eventually became apparent to the board that the top fifteen nuclear engineers in the new Office of

Nuclear Power were not up to speed in their depth and experience. Yet efforts to pay higher salaries to such people had been stopped by Congress, including Senator Sasser. As a result, according to Willis, "In the summer and fall of 1985 the thing started coming apart. We knew we had to totally stop and totally rebuild the nuclear organization. We could not survive otherwise. We knew two years in advance that we were in deep trouble but we were too undermanned to do anything. We looked for the toughest, hardheaded s.o.b. we could find and decided to bring in Steve White. We should have done it a year earlier."[97]

All four directors—the two Freemans, Dean, and Waters—agreed in retrospect that the central problem was that TVA did not have enough good nuclear engineers and managers. Congress had resisted TVA efforts to pay higher salaries to such experts in order to attract and keep good people for the nuclear program. Both Admiral Steven White and Marvin Runyon were later able to hire high-priced talent, with congressional acquiescence, but only because it seemed the only way to get the reactors running again. Congressional views were always behind events, and oversight was superficial. David Freeman had put his principal energies into cutting back, rather than managing, the nuclear program, but he admitted that management problems were severe: "The job of management was cutting the programs down to size. There is no good in perfect management if we are wasting our money. The first job is to be working on getting the right agenda. But we did not cure the management problem, which was largely incurable. You can't micromanage." Then, on reflection, he added, "Maybe I was too hard on TVA staff but if I had been less aggressive, I might have faded into the woodwork." The fundamental problem, according to Freeman, was that TVA should not have tried to build so many reactors. "We began to build plants before the design was completed."[98]

John Waters reported the views of many TVA managers about Freeman's management style: "Dave was said to be a terrible manager. TVA would have board-staff conferences of fifty or sixty people. Willis would open the meeting and introduce x, y and z. Freeman would then tear people to pieces."[99] John Bynon felt that both Freemans had a defective management style: "They were so aggressive and critical of TVA professionals in board-staff meetings that the TVA tradition in which senior persons defended their recommendations to the board was killed."[100]

However, it was not apparent that the more passive management style practiced by both Dean and Waters was any more effective in eliciting truth telling by TVA managers. The problems of organizational culture were simply too complex for any management style to be effective. Sandra Seeley's analysis of the TVA nuclear bureaucracy is a description of an organization in turmoil. The original idea had been to create an agency that would combine the accountability of government with the efficiency of a business corporation. Seeley saw it differently: the worst features of government and business were combined. Hiring was through a tight network of family connections, and money was spent freely without regard to cost.[101] She reported that Nuclear Regulatory Commission officials in Atlanta thought that the board and general manager were "irrelevant" to TVA's nuclear failures. In the absence of control from above, the separate divisions of the organization engaged in a rivalry of "fiefdoms."[102] She painted a sharp picture of TVA management:

> Top quality managers, vital to help adapt a cumbersome and unresponsive giant to the demands of a nuclear program, did not always stay, or reach the top in the TVA system. In the years prior to nuclear power, the top ranks were filled by people from all over the world. Over an extended period, however, the regional influence began to be felt as TVA became inbred, failing to seek or attract top managers from outside. The government pay cap may also have been a hindrance. The promotion system at TVA caused problems for some top quality people. Whereas the early TVA had a strong cadre of professionalism, many of the most talented TVAers accomplished their goals and left or retired. TVA had become a very closed agency. Jobs (including many technical positions) at the M-4 level and above were not advertised, and, as a consequence, the "good ol' boy" system became entrenched at TVA. Top managers were not brought in; they were brought up, in the image of the boss.[103]

The watchwords for success were "don't rock the boat" and "a team player," which affected the information the board received. Seeley also felt that TVA had so insulated itself that it could not tell what was happening within the nuclear industry.[104] A sample of such insulation can be seen in a note that David Freeman wrote on his copy of a letter that Dean had sent to the executive vice-president of the Atomic Industrial Forum, an association of the nuclear utility industry. Dean responded positively to a request to serve on a study committee. Richard Freeman had asked that the letter be changed to indicate that Dean was acting for himself, not the board. David Freeman added: "I agree with Dick's comments. TVA ideas on how to revitalize the nuclear system can be presented much more effectively in TVA. I can't object to your personal participation, but TVA needs to continue to keep its identity on policy issues, a policy that has been useful."[105]

Freeman wished TVA to have an independent policy stance because he wanted it to be a leader in environmentalism and energy conservation. But that separateness may also have walled the organization off from developments in the nuclear industry. According to Seeley, many TVA employees were greatly concerned about nuclear safety and were frustrated because the board was, to some extent, kept in the dark by nuclear power managers. Neither the personnel system nor the Office of the General Counsel were seen by employees as conduits for this concern because they appeared to represent top management. Seeley also reported that the NRC, for all its criticism of TVA, was respectful of the autonomy Congress had given TVA and was patient—until the nuclear collapse of 1985. The board was thus, according to Seeley, not fully aware of the seriousness of the situation until 1985.[106]

Certainly Dean and Waters felt themselves to be in a vacuum. They came to realize that program analysts in the general manager's office had not been able to penetrate either the Office of Engineering Design and Construction or the Office of Power and decided belatedly that the board should have had its own nuclear experts.[107] Dean did not realize how serious the problems were until 1985. He stated that he did not recall that either the Nuclear Regulatory Commission or the Institute of Nuclear Power Operations had given the board a strong negative report on TVA before 1985. Nor did the Office of Management and Budget or the congressional oversight committees say a word about nuclear issues until 1985.[108] It was ironic that Waters had to visit INPO in Atlanta, after the TVA units were shut down, in order to learn that the big utilities were critical of TVA because its failures were hurting the industry.[109] Richard Freeman admitted that the board had failed to get control of nuclear operations. He did not think TVA engineers were qualified to build nuclear plants and felt that George Kimmons should have been moved aside.[110] However, John Stewart remembered that no one thought the situation was as bad as it turned out to be. The real villain, Stewart thought, was "the TVA culture" in which the board relied on division and office heads, "who let them down."[111] These are all impressionist comments after the fact of the 1985 failures, but they represent honest efforts of those involved to understand the problem. Bill Willis summed it all up: "The TVA (decentralized) model is good if you know your mission. You turn folks loose and you get strong implementation. But you need strong centralization in periods of transition."[112]

CONGRESSIONAL OVERSIGHT

Whereas congressional committees exercised considerable oversight of TVA from 1981 to 1985, little attention was given to the management of the nuclear program. Ken Gray, head of TVA's Washington office, was very critical of Congress: "I see TVA as a great failure of American public administration because of the inability to make the nuclear plants work as a yardstick. The nonpower programs are hard to justify. But the mistakes of the Wagner, and even Freeman, years was the failure to critically assess the nuclear building program. OMB [Office of Management and

Budget] and Congress were very much at fault for permitting TVA to get in such trouble."[113]

Gray thought that the most serious lapse was the failure of either the Office of Management and Budget or Congress to do a thorough investigation in 1979 when the TVA board asked for a doubling of the debt limit from $15 to $30 billion in order to complete the massive nuclear program. Senator Jim Sasser agreed. But he also remembered that the nuclear programs were popular in Congress. It was highly unlikely, in his judgment, that the Freemans could have cut back the nuclear construction program any sooner than they did, because of its popularity.[114]

This need for oversight was certainly not the predominant view within TVA. In early 1982 David Freeman wrote an internal memo in response to a General Accounting Office report on the oversight of TVA: "The most dangerous suggestion in the report is that OMB review our power budget. Let's not give that any attention, but I do want to see a legal opinion confirming that OMB has no right to change our power budget."[115]

About the same time, Senator Sasser said at a hearing in Memphis that Congress could not effectively supervise the bond ceiling. He said that he "vividly" remembered David Freeman telling him that if TVA was not allowed to build all the nuclear plants initially scheduled that "the lights would go out in the Valley."[116] David Freeman acknowledged this reality in a retrospective analysis: "When the region is in love with nuclear power, senators will not investigate nuclear issues. There will never be oversight on nuclear matters. The valley delegation agreed to double the debt [in 1979]. I had no idea we would shut down eight reactors."[117]

Periodic reports from Ken Gray to Bill Willis give a good general picture of the kind of congressional oversight that actually occurred. Most of it was simply inquiry by members about TVA programs in their districts or states. In a memo describing congressional activities regarding TVA for 1981, Gray described a large number of contacts. TVA officials met with both members and staff of the Senate and House Appropriations subcommittees and the Senate Environment and Public Works Committee. There were two meetings with the valley delegation. Committee staff members visited the valley. Dean's confirmation hearing and hearings on TVA pay policies provided opportunities for discussion of general issues. Ninety-six members of Congress wrote TVA with questions, all of which were answered. The letters covered 1,173 subjects, the largest items being personnel policies and natural-resource questions, with 373 and 147 entries respectively. Nuclear construction received 27 queries and was far outdistanced by 88 questions about power rates. Board members called on most of the thirty-seven members of the valley delegation at least once a year and saw the leaders far more often. TVA's Washington office was in continual communication with congressional offices.[118] There was plenty of opportunity for oversight in a procedural sense. Gray's reports for 1984 and 1985 reveal that members of the valley delegation put their energies into protecting TVA nonpower programs from the Reagan administration. TVA relied on thirteen or fourteen members to protect its appropriated budgets. An even smaller number sat on the pertinent appropriations subcommittees: Tom Bevill, Jamie Whitten, and Bill Boner, the Nashville congressman, in the House, and Sasser, Stennis, and Huddleston, of Kentucky, in the Senate.[119] These few members and their staffs were described by Gray as the people "who largely determine Congress's decisions about TVA appropriations or legislation attached to appropriations bills." The Public Works and Government Operations committees in both houses, which had primary jurisdiction for oversight and legislation regarding TVA, were not active. Writing in 1984, Gray reported: "The recent decline in conflict over TVA in the Valley, the departure from the House Committee of senior Valley members, the TVA's reduced need for additional borrowing authority have virtually eliminated for now the Houses's active interest in TVA."[120]

Gray warned that Senator Baker's impending retirement would harm TVA, that the Senate Appropriations Committee staff was unfriendly, and that OMB was still hostile. However, "valley grass roots support, and thus member support, continues to increase because of low rate increases, perceived good management of non-power programs, manager's constituency building work and the continued good feeling from the 50th anniversary."[121] Congressional criticism of TVA only developed after the 1985 nuclear debacle, and then it was loud and angry. Those failures had not caused a stir in Washington outside the valley delegation but gave members of the delegation a license to shout at TVA after the barn door was open and the horse gone. Gray described one meeting: "Representative [Ronnie] Flippo (D-Alabama) held on Sept. 19 a caucus hearing to criticize in public the Board [members] and staff who attended to explain their handling of TVA's nuclear program." Those members who attended were "extremely critical" due to "cumulate concerns none of which was a major event in 1984: the FY'86 rate increase, nuclear plant closings, fear of being held responsible for costs which might result from Board decisions to close the operating nuclear units, escalating NRC criticism of TVA's nuclear program, the Watts Bar employee complaints, Mr. Flippo's wish to stop the Board's efforts to secure exemption from the pay cap for top nuclear managers."[122]

Within a month, Flippo and fourteen cosponsors had held a press conference to announce the introduction of a bill to give TVA an Inspector General. Senators Sasser and Gore also held a press conference, with two TVA board members present, at which they called for an inspector general and asked that the TVA board immediately appoint a "nuclear czar."[123] All of this was after the fact. However, if the board itself did not fully realize that TVA had deep organizational problems with its nuclear program, how could members of Congress, who were so far from the valley, have been expected to learn about such problems?

ADMIRAL STEVEN WHITE: THE NUCLEAR CZAR

Steven White, a veteran of Admiral Hyman Rickover's nuclear navy, was hired by the board in early 1986 to head the Office of Nuclear Power on a temporary basis to get TVA right with the Nuclear Regulatory Commission. It was assumed that White's appointment was temporary and that his assignment was to get Browns Ferry and Sequoyah back into operation. The considerable delegation of authority to White caused Richard Freeman to resign abruptly from the board rather than sign the contract of agreement between the board and White. Freeman never gave a reason for his resignation, either privately or publicly, but those close to the situation believed him to be uncomfortable with a potential conflict-of-interest situation. White was to be paid through the consulting firm of Stone and Webster, for whom he worked, and at the same time was to use engineers from that firm for TVA work.[124] Another possible explanation is that Richard Freeman realized that he had lost control of the board. One TVA lawyer who helped negotiate the contract with White remembered Freeman saying, "After Dave left I would stay only as long as I had voting control. Today I've lost control of the board and I am gone."[125] Observers also agree that after David Freeman left, Richard Freeman was a great force on the board because of his strong personality and intelligence and the support of Herbert Sanger, the general counsel with whom he was close, as well as the facilitating management of Bill Willis, who worked hard to repair disagreements.[126]

White may have also been hired because of the strong pressure from Senator Sasser to hire a nuclear adviser.[127] White had originally been brought to TVA as a consultant by Hugh Parris. After White met with the board, Dean and Waters decided they would ask him to salvage the nuclear program. They had lost confidence in Parris.[128] When he was offered the job in a subsequent meeting, White did not demand that Parris leave but did say that it would be a very difficult situation for Parris to work for him, as the board suggested.[129] In any event, Parris left TVA.

There was a controversy later in 1986 about conflicts of interest between White's job with Stone and Webster and his use of their people in TVA. There was even more hullabaloo about White's salary of $355,000 a year. The adverse publicity forced him to take a leave of absence for several months until a new contract was written.[130] White had initially resisted being anything more than a consultant to TVA. E. P. Wilkinson of the Institute of Nuclear Power Operators, also a former navy officer, told White, "Steve, you have to do this for your country." White was persuaded by this appeal but set very tough conditions that would give him absolute authority within the Office of Nuclear Power to hire and fire, and the board agreed, contrary to his expectation.[131]

It did not take White long to learn about the TVA bureaucracy and its culture, which he described as having the following characteristics: (1) the belief that TVA could do things better than anyone else; (2) entrenched "old boys" who closed ranks against outsiders; (3) a culture that told whistle-blowers not to make waves; and (4) a lack of high standards for nuclear construction and operation. He described a conversation with a senior nuclear manager, who had initially been critical of White but later said he wished he had cooperated earlier. It was necessary that White understand, he told him, that TVA managers were trained not to make waves and never criticize anyone else in the organization. According to White, only a few people in the Office of Nuclear Power wished to be "set free" of this culture.[132]

White believed that Parris had not been frank with the board about TVA's nuclear problems. He remembered the distress of board members when he initially told them of the extent of the problems, much of which he had learned from the Institute of Nuclear Power Operators: "The board was agitated and asked, 'why aren't our people telling us this?' They suspected but didn't have the facts. They were eager to have someone who would tell them the truth. Willis's role had been that of a pacifier, keep things running quietly and keep the board quiet and let the organization run TVA."[133]

White's strategy for turning things around was to bring in a handful of managers to repair the damage. In addition to Stone and Webster employees, they were former nuclear navy people and people on loan from private utilities. White did not rely on permanent TVA people for this leadership effort because he doubted their commitment to reform. A main task was to convince the Nuclear Regulatory Commission that TVA was serious about correcting defects. Much had been discovered, but little had been done to correct failures. White assigned task forces to each plant, which as he said, "was a terrible trauma for upper TVA management. They were accustomed to self-evaluation. Some left. The general feeling of managers was to give me rope to hang myself. They could outwait me for the two years I had said I would stay."[134]

A few TVA people volunteered to help. A small number actively opposed White in an underground way, and the vast majority simply watched and waited.[135] White decided to deal directly with the board, bypassing Willis, to educate Dean and Waters by taking them to nuclear plants and showing them the kinds of problems to be solved. He moved quality assurance to a high level reporting directly to him. He soon discovered the tensions between design and construction engineers and plant operators, which Parris had not resolved. Operations had the upper hand, and White found that they often did not listen to the advice of their rivals. Parris had established the "owner-operator" concept in which plant managers had authority over design and construction engineers. White tried his best to reverse that situation.

He was critical of the board for its passivity. They seemed unaware of what was happening in the organization and did not seem to know how to get control of it. Often they would find ways not to confront issues. White began to understand why Hugh Parris might have thought it better to keep the board in the dark since they could not help him with his concrete problems. However, when the NRC eventually learned of the board's limited control, the game was up for TVA. In White's opinion, the NRC should have intervened earlier, but he felt that its inspectors had been too deferential because TVA was highly autonomous by law. But once the NRC did move, it was extremely tough in order to compensate for its previous softness.

White also discovered that most members of the valley congressional delegation had no respect for either Dean or Waters and were often rude to them when they came calling. As a result, the two board members told White that they expected him to deal with Congress for them. The same pattern emerged in dealing with the press. White had to stand in for the board members. It was White's perception that congressional delegates from the valley were not knowledgeable about the issues with which he was dealing. Instead they focused on symbolic issues like his high salary and the Stone and Webster contract. White described one senator who was publicly critical of TVA and White, but when White called with an offer to explain a particular matter, the senator told him not to pay any attention to his public statements, and that he, White, was doing fine.

White gave credit to both Sandra Seeley and Dan De Ford for teaching him about TVA, and they, in turn, respected him. However, like both Seeley and De Ford, White understood that not all whistle-blowers were disinterested. Some were opportunists, and White knew which ones he could rely on. After he returned to TVA in January 1987, and until he left in November 1988, White used his temporary lieutenants to correct the design and construction errors and ensure that procedures were consistent with NRC requirements. Many TVA officials contended that their own employees could have done the work as easily, but White lacked confidence in the regular staffs. When he left in 1988, Sequoyah was back in business but Browns Ferry was not. It was very slow going. In March 1987, James G. Keppler, director of the new Office of Special Projects of the NRC, said that "lingering discord and distrust among TVA managers" was the major obstacle to restarting Sequoyah. The plant would stay shut, he said, until TVA could prove that its top managers were "pulling in the same direction."[136]

White's watchword to his top managers was "accountability." In June 1986 he described the rank and file of middle managers as "good people" but said that management had been "rotten from the top." Job descriptions were rewritten to tell supervisors, in White's words, "here are the things you're responsible for . . . and you're going to be held accountable for them."[137] But it was a long, slow process. In February 1987, the NRC had created an Office of Special Projects which would focus on the two utilities the NRC believed needed the most improvement, TVA and Texas Utilities.[138] The NRC requirements were massive. For example, in April the board approved four contracts for seven hundred engineers for the Watts Bar plant at a cost of $170 million, with the sole purpose of correcting existing deficiencies. White recommended that a similar contract be approved for Browns Ferry.[139] Even so, the NRC would not permit either plant to return to service in 1987.

Nuclear plants around the country were suffering unanticipated start-up problems. TVA was not unique. And several veterans of the nuclear navy had been hired by utilities as troubleshooters. White was not optimistic about either TVA or the future of nuclear power in the United States. He did not believe that the utilities in general would be willing to make the necessary financial investment in nuclear expertise to keep complex plants functioning.[140] In mid-1987 he told a group of Tennessee congressmen that it would take "at least seven years for the TVA nuclear program to recover."[141]

Both Dean and Waters thought highly of White. For one thing, he was able to pay consulting engineers more than comparable TVA employees could receive. A lot of money was therefore spent without too much concern about the total cost. Dean felt that it was necessary for White to superimpose "hundreds of people" on the organization. But he also recognized that when White and the outsiders left, TVA would be largely as it had been before their arrival.[142] Waters was even more enthusiastic about White:

> We had to have a Steve White. Anything else would not have lasted here. He had a big ego but it was worth millions of dollars. If he wanted to talk to someone at GE [General Electric] he talked to the president. He had prestige, credibility and guts. He is a crisis manager. . . . The TVA way had been to rely on old timers to handle new problems. White would ask, "who's the best guy in the country on this?" TVA would not ask that. And he would find him at Bechtel.[143]

Dan De Ford thought highly of White: "Most of the people at working level feel he was someone we could trust. He was the first leader since Red [Wagner] who had the employees starting to trust him."[144] George Dilworth found himself subordinated in quality assurance work to White's appointees, but he tried to be cooperative. He was critical of paying consultants by the hour because they were spending great amounts of time to redo procedures. But he also recognized that White had credibility with the NRC and Congress and that the board had lost all credibility.[145] Herb Sanger, the general counsel, clashed with White on the conflict-of-interest issue and had a less admiring view of the navy man "There was not much done. There were no hardware changes. Much money was spent proving that what was there *was* there. White did not correct any of the basic internal problems of TVA and the failure to document actions. He threw money at it and TVA did not learn from that. . . . The board was willing to turn it all over to contractors. That doesn't fix the institutional part. And the board was willing to let White speak for the board."[146] Bill Mason, also a TVA lawyer who worked closely with White, believed that TVA employees could have done the necessary documentation to satisfy the NRC—although he did agree that much TVA construction had altered design plans at the point of construction.[147]

The pattern of attitudes toward White, when matched with his own insights, gives a fairly coherent picture of two and one-half years of crisis management, all for the purpose of getting the plants back in commission and building the new plants properly. There was general agreement that White and his men did not change the TVA culture. Sandra Seeley was not optimistic in 1989: "Steve White could not remake the organization. He had to get the plants on line. . . . It may be worse now than it ever was because the real analysts are gone."[148] She heard TVA employees with a "siege mentality" refer to White and his people as "carpetbaggers" whom they could outwit. This was ironic because many early opponents of TVA had seen its first wave of engineers as carpetbaggers. According to Seeley, such people failed to cooperate with White. No one would ever admit to having made a mistake because "so much was concentrated on promotions." The organization could not be changed in two or three years. For one thing, White could not fire anyone. His announcement that he would only stay two years encouraged the career people to wait him out.[149]

A Critical Study

In December 1986, Virginia governor Gerald Baliles, acting as chairman of the Southern States Energy Board, established an advisory committee to look into the troubles of TVA and recommend steps by which TVA might regain a leadership role in the industry. A healthy TVA was presumed to be important for the southeastern states. The committee issued its report in September 1987.[150] The committee members included the presidents of the Alabama and Virginia power companies; the president of Reynolds Metal company; the president of Resources for the Future; a former member of the NRC; the retired chairman of Consolidated Edison of New York; a former director of the American Public Power Association; the chairman of Federal Express; and a retired former admiral who was president of the Institute of Nuclear Power Operators. There was speculation that Baliles had a secret agenda to denigrate TVA in order to create more business in the southeast for Virginia Power. Others suggested that perhaps the purpose of the study was to suggest that TVA should be privatized. But according to one committee member, the more the situation was studied, the more it seemed undesirable to break up TVA because no one would want the problems. TVA could not easily be picked apart for only the good parts to be taken.[151]

The report of the Baliles Committee was consistent with analyses of TVA going back to the 1970s. The committee recognized that other utilities also had organization and management problems similar to those of TVA: skyrocketing construction costs, safety concerns, negative effects of the Arab oil embargoes, the obsolescence of steam plants. TVA's problems were on a larger scale. Large scale may have been one reason that neither the NRC nor top TVA management had recognized the "generic weaknesses" of the TVA organizational structure and culture in their haste to resolve particular problems.[152] It also pointed out that about the time the problems began to be identified, TVA began to lose experienced nuclear managers because of the federal pay-cap. TVA was said to have reacted to the Three Mile Island crisis more slowly than most other utilities, as seen in the subsequent number of larger-than-average deficiencies cited by the NRC. According to the report, both the NRC and the Institute of Nuclear Power Operators should have acted decisively to identify problem areas in TVA sooner than they did.[153]

The report was critical of TVA's failure to adjust its plans for growth to the great increases in energy prices in 1973 and later. Most utilities cut back, but TVA's very ambitious plan for seventeen nuclear reactors by 1984 was unrealistic.[154] The study was particularly critical of TVA management for failing to discover existing and impending problems. The board had taken steps to correct organizational flaws: "But TVA's management problems are deeply rooted in its peculiar form of governance. They have been amplified by the corporation's virtual freedom from accountability and the harmful effects of the Federal pay ceiling to which TVA is subject."[155]

The biggest problem, according to the report, was that the legal power vested in the board prevented the general manager from operating as a chief executive officer. The traditional TVA structure was inimical to executive leadership and decision making. Divided responsibility for management results fostered insularity and limited exposure to external viewpoints.[156] A major mistake had been to fail to recognize the special demands of nuclear plants and the assumption that staffs with conventional power-plant experience could build and operate nuclear plants using the old distinctions among design, construction, and operations. That division of labor did not work for the seamless web of nuclear plants.[157] By the same token, TVA's power to set its own electric rates did not subject it to the discipline required in well-regulated utilities. Public comment on TVA rate making had merit but lacked rigor, and the persons who made the plans also judged them.[158]

The Baliles Committee's report made several recommendations. The position of chief executive officer should be created by law and that person should be responsible to the board for managing TVA, in short a stronger general manager, an old idea that had returned. The board should be expanded to nine directors, all part-time, who would serve staggered terms and set general policy. The board would hold the CEO responsible for TVA performance. The statutory pay-cap should be eliminated. The committee rejected the idea of TVA rates being regulated by the Federal Energy Regulatory Commission because the larger TVA board would be responsible to the president and Congress, just as the commission was. However, it was strongly recommended that the Office of Management and Budget increase its oversight of TVA and require detailed financing plans from TVA that it would scrutinize.[159]

The prescriptions were taken largely from a paper that Alex Radin had written for the Tennessee Valley Public Power Association. Radin, who was a member of the Baliles Committee, was a former executive director of the American Public Power Association. He made his report available to the committee and had considerable influence on the diagnosis of organizational problems and the suggested remedies. His report was based on thorough interviews with past and present board members, as well as the heads of other utilities in Toronto, New York, and elsewhere.[160] Radin strongly believed that TVA's organizational structure was flawed: "I felt that TVA needed a strong CEO and a policy board. . . . The problem with TVA now is that the board is both a policymaking and an administrative board. These should be separated. The board is supposed to be a policy board and the general manager is supposed to run the agency. But the chairmen of the board have not permitted that.[161]

Radin was critical of the weak congressional oversight: "The reality is that you don't have a degree of oversight without appropriations. You only have it when TVA gets into deep trouble, e.g. rate rises, valley politics. Members will begin to look but there is too much competition for their attention. The Bonneville Power Administration gets more scrutiny because it submits its bond budgets to Congress."[162]

Radin also lamented the weak scrutiny that publics in the valley were able to give TVA:

The culture of the agency is important but the culture of the region is also important. The culture of the northwest is so different from Tennessee Valley culture. There is a lot more public input in Bonneville in that the people of the area are more concerned about the environment and what the agency does. If these environmental issues were of greater concern to the people of the Tennessee Valley, TVA would be more responsive. TVA open board meetings are not real scrutiny. Bonneville has a series of meetings throughout the region in which they lay out their plans. There is a lot more activism there and also more give and take. The northwest public power systems existed before Bonneville was created. It was just the reverse in the valley. TVA stimulated the creation of distributors. Bonneville does not have 100% responsibility for power in the northwest. There is a give and take between power systems.[163]

There was nothing new in either the diagnoses or prescriptions of the Baliles Committee's report. Many of the issues that it raised had been discussed since the 1930s. The Draper Committee that looked at TVA for President Franklin Roosevelt had recommended a stronger general manager as a chief executive. At about the time that the Baliles Committee's report came out, Charles Dean said publicly that it was essential that one person run the agency.[164] Dean was about to get his wish in a de facto manner, for in January 1988 Marvin Runyon was named chairman of the TVA board in his place. Runyon left the presidency of Nissan-USA to succeed Dean, who remained on the board. The new chairman was to take advantage of the crisis to create a new executive structure, which he would dominate, as a first step toward changing the TVA organizational culture. The old myth was dead. A new myth was nascent.

New Departures

MARVIN RUNYON became chairman of the TVA board in January 1988 at the age of sixty-three. He had been a production executive with the Ford Motor Company for many years and, since 1980, president of the Nissan Motor Manufacturing Corporation, USA, in Smyrna, Tennessee. His reputation at Ford, and later at Nissan, had been that of an innovator.[1]

Runyon's central objective was to increase the "competitiveness" of TVA's electricity program. He created a top-management committee that met every week and appointed six task forces to examine every aspect of TVA activity. His watchword was that TVA should be "run like a business." TVA's debt was $17.4 billion, about half of which was the result of slow nuclear construction. Runyon announced that getting the nuclear plants up and running was a high priority.[2] He restructured the organization. Willis became executive vice-president and chief operating officer. Five vice-presidents, who reported to the board, were created: corporate, which included finance and legal affairs, as well as the inspector general and governmental relations; power; nuclear power; resource development, which encompassed the fertilizer, river basin, forestry, and economic development operations; and human resource services. The unit for program planning was abolished. Each of the directors took special responsibility for one sphere, with Dean overseeing power and Waters natural resources. Runyon reserved management services for himself, but in fact he functioned as a chief executive officer for all divisions.

Runyon understood clearly that TVA's unpopularity was due primarily to the skyrocketing electric rates and promised at the outset that rates would not be raised for three years. In fact, they had not been raised by 1992 when he left TVA to become postmaster general. This commitment required a top-to-bottom pruning in which TVA got rid of 12,500 of its 32,000 employees, largely by early retirement and attrition, but 7,500 were let go. The number of management layers was reduced from 13 to 8. The in-house construction force was eliminated altogether. TVA left the Federal Financing Bank, which had issued its bonds in the past, to take advantage of lower interest rates available in the public markets, and then refinanced $10.5 billion in long-term debt, saving about $125 million annually in interest expenses.[3]

Once inside TVA, Runyon found it to be "very bureaucratic." When he suggested changes, he was invariably told that it couldn't be done because of the TVA act. He soon discovered that the act was quite flexible and provided much discretion.[4] He was dismayed to learn that the office managers had no plans at all to control costs. Runyon was surprised to discover that top managers in each office did not know each other well. He quite self-consciously intended to create a new organizational culture and a new generation of TVA leaders. The theme of the new culture would be the accountability of managers for results. A system of executive bonuses, above salary, was initiated, with the silent consent of Congress, in order to keep and reward talent.[5] Any proposals for new programs had to be accompanied by recommendations for budget cuts in the same area. And the practice of simply raising the electricity rates in order to meet rising costs came to an end.[6]

Runyon regarded all line managers as staff to the board and had little use for program "analysts" who "can't run a business. The line has to run the business." Runyon saw his vice-president for finance as the natural adversary of and check on line managers; he could get the managers' attention in a way that staff analysts could not because he controlled their budgets. Runyon's experience and self-confidence told him he could ferret out the information he needed for decisions by pressing managers to make sure they understood their programs. He was often disappointed to learn they were not always as knowledgeable as they pretended to be.[7]

Runyon discovered on his arrival that TVA was spending $800,000 a year for electric car research that should have been left to car manufacturers.[8] The energy-conservation programs were also curtailed and shifted to the customer service departments of local utilities. Runyon did not think it was cost-effective to spend money to convince customers to use less electricity when TVA had a surplus of power.[9]

By early 1992, Runyon's leadership appeared to have been effective on many fronts. The two nuclear reactors at Sequoyah and two of the three Browns Ferry reactors had been restarted, with Nuclear Regulatory Commission approval. Electric rates had held steady. Wall Street had bought $10.5 billion in TVA bonds. The head of the valley congressional delegation, Representative Jim Cooper, Democrat of Tennessee, called Runyon the "best TVA director in modern history." However, there were problems. Environmentalists were angry because of the dismantling of energy-conservation programs. About $11 billion invested in the uncompleted Watts Bar and Bellefonte nuclear plants would have to be written off as debt when they began to function in the year 2000. More than $2 billion would be required to bring old coal-fired plants into compliance with the Clean Air Act. The Department of Energy cut its need for TVA power from $457 million to $160 million in 1992, with no requirements at all expected by 1994.

These many changes damaged the morale of many TVA employees and

were dubbed "Runyonitis" by Jo Anne Howell, president of the Knoxville chapter of Federally Employed Women. The symptoms were said to
be rushed and redone work, high stress, loss of good judgment, high
paper usage, uncertainty, and clean offices. Runyon's style of asking employees about what they were doing and why and whether it could be
done more efficiently was said to have triggered the epidemic of Runyonitis. However, Howell and other TVA managers believed that the condition was a temporary but necessary transition cost toward the achievement of important objectives.[10]

Runyon's board colleagues and senior managers generally approved of
his objectives and leadership style. Dean saw him as hardworking and
innovative but not suited to a three-member board. He received far more
information than Dean and Waters, and they deferred to him. Bill Willis
admired Runyon's forcing of management-team discussions, even on
seemingly trivial matters. He saw Runyon using such meetings to push
managers to think creatively together about how to improve operations.
David Freeman had done this too, but the difference with Runyon, according to Willis, was that "Marvin brings it out of you and Dave lays it
on you."[11] Craven Crowell, director of public information under both
Freeman and Runyon, described how Runyon took the top office managers on a retreat to set goals for the agency. Runyon said little but used
a consultant facilitator who worked to pull goals for the agency out of its
managers. A consensus that rates should not be raised and that peripheral
activities should be jettisoned was finally reached, and Runyon announced it publicly, making his managers accountable for achieving the
goals. The possibility of laying off 20 percent of the workforce did not
occur to anyone, but it followed logically. According to Crowell, Runyon
was so detail oriented in management meetings because he wanted to
drive concern for details all down the line. The bottom line was what
mattered. Runyon used well-tested management strategies. He was a production man.[12] However, Jerry Campbell, executive director of the Tennessee Valley Public Power Association, was not optimistic for the long
run in 1992: "Marvin Runyon has brought TVA a very long way in a very
short time. He has had to do unpopular things and there is still a lot of
restlessness among the good old boys. The morale over there is rotten."
Campbell admired what Runyon had done and believed that "only a
strong chief executive can save TVA. The board system perpetuates the
old boy network. A poor board will not face real problems. . . . This
structure will not permit a Marvin Runyon-type CEO."[13]

A 1992 analysis of the future for TVA by Allan Pulsipher, the former
TVA chief economist, raised hard questions about whether anyone could
solve TVA's problems as an electric utility. When compared with private
utilities in North Carolina, Alabama, and Kentucky, TVA rates were

higher and TVA costs would also be higher because of the $8 to $10 billion invested in unused nuclear reactors. The Department of Energy was losing its need for TVA electricity. The Clean Air Act would hit TVA much harder that its regional counterparts because of the large number of old, dirty fossil plants. Pulsipher predicted that TVA distributors would increasingly cut their ties with TVA and begin to buy power from other regional utilities.[14] He blamed TVA failures on the TVA Act itself which provided for minimal supervision of TVA decisions, especially rates, by higher levels of government. The charter provided no incentives for efficiency, for participation by consumers, or for tests of management effectiveness. Pulsipher suggested that the only way out of the impasse was through a regional, interstate compact that would create TVA responsibility to the valley states. TVA rates should be set, he felt, by the Federal Energy Regulatory Commission. Despite Runyon's successes, Pulsipher thought that more fundamental changes were required: "The prudent policy, regionally and nationally, is to give TVA a structure that is consistent both with the unique nature of the short run problems it faces and the economic realities of the next century—not to continue to rely on a structure which largely reflects Rooseveltian notions popular half a century ago, at the depths of the Great Depression."[15]

Jerry Campbell was also worried that distributors would leave the TVA system in a search for cheaper electricity. Memphis had almost left, but Runyon persuaded them to stay.[16]

In the summer of 1992, Marvin Runyon left TVA to become the U.S. postmaster general. President Bush appointed John Waters to be TVA's new chairman, but his term expired in 1993 and President Clinton nominated Craven Crowell for the chairmanship. Crowell was at the time Senator James Sasser's chief of staff, but he had been director of public information at TVA in the Freeman, Dean, and Runyon years.

It is too soon to say whether the changes initiated by Runyon can actually change the TVA culture or enable it to confront challenges to its missions. If the reader compares this epilogue with the epilogue to Part I, it will be apparent that the virtues of the decentralized TVA organizational structure and culture in the 1930s had become serious liabilities by 1988. Runyon had an opportunity not available to his predecessors to change the culture and structure after the shock of failure. But can a phoenix rise from the ashes?

CHAPTER 10

Reflections

THE TASKS of leaders are very different at different sequences in the history of an organization. The founding is an exercise in the creation of meaning. Purpose and direction may be provided by the founding charter, but the first generation of leaders must match statements of purpose to the political resources and constraints in the environment of the organization, and this requires a period of trial and error, and perhaps conflict, until purpose and politics can be brought together. A parallel task is to imbue the ranks of the organization, itself with purposive cohesion so that bureaucratic processes are consistent with environmental demands. Leaders must weave a seamless web of purpose, politics, and process out of many disparate elements in the early life of an organization. This is a task that no one else can perform for them. The legislators who have created the organization and those political executives who oversee it are not able to do that work. They may write the charter, but they then turn to other charters; the leaders of the new organization are the only people who are in a position to match the aspirations of the charter to the realities of politics and bureaucracy.[1] The mosaic of purposes will be expressed in different ways in what I have called organizational myth, a set of aspirations that never fully match reality but are a continual spur to action.

The next generation of leaders must be good at the institutionalization of myth. Their task is to nurture the harmony developed in the founding period, between internal capacities and external expectations and demands. Such leaders need not be as imaginative and creative as the founding generation of leaders. Some organizations never require any other type of leadership, if the mission is stable and support for it continues to be strong. However, the political environment may change. Old missions may become less relevant to the politics of the time. The initial missions may have been achieved with a corresponding search for new purposes. Whatever the stimulus, uncertainty is the result. A new compact among purpose, politics, and process must be developed. At this juncture there is no clear sense of direction, and the task of leadership is to address the ambiguity of the situation and provide plausible solutions around which people may rally. One kind of leader who may appear in this sequence of renewal is a creative articulator of purpose who attempts to adapt and refocus the original organizational myths to encompass new purposes and politics. Adaptation will work within strong continuity with the past. At this juncture it may be difficult to scale back the collective sense of purpose to less ambitious goals because those in the organization and their constituents expect boldness and creativity. However, the very effort to revive and adapt the vitality of myth, although it may work to a certain extent, may also create a discordant politics by trying to revive a coalition that is no longer strong or unified. The raw materials for success are simply not available, and their invocation may create new divisive conflicts. Such leaders, no matter how creative and successful, are ultimately prisoners of myth. An alternative leadership strategy at this critical juncture in organizational history may be to scale back myths and find niches in the environment for stable and steady missions of less heroic cast than those set out at the founding. However, this more cautious leadership cannot always find a voice when the dilemma is presented as one of stagnation in routine versus adaptation and new dynamism. Such a voice may seem fainthearted and may win support only after the dynamic period of adaptation has either failed or produced great discordance. Should such failures occur, then the opportunity is ripe for an altogether new kind of leadership that takes advantage of the shock of failure to create new myths and a new congruence among purpose, politics, and process.

There is no necessary sequence of stages in the history of an organization. The interactions of an organization with its environment often reflect the changing character of that environment as much or more than any predictable organizational life cycle.[2] But the organization is not simply a mirror of its environment. It develops a structure and culture with which it engages the world and which can be employed to change that world as much as the world attempts to change it. It is therefore important to ask at every critical juncture in the organization's history about how past decisions may be influencing the perception of current dilemmas and provide precedents for their resolution.[3] Cross-sectional analyses of organizations cannot tell us whether an organization's birth and history explain the actions of contemporary leaders. Indeed, cross-sectional analyses may underestimate the importance of leadership in steering the organization. Structure and culture may dominate the cross-sectional picture without taking account of the role of leadership in creating and adapting structure and culture.[4] By the same token, leadership may be less important in stable periods in which the organization is highly congruent with its environment.[5]

David Lilienthal was the archetype of a founding leader. He performed a task that neither Senator Norris nor President Roosevelt could have carried out, that of defining and articulating TVA's missions and creating political support for those missions in the Tennessee Valley and the nation. Both the senator and the president had too much else to do and were too remote from TVA to do that work. And it had to be done, as the abortive career of A. E. Morgan revealed. Morgan's conceptions of what TVA was to be were not congruent with either the culture of the valley or the politics of Washington. He would surely have failed had he been given full scope to carry out his ideas. But there was no guarantee in history that TVA would succeed. Lilienthal made it work. He was singularly lucky. His talent for articulation and rhetoric exploited the strong political resources of New Deal politics in a depression and an economically backward region. He understood the magical appeal of electricity, both as symbol and reality. His luck can be seen by comparing his leadership of the postwar Atomic Energy Commission, in which he tried many of the strategies of rhetorical and managerial leadership that had worked at TVA. But his talents were mismatched for the mission of producing weapons that was caught up in the partisan politics of the emerging Cold War and in an organization that required centralization and secrecy by virtue of its mission.[6]

Lilienthal did not create the TVA management system, but he supported the work of John Blandford and Gordon Clapp and romanticized it in his speeches and writing so that its decentralization became part of the myth of grass roots democracy which he so effectively popularized. He borrowed much from H. A. Morgan here, an inarticulate man, but it was Lilienthal's voice and his feel for the political task at hand that ensured the success of the TVA experiment. Lilienthal was also able to articulate the uncertainties of the future, perhaps because he understood so well how to defeat those uncertainties in his own time. He worried about a future day when most of the TVA missions would have been achieved. He believed passionately in the governmental structure of a public authority that carried out multiple purposes within one region as an alternative to top-heavy and fragmented national government and splintered and ineffective state and local governments. Therefore the form was not in doubt but only the question of mission. What would the TVA of the future do in behalf of regional development? This question permeated Lilienthal's wartime journal and was asked with increasing anxiety in the immediate postwar years by his successors. However, it did not have to be answered because the missions of the 1930s continued into the next decades. In the process, TVA myths became protective defenses against TVA's enemies. Myth gradually became less of an inspiration to action and more of an invocation of legitimacy.

Gordon Clapp and Herbert Vogel were consolidating leaders who succeeded in implementing Lilienthal's vision. Clapp was the custodian of the TVA management system and organizational culture. He was Lilienthal's lieutenant who carried out those administrative steps that Lilienthal left to others and thereby gave solidity to the experiment. It is not a coincidence that once Lilienthal had decided to replicate the TVA adventure on a worldwide basis, he asked Clapp to be his lieutenant in the Development and Resources corporation. However, because Clapp was an administrator and lieutenant, rather than a captain, he could not resolve the hard political question of how to finance the power program. He lacked both the skill and the political support necessary for the task.

Vogel solved the political problem because he was skillful and the time for resolution was ripe. The Dixon-Yates imbroglio had brought the political conflicts over TVA to a dead end, and both the Republican president and the Democratic Congress were open to a resolution. Vogel, with much help from his organization, supplied that resolution. But his success gave TVA autonomy in the management of its power program that it had never had. TVA ceased to be a national institution. Without anyone intending it, TVA became dependent upon future public confidence in the valley for its well-being. Its national patrons, both presidents and Congress, paid little attention except when people in the valley spoke to them. And as long as TVA was building and expanding without escalating costs, there was little discontent.

Aubrey Wagner was a true believer in the TVA myth who carried the charter to logical extremes in efforts to revitalize the authority. The Tributary Development Program, the Tellico, Normandy and Columbia dams, the Land Between the Lakes, and plans for seventeen nuclear reactors in nine plants were all products of his vision. He wanted a heroic TVA, yet he embodied its contradictions in his person. He believed in the grass roots ideal and tried to implement it in the Tributary Area Development program. He both lamented the fact that TVA had become a power company and sought to compensate by other inventions, but he also embraced the myth of electricity and the credo that TVA could do anything bigger and better than any other organization of its kind. Perhaps above all, he believed in the lesson of the Douglas Dam story, that TVA should not surrender its autonomy to make sound professional decisions to anyone, whether politicians or public.

But Wagner was increasingly at odds with a changing environment. The running controversies over strip-mining, clean air, and the escalating costs of electricity were not supposed to happen in his conception of TVA. And in trying to cope with these problems, he became a prisoner of the TVA management system that he had presided over, knew well, and believed in so strongly. The system did not permit him to learn what he needed to know about TVA's self-defeating actions. Instead, he escalated his commitments as the opposition grew stronger. He would prevail, just as Lilienthal had prevailed, with the Douglas Dam and when Dixon-Yates had been faced down. Wagner kept the support of the core TVA constituencies to whom he looked for support—the distributors, the valley delegation in Congress, and his own lieutenants. His leadership style was imperious, in part because of temperament but also because he believed that the charter gave him freedom to act as he thought right so long as he stayed within its terms. But politics is no respecter of charters. The unpopularity of TVA was Wagner's legacy.

David Freeman corrected Wagner's mistakes. He preached the environmental cause, practiced energy conservation, and after a period of hesitation, led the cutback of the nuclear-power program. He was as possessed with the TVA myth as Wagner had been. The content was different, but Freeman believed very strongly that TVA could and should not exist if it were not a national institution that carried out national policies. Thus it was logical that TVA should be the energy lab of the nation and that new ways should be found to integrate energy programs and economic development. This was all very plausible, indeed desirable, in the sense that most people agreed that TVA had to conserve energy and respect the natural environment. Whether it could or should actually become a center for experimentation and demonstration for new uses of energy was more problematic. But Freeman was trying to answer the queries that Lilienthal kept posing in his wartime diaries. How will TVA be heroic in the present and future? Freeman had no strong constituencies for these purposes. He lost the support of the key TVA constituencies—the distributors and the valley delegation—and he never really had the support of his professional lieutenants in the organization, with a few exceptions. But even worse, he lost the support of the public.

Freeman tried to reform the TVA management system, but to a great extent he became its prisoner. He clearly understood how that had happened to Wagner. All of the criticisms of the administrative system that were voiced by experts and observers in the Wagner years were known to both Freemans. But as events after 1981 revealed, the Freemans were never actually able to get control and were finally defeated by the organizational culture.

Charles Dean presided over the disintegration of the TVA organizational structure and culture, though he was not to blame. His leadership style was consistent with that culture, and he therefore did not challenge it. But the genie was already out of the bottle, and it became apparent in 1985.

Each of these leaders attempted, with varying degrees of success, to forge a unity between their purposes, the politics of the TVA environment, and the bureaucratic processes of TVA decision making and implementation. Their skills at this work varied greatly, as did the strength of resources and constraints in their environments. The most favorable combination of skill and context was seen in Lilienthal's leadership. Neither Aubrey Wagner nor David Freeman was able to marshall the political resources that would have sustained their conceptions of TVA's missions. Neither was as skillful a political leader as Lilienthal, but they were both strong and forceful enough that they might have duplicated his achievements had the historical context been more favorable. The interesting question is why they failed to discern this fact. Clapp and Vogel discerned their environmental situations, in relation to their own skills and their ambitions for TVA, more realistically than any chairmen after Lilienthal, and certainly more than Wagner and Freeman. But their ambitions were less. Dean came to appreciate the constraints that his environment placed upon achievement at TVA, but he was much more hobbled by that environment than either Clapp or Vogel had been. Only Marvin Runyon was in a position to unite purpose, politics, and process in creative ways, not only because of his abilities but because he had something of a fresh start after a major shock to the organization.[7]

A Theory of Organizational Failure

The theoretical problem that was posed in Chapter 1 was to ask how and why organizations fail in the effort to perform feats of achievement comparable to past glories. The initial insight was that failure in such cases is not due to sluggishness or routinization after the creativity of the founding era. Rather, failure is somehow associated with new efforts at creativity and innovation by organizational leaders who have taken founders and other creative leaders in the history of the institution as their exemplars. This study of TVA suggests at least three kinds of organizational failure that can be subsumed under the umbrella question and can be elaborated as separate and complementary theoretical insights.

First, organizations may fail because of "persistence in the face of success."[8] TVA engineers believed that their ability to design and build dams, and then steam plants, qualified them to construct nuclear installations. Why not? They were the best around, or at least had been. This variety of failure seeks organizational glory in a linear fashion. A certain institutional hubris overwhelms humility. The organization overreaches its capacities. This was the problem of the last years of the Wagner era.

Second, organizational leaders who seek to arrest organizational decline through reform and innovation may fail because they are unable to overcome the opposition of those persons, groups, and constituencies that have strong stakes in the practices that are to be changed.[9] This is the story of David Freeman's failure. He entered TVA like a whirlwind, conscious of Wagner's failures of "persistence in the face of success," but was also possessed, as was Wagner, with the belief that TVA had to have a national mission to thrive and survive. The most important actors within TVA and in its environment—high bureaucrats, members of the congressional valley delegation, and the distributors—only grudgingly agreed with Freeman's policy objectives and succeeded in arranging his demise. They were still living in Wagner's time warp, even though there could not be a return to Wagner's policies, and Freeman's commitments to environmental values continued.

Third, in the absence of effective "political leadership," the "technical rationality" that has sustained the core functions of the organization is not sufficient for constructively relating the organization to new demands from its environment.[10] The nuclear debacle under the Dean board, in which the technical core not only could not be related to the environment in constructive ways but could not perform at a minimal level, is an illustration of this theoretical insight. After the Freemans' reform efforts had failed, TVA was rudderless and without effective leadership, and the technical tasks could not be sustained. The possibility of fundamental redirection of missions for TVA then seemed realistic, and the Runyon chairmanship was feasible.

We must do more than restate our historical stories in propositional language. What were the shifting, but perhaps predictable, factors that made Aubrey Wagner, David Freeman, and Charles Dean fail? The three stories, taken together, can be unpacked to reveal complementary insights.

PERSISTENCE IN THE FACE OF SUCCESS

Aubrey Wagner believed in his policies. This was surely the most important source of his actions. His personal abilities, the tasks he set himself, and the favorable support for his goals among TVA's most important constituencies were all congruent. A chairman of lesser force of personality would perhaps not have been such a dynamic leader, but it is difficult to argue that policy would have been significantly different in the Wagner years. The 1959 Bond Revenue Act gave TVA the autonomy to finance its power program with minimal oversight from Washington. The structure of the organization and its relative autonomy to operate in the region as it wished were protected by congressional politicians from the valley and abetted by the disinterest of successive presidents. Wagner and his principal lieutenants in TVA had grown up together in the organization, learned TVA myths from Lilienthal and Clapp, and used their leadership positions to build new programs on the basis of the old idealism. Wagner's addition to the mix of factors favorable to action was to provide bold and strong leadership.

To emphasize that TVA's leaders in the Wagner years believed in what they were doing and acted accordingly is so straightforward that it hardly seems to be a political-science insight. It is open and shut history that explains action by the intentions of actors. But intentionality must be included in theoretical statements if we are to be accurate.

The autonomy to act in accord with one's beliefs was matched to support for such actions from key constituencies. Organizational structure permitted highly autonomous action, but there was very little disagreement among important constituencies about the right thing to do. In addition, the emphasis upon growth of all TVA programs, power and non-power—was feasible because budgets were expanding. Growth always augments choice in that all constituencies can be squared and none denied what they wished.

Arthur Stinchcombe anchors the beliefs and actions of institutional leaders in the history of their institutions: "One of the main determinants of what a man thinks about is what he gets paid for thinking about. Directly, or indirectly, power holders get paid for thinking about how to achieve and preserve the values and interests embodied in an institution."[11]

One of the prime tasks of such leaders is to win support for their institution by linking it to values widely held among publics and elite supporters.[12] This is more powerfully done if values and interests are inseparable, which was certainly the case with TVA constituencies. It was in part a pork barrel for the Tennessee Valley, but it also expressed a long-standing set of aspirations for the development of an economically backward region which could not be reduced to the interests and claims of particular groups.

The capacities and momentum of TVA as an organization of talented professionals provided a strong bias toward action. TVA engineering capacities were a "permanently useful resource" just waiting to be used and were "sunk costs" in this respect. This capacity to alter the physical environment is perhaps irresistible when the cost of deploying such a resource seems reasonable in terms of expected benefits and alternative uses. The "permanence" of such a resources comes about by means of "constant effort." Such specialized resources are enhanced when they are self-generating and do not depreciate in value to the organization.[13]

Such strong continuity is enhanced within institutions if those in power select their own successors and control the socialization of elite recruits, all of which is given tremendous emotional power if past leaders are made heroes and exemplars for present and future leaders.[14]

Such institutional leadership can only be sustained for a long period of time if successive leaders are able to rally the support of a coalition in the environment in case of challenge from critics. Tending such a coalition is a political act in which one must never give up.[15] Thus Wagner's dismay and incredulous silence when Tennessee governor Winfield Dunn told him on the telephone that he was opposed to the Tellico Dam. That was not supposed to happen.

These insights begin to explain the intransigence of Wagner and his lieutenants in the face of strong and hostile opposition, to the Tellico Dam, to air pollution, and to the costs of the nuclear-construction program. The leaders of a historically successful bureaucracy like TVA will often try to override strong criticism as an alternative to compromising with critics and thereby softening the controversial policies. The Wagner TVA even resorted to an escalation of commitment on much-criticized projects, most dramatically in the case of the Tellico Dam but also with the nuclear-construction program, in response to the crescendo of intense opposition. Why does this happen? Barry Staw suggests several reasons. "Sunk costs" have already been invested, and the organization is not about to waste such resources which are the basis of its raison d'etre. The decision to deploy resources to their full use is not an isolated choice but a reflection of a larger pattern that, if reversed, would call the rationale for the entire organization into question. Not only past but future decisions must be protected from such questioning.[16]

The escalation of commitment, perhaps beyond what a prudent person would feel are the objective facts that might justify the escalation, is understandable as an effort to justify the rationale of earlier decisions. This may be a psychological element in the determination of leaders, for they wish to prove themselves to have been not only right but consistent. Engineers, of all people, wish to appear rational in the decisions they make, and consistency with past arguments and decisions is therefore highly desirable to them.

One then may see a kind of "retrospective rationality" which is intended to justify future as well as past actions.[17] The strategy of escalation of commitment in the face of opposition is likely to be tried if it has worked successfully in the past and is part of the institutional folklore. The fight for the Tellico Dam was simply the Douglas Dam story all over again in the minds of Wagner and his lieutenants. And TVA won that fight. The whole experience of TVA with opposition in the valley and in Washington—with the private power companies, with people needing to be resettled, in the Dixon-Yates fight, with massive projects like the Land Between the Lakes, and with the construction of dams and power plants—had been to drive ahead because the combination of organizational autonomy to act and supportive constituencies in key places meant that TVA could eventually overwhelm its critics. Wagner's generation within TVA learned how to rally grass roots opinion in favor of their projects by having watched Lilienthal and his colleagues invent the strategy in the power fight of the 1930s. This may be especially the case if the strongest opponents are outside the organization. One can hope to over-power critics by escalation of action.[18]

In organizations like Wagner's TVA, the institution will carry solutions that are used to chase problems, especially if such actions are stimulated by a sense of competence and past successes, thus reinforcing the "institutionalist" maxim that institutions need not be "efficient" to survive.[19] Even after they have worn out their welcome with critics in their environment, they may be able to carry on for some time before the forces of change overtake them.[20] Wagner's TVA was thus an instance of predominantly "proactive" rather than "enactive" learning in relation to the political context.[21] This was certainly Wagner's personal style, but it also permeated the organization.

The argument has been made that TVA's great physical achievements have been much overrated and that in fact TVA has been no more than a massive political machine that has sustained itself by continuous economic and political payoffs to those who would protect it from careful scrutiny. For example, Chambers presents data in behalf of the plausible thesis that TVA's work in the Tennessee Valley did no more for the economic development of the region than what alternative means achieved for the economic growth of the rest of the south, and the data appear to support this assertion.[22] Certainly Wagner's TVA did not concern itself with such questions. The idea of policy analysis in which the costs and benefits of alternatives might have been debated was not congenial to the leadership of the organization. Wagner and his friends were "true believers," and it would have been impossible for them to have rejected the premises of the TVA Act. Indeed, each new board member must swear under oath that he or she believes in the purposes of TVA as described in the act. Therefore, fundamental failures of TVA, perhaps such as Tellico, could not be faced by its leaders. To do so would have been to question their entire careers which had given meaning to their lives.

The Uncertainty of Reform

By 1978 Aubrey Wagner's leadership and the policies for which he stood had become pretty well discredited among environmentalists, advocates for the efficient use of energy, and others who saw TVA as a juggernaut out of control. Even the strongest TVA supporters in Congress understood that something had to be done to adapt TVA to new policy demands for a clean environment and energy conservation. Whereas some were ambivalent about David Freeman's own commitment to the historic TVA canons, they also told him privately that change was needed. However, the principal TVA constituency in the valley, the distributors of electrical power, were not so keen on change. The development of a theory of failure therefore must ask if Freeman failed, in both policy and politics, and whether the degree of failure can be explained by more general insights about the reasons for failure of organizational reform efforts.

Marshall Meyer and Lynne Zucker have formulated a theory of organizational failure that can be adapted to help explain David Freeman's successes and failures as TVA chairman. They try to explain why organizations with low levels of performance persist in that condition for long periods of time. They call this a situation of "permanent failure." They do not seek to explain the reasons for the initial organizational failures. Rather, they wish to explain the failure of internal reformers to carry the day for innovations that might overcome the conditions sustaining permanent failure. Their answer is that the coalition of "dependent actors" whose fortunes and fates are linked to the organization as it is, even in such a condition, will resist and overpower reformers.[23] They believe that in most such cases in which poor performance and organizational survival coexist, the winning coalition is strong enough to stop reform. The irony to be explained is how low performance can trigger not only reformers but voices seeking to maintain the combination of low performance and high resistance to reform. Those who fully depend upon an organization may benefit from its very existence and have few alternatives to it. They do not "choose between success and failure (for the organization). They choose instead whether or not to pursue success (reform) and thereby to risk failure."[24] They are fearful that highly innovative action, even more than low performance, may risk the life of the organization as well as their own careers.

There is also not necessarily agreement within the organization on the correct steps to take to improve performance. Uncertainties create disagreement, and one must not assume that reformers, who eventually lose their fight, presented a clear-cut case for reform that was clearly antithetical to the interests and values of resistors. Rather, disagreement, bolstered by uncertainty, may make it difficult or impossible for any reform coalition to win. In such cases there will very likely be multiple and contradictory organizational objectives. The major operating parts of the organization, with separate missions, may be clear about their objectives, but overall goals for the institution may be elusive.[25]

Reformers are likely to attempt several predictable strategies. Reorganization, the use of "strategic planning" and planners to challenge operating arms, and various forms of "strategic management" will likely be attempted. The objective will be to widen the number of policy alternatives to be considered; to increase the reach of central actors, i.e., reformers and their staffs, over the separate divisions; and to provide new incentives and rewards for increased performance.[26] However, such strategies may not be persuasive: "Were disparate interests commensurable . . . were simple incentives capable of aligning diverse interests, the problem of permanent failure would not arise."[27]

Meyer and Zucker developed their theory to apply to business firms, but they suggest how it might be adapted to public bureaucracies. The dependencies surrounding public agencies are greater than those around private firms, which must respond to markets. Public agencies may be monopolies, or they may provide vital services that cannot easily be provided in any other way. Crucial missions cannot be abandoned.[28] The constraints on leadership are even greater than in firms.

The story of David Freeman matches this theory quite well. James March recommends organizational "foolishness" as a way of breaking the hold of traditional ideas on a bureaucracy and fostering fresh thinking.[29] This was exactly what Freeman did in his first year at TVA in his "Dave-o-grams" to staff members. Meyer and Zucker suggest that public managers who would be reformers like Freeman will propose fresh ideas that are "neither derived from first principles nor entirely consistent with one another."[30] They are just trying to shake up things. Such seemingly "nonrational" actions may be required in the management of large organizations. But the ideas themselves may appear to others to be so off the wall that failure is predicted if they are followed. The power of manager reformers is therefore, and perhaps paradoxically, strongest after an outright failure of old policies. That power is weakest when outright failure cannot so easily occur, as in essential public services or when competition is low. This was certainly Freeman's dilemma. He was thought to be crazy by several TVA professionals and never really was able to get control of the organization as Runyon did after the dramatic failures of 1985. Freeman initiated the appropriate reform strategies—reorganization and attention to strategic planning—but they were weak reeds in the face of his inability to build a winning coalition within TVA and in its environment. The handful of environmentalists and energy conservationists in the valley were no substitute for the political influence of the distributors. However, Freeman was able to invoke the power of law and his administrative authority to force TVA to comply with environmental legislation and to embark on a series of actions to conserve energy. The distributors supported neither step, and they were able to force Freeman out of the chairmanship, not by direct action so much as by contributing to the congressional perception that he was highly unpopular in the valley. The distributors could not stop Freeman's policies, however, because environmental policy was supported by law, and energy conservation in the face of energy shortages could not be ignored. Freeman's failure was thus partly political.

The distributors, who had been coopted by TVA in the founding and middle years, gradually reversed the relationship after the 1959 Bond Revenue Act. The pressure on TVA to provide the greatest amounts of electricity at the least possible cost, all for regional economic development, became their war cry. TVA did not create new forms of representation for environmentalists and energy conservationists, so the distributors, with the advocacy of maximum growth, continued their special relationship with TVA. This was the very group that Lilienthal had created. Their opposition to Vogel presaged their hostility to Freeman. Freeman knew that each kilowatt of generating capacity cost more than the previous one, and he hoped that conservation would reduce demand and therefore lower costs. The distributors believed, in contrast, that maximum utilization would lower their operating costs, and just as important, they wanted a growing supply of power to attract industry to the valley. The Tennessee Valley Public Power Association's idea was to stop the lower TVA rates for residential users, as required by the TVA Act, and charge some of the costs of growth to them. Freeman rejected this idea and did succeed in reducing the demands of industry for power through conservation measures. Cooptation is thus a continuous process in which the balance of influence may shift over time in response to changes in the environment. Freeman was trying to strengthen grass roots democracy as Lilienthal had preached, but Freeman's task was far more difficult. Lilienthal had seen the first generation of distributors as the agents of democracy at the grass roots. Freeman wished to appeal to the public at large against the distributors but found no way to do this effectively.[31] He was trapped by the very institutions that had sustained Lilienthal and Wagner.

Meyer and Zucker suggest that one alternative available to reformers is to accept that "organizations should do what they do efficiently rather than change what they do to reap greater profits."[32] This question could be asked of Freeman. Rather than crusading for a newly innovative TVA, why not focus on TVA carrying out traditional missions more efficiently? One answer is that Freeman explicitly rejected such a TVA. He was convinced that there was no justification for the existence of TVA without a national mission and therefore sought to invent new ones to carry the organization to new achievement and to pull it out of the doldrums. Wagner was more comfortable with TVA as an institution for the valley and less ambitious for TVA to be considered an institution with a national mission. But both he and Freeman understood that TVA had to be animated by a vision if normal bureaucratic politics of stasis and routinization were to be avoided. In this sense, both chairmen were prisoners of TVA myths and the mythic appeal, although with somewhat different visions, because they regarded the inspiration of myth as inherent in

TVA's purposes and as the best way to galvanize the organization. For Freeman to have tried to make TVA simply an efficient power company would, in his view, have denied the very ideals that could make TVA great.

THE GENIE OUT OF THE BOTTLE

James Thompson suggests that complex organizations must do more to adapt to their changing environments than simply address particular problems in an ad hoc way. Rather, in times of major change, organizations must also be able to practice "opportunistic surveillance" of their environments in order to keep up with external change. Such a search should be found at the "institutional" level of the organization, in which in Selznick's conception, leadership infuses the institution with value. Yet, Thompson says, cases are numerous in which "once robust organizations decline or pass through crises because they have failed to anticipate institutional changes." He suggests two hypotheses that might explain the absence of "opportunistic surveillance": the attributes of top administrators as individuals, and the structure of the situation in which they operate. The two factors are not easily separated in real life.[33]

If administrators have an "office holding" view of their tasks, they are not likely to initiate opportunistic surveillance. Conventional routine will seem fine to them. Such leadership is more likely to be found in organizations that are sheltered from interference by actors in their "task environment." Thus, to the degree that the organization is relatively autonomous and is able to function according to the rationality of the missions at its "technical core," opportunistic surveillance may be limited. This kind of stasis is especially likely if influence within the organization is dispersed and management of technical tasks is strong or stronger in influence than the management of "institutional" tasks.[34] There is no "inner circle" to give clear direction to the organization.

In Thompson's view, every bureaucratic organization must find a "technology" that satisfies the "task environment," and demands in this regard are continually changing. But responsiveness does not happen spontaneously. The failure of General Billy Mitchell to persuade the army of the uses of air power in the 1920s is an example.[35] Institutional leadership must establish a "coalignment of technology and task environment with a viable domain, and of organization design and structure appropriate to that domain."[36] In concrete terms, TVA had to find ways to match its nuclear technology with regulatory demands from the task environment, and that match was to be secured by "opportunistic surveillance" and through an organizational design responsive to that search. This was the requirement that the post-1981 TVA board failed to fully meet. Organizational goals, as set at the highest level, from an institutional perspective, must direct the uses of the "technical core" of the organization. In this sense administration is a process in which all levels of the organization work together dynamically to be responsive to the task environment. This is a responsibility beyond simple management. Technical levels of the organization are dependent on higher, institutional levels for direction. The tension in such a task is between the desire for "certainty" and the need for joining slack resources to adaptability. The desire for certainty may prevail in the short term, but "freedom from commitment" in order to match tasks to the environment in the long run is the key to the organization's effectiveness. Only then can new possibilities suggested by environmental change be incorporated into organizational routines. Direction and adaptation must be balanced as decisions are made about how fast to change the design, structure, or technology of the organization. The task of leadership is to keep the organization at the "nexus" of connecting streams between the institution and its environment, and as the streams may be moving at different speeds, the nexus may be difficult to find.[37]

This abstract language perhaps comes to life when applied to the dilemmas facing the TVA board after 1981. Chairman Charles Dean took an "office holding" view of his job and did little to challenge the technical core of TVA to adapt to urgent demands from the task environment. After 1981, the two Freemans did practice "opportunistic surveillance" in their actions to cut back the nuclear construction program. This was a successful effort which reduced TVA's debt and matched its capacities to future energy needs of the valley in a realistic way. This was a concern with policy rather than administration. Dean and the Freemans did not fully grasp the challenges from the task environment for the regulation of nuclear safety until it was too late. The nuclear power organization within TVA was permitted to operate for too long in terms of its own ideas of "technical rationality" without much effort to join that mission to organizational redesign to foster greater responsiveness to both the internal and external regulation of nuclear safety. Of course, there were reorganizations, special task forces, and elaborate networks of safety specialists, but the TVA organizational culture developed in the 1930s prevailed over such palliatives until the shock of 1985 permitted radical change.

The technical problems of nuclear safety and the difficulties TVA experienced in correcting them were at bottom organizational issues. In discussing ways to manage change in "loosely coupled" bureaucratic organizations, Karl Weick recognizes that "multiple realities" are a consequence of "bounded rationality" in complex organizations with many specialized divisions. Such organizations work best on "trust and presumption."[38] This was the traditional TVA way; people trusted each other and relied upon the analysis and information supplied by those in other divisions. Such trust and presumption appear to have broken down in the late 1970s and early 1980s. TVA institutional leaders were unable to establish new bonds and loyalties as those derived from traditional missions gradually eroded.

Todd La Porte and his colleagues have explored the characteristics of complex organizations that work with high degrees of "reliability," that is they do not have dramatic mishaps that would be catastrophes. They have found that aircraft carriers and air-traffic control operations that work smoothly practice something other than simple "trial-and-error" ways to discover how to prevent failure. The contrasts with the TVA nuclear organization are striking. In the high-reliability organizations, physical technologies are tightly coupled so that the results of operational failures are quickly and immediately visible. Routine failure shuts down everything immediately, and long-term reliability is valued over short-term efficiency. Error cannot be tolerated because the consequences are too great, so analysis and search for the causes of error are continuous. Routine tasks are carried out by detailed standard operating procedures. In situations of high tempo and emergencies, routine work is transformed into small working groups that can manage the challenges according to prearranged conceptions. Yet whereas the organization is tightly coupled, there is continuous feedback from below upward. The whole is cohesive. The authors report that their "most vivid impression" is one of "close interdependence, especially during high-tempo or emergency activities" in which "relationships are complex, tightly coupled and sometimes intense and urgent."[39]

In the judgment of LaPorte and his colleagues, organizations that must function with high reliability are not like ordinary "trial-and-error" organizations, but too many people assume them to be so.[40] This is the same model suggested by Meyer and Zucker and by Thompson. These authors are all reaching for organizational capacities that go beyond simple "problemistic search." Society relies on such complex organizations, and if they fail, we are often surprised. Overseers in the task environment are often too late to "salvage troubled organizations" until the mishaps have occurred.[41] La Porte's study of the relations of the Nuclear Regulatory Commission with the Diablo Canyon nuclear plant in California, which has operated with high reliability, presents a clear contrast to TVA and the regulation of nuclear operations during the early 1980s. LaPorte and his colleagues approached the study with the notion that conventional "capture" theory would probably explain the relation of plant operators to the NRC inspectors.[42] Outside regulators would become sympathetic to the problems of the regulated, with the result that compliance by the plant with regulations would be minimal.[43] Since the cost of shutting down nuclear operations is very great, it was plausible to think that operators would receive pressures from management to "fudge" on standards.[44] The remarkable thing to LaPorte and his colleagues was that they found just the opposite. Plant operators believed that it was best if they found operating problems and disclosed them to NRC staffs so that it would be clear that the operators were working continuously to prevent error. Internal safety staffs were accorded high prestige and were encouraged to compete in the discovery of problems.[45] Attention was given to the "root causes" of errors. For example, the divergence between construction drawings and the actual construction were treated as potentially very serious because the integrity of all drawings could then be challenged. Such conditions were fostered by the high recognition of the hazards of nuclear power, the emphasis upon high technical quality in operators, and the external pull from the NRC and the state public service commission for regulation which was matched by internal competition for compliance with safety standards.[46] The La Porte team is cautious about stating a theory that will explain effective regulation of organizations requiring high reliability because there has been very little research on the regulation of nuclear plants. The seeds of a theory are latent in the comparison of TVA operations with the organizations described in the La Porte team's study. And, indeed, such insights are compatible with earlier criticisms of TVA's failure to regulate internally for environmental quality. The internal regulators were accorded low prestige. External regulators were regarded as enemies. The links of responsiveness between operating and policy levels were broken and uncertain. In short, the TVA organizational culture of high operational discretion and self-evaluation by operating divisions had become seriously flawed in the face of technology far more complex than hydroelectric projects.

A study of possible organizational correlates of the 1986 *Challenger* disaster in which a space shuttle blew up just after launching provides some interesting comparative insights.[47] Disasters are said to have long incubation periods, and retrospectively it was possible to identify the failure of officials of the National Aeronautic and Space Administration who did not follow up pieces of isolated evidence of the problem with the O rings on the shuttle that caused the explosion.[48] The relevant external regulatory body was advisory in nature and supposed to be responsive to the concerns of the NASA administrator. That official also had discretion on how to respond to external advice. External reviewers were dependent on the NASA operators for information and were several steps removed from operations.[49] There were two groups of internal safety regulators, both of whom were shorthanded and pressured by the tensions between cost-savings and deadlines on the one hand and safety on the other. Financial incentives were available for cutting costs and meeting deadlines rather than for discovering safety problems. The two staffs were under the supervision of the operators they were supposed to regulate. No sanctions were imposed on operators who were responsible for mishaps, even those in the *Challenger* case. Congress, as an external regulator several times removed from NASA operations, could not make judgments about technical controversies and was also dependent on NASA's monopoly of U.S. space activities.[50] This brief summary suggests important similarities between the regulator ethos of TVA and NASA, which were very different than the atmosphere and practices found by La Porte and his colleagues in organizations of high reliability.

It is an ironic possibility that the very creativity and innovativeness of the TVA and NASA organizations in their founding years were due to the loosely coupled separateness of the operating arms which had learned to collaborate in behalf of inspiring cross-departmental missions. In subsequent years, loose coupling simply fostered separateness. The effort of subsequent leaders to inspire new visions may have been a response to this stagnation. The administrator who was called out of retirement to pull NASA out of the *Challenger* problems was the same one who had pushed the controversial space shuttle in the first place, and he was the subsequent author of the much debated idea of a space station.[51] The parallels with Aubrey Wagner are striking.

The consequence of leadership failures at TVA in regard to nuclear operations were organizational drift and defensiveness in nuclear operations. The warning signs kept surfacing, but no action was taken. If operators on the ground could be blamed for particular mishaps, then the organizational structure and culture could escape analysis and blame. I draw the perhaps paradoxical conclusion that more sophisticated "political" leadership by the TVA chairman and board might have seen the potential threat of nuclear malfunctions to the entire institution and its external reputation. Greater political sensitivity might have produced more effective management.

POLITICAL ACCOUNTABILITY

TVA is an exemplar of the dream of American progressives that politics can and should be separated from administration.[52] This assumption was made explicit in Lilienthal's vision of grass roots democracy as the TVA ideal. The national government would set a policy of unified resource development in a region, and then the government corporation, empowered with the autonomy to act, would implement that policy in the region, close to the people. Lilienthal did not dwell much on the other part of the New Deal dream that there would be several TVAs in the major regions, all of which would be guided by national planning for resource development under the aegis of the National Resources Planning Board or some such entity. The political scientist John Gaus pointed out in 1937 that in the absence of such an overall guiding structure, the new public authorities, such as TVA, might be difficult to control and would engage in competition with federal, state, and local agencies.[53] This was perhaps one reason why secretary of the interior Harold Ickes tried to put TVA under the umbrella of his department. TVA advocates can of course argue that such a fate would have destroyed TVA's creativity, and they might be correct. American government exhibits two extremes of political and administrative control.[54] Some agencies, like TVA and other public authorities and independent corporations and regulatory bodies, have great autonomy but are not easy to control. Accountability is often in question. Other agencies, certainly the majority, are so tightly bound into political and administrative controls that independence, discretion, and creativity are rare indeed. Such agencies are pushed first one way and then the other because of shifting vagaries of public policy. Caution becomes the byword, and administrative improvements are incremental at best. This might have been TVA's fate had it landed in the Department of the Interior. But it might also have been the case that such a TVA would never have tried to build seventeen nuclear reactors. One can never know. Plenty of federal pork-barrel projects are no more inspiring than the Tellico Dam, or, for example, the Tombigbee Waterway along the lower Mississippi River. But in such cases the initiative for the projects comes from congressional politicians. Distributive politics rule the day. The TVA case is somewhat different in that the initiatives came from the organization itself. The limited surveillance exercised over TVA and the high degree of protection that the congressional members from the Tennessee Valley gave the authority might have been the same had TVA been tied closer to a federal department, but it might have been more difficult for TVA executives to engage in unilateral adventurism.

What is perhaps more important is that both the Congress and the president declined to give TVA any kind of careful oversight after it became virtually financially independent of the federal government in 1959. The Bureau of the Budget fought like a tiger to keep the power of approval over TVA expenditures, even those from revenue bonds, but the compromise of 1959 cut TVA loose from such control. Congress retained the authority of oversight but did not exercise it to any extent except in highly emotional defensive actions, as in the Dixon-Yates story. It was only when the people of the valley themselves turned on TVA that Congress began to pay attention, and the nuclear mishap of 1985 then permitted a degree of temporary congressional intervention. TVA had shifted incrementally from a national to a regional mission without a matching shift in mechanisms of accountability. For example, the idea that the valley states might exercise some oversight over electricity rates was knocked down easily in the early days. A federal corporation could not be subject to state regulation. But the very absence of a grass roots politics of accountability and control that resulted permitted TVA to operate in a political vacuum for many years.

Thompson suggests that relying on task environments to "salvage troubled organizations" is likely to be too late and too expensive. "Preventive care" is better.[55] His remedy is to suggest the incorporation of single agencies into "multiorganizational complexes" such as the space agency, interuniversity consortia, and gigantic hydroelectric projects. But he goes on to point out that there can be pockets in society in which several organizations may operate in mutual support in a network which is itself difficult for society to control.[56]

In fact, the more complex the bureaucracy, the more difficult it is for the national government to control it. Congress is almost never a "principal" that can give unchallenged direction to its bureaucratic "agent." Agencies with easily designed tasks that can be clearly and efficiently implemented and that have strong client support are perhaps more easily controlled by Congress. But agencies with difficult, complex tasks that are hard to specify and evaluate often elude congressional oversight and control.[57] The federal executive is in no better position, because to the degree that an administrative agency is complex, has multiple clients, is protected by congressional patrons, and is not central to the policy objectives of presidents, executive control is limited.

To the degree that federal agencies are autonomous and subject to only limited central oversight and control, their leadership positions will more likely be filled with administrators who are more responsive to the "technical rationality" of the agency than to the politics of policy and accountability. Thompson warns that "there is no guarantee that the society which assigns such importance to complex organizations will be able to provide them with administrators equal to the task."[58] Few public administrators really understand much about complex administrative processes. A few may have private insights derived from experience, "but the conversion of private insight into sharable—teachable and learnable—understanding is not an automatic process."[59] There is too much insistence on competence in the work of the technical core of organizations—whether hospitals, schools, or social welfare organizations—with the result that technical management is frequently equated with administration, thus ignoring Selznick's depiction of the crucial importance of "institutional" leadership.[60]

After Lilienthal, the TVA chairmen were administrative managers with considerable, but varying, technical skills. Vogel had such a background, but his experience in the Army Corps of Engineers had given him the opportunity to develop the political skills necessary for getting along with regional politicians and Congress. Wagner was the archetypal apostle of "technical rationality," and like most chairmen, he did not attempt to work Congress himself but relied heavily on TVA's Washington staff, who cultivated the support of key legislators like Lister Hill and Bob Jones. David Freeman had worked as a staff person in both Congress and the White House and understood Washington politics, but before becoming chairman he had never had the experience of providing "institutional" leadership for a large organization. The cast of his mind was one of "technical rationality," albeit with considerable policy vision. The TVA chairmen were not selected from a pool of politically experienced administrators, as is often the case with federal cabinet heads, subcabinet officers, and even career heads of agencies and bureaus. This has proved to be unfortunate for the "institutional" leadership of TVA. The administration of a complex public bureaucracy is a process of coping with uncertainty and unpredictable contingencies. There is no blueprint for carrying an institution through difficult periods of change because there is no predictable evolutionary line. The ability to discern plausible paths and to convince others is a political skill and is the prime basis for the influence of the institutional leader.[61]

PUBLIC AUTHORITIES AND ACCOUNTABILITY

The comparative study of American government corporations reveals much in common in their histories and actions. Because they are exempted from the private market and are likely to be monopolies, they are likely to charge prices necessary to meet their costs without regard for cost controls. This can lead to misallocation of resources in the absence of market tests or cost-benefit analyses.[62] The highly technical specialization found in most authorities may make them less innovative over time because new problems will arise for which the organizational professionals are less suited. Construction engineers, for example, do not easily become sensitive to environmental impact analysis.[63] Two central but conflicting themes often found in public authorities are their "faith in participatory democracy and their suspicion of elected politicians."[64] To keep politicians at bay, authorities will invoke the values of grass roots democracy in nonpartisan terms, all of which was once part of "progressive dogma."[65] In such cases, local elites, like businesspeople, may be taken as the surrogates of democracy. Annemarie Walsh finds that public authorities as a class show common tendencies to borrow and build with minimal delay, to select projects with financial revenues, to rely on established methods, and to emphasize physical rather than social projects. These tendencies reinforce each other. Avoidance of delay is a way to limit political debate about projects and thus permits development to move ahead more easily than otherwise. Physical projects that produce revenues are thereby favored.[66] Those parts of a region or economic group that do not benefit from such projects have very little leverage over authorities.[67] Walsh suggests that public authorities, in their great autonomy, are a symptom of "pluralism run rampant." They pursue the logic of their "technical rationality" quite apart from any larger or overriding social goal. She does not blame the authorities but the politics that has produced them in which such bureaucracies have not been directed by either general theories of the purposes of public enterprise or definitions of the public interest.[68]

Walsh's insights provide a shock of recognition for a student of TVA, and indeed she gives many TVA examples as evidence for her propositions. Does this mean that the attention given the leadership of TVA in this study is less important than has been suggested because they have simply been puppets in a larger story found in many public authorities? I do not think so. Each public authority has its own history, and the institutions may diverge greatly in ways not learned from a study of what they have in common. For example, the New York Port Authority appears to have weathered the years in better shape than TVA, perhaps because it is less dependent on complex technology for its work, and also because it is the child of the state governments of New York and New Jersey and is therefore far more responsive to politics and politicians than TVA.[69] Yet NASA and TVA appear to have become prisoners of myth in their more recent histories.

The point is, it is useful to compare types of institutions, within the same framework, as Walsh has done, but it is also important to trace the uniqueness of institutional histories and then compare them for similarities and differences. The comparative study of institutions that relies on individual histories can be theoretical as differences in development are explained.

Conceptions of Organizational Leadership

The study of one or more organizations across time may permit an assessment of the relative importance of institutional leadership that is less easily seen in cross-sectional studies at one period of time.[70] Leadership may prove to be important for organizational action and development during critical historical junctures when someone must probe the uncertainties and provide a plausible course of action, subject, of course, to prevailing resources and constraints. And by the same token, leaders in times of stability may simply act out the expectations of fixed institutional roles, although with varying degrees of personal skill. Leaders may also be effective in deliberately resisting change.

The most effective opportunities for creative leadership are those in which the leadership skills, the tasks to be performed, and the political context are congruent in positive ways. Success cannot be reduced to any one factor.[71] Thus Lilienthal's rhetorical abilities, the requirement that the TVA idea be sold to the people of the valley, and the favorable politics of the New Deal all worked to help him provide the public leadership that the new authority desperately needed. Dean's passivity was not favorable to managing a nuclear program that was out of control in a hostile regulatory climate. Skills can be appropriate for one task and time and not another. Wagner's driving, building abilities were appropriate for the period of construction and expansion in the 1960s and matched the political climate of the Great Society. But Wagner was ill-suited to cope with the challenges of the new environmental politics or the energy crisis. David Freeman might have been as creative a leader of TVA as Lilienthal if there had been stronger support for environmental values and energy conservation in the valley, especially among the distributors and among TVA's congressional patrons. Freeman's stubbornness and persistence, along with that of Richard Freeman, paid off in cutting back the nuclear program after David was forced from the chairmanship. He had nothing to lose by boldness.

Effective leadership is not possible if the leader does not "discern" the historical possibilities for action at a given time and the degree to which his or her skills match the tasks required and available political support. David Freeman perhaps failed to discern accurately the real possibility that TVA could become an "energy lab for the nation," with the consequence that he alienated the distributors on that score without any compensating gain. Acute discernment can make one sensitive to what cannot be done perhaps more easily than to what can potentially be done.

One aspect of discernment is self-knowledge. One must be careful not to take on tasks that run counter to one's strengths as a leader, and it follows that one should look for promising opportunities to use such skills. But skills may chase problems just as inappropriately as solutions do.

The aspect of discernment that is even more tricky is to know whether manifest or latent political resources can be summoned to support leadership actions and strategies. It may be easier to discern political constraints, perhaps because they are likely to be more visible. Because political support may be latent, one cannot always know whether a bold step is possible until one tries and others follow or fail to do so. The trade-off between boldness and caution is one that every institutional leader must make. James Wilson cautions organizational leaders to balance core and

peripheral tasks, to understand the culture of the organization, to negotiate with political superiors to get agreement on essential constraints, and
to match the distribution of authority and the control over resources to
the tasks of the organization.[72] Such prudential maxims are the ingredi-
ents of discernment.

If leadership ability is a potential factor for boldness and innovation in
organizational history, then predicting the success of such leaders before
the fact will be difficult if not impossible. The importance of intentionality, including both will and skill in leaders, is a constraint on political
science prediction, although not to theory. The intentionality factor must
be included in theoretical propositions. Wagner's great determination
and his strong beliefs in the TVA mission were crucial to both his successes and failures. The structural and political factors surrounding action cannot permit predictions unless it is determined that leadership is
not an important factor in a given case. Lilienthal could have lost the
power fight to Wilkie if the Supreme Court had decided differently. Vogel
could not have been sure he could persuade Eisenhower to sign the Bond
Revenue Act. If leadership is solely a dependent variable, then intentionality matters less and prediction may be easier. Since leadership is both an
independent and dependent factor, we must always consider it as a possible cause of action. Wilson suggests that this is why little progress has
been made in developing a theory of organizational innovation. Deliberate change is so dependent on executive interests and beliefs that "the
chance appearance of a change-oriented personality is enormously important in explaining organizational change." Likewise, a "perverse"
executive can delay change for years.[73]

CONCLUSION

In retrospect, I now "discern" more clearly the ideas running throughout
this study of TVA than I did at the outset. These ideas have been slowly
incubating in my mind in the past few years as I have tried to sharpen and
refine my understanding of institutional leadership.

First, I have wished to satisfy myself that I understand the failures of
TVA since I first began to observe the authority in 1979. In particular I
have tried to understand how failure could be connected to past successes. The idea of organizational leaders as prisoners of myth developed
as I read Selznick and saw how I might complete the task that he began.
Our two books should be read together.

Second, this book is the fullest expression of my evolving thinking in a
sequence of writings about political/organizational leadership.[74] I have
tried to understand the character of and conditions for "entrepreneurial
leadership" in public administration, the conditions affecting creativity in

the career line of individual administrators, the relation of historical context to the success of personal political skill in leaders, and the kinds of leadership required in different contexts. The central insight that emerges is that accurate "discernment" of the possibilities for action inherent in the historical situation is the central task and most important skill required of "political" leaders.

Finally, for some years I have been trying to understand how to develop theories about leadership from historical analysis. This has led me, perhaps without my fully realizing it, toward an interest in narrative as a means of capturing the moment of action. But at the same time, I affirm the importance of comparing historical stories to produce generalizations, even as one respects particular historical contexts. In my judgment, narrative is the vehicle for interpretation and the friend of theory.

Notes

PREFACE

1. *Summer Policy Study: The Role of TVA in Regional Development* (Knoxville: Tennessee Valley Authority, 1981).

2. Erwin C. Hargrove, "The Task of Leadership: The Board Chairmen," in *TVA: Fifty Years of Grass-roots Bureaucracy*, ed. Erwin C. Hargrove and Paul K. Conkin (Urbana: University of Illinois Press, 1983).

3. Jameson W. Doig and Erwin C. Hargrove, "Leadership and Political Analysis," in *Leadership and Innovation: A Biographical Perspective on Entrepreneurs in Government*, ed. Doig and Hargrove (Baltimore: Johns Hopkins University Press, 1987).

4. Erwin C. Hargrove, *The Power of the Modern Presidency* (New York: Alfred A. Knopf, 1974), chap. 6.

5. Erwin C. Hargrove, *Jimmy Carter as President: Politics and Leadership for the Public Good* (Baton Rouge: Louisiana State University Press, 1988).

6. Herman Finer, *The Administrative History of the Tennessee Valley Authority*, unpublished manuscript, 1938. Finer did publish a sanitized version, *The TVA, Lessons for International Application*, International Labor Office, Montreal, 1944). Also see C. Herman Pritchett, *The Tennessee Valley Authority: A Study in Public Administration* (Chapel Hill: University of North Carolina Press, 1943).

7. George Gant, a TVA general manager in the 1950s, told an interviewer in 1971 that the Finer manuscript was controversial within TVA and that "someone managed to get its publication squelched." But he did not know any details. Oral History Interviews, Memphis State University, December 28, 1971, part 2:14.

8. Personal communication to the author from Pendleton Herring, former head of the Social Science Research Council, April 1989.

9. The committee members were Ernest Draper (an assistant secretary of Commerce), Herbert Emerich, and Admiral A. E. Parsons.

10. The Freedom of Information Act contains a provision for "deliberative privilege" which permits an agency to withhold documents from inquiry if the material describes internal debate and decision making. This provision makes sense for current work, but there is no reason why material twenty or even ten years old cannot be read by anyone. TVA lawyers argued to me that if I were to see material, then anyone could see it. They were gun-shy from having faced so many lawsuits from "whistle-blowers" about the nuclear construction program. My response to this argument is that anyone should be able to see such material. But a lone scholar cannot do much against a giant bureaucracy.

11. John Briggs and F. David Peat, *Turbulent Mirror: An Illustrated Guide to Chaos Theory and the Science of Wholeness* (New York: Harper and Row, 1989), 83.

CHAPTER 1

1. Philip Selznick, *Leadership in Administration: A Sociological Interpretation* (New York: Harper and Row, 1957).

2. Philip Selznick, *TVA and the Grass Roots: A Study in the Sociology of Formal Organization* (New York: Harper Torch Books, 1966).

3. Citation for FDR's message to Congress.

4. Selznick, *TVA and the Grass Roots* , 57.

5. Ibid., 58–60, 64–67.

6. Gordon Clapp, *The TVA: An Approach to the Development of a Region* (Chicago: University of Chicago Press, 1965).

7. James G. March and Johan P. Olsen, *Rediscovering Institutions, The Organizational Basis of Politics* (New York: Free Press, 1989).

8. Theda Skocpol, ed., *Vision and Method in Historical Sociology* (Cambridge: Cambridge University Press, 1984), 362–363.

9. Ibid., 368.

10. Ibid., 372.

11. Ibid., 377.

12. Ibid., 378–379.

13. Ibid., 383.

14. Paul Diesing, *Patterns of Discovery in the Social Sciences* (Chicago: Aldine-Atherton, 1971), 138.

15. Ibid., 149.

16. Ibid., 182.

17. Larry Griffin, "Narrative, Event Structure Analysis and Causal Interpretation in Historical Sociology," *American Journal of Sociology* 98 (March 1993): 1094–1133.

18. John R. Kimberly, "The Life Cycle Analogy and the Study of Organizations: Introduction," in *The Organizational Life Cycle: Issues in the Creation, Transformation, and Decline of Organizations*, ed. John R. Kimberly, Robert H. Miles, and Associates (San Francisco: Jossey-Bass, 1980), 13.

19. Ibid., 12–13.

20. Kimberly, "Initiation, Innovation and Institutionalization in the Creation Process," in Kimberly et al., *The Organizational Life Cycle*, 39–43.

21. Robert H. Miles and W. Alan Randolph, "Influence of Organizational Learning Styles on Early Development," in Kimberly et al. *The Organizational Life Cycle*, 51–52.

22. Ibid.

23. Ibid., 75–78.

24. Robert H. Miles, "Findings and Implications of Organizational Life Cycle Research: A Commencement," in Kimberly et al., *The Organizational Life Cycle*, 443.

25. Mary Douglas, *How Institutions Think* (Syracuse: Syracuse University Press, 1986), 41.

26. Ibid., 45, 47, 65.

27. Ibid., 124.

28. Ibid., 83, 120, 128.

29. Ibid., 69.

30. Ibid., 42.

31. W. Richard Scott, "Unpacking Institutional Arguments," in Walter W. Powell and Paul J. DiMaggio, *The New Institutionalism in Organizational Analysis* (Chicago: University of Chicago Press, 1991), 170.

32. John Van Maanen and Stephen R. Barley, "Cultural Organization, Fragments of a Theory," in *Organizational Culture*, ed. Peter J. Frost et al. (Beverly Hills: Sage Publications, 1985), 39–48.

33. Scott, "Unpacking Institutional Arguments," 263.

34. March and Olsen, *Rediscovering Institutuions*, 740.

35. The organizing ideas of the TVA study developed from previous work. See Doig and Hargrove, *Leadership and Innovation*, and Erwin C. Hargrove and John C. Glidewell, *Impossible Jobs in Public Management* (Lawrence: University Press of Kansas, 1989).

36. James Q. Wilson, *Bureaucracy: What Government Agencies Do and Why They Do It* (New York: Basic Books, 1989), 228.

37. Doig and Hargrove, *Leadership and Innovation*, and Hargrove and Glidewell, *Impossible Jobs*.

38. Peter B. Smith and Mark F. Peterson, *Leadership, Organizations, and Culture* (Beverly Hills: Sage Publications, 1988), 159.

39. James D. Thompson, *Organizations in Action: Social Science Bases of Administrative Theory* (New York: McGraw-Hill), 1453.

40. Smith and Peterson, *Leadership*, 160.

41. Ibid., 162.

42. Norman Frohlick and Joe A. Oppenheimer, *Modern Political Economy* (Englewood Cliffs, NJ: Prentice-Hall, Inc., 1978), 85–88.

CHAPTER 2

1. Paul K. Conkin, "Intellectual and Political Roots," in Hargrove and Conkin, *TVA: Fifty Years*.

2. Franklin D. Roosevelt, "A Request for Legislation to Create a Tennessee Valley Authority—A Corporation Clothed with the Power of Government but Possessed of the Flexibility and Initiative of a Private Enterprise" (president's address to Congress, April 10, 1933, White House copy).

3. Walter L. Crease, *TVA's Public Planning: The Vision, the Reality* (Knoxville: University of Tennessee Press, 1990), 35.

4. Ibid., 38–39.

5. Ibid., 42–43.

6. Ibid., 50.

7. Conkin, "Intellectual and Political Roots," 25–26.

8. Ibid., 26–32.

9. Frederick Gutheim to Herman Finer, December 30, 1937, Washington, D.C.

10. The Tennessee Valley Authority Act, 73rd Congress, 1st Session [HR 5081], May 1933.

11. Herman Finer, section 1, chapter 12, *The Administrative History*, 18.

12. Roy Talbert, Jr., *The Human Engineer: Arthur E. Morgan and the Tennessee Valley Authority*, Master's thesis, Vanderbilt University, 1967, 13.

13. Thomas K. McCraw, *TVA and the Power Fight, 1933–1939* (Philadelphia: J. B. Lipincott, 1971), 44; David E. Lilienthal, *The Journals of David E. Lilienthal*, vol. 1, *The TVA Years, 1939–1945* (New York: Harper and Row, 1964), 102.

14. H. A. Morgan, personal papers, University of Tennessee Library, Knoxville, transcript of recording, spool 5,1, 13–14.

15. Raymond Moley, *The Spirit of the New Deal* (New York: Harcourt, Brace and World, 1966), 331.

16. Ibid., 328.

17. Roy Talbert, Jr., *Beyond Pragmatism: The Story of Arthur E. Morgan*, Ph.D. diss., Vanderbilt University, 1971, 148.

18. Robert Crunden, *Ministers of Reform: The Progressive Achievement in American Civilization, 1889–1920* (New York: Basic Books, 1982).

19. Roy Talbert, Jr., *FDR's Utopian, Arthur E. Morgan of the TVA* (Minneapolis: University Press of Minnesota, 1987), 9.

20. Ibid., 9–10.

21. Ibid.

22. Ibid., 16–17.

23. Ibid., 19.

24. Ibid., 70.

25. Ibid., 18, 218, 131.

26. Ibid., 137–139.

27. Ibid., 137–139, 140–141.

28. Ibid., 64–65.

29. Ibid., 24.

30. Ibid., 65–68.

31. Ibid., 119.

32. Ibid., 61–62, 119–120.

33. Ibid., 54, 126.

34. Ibid., 41, 54.

35. Finer, *The Administrative History*, section 2, chapter 3, 10. Aubrey Wagner told me a story of how he and other young engineers who lived in Norris would put beer bottles on Wagner's front porch in sight of Mr. and Mrs. Morgan's windows. As the line of bottles got longer, the Morgans would peek out of their windows in shock.

36. John Muldowny, University of Tennessee historian of TVA, to the author, 1979, Knoxville, TN.

37. Talbert, *FDR's Utopian*, 77.

38. Neal Bass to author, 1981, Nashville, TN.

39. Floyd Reeves to Herman Finer, December 30, 1937, Knoxville, TN, 11–12.

40. Finer, *The Administrative History*, section 2, chapter 4, 17.

41. Neal Bass to author, 1981, Nashville, TN.

42. David E. Lilienthal, Memphis State Oral History Project, part 1, 26.

43. John Ferris, Memphis State Oral History Project, part 2, 4.

44. Herman Finer to H. A. Morgan, September 10, 1936, 1–2.

45. John Ferris, Memphis State Oral History Project, part 2, 8.

46. David E. Lilienthal, *The Journals of David E. Lilienthal*, 7 vols. (New York: Harper and Row, 1964–1984).

47. Ibid., vol. 7, *Unfinished Business, 1968–1981*, 782.

48. Ibid., vol. 1, *The TVA Years*, 4–5.

49. Ibid., 6–7.

50. Ibid., 8.

51. John Brooks, *Business Adventures* (New York: Weybright and Talley, 1969), 273. Lilienthal was referring to Senator Kenneth McKellar, of Tennessee, who made life difficult for him with pressure to make patronage appointments to TVA and with attacks on board autonomy.

52. Lilienthal, *The TVA Years*, 13.

53. Ibid., 6.

54. Joseph Swidler to author, June 4, 1981, Washington, D.C.

55. Lilienthal, *The TVA Years*, 14.

56. Ibid., 14–15, 16–17.

57. Eli W. Clemens, *Public Utility Regulation in Wisconsin Since the Reorganization of the Commission in 1931*, Ph.D. diss., University of Wisconsin, 1940, 11.

58. Lilienthal, *The TVA Years*, 16–17.

59. Ibid., 21.

60. Ibid., 26.

61. Talbert, *FDR's Utopian*, 28.

62. Edward Falck to author, July 21, 1981, Washington, D.C.

63. Arthur E. Morgan, radio address, National Broadcasting Company, August 15, 1933, Harold Denton's card file of A. E. Morgan speech materials, TVA Technical Library, Knoxville, TN.

64. Herman Finer, *The Administrative History*, section 2, chapter 3, 13, 14.

65. Ibid., 15.

66. Talbert, *FDR's Utopian*, 133.

67. Ibid., 127–129.

68. Finer, *The Administrative History*, section 2, chapter 3, 15–16, 17.

69. Finer interview with A. E. Morgan, September 13, 1937, Knoxville, TN, 6–9.

70. Ibid.

71. Ibid.

72. Finer, *The Administrative History*, section 2, chapter 3, 30.

73. Ibid.

74. I have been told this story by several construction engineers, some of whom were present at the beginning. The practice of adapting plans at the site has been common and legitimate within TVA. The story of nuclear construction in Chapter 9 suggests that this practice continued in that area, with great detriment to nuclear safety.

75. G. David Hudson to Herman Finer, February 11, 1938, Knoxville, TN, 5–6.

76. A. E. Morgan to Herman Finer, October 4, 1937, Knoxville, TN, 3.

77. A. E. Morgan to Herman Finer, November 23, 1937, 3.

78. Ernest Draper, Memphis State Oral History Project, December 30, 1969, 19.

79. John Ferris, Memphis State Oral History Project, December 7, 1969, part 3, 12.

80. H. A. Morgan, personal papers, University of Tennessee Library, Knoxville, spool 7.

81. Ibid., spool 5, part 2, 13.

82. Ibid., spool 3, 3.

83. Ibid., spool 6, 9.

84. Ibid., spool 6, 7–8.

85. H. A. Morgan to Herman Finer, December 16, 1937, Knoxville, TN, 2.

86. H. A. Morgan, personal papers, spool 5, 6–8.

87. H. A. Morgan to Arthur E. Morgan and David E. Lilienthal, "Proposed Statement of Policy in the Planning Activities of the Tennessee Valley Authority," October 3, 1933, A. E. Morgan File, VIB, "Morgan's Board Relationships," U.S. Archive, East Point, GA.

88. John Ferris, Memphis State Oral History Project, December 6, 1969, 16.

89. Barrett Shelton, Memphis State Oral History Project, June 18, 1970, 9–10.

90. David Lilienthal, "Some Observations on the TVA," A. E. Morgan File, VIB, "Morgan Board Relationships," U.S. Archive, East Point, GA.

91. Ibid.

92. David E. Lilienthal, Memphis State Oral History Project, February 6, 1970, 4.

93. Ibid., 6.

94. Minutes of Meeting of the Board of Directors of the Tennessee Valley Authority, July 30, 1933, A. E. Morgan File, VIB, U.S. Archive, East Point, GA.

95. Finer, *The Administrative History*, section 2, chapter 2, 25–26.

96. H. A. Morgan and David E. Lilienthal, "Memorandum on Reorganization," August 3, 1933, Curtis, Morgan, Morgan, 24H26, 321 (1), "Creation of Division," U.S. Archive, East Point, GA; Harcourt A. Morgan, personal papers, University of Tennessee Library, Knoxville, spool 9, 5–7; David E. Lilienthal, Memphis State Oral History Project, part 1, 15.

97. David E. Lilienthal memo to A. E. Morgan and H. A. Morgan, October 13, 1933, and A. E. Morgan's reply, November 11, 1933, "Morgan's Board Relationships," VIB, U.S. Archive, East Point, GA; Talbert, *FDR's Utopian*, 4.

98. Talbert, *FDR's Utopian*, 189–190, A. E. Morgan memo about real estate, June 5, 1933, VIB, "Morgan Board Relationships," A. E. Morgan File, VIB, U.S. Archive, East Point, GA.

99. Earle S. Draper memo to TVA Board, "Program for Regional Planning Project, RP1, Tennessee Valley Section of the National Plan," March 26, 1934, Chairman's Office Files, Land Planning, 913.2, U.S. Archive, East Point, GA.

100. David E. Lilienthal to H. A. Morgan and A. E. Morgan, "Re: Project RP1," Chairman's Office Files, Land Planning, 913.2, U.S. Archive, East Point, GA.

101. Neal Bass to author, May 20, 1981, Nashville, TN.

102. Ibid.

103. A. E. Morgan to H. A. Morgan, August 3, 1934, Box 1, Folder 1, U.S. Archive, East Point, GA.

104. Marvin H. McIntyre to Arthur E. Morgan, November 24, 1933, White House Correspondence, 1933, VIA, "Establishment of TVA," U.S. Archive, East Point, GA.

105. Ruth Falck to author, July 22, 1981, Washington, D.C.

106. Finer, *The Administrative History*, section 2, chapter 5, 19.

107. Ibid.

108. Ibid.

109. Minutes of Board Meeting, July 11, 1933, A. E. Morgan, "Board Relationships," VIB, U.S. Archive, East Point, GA.

110. Memo from A. E. Morgan to H. A. Morgan and David E. Lilienthal, August 14, 1933, "On Principles of Publicity," A. E. Morgan File, VIB, "Morgan Board Relationships," U.S. Archive, East Point, GA.

111. David E. Lilienthal, "Memo in Opposition to the Proposal of the Chairman, Arthur E. Morgan, for Territorial Division Agreement and cooperation between the Tennessee Valley Authority and Private Utilities," August 16, 1933, A. E. Morgan File, VIB, "Morgan's Board Relationships," U.S. Archive, East Point, GA.

CHAPTER 3

1. Joseph Swidler, Memphis State Oral History Project, December 8, 1981.

2. John Oliver to author, June 9, 1981, Signal Mountain, TN.

3. George Palo to author, May 28, 1981, Knoxville, TN.

4. Bernard Frank to Herman Finer, January 31, 1938, Knoxville, TN.

5. Lilienthal *The TVA Years*, 106–107.

6. David E. Lilienthal, *Management: A Humanist Art* (Carnegie Institute of Technology, distributed by Columbia University Press, 1967), 35.

7. Lilienthal, *The TVA Years*, 52–53.

8. Ibid., 55–56, 63.

9. Joseph Swidler to author, June 4, 1981, Washington, D.C.

10. David Lilienthal, interview with Ross Spears, Princeton, NJ, for the film "The Electric Valley," May 1980.

11. McCraw, *TVA and the Power Fight*, 63–66. My story of TVA's relations with the private utilities relies heavily upon McCraw's definitive account.

12. McCraw, *TVA and the Power Fight*, 67–70.

13. Edward Falck to author, July 21, 1981, Washington, D.C.

14. David Lilienthal, interview with Ross Spears, May 1980.

15. McCraw, *TVA and the Power Fight*, 74.

16. Speech by President Roosevelt in Tupelo, Mississippi, November 10, 1934. A stenographic report. David E. Lilienthal Files, 031, U.S. Archive, East Point, GA.

17. Joseph Swidler to author, June 4, 1981, Washington, D.C.

18. Lilienthal, *The TVA Years*, 54, 52.

19. McCraw, *TVA and the Power Fight*, 124.

20. U.S. Attorney General Homer Cummings to President Roosevelt, February 28, 1935, RG 142 040 Justice Department, U.S. Archive, East Point, GA.

21. *Ashwander v. TVA*, 297 U.S. 288 (1936).

22. Richard Lowitt, "The TVA, 1933–45," in Hargrove and Conkin, *TVA: Fifty Years*, 42–43.

23. Lilienthal, *The TVA Years*, 119–120.

24. David Lilienthal, interview with Ross Spears, May 1980.

25. Herman Finer, *The Administrative History*, section 2, chapter 9, 36–38.

26. Floyd Reeves to Herman Finer, December 30, 1937, Washington, D.C., 13.

27. Ruth Falck to author, July 22, 1981, Washington, D.C.

28. Roosevelt letter to Arthur Morgan, May 15, 1936. Arthur E. Morgan, White House Correspondence, 1936, Group 6 A, Box 535898, U.S. Archive, East Point, GA.

29. Lilienthal, *The TVA Years*, 62.

30. Ibid., 64.

31. Memo from Marguerite Owen, head of TVA Washington office, to Forest Allen, in Mr. Lilienthal's office, April 29, 1938. David E. Lilienthal Files, 031, 295, U.S. Archive, East Point, GA.

32. David E. Lilienthal, *TVA: Democracy on the March* (New York: Harper and Brothers, 1944).

33. Philip Selznick, *Leadership in Administration*, 17–19, 138–140, 150–152.

34. Lilienthal, *The TVA Years*, 116.

35. *Reorganization of the Excutive Departments*, message from the President of the United States transmitting a report on the reorganization of the Executive Department of the government, January 12, 1937, U.S. Government Printing Office, Washington, D.C., 1937.

36. Memo, William C. Fitts, Jr., to Lilienthal, September 7, 1939, 031, White House, 1939, RG 142 Board of Directors, David E. Lilienthal, General Correspondence, 1933–46, U.S. Archive, East Point, GA.

37. Memo, Earl S. Draper to John B. Blandford, Jr., August, 1939, Chairman's Office Files, 031.1, 095, 320, U.S. Archive, East Point, GA.

38. Harcourt A. Morgan to President Roosevelt, "Memorandum for the President, From the Board of Directors of the Tennessee Valley Authority," September 23, 1939, 1, Chairman's Office Files, 031.1, 095, Department of the Interior, U.S. Archive, East Point, GA.

39. Lilienthal, *The TVA Years*, 123, 125, 138, 266–270; David E. Lilienthal to Files, October 2, 1939, "Conference with Senator Norris, morning of October 2," 031.1, 032.2, Norris, George W., 095, 320, U.S. Archive, East Point, GA.

40. McCraw, *TVA and the Power Fight*, 158.

41. Lilienthal, *The TVA Years*, 667.

42. Ibid., 142.

43. Ibid.

44. Ibid., 81.

45. Ibid., 80.

46. Joseph C. Swidler to author, June 4, 1981, Washington, D.C.

47. Lilienthal, *The TVA Years*, 146.

48. McCraw, *TVA and the Power Fight*, 146–148.

49. Lilienthal to Dr. Alvin Johnson, October 29, 1938, RG 142, 095, New A–Z, U.S. Archive, East Point, GA.

50. Lilienthal, *The TVA Years*, 149.

51. Ibid., 146.

52. Ibid., 155.

53. Lilienthal to E. J. Coil, July 13, 1942; Coil to Lilienthal, July 17 and 27 and August 1, 1942; Alvin Hansen to Lilienthal, July 3, 1942; Lilienthal to Hansen, July 15, 1942; all from 095, 040, 032.1, Hansen, Alvin, National Planning Association, U.S. Archive, East Point, GA.

54. Selznick, *TVA and the Grass Roots*.

55. Ibid., 3, 4, 5.

56. Lilienthal, *TVA: Democracy*, 80–81.

57. Selznick, *TVA and the Grass Roots*, chapter 4.

58. Selznick, *TVA and the Grass Roots*, 238–242.

59. Victor C. Hobday, *Sparks at the Grass Roots: Municipal Distribution of TVA Electricity in Tennessee* (Knoxville: University of Tennessee Press, 1969), 38–50, 60, 71, 233, 240.

60. Hobday, *Sparks at the Grass Roots*, 32–33, 236.

61. Lilienthal, *The TVA Years*, 392.

62. David E. Lilienthal, *The Journals of David E. Lilienthal*, vol. 2, *The Atomic Energy Years, 1945–1950* (New York: Harper and Row, 1964), 187.

63. Lowitt, "The TVA, 1933–45," in Hargrove and Conkin, *TVA: Fifty Years*, 46–49; Lilienthal, *The TVA Years*, 344–348, 359–363, 365–367.

64. Clapp, *The TVA*, 38–45. Clapp told the Douglas Dam story in the Walgreen Lectures at the University of Chicago.

65. Lilienthal, *The TVA Years*, 396–397.

66. Ibid., 384–386.

67. Clapp, *The TVA*, 42.

68. Lilienthal, *The TVA Years*, 403.

69. Ibid.

70. Ibid., 425.

71. Ibid., 482.

72. Ibid., 483.

73. Ibid., 482–483.

74. Ibid., 483–484.

75. Ibid., 498, 519.

76. Ibid., 111–112.

77. David Lilienthal to board and general manager, October 4, 1939, "New Policies," Chairman's Files, 321(2), 321–70–1(2), 095, U.S. Archive, East Point, GA.

78. Lilienthal, *The TVA Years*, 143.

79. Ibid., 290.

80. Ibid., 291–292.

81. Memo to President Roosevelt, from the Board of Directors of the Tennessee Valley Authority, October, 1939. Harcourt Morgan Files, 031, 050–63, 000.41, 095, U.S. Archive, East Point, GA.

82. Memo to President Roosevelt, from the Directors of the Tennessee Valley Authority, June 12, 1940, Harcourt A. Morgan Papers, 031, 951.11,000.41, 679 (1356), U.S. Archive, East Point, GA.

83. Annual Report, 1942–43, 1–2, Tennessee Valley Authority.

84. Annual Report, 1944–45, Tennessee Valley Authority, 1, 5.

85. Ibid., 35, 57.

86. Roland Kampmeier, Memphis State Oral History Project, part 1, 4.

87. Julius Krug, Memphis State Oral History Project, September 24, 1969, 20–21.

88. David Lilienthal from Gordon Clapp, March 20, 1942, Clapp Papers, 031, 095, U.S. Archive, East Point, GA.

89. Lilienthal, *The TVA Years*, 394.

90. Ibid., 638–639.

91. Ibid., 654–655.

92. Ibid., 660.

93. George Palo to author, May 28, 1981, Knoxville, TN.

94. John Ferris, Memphis State Oral History Project, December 7, 1969, part 3, 27–28.

95. "A Reassessment of Tennessee Valley Authority Objectives," February 4, 1944. H. A. Morgan, personal papers, University of Tennessee Library, Knoxville.

96. Lilienthal, *The TVA Years*, 643.

97. Memo to Lilienthal from Gordon Clapp, August 18, 1943, Lilienthal Files, 061, 185, U.S. Archive, East Point, GA.

98. Earle Draper, Memphis State Oral History Project, December 30, 1969, 68, 73.

99. Paul Ager, Memphis State Oral History Project, April 15, 1970, 14.

100. Crease, *TVA's Public Planning*, xvi, 33, 54.

101. Rexford G. Tugwell and E. C. Banfield, "Grass Roots Democracy—Myth or Reality?" *Public Administration Review*, 10 (Winter 1950): 47–55.

102. Crease, *TVA's Public Planning*, 273.

103. Richard A. Couto, "Heroic Bureaucracies," unpublished paper, September 6, 1987. Couto is a faculty member at the University of Richmond. He identifies as "heroic bureaucracies" the Freedman's Bureau after the Civil War, the Resettlement Administration of the New Deal, and the Office of Economic Opportunity of the War on Poverty. Such agencies, according to Couto, are "demonstration endeavors" which attack a large social problem in new ways.

CHAPTER 4

1. Louis Brownlow to Herman Finer, December 6, 1937, Chicago, IL, 1.

2. Floyd Reeves to Herman Finer, December 30, 1937, Washington, D.C, 5.

3. Ibid.

4. A. E. Morgan to Herman Finer, September 13, 1937, Knoxville, TN, 7–8.

5. John Blandford to Herman Finer, November 10, 1937, Knoxville, TN, 4.

6. Herman Finer, *The Administrative History*, section 3, chapter 3, 13–14.

7. Pritchett, *The Tennessee Valley Authority*, 156–157; David Lilienthal, interview with Ross Spears, May 1980.

8. Pritchett, *The Administrative History*, 162–163.

9. John Blandford to Herman Finer, November 10, 1937, Knoxville, TN, 2.

10. Ibid.

11. Ibid., 3.

12. Finer, *The Administrative History*, section 3, chapter 1, 23, 45–46; chapter 2, 5, 12–15; chapter 3, 5, 6–7.

13. Forest Allen to Herman Finer, April 7, 1938, Knoxville, TN, 4–6, 13.

14. A. E. Morgan to President Roosevelt, May 18, 1936, 031, 095, 320. U.S. Archive, East Point, GA.

15. John Blandford to Herman Finer, November 10, 1937, 9.

16. Harry Wiersma, a TVA engineer and confidant of A. E. Morgan, related that Morgan would ask him to travel to meet his train before it reached Knoxville so that he might be told what the other two directors had done during his absence. Interview with author, May 13, 1981, Knoxville, TN.

17. John Blandford to Herman Finer, November 17, 1937, 4.

18. Louis Brownlow to Herman Finer, December 6, 1937, Chicago, IL, 3.

19. Herbert Emmerich to Herman Finer, December 5, 1937, Chicago, IL, 6–10.

20. Ibid., 2.

21. Ibid., 9.

22. The Draper Committee report, "Administrative Organization of the Tennessee Valley Authority," is not in Finer's papers. But Finer read it and summarized its recommendations in his text. A. E. Morgan's papers contain the main analysis and recommendations of the report, which Draper sent to Morgan on June 3, 1937. VIC2, U.S. Archive, East Point, GA.

23. Finer, *The Administrative History*, section 3, chapter 7, 9–11.

24. Herbert Emmerich to Herman Finer, December 5, 1937, Chicago, IL, 9.

25. Ibid., 9–10.

26. Ibid., 10.

27. The Draper Committee interviews and papers are in the Herman Finer Files in the National Archives, labeled "Interviews, March–May, 1937." Harry A. Curtis to Herman Finer, April 27, 1937.

28. C. A. Bock to Draper Committee, April 27, 1937.

29. Earle S. Draper to Draper Committee, April 28, 1937.

30. John Blandford to Draper Committee, May 1, 1937.

31. Gordon R. Clapp to Draper Committee, April 28, 1937.

32. John Gaus memo to Draper Committee, March 29, 1937.

33. John Gaus letter to Herbert Emmerich, April 19, 1937.

34. John Gaus letter to Ernest Draper, April 22, 1937.

35. Herbert Emmerich to Herman Finer, December 5, 1937, Chicago, IL, 7–8, 4.

36. "Report on Administrative Organization", John B. Blandford, Jr., Box 1, Herman Finer Papers, National Archives, Washington, D.C.

37. John B. Blandford to Herman Finer, November 17, 1937, Knoxville, TN, 4.

38. Ibid., 10.

39. John B. Blandford to Herman Finer, June 8, 1937, Knoxville, TN, 1.

40. Ibid., 1.

41. Finer, *The Administrative History*, section 3, chapter 3, 29–30.

42. Tennessee Valley Authority, List of Official Titles and Stations, 1937. Arthur E. Morgan Papers, VIC2, U.S. Archives, East Point, GA.

43. "Proposed Resolution Designating the General Manager as the Chief Administrative Officer of the Tennessee Valley Authority," July 29, 1941. Chairman's Office Files, 321–700-2(2), U.S. Archive, East Point, GA.

44. Finer, *The Administrative History*, section 3, chapter 5, 4.

45. Ibid.

46. Ibid.

47. Ibid.

48. Herman Finer, memo titled "Board Meeting," dated December 20, 1937.

49. Lilienthal, *The TVA Years*, 280.

50. Morris Leven to Herman Finer, December 30, 1937, Knoxville, TN.

51. John B. Blandford to Herman Finer, November 17, 1937, Knoxville, TN, 10.

52. William Hayes, Memphis State Oral History Project, December 29, 1970, 8–9.

53. Finer, *The Administrative History*, section 7, chapter 1, 28–30.

54. Gordon Clapp to members of the TVA board, July 3, 1943. "Staff Assistance to the General Manager in Various Phases of Over-All Management." Curtis, Morgan, Morgan File, General Manager's Office and Duties, 321–70–2(2), 095, U.S. Archive, East Point, GA.

55. Robert E. Sessions, "Notes on Conference with Mr. Ager," January 28, 1944, Administrative Files, 337, 404, 441, 095, U.S. Archive, East Point, GA.

56. Pritchett never read Finer's manuscript. Personal communication from C. Herman Pritchett, April 1989.

57. Pritchett, *The Tennessee Valley Authority*, 167. Pritchett's source was Gordon R. Clapp, "The Problems and Methods of General Management in a Multiple-Purpose Regional Agency," Seminar on the Economics of River Development Programs, May 22, 1941. Chairman's Office Files, 913, 001.32 (Clapp, G. R.) 321C4, U.S. Archive, East Point, GA.

58. Pritchett, *The Tennessee Valley Authority*, 167–170.

59. George F. Gant, Memphis State Oral History Project, December 28, 1971, Madison, WI, part 6, 3–4. A group of this kind continued to meet for lunch up through Aubrey Wagner's tenure as chairman. Hugh Parris and David Patterson to author, July 1979.

60. Gant, Memphis State Oral History Project, part 3, 14–15.

61. John Oliver, Memphis State Oral History Project, 13.

62. Lilienthal, *Unfinished Business*, 269.

63. David E. Lilienthal memo to board and general manager, "New Policies," October 4, 1939. Chairman's Office Files 321(2), 321–70–1(2), 095, U.S. Archive, East Point, GA.

64. Lilienthal, *The TVA Years*, April 9, 1942, 465.

65. Clapp, "The Problems and Methods of General Management in a Multiple-Purpose Regional Agency," May 22, 1941, seminar.

66. Edward Falck, Memphis State Oral History Project, September 25, 1970, Washington, D.C., 12.

67. Harry Case, Memphis State Oral History Project, March 6, 1970, East Lansing, MI, 18–19.

68. John Oliver, Memphis State Oral History Project, December 9, 1969, Chattanooga, TN, 6.

CHAPTER 5

1. Crease, TVA's Public Planning, 27.

2. Frederick Gutheim to Herman Finer, December 30, 1937, Washington, D.C., 2.

3. Louis Brownlow to Herman Finer, December 6, 1937, Chicago, IL.

4. Gordon Clapp to Herman Finer, October 30, 1937, Knoxville, TN.

5. A. E. Morgan to Franklin D. Roosevelt, September 25, 1933. White House Correspondence, 1933, Group 6 A, The Establishment of TVA, Arthur E. Morgan Papers, U.S. Archive, East Point, GA.

6. E. S. Draper to TVA board, "Program for Regional Planning Project, RPI—Tennessee Valley Section of the National Plan," March 28, 1934, Chairman's Office Files, 913.2, U.S. Archive, East Point, GA.

7. Earle S. Draper, "Regional Planning and the Tennessee Valley Authority," School of City Planning, Harvard University, January 14, 1935, 7, Draper, E. S., 001.32, 913, U.S. Archive, East Point, GA.

8. Crease, TVA's Public Planning, 324–327.

9. Earle S. Draper to TVA board, "Program for Regional Planning," 12.

10. Earle S. Draper, Memphis State Oral History Project, December 30, 1969, 29.

11. Lilienthal to A. E. Morgan and H. A. Morgan, March 26, 1934, Project RPI, Tennessee Valley Section of the National Plan, submitted as of February 20, 1934, by E. S. Draper, Director of Land Planning and Housing. Chairman's Office Files, Land Planning, 913.2, U.S. Archive, East Point, GA.

12. David E. Lilienthal, "Plans and Planners—American Style," an address at the fall meeting of the American City Planning Institute, October 11, 1937, Norris, TN, 10–11. A speech by Lilienthal, from TVA collection of speeches by the chairmen of the board.

13. Ibid., 11–12.

14. Forest Allen to John B. Blandford, Jr., August 17, 1936, "Program Planning," Lilienthal Papers, 320, 095, 300.4, U.S. Archive, East Point, GA.

15. Forest Allen to John B. Blandford, Jr., November 9, 1936, "Mr. Augus's Memo, October 6, on Outline of Regional Planning Report." Lilienthal Papers, 913, 095. U.S. Archive, East Point, GA.

16. Earle S. Draper, Memphis State Oral History Project, December 30, 1969, 25.

17. Lawrence L. Durisch and Robert E. Lowry, "The Scope and Content of

Administrative Decisions: The TVA Illustration," *Public Administration Review* 13 (1953): 225.

18. Pritchett, *The Tennessee Valley Authority*, 122–125.

19. Daniel Schaffer, "Environment and TVA: Toward a Regional Plan for the Tennessee Valley, 1930s," Tennessee Valley Authority Cultural Resources Program, undated paper, written in the 1980s, 22. Schaffer was a TVA historian.

20. Ibid., 27.

21. Crease, *TVA's Public Planning*, 269.

22. Ibid. A. J. Gray, a longtime TVA planner, told the same story in his oral history interview, Memphis State Oral History Project, December 20, 1974, Knoxville, TN, 4–9.

23. Crease, *TVA's Public Planning*, 380, citing Howard W. Odum and Henry Estil Moore, *American Regionalism: A Cultural-Historical Approach to National Integration* (Gloucester, MA: Peter Smith, 1966), 107.

24. Gordon R. Clapp, "Some Aspects of Regional Planning in the Tennessee Valley Authority," paper given at a joint meeting of the American Political Science Association and the American Society for Public Administration, December 30, 1940, Chicago, IL. Cited in Pritchett, *Tennessee Valley Authority*, 121.

25. Herman Finer, *The Administrative History*, section 2, chapter 5, 28.

26. Ibid., section 3, chapter 6, 6.

27. Ibid., section 4, chapter 2, 46–47.

28. Crease, *TVA's Public Planning*, 79.

29. Lilienthal to Frederic Delano, December 15, 1942. H. A. Morgan Files, 307, NSB, 031–6–3, 095, U.S. Archive, East Point, GA.

30. Clapp, "The Problems And Methods of General Management In A Multiple-Purpose Regional Agency," May 22, 1941, seminar.

31. Gordon R. Clapp to George F. Gant, Acting Director of Personnel, August 22, 1941, "Changes of Delegation Within the Personnel Department," Chairman's Office Files, 321–71–1(1), 320–8, 095, U.S. Archive, East Point, GA.

32. G. Donald Hudson to Herman Finer, February 11, 1938, Knoxville, TN, 5–6.

33. Forest Allen to Herman Finer, April 7, 1938, Knoxville, TN, 12–13.

34. T. Levron Howard, "The Social Scientist in the Tennessee Valley Authority Programs," March 11, 1936, 001.32 (Howard T. Levron), 901.03, 901.04, U.S. Archive, East Point, GA.

35. C. A. Bock to Herman Finer, October 13, 1937, Knoxville, TN, 6–7.

36. Forest Allen to Herman Finer, April 7, 1938, Knoxville, TN, 8, 9.

37. G. Donald Hudson to Herman Finer, February 11, 1938, Knoxville, TN, 3.

38. A. J. Gray, Memphis State Oral History Project, December 20, 1974, Knoxville, TN, 5.

39. Bernard Frank to Herman Finer, January 31, 1938, Knoxville, TN, 2–4.

40. Ibid., 6.

41. Neal Bass to author, May 20, 1981, Nashville, TN.

42. Willis M. Baker, Memphis State Oral History Project, February 8, 1970, Media, PA, 12.

43. H. A. Morgan to A. E. Morgan and David Lilienthal, "Proposed State-

ment of Policy in the Planning Activities of the Tennessee Valley Authority," October 3, 1933, Chairman's Office Files, 241 and 265, 321(2) Duties and Activities, etc. 913, U.S. Archive, East Point, GA.

44. Durisch and Lowry, "The Scope and Content," *Public Administration Review*, 13 (1953): 224.

45. John P. Ferris, "A Unified Terminal System for the River," Chairman's Office Files, 001.32 (Ferris, John P.), U.S. Archive, East Point, GA.

46. Lilienthal, *TVA: Democracy*, 105.

47. Pritchett, *The Tennessee Valley Authority*, 137–140.

48. Selznick tells this story fully in *TVA and the Grass Roots*, 169–179.

49. Lilienthal, *The TVA Years*, 493–495.

50. "Notes on Reorganization Problem," (Jandry, Reichle, and Sessions) September 16, 1939, 321 (1), U.S. Archive, East Point, GA.

51. Herman Finer, memo, October 5, 1937.

52. Herman Finer, *The Administrative History*, section 4, chapter 8, 15–16.

53. Dorothy H. Clayton, "Intergovernmental Relations and TVA," conference paper, Vanderbilt University, Nashville, TN, December 3–5, 1981, 26.

54. George F. Gant to Gordon R. Clapp, "Report on Administrative Conferences," Administrative Files 333.1, 337, 095, 926.9–29, U.S. Archive, East Point, GA.

55. Gordon R. Clapp to TVA board of directors, March 13, 1943, "Basic Considerations for Regional Development Programs," H. A. Morgan Files, 913, 915, 095, U.S. Archive, East Point, GA.

56. John McAmis, Memphis State Oral History Project, March 11, 1970, 17–25.

57. Neal Bass to author, May 20, 1981, Nashville, TN.

58. Finer, *The Administrative History*, section 4, chapter 10, 8.

59. Ibid., 13–14.

60. John McAmis, Memphis State Oral History Project, March 11, 1970, 1–2.

61. John Ferris, Memphis State Oral History Project, December 7, 1969, part 1, 11; part 2, 9–10.

62. Lilienthal, interview with Ross Spears, May 1980.

63. Leland Allbaugh to author, May 28, 1981, Knoxville, TN.

64. Finer, *The Administrative History*, section 4, chapter 10, 14.

65. Ibid., section 4, chapter 10, 25–26.

66. Ibid., section 6, chapter 12, 1–2.

67. Ibid., section 4, chapter 10, 26–27.

68. Ibid., section 3, chapter 6, 18–19.

69. Ibid., section 4, chapter 10, 20–21.

70. Ibid., section 4, chapter 10, 28–29.

71. Ibid., section 4, chapter 11, 1–5, 9–10.

72. Norman Wengert, *Valley of Tomorrow: The TVA and Agriculture*, (University of Tennessee: Bureau of Public Administration, 1952), 119.

73. Ibid., 119–120.

74. Ibid., 121–122.

75. Ibid., 122–123.

76. Ibid., 123–124.

77. Ibid., 125–127.

78. Hobday, *Sparks at the Grass Roots*, 16.

79. Pritchett, *The Tennessee Valley Authority*, 36–37.

80. George E. Rawson, *The Process of Program Development: The Case of TVA's Power Program*, Ph.D. diss., University of Tennessee, 1978, 54–55.

81. Wilmon H. Droze, "The TVA, 1945–80: The Power Company," in Hargrove and Conkin, *TVA, Fifty Years*, 68–69.

82. Floyd Reeves to Herman Finer, December 30, 1937, 13.

83. Annual Report, 1942–43, 2, Tennessee Valley Authority.

84. Annual Report, 1944–45, 1, 5, Tennessee Valley Authority.

85. Pritchett, *The Tennessee Valley Authority*, 141–144.

86. Ibid., 33, 53.

87. John Ferris, Memphis State Oral History Project, December 7, 1969, part 3, 27–28.

88. Hobday, *Sparks at the Grass Roots*, 32–33.

89. Elliott Roberts, *One River-Seven States: TVA-State Relations in the Development of the Tennessee River* (Knoxville: Bureau of Public Administration, University of Tennessee, 1955), 68, 70.

90. Finer, *The Administrative History*, section 10, chapter 14, 9–14, 29; Rawson, *The Process*, 54–55.

91. Finer, *The Administrative History*, section 10, chapter 14, 4, 11.

92. Ibid., section 4, chapter 5, 15.

93. Hobday, *Sparks at the Grass Roots*, 38–40, 60, 71, 145–147, 233, 238–239; Pritchett, *The Tennessee Valley Authority*, 83–84; Selznick, *TVA and the Grass Roots*, 142–143.

94. Hobday, *Sparks at the Grass Roots*, 240, 236.

95. Lilienthal, *The TVA Years*, 585.

96. Pritchett, *The Tennessee Valley Authority*, 105–107.

97. Roberts, *One River*, 73–78; Hobday, *Sparks at the Grass Roots*, 30; Finer, *The Administrative History*, section 4, chapter 13, 12–14.

98. Finer, *The Administrative History*, section 4, chapter 11, 15.

99. Marguerite Owen, *The Tennessee Valley Authority* (New York: Praeger, 1973).

100. Selznick, *TVA and the Grass Roots*, 57.

101. Ibid., 587.

102. Julius A. Krug, "New Hopes for Rural Electrification," May 17, 1940. 001.32 (Krug, J. A.), U.S. Archives, East Point, GA.

103. Pritchett, *The Tennessee Valley Authority*, 373.

104. Ibid., 313–315.

105. Ibid., 315–316.

106. Ibid., 321–323.

107. Crease, *TVA's Public Planning*, 178.

108. Luther Gulick, "Large Scale Planning as Illustrated by the TVA," National Resources Planning Board, March 2, 1944, 031.6–3,095.913 U.S. Archives, East Point, GA.

109. Lilienthal, *The TVA Years*, 595–596.

110. Selznick, *TVA and the Grass Roots*, 48–49.

111. Ibid., 50–56.

112. Ibid., 49.

113. Ibid., 57.

114. Ibid., 58–59.

EPILOGUE: PART I

1. Edgar Schein, *Organizational Culture and Leadership* (San Francisco: Jossey-Bass Publishers, 1985), 2.

2. Schein, *Organizational Culture*, 9.

3. Lilienthal's notes in his journal about the intensity he gave to writing *TVA: Democracy* attest to his very great, personal investment and commitment. See Lilienthal, *The TVA Years*.

4. March and Olsen, *Rediscovering Institutions*, 39–40.

5. Ibid., 46–47.

6. Schein, *Organizational Culture*, 45.

CHAPTER 6

1. George Gant, Memphis State Oral History Project, December 28, 1971, Madison, WI, part 2, 12–13; Paul Ager, Memphis State Oral History Project, April 15, 1970, Hollywood, CA, part 2, 19; Paul Evans to author, August 11, 1981, Norris, TN; A. J. Gray to author, May 12, 1981, Knoxville, TN; John Oliver to author, June 9, 1981, Signal Mountain, TN.

2. John Oliver to author, June 9, 1981.

3. Harry L. Case, Memphis State Oral History Project, March 6, 1970, East Lansing, MI, part 2, 35.

4. Aubrey Wagner to author, May 28, 1981, Knoxville, TN.

5. Leland Allbaugh to author, May 28, 1981, Knoxville, TN.

6. John Oliver to author, June 9, 1981.

7. Harry L. Case, "Gordon R. Clapp: The Role of Faith, Purposes and People in Administration," *Public Administration Review* 24 (June 1964): 90–91.

8. John Rozek to author, August 8, 1989, Knoxville, TN.

9. Gordon R. Clapp, *Volts and Jolts*, vol. 4, no. 9, Knoxville, TN., October, 1954, 3.

10. Neal Bass to author, May 20, 1981, Nashville, TN.

11. Harry Wiersma to author, May 13, 1981, Knoxville, TN.

12. Edward Falck to author, July 21, 1981, Washington, D.C.

13. George F. Gant, Memphis State Oral History Project, part 4, December 29, 1971.

14. John Oliver to author, June 9, 1981.

15. Marguerite Owen to author, July 21, 1981, Washington, D.C.

16. Gordon R. Clapp to TVA board, July 3, 1943, "Staff Assistance to the General Manager in Various Phases of Over-All Management," 6. H. A. Morgan Files, 321–70–2(2), 095, U.S. Archive, East Point, GA.

17. "Notes on Washington Conferences," July 30, 1945, Administrative Files, 337, 031.6–2, 095, U.S. Archive, East Point, GA.

18. A. J. Gray, Memphis State Oral History Project, May 12, 1981, part 2, 5, 16–17.

19. William J. Hayes, Memphis State Oral History Project, December 29, 1970, 21–22.

20. Leland Allbaugh to author, May 28, 1981.

21. George F. Gant, "TVA Management and Policies," March 8, 1949, H. A. Curtis Files, 001.32 (Gant, G. F.), U.S. Archive, East Point, GA.

22. Ibid., 6.

23. George F. Gant, "Management Improvement in TVA," October 28, 1949, 321 (2), 031.6–2, 110.011–51, U.S. Archive, East Point, GA.

24. George F. Gant to Harry Case, "Informal," January 11, 1951, 337–1, 321 (4–5), 110.011–52, 095 (1), U.S. Archive, East Point, GA.

25. John Oliver, "To Those Listed," May 6, 1952, Administrative Files, 337.1, U.S. Archive, East Point, GA.

26. John Oliver, "Report on Staff Conference," Administrative Files, 337.1., U.S. Archive, East Point, GA.

27. Gabriel Wessenauer to author, June 9, 1981, Knoxville, TN.

28. Leland Allbaugh to author, May 28, 1981.

29. The Tennessee Valley Authority Act, 73rd Congress, 1st Session [H.R. 5081], May 1933, Sec. 4 (j).

30. "Financial Results and Financial Requirements of the TVA Electric Power Program," Statement by the TVA Board of Directors, 3–4, H. A. Morgan Files, 951.01, 131.011, 095. U.S. Archive, East Point, GA.

31. Neal Bass to author, May 20, 1981.

32. David E. Lilienthal, "The Road Ahead," February 23, 1944, 001.32 (Lilienthal, D. E.), 095, 951.01, U.S. Archive, East Point, GA.

33. Neal Bass to author, May 20, 1981.

34. Annual Report, 1946–47, 85, Tennessee Valley Authority.

35. Gordon R. Clapp, testimony to the subcommittee of the Committee on Appropriations, House of Representatives, Government Corporations Bill for 1949, 80th Congress, 2nd Session, 1948, 422–3.

36. Rawson, *The Process*, 60–62.

37. Annual Report, 1949–50, 17, Tennessee Valley Authority.

38. TVA press release, January 1, 1954, H. A. Curtis File, 321-(45), 5, U.S. Archive, East Point, GA.

39. Hobday, *Sparks at the Grass Roots*, 63–64.

40. Annual Report, 1951, 3, Tennessee Valley Authority.

41. James P. Pope to President Truman, October 25, 1949, H. A. Curtis File, 307, U.S. Archive, East Point, GA.

42. Gordon R. Clapp to Kenneth McKellar, chairman, Committee on Appropriations, U.S. Senate, May 9, 1951, Chairman's Office Files, CV 131, U.S. Archive, East Point, GA.

43. Gordon R. Clapp, *The TVA*, 93–94.

44. John Oliver, talk to the Tennessee Valley Public Power Association, Memphis, TN, March 31, 1952, 3, 095, 001.32 (Oliver, John), U.S. Archive, East Point, GA.

45. Aubrey Wagner to author, May 28, 1981.

46. Stefan A. Roback, chief industrial economist, talk to the Tennessee Valley Public Power Association, April 7, 1953, 095, 001.32 (Roback, Stefan A), 8, U.S. Archive, East Point, GA.

47. Roscoe C. Martin, "Retrospect and Prospect," in Roscoe C. Martin, ed. *TVA: The First Twenty Years: A Staff Report* (Birmingham: University of Alabama Press, 1956), 266–267.

48. Louis Van Mol, Memphis State Oral History Project, September 8, 1972, 7.

49. Louis Van Mol, Memphis State Oral History Project, November 29, 1972, part 2, 11–12.

50. Annual Report, 1951, 34, 54, Tennessee Valley Authority.

51. George F. Gant to TVA board, "Study of TVA Organization—Progress Report," December 17, 1947, H. A. Morgan Files, 321(1), U.S. Archive, East Point, GA.

52. Wengert, *Valley of Tomorrow*, 93.

53. Ibid., 124–127.

54. Ibid., 136.

55. Willis Baker to Neal Bass, "Reassessment of TVA Objectives," January 25, 1944. H. A. Morgan Files, 321(2), 095, 901.01, 901.02, U.S. Archive, East Point, GA.

56. Leland Allbaugh to author, May 28, 1981.

57. Ibid. Allbaugh refers here to an earlier time.

58. John Oliver to author, June 9, 1981.

59. Leland Allbaugh, Memphis State Oral History Project, April 10, 1970, part 2, 8, 13, 29.

60. Louis Van Mol, Memphis State Oral History Project, November 29, 1972, part 2, 15.

61. Martin, *TVA: The First Twenty Years*, 267.

62. Ibid., 267.

63. Clapp, *The TVA*, 27–28.

64. John Krutilla to author, Nashville, TN, September 8, 1986.

65. Ibid.

66. Richard Freeman to author, May 1, 1986, Knoxville, TN.

67. George F. Gant to TVA board, "Proposed Revision in TVA Organization," February 3, 1948, H. A. Morgan Files, 321(1), 321–75–0, 032.21 (Aiken, George D.), U.S. Archive, East Point, GA.

68. John P. Ferris, Memphis State Oral History Project, December 7, 1969, 34–35.

69. Revised Organizational Bulletin, December 6, 1953, H. A. Curtis Files, 321(1), U.S. Archive, East Point, GA.

70. Roscoe C. Martin letter to TVA board, December 2, 1952, 3, "Preliminary Investigation of the Desirability of a General 'Social Science' Survey of the Tennessee Valley Authority," 321(2), 002 (Syracuse University), 095(2), 680.91, 901.03, U.S. Archive, East Point, GA.

71. Martin, *TVA: The First Twenty Years*.

72. Roscoe C. Martin to Gordon R. Clapp, enclosing letter sent to prospective authors, 321(2), 002 Syracuse University, 095(1), October 22, 1953, U.S. Archive, East Point, GA.

73. Ralph F. Garn, *Tributary Area Development in Tennessee: TVA's Changing Perspective*, Ph.D. diss., University of Tennessee, Knoxville, 1974, 63.

74. Ibid., 65.

75. Richard Kilbourne, Memphis State Oral History Project, March 13, 1970, Norris, TN, part 2, 17.

76. Marguerite Owen to author, July 21, 1981.

77. George F. Gant, Memphis State Oral History Project, part 4, 11.

78. Garn, *Tributary Area Development*, 69–72.

79. Aubrey Wagner to author, May 28, 1981.

80. Garn, *Tributary Area Development*, 61–62.

81. Harry Curtis, July 3, 1951, 913.2, 819, 913.3, 811–59–26, U.S. Archive, East Point, GA.

82. John Oliver to Harry Curtis, July 5, 1951, 913.2, 819, 913.3, 811–59–26, U.S. Archive, East Point, GA.

83. Garn, *Tributary Area Development*, 80–81.

84. Richard Kilbourne, Memphis State Oral History Project, March 12, 1970, Norris, TN, part 2, 24–25.

85. Gordon R. Clapp, untitled paper, September 24, 1952, 320, 001.32 (Clapp, G. R.), U.S. Archive, East Point, GA.

86. Crawford D. Goodwin, "The Valley Authority Idea—The Fading of a National Vision," in Hargrove and Conkin, *TVA: Fifty Years*, 265.

87. Ibid., 266–274.

88. Ibid., 274–275.

89. Ibid., 284–287.

90. Droze, "The TVA, 1945–80," 70–72.

91. Gordon R. Clapp letter to Joseph M. Dodge, director of the Bureau of the Budget, February 15, 1953, CV, 131, 072A, 121, 201, 350, A(1), U.S. Archive, East Point, GA.

92. John Oliver memo to Marguerite Owen, June 8, 1953, CV, 131, 012A, 312, A(1), U.S. Archive, East Point, GA.

93. Legislative History, Regular Appropriations, Fiscal Year 1954, June 20, 1953, CV131, U.S. Archive, East Point, GA.

94. David E. Lilienthal to Gordon R. Clapp, July 18, 1953, CV 131, U.S. Archive, East Point, GA.

95. Sherman Adams to Frank Clement, March 1, 1954, CV 131, U.S. Archive, East Point, GA.

96. "Revenue Bonds Wouldn't Work for TVA, Clapp Says," interview with Gordon R. Clapp by the Knoxville *News-Sentinel*, August 9, 1953, CV, 133, 131, A(2), U.S. Archive, East Point, GA.

97. George F. Gant, Memphis State Oral History Project, December 28, 1971, part 2, 16.

98. Gabriel Wessenauer to author, June 9, 1981.

99. Joseph Swidler to author, June 4, 1981, Washington, D.C.

100. Aubrey Wagner to author, May 28, 1981.

101. John Oliver to author, June 9, 1981.

102. Marguerite Owen to author, July 21, 1981. Her methods of working were described in the same way by two longtime cohorts of TVA, Alex Radin and J. D. Brown, director and deputy director of the American Public Power Association, to the author, June 16 and 17, 1992, Washington, D.C.

103. Alex Radin to author, June 17, 1992, Washington, D.C.

104. John Oliver to author, June 9, 1981.

105. Marguerite Owen to author, July 21, 1981.

106. Aubrey Wagner to author, May 28, 1981.

107. Herbert Vogel, Memphis State Oral History Project, January 9, 1970, 8.

108. Paul Evans to author, August 11, 1981.

109. Herbert Vogel to author, June 5, 1981, Washington, D.C.

110. A.R. Jones, Memphis State Oral History Project, December 28, 1969, Sun City, FL, part 2, 38.

111. A. J. Gray to author, May 12, 1981, Knoxville, TN.

112. Herbert Vogel, Memphis State Oral History Project, January 9, 1970, 7.

113. Ibid., 9.

114. Paul Evans to author, August 11, 1981.

115. Dwight D. Eisenhower to Herbert Brownell, August 17, 1954, CV, 363(ACE), 013M(AEC), 012, 013E (Att. Gen.), A(2), U.S. Archive, East Point, GA.

116. R. V. Taylor to President Eisenhower, July 6, 1954, CV, 363 (AEC), 350, 012, A(2), U.S. Archive, East Point, GA.

117. Joseph Swidler to author, June 4, 1981; Gabriel Wessenauer to author, June 9, 1981.

118. Harry Curtis to Rowland Hughes, director of the Bureau of the Budget, July 2, 1954, CV, 363 (AEC), 013M (AEC), 131, 012 A, A(1), U.S. Archive, East Point, GA.

119. Herbert Vogel, Memphis State Oral History Project, January 9, 1970, 10.

120. Ibid., 11–12.

121. Herbert Vogel to Charles C. Fichter, November 26, 1954, CV, 363 (AEC), 013 (AEC), A(2), U.S. Archive, East Point, GA.

122. Herbert Vogel, Memphis State Oral History Project, January 9, 1970, 12–13.

123. Ibid., 14.

124. Marguerite Owen to author, July 21, 1981.

125. John Oliver to author, June 9, 1981.

126. Aubrey Wagner to author, May 28, 1981.

127. Marguerite Owen to author, July 21, 1981.

128. Paul Evans to author, August 11, 1981.

129. Herbert Vogel to author, June 5, 1981.

130. Harry L. Case, Memphis State Oral History Project, March 6, 1970, part 2, 25–27.

131. Aubrey Wagner to Administrative Files, December 27, 1954, "Proposed Management Survey of TVA," 321 (2), U.S. Archive, East Point, GA.

132. Rowland Hughes to Herbert Vogel, December 20, 1954, CV, 131, Chairman's Office File, U.S. Archive, East Point, GA.

133. Herbert Vogel to Rowland Hughes, December 6, 1954, CV, 131, Chairman's Office Files, U.S. Archive, East Point, GA.

134. Herbert Vogel to author, June 5, 1981.

135. Charles McCarthy to author, June 20, 1981, Washington, D.C.

136. Herbert Vogel to Congressman Joe L. Evins, October 10, 1960, J. McBride—A. R. Jones Files, 650, U.S. Archive, East Point, GA.

137. Herbert Vogel to author, June 5, 1981.

138. Paul Evans to author, August 11, 1981. Evans added that Vogel and Curtis "got along like fire and water."

139. Gabriel Wessenauer to author, June 9, 1981.

140. Herbert Vogel to author, June 5, 1981.

141. Garn, *Tributary Area Development*, 89–91.

142. Ibid., 94, 97–98, 102, 124.

143. Ibid., 84–85.

144. William Bruce Wheeler and Michael J. McDonald, *TVA and the Tellico Dam, 1936–1979* (Knoxville: University of Tennessee Press, 1986), 34.

145. Richard Kilbourne, "Meeting of TVA Board and Staff with Tennessee River and Tributary Association," November 17, 1961, Knoxville, TN. Tributary Area Development Files, Chairman's Office Files, T, 220 (Elk River), 601, A (9), 208, U.S. Archive, East Point, GA.

146. William L. Sturdevant, Jr., to Herbert Vogel, March 16, 1955, with Vogel's reply of March 17, CV, 320, 321–70–1(2), 095 (2) General Manager Files, U.S. Archive, East Point, GA.

147. Memphis *Press-Scimitar*, July 12, 1955.

148. Louisville *Courier Journal*, June 19, 1956.

149. Knoxville *News-Sentinel*, October 28, 1954.

150. Nashville *Tennessean*, September 6, 1955.

151. Chattanooga *News-Free Press*, October 19, 1955.

152. Hammon, TN, *Record*, August 25, 1955.

153. Nashville *Banner*, January 16, 1959.

154. A. J. Wagner to Administrative Files, "Chairman's Report on TVA to the President," January 26, 1955, U.S. Archive, East Point, GA.

155. TVA report and press release, January 7, 1954, 5. H. A. Curtis Files, 321(4–5), U.S. Archive, East Point, GA.

156. A. J. Wagner to Board of Directors, December 22, 1954, CV, 131, Office of the General Manager, U.S. Archive, East Point, GA.

157. A. R. Jones, "An Up to Date Picture of TVA," address to annual meeting of the Electrical Power Distributors, September 12, 1958, 3.E, 185 (A. R. Jones), U.S. Archive, East Point, GA.

158. A. J. Wagner to Board of Directors, "Future Financing of the TVA Power System," March 18, 1955, 133, 300, A(1), Chairman's Office File, U.S. Archive, East Point, GA.

159. A. J. Wagner to Administrative Files, "Meeting of TVA Power Distributors Representatives with TVA Board Re Power Financing Plan," April 12, 1955, 133, A(1), Chairman's Office File, U.S. Archive, East Point, GA.

160. A. J. Wagner to Administrative Files, "Financing Plan," May 29, 1955, CV, 133, 012A, U.S. Archive, East Point, GA.

161. Herbert Vogel to States Rights Finley, December 8, 1955, CV, 133, 131, 012A, A(2), Chairman's Office Files, U.S. Archive, East Point, GA.

162. Herbert Vogel to President Eisenhower, September 9, 1955, 0955(6), 810.01, 951, 031.6–2, 031, Chairman's Office Files, U.S. Archive, East Point, GA.

163. Herbert Vogel to Senator Dennis Chavez, chairman, Committee on Public Works, July 25, 1956; Senator Albert Gore to Raymond R. Paty, July 26, 1956. 133. 131. 171A (SB 3964, 84th Congress), 011A1 (Chavez, Dennis; Gore, Albert). U.S. Archive, East Point, GA.

164. James E. Watson, "Discussion with Bureau of the Budget on Financing," January 17, 1957, Manager's Files, Chattanooga, CV, 133, 012A, U.S. Archive, East Point, GA.

165. Gabriel Wessenauer, testimony before Subcommittee on Public Works, U.S. Senate, March 29, 1957.

166. *New York Times*, May 8, 1959; July 10, 1959; July 24, 1959; July 27, 1959; July 30, 1959; Rawson, *The Process*, 66–67.

167. List of Material Assembled for the Board Members in Connection with Conference with President Eisenhower on July 29, 1959, J. McB. 133, Office of A.R. Jones, U.S. Archive, East Point, GA.

168. Herbert Vogel to author, June 5, 1981. Also see Vogel, Memphis State Oral History Project, January 9, 1970; and A. R. Jones, Memphis State Oral History Project, December 28, 1969.

169. Charles McCarthy to author, June 20, 1981.

CHAPTER 7

1. Aubrey Wagner to author, May 13, 1981, Knoxville, TN.

2. Ibid.

3. Ibid.

4. Rawson, *The Process*, 73.

5. Leland Allbaugh to author, May 28, 1981, Knoxville, TN.

6. Louis Nelson to author, July 26, 1979.

7. Billy Bond to author, August 8, 1989, Knoxville, TN.

8. S. David Freeman to author, June 15, 1992, Washington, D.C.

9. Aubrey Wagner to author, May 13, 1981.

10. Author's interviews with Paul Evans, August 11, 1981; John Bynon, August 2, 1989; Tom Ripley, July 31, 1989; John Baron, August 4, 1989; and Bevan Brown, 1989. Evans was interviewed in Norris, TN, the others in Knoxville.

11. Paul Evans to author, August 11, 1981, Norris, TN.

12. S. David Freeman to author, June 15, 1992.

13. Frank Smith to author, May 5, 1981, Nashville, TN.

14. William Jenkins to author, May 29, 1981, Rogersville, TN.

15. Phil Ericson to author, August 8, 1989, Knoxville, TN.

16. John Bynon to author, August 2, 1989, Knoxville, TN.

17. David Patterson to author, August 3, 1989, Knoxville, TN.

18. Hugh Parris to author, August 15, 1979.

19. John Bynon to author, August 2, 1989.

20. Aubrey Wagner to author, May 13, 1981.

21. Paul Evans to author, August 11, 1981.

22. Gabriel Wessenauer to author, June 9, 1981, Chattanooga, TN.

23. Hugh Parris to author, August 15, 1979, Knoxville, TN.

24. Aubrey Wagner to author, May 13, 1981.

25. Brooks Hays to author, 1981, Washington, D.C.

26. Billy Bond to author, August 8, 1989.

27. Frank Smith to author, May 5, 1981.

28. David Patterson to author, August 3, 1989.

29. These comments are respectively by John Rozek, August 8, 1989; Dan De Ford, August 10, 1989; James Robert Durall, August 9, 1989; and Tom Ripley, July 31, 1989. Ripley was interviewed in Nashville, the others in Knoxville.

30. Aubrey Wagner to author, May 13, 1981.

31. Paul Evans to author, August 11, 1981.

32. Frank Smith to author, May 5, 1981.

33. John Rozek to author, August 8, 1989.

34. Aubrey Wagner to author, May 13, 1981.

35. George Palo to author, May 28, 1981, Knoxville, TN.

36. Tom Ripley to author, July 31, 1989.

37. I first met Wagner in 1976 at Vanderbilt University. Wagner was surrounded by a retinue of aides, and at a small dinner with a few faculty members, they gave the impression that they had closed the wagons and would defend the correctness of all their actions no matter what the issue. At the time I felt as if I had had dinner with J. Edgar Hoover and his aides. However, when I later interviewed Wagner in 1981, I found him to be warm, open, and extremely cordial. I could see how and why he could foster loyalty. But that same loyalty could perhaps lead to a kind of "group think."

38. Paul Evans to author, August 11, 1981.

39. George Palo to author, May 28, 1981.

40. Aubrey Wagner to author, May 13, 1981.

41. Marguerite Owen to author, July 21, 1981, Washington, D.C.

42. Frank Smith, Memphis State Oral History Project, August 2, 1973, part 2, 20.

43. Marguerite Owen to author, July 21, 1981.

44. Aubrey Wagner to author, May 13, 1981.

45. Ibid.

46. Frank Smith to author, May 5, 1981; Paul Evans to author, August 11, 1981.

47. This description of TVA activities in the 1960s and 1970s was drawn from a paper by Charles M. Stephenson, chief of the Government Relations staff, Division of Navigation Development and Regional Studies, entitled "Administrative Decisions Revisited: TVA Experience Since 1953," October 15, 1975. TVA Archive, Knoxville, 353.00823, S839.

48. William J. Hayes, Memphis State Oral History Project, December 29, 1970, Knoxville, TN.

49. A. J. Gray, Memphis State Oral History Project, December 20, 1974, Knoxville, TN, part 2. 10–11.

50. George Palo to author, May 28, 1981.

51. Ibid.

52. Hugh Parris to author, August 15, 1979.

53. William Willis to author, August 7, 1990, Knoxville, TN.

54. John Bynon to author, August 2, 1989.

55. Phil Ericson to author, August 8, 1989.

56. H. Knop, ed., *The Tennessee Valley Authority: A Field Study* (Laxenburg, Austria: International Institute for Applied Systems Analysis, 1979).

57. Ibid., 46–47.

58. Ibid., 48.

59. Ibid.

60. Ibid., 48–49.

61. Ibid., 52.

62. Ibid., 57.

63. Ibid., 57–58.

64. Ibid., 68–71.

65. Ibid., 79–80.

66. Ibid., 99.

67. Ibid., 101–107.

68. Ibid., 107–114.

69. Ibid., 174.

70. Marc J. Roberts and Jeremy S. Blum, "The TVA," in *The Choices of Power: Utilities Face the Environmental Challenge*, ed. Marc J. Roberts and Jeremy S. Blum. (Cambridge: Harvard University Press, 1981), 87.

71. Ibid., 81.

72. Ibid., 82.

73. Ibid., 83–84.

74. Ibid., 85.

75. Ibid., 85–87.

76. Ibid., 88.

77. Ibid., 88–89.

78. Ibid., 90–91.

79. To Marguerite Owen, Washington representative, from Richard Kilbourne, director of the Tributary Area Development Program, "TVA's Tributary Area Development Program—Historical Background." Knoxville, TN, July 30, 1962. Smith, 601B, Director's Office, TVA Archive, Knoxville, TN.

80. A. J. Wagner, "TVA Tributary Area Development Program," September 8, 1961, Smith et al., Director's Files, 601, 185, (Wagner, A. J.), TVA Archive, Knoxville, TN.

81. Wheeler and McDonald, *TVA and the Tellico Dam*, 170–171.

82. Ibid., 171.

83. Ibid., 172.

84. Ibid., 173–174.

85. Ibid., 174.

86. Garn, *Tributary Area Development*, 224.

87. John Bynon to author, August 2, 1989.

88. Garn, *Tributary Areas Development*, 227.

89. Ibid., 156–157, 173, 184.

90. John Bynon to author, August 2, 1989.

91. Donald T. Wells, *The TVA Tributary Area Development Program* (University of Alabama: Bureau of Public Administration, 1964), 60–62, 123–124.

92. John Baron, former Tributary Area Development director, to author, August 4, 1989, Knoxville, TN.

93. Bevan Brown to author, August 10, 1989, Knoxville, TN.

94. George Palo to author, May 28, 1981.

95. William Willis to author, August 7, 1990.

96. Wheeler and McDonald, *TVA and the Tellico Dam*, 3. My account relies on these authors who have worked with the primary sources and conducted numerous interviews. They advance the thesis that Wagner was trying to use Tellico as a means to strengthen the TVA economic development mission, which is consistent with my argument. They also agree that the Tributary Area Development program was a precursor of Tellico. The sequence of events is also well reported by Stephen J. Reichichar and Michael R. Fitzgerald, *The Consequences of Administrative Decisions: TVA's Economic Development Mission and Intragovernmental Regulation* (University of Tennessee: Bureau of Public Administration, 1983).

97. Wheeler and McDonald, *TVA and the Tellico Dam*, 4.

98. Ibid., 8–9.

99. Leland Allbaugh to author, May 28, 1981.

100. Wheeler and McDonald, *TVA and the Tellico Dam*, 11. The report was written by Arthur Jandrew, an assistant general manager.

101. Ibid., 14–16.

102. J. D. Brown to author, June 16, 1992, Washington, D.C. Brown worked at TVA in Chattanooga after the war as a public information officer and was subsequently assistant director of the American Public Power Association in Washington, D.C., with special responsibilities for TVA.

103. Wheeler and McDonald, *TVA and the Tellico Dam*, 20, 23.

104. Ibid., 175.

105. Ibid., 39.

106. Ibid., 37.

107. Ibid., 37–38.

108. Ibid., 37–39.

109. Ibid., 43–44.

110. Reichichar and Fitzgerald, *The Consequences*, 10–11.

111. Ibid., 12–14.

112. Ibid., 14.

113. Wheeler and McDonald, "The 'New Mission' and the Tellico Project, 1945–70," in Hargrove and Conkin, *TVA: Fifty Years*, 63.

114. Reichichar and Fitzgerald, *The Consequences*, 16.

115. Ibid., 15–17.

116. Wheeler and McDonald, *TVA and the Tellico Dam*, 88.

117. Ibid., 92–93.

118. Ibid., 101–103.

119. Ibid., 109–110.

120. Ibid., 109–110.

121. Reichichar and Fitzgerald, *The Consequences*, 27; Wheeler and McDonald, *TVA and the Tellico Dam*, 134.

122. Reichichar and Fitzgerald, *The Consequences*, 27–31.

123. Professor Edward Thaxton, an engineer on the Vanderbilt University faculty, was on Governor Dunn's staff at the time. Thaxton remembered that Governor Dunn called Wagner before he spoke publicly to tell Wagner what he was going to say. Wagner could not believe it possible that a Tennessee governor would oppose TVA and was so shocked that he hardly talked during the conversation.

124. Reichichar and Fitzgerald, *The Consequences*, 34.

125. Ibid., 34–37.

126. Ibid., 60.

127. Ibid., chapters 3 and 4.

128. Ibid., 67–73,

129. See Dean Hill Rivkin, "TVA, the Courts, and the Public Interest," in Hargrove and Conkin, *TVA: Fifty Years*, 200–201.

130. Ibid., 201.

131. Paul Evans to author, August 11, 1981.

132. Reichichar and Fitzgerald, *The Consequences*, 4–5.

133. Ibid., 17–25.

134. Aubrey J. Wagner to Robert F. Durant, February 18, 1981, Knoxville, TN, in Robert F. Durant, *When Government Regulates Itself: EPA, TVA, and Pollution Control in the 1970's* (Knoxville: University of Tennessee Press, 1985), 40.

135. William Ruckleshaus to Aubrey J. Wagner, February 24, 1971, Chairman's Office Files, 805, 013, R258, A (1), TVA Archive, Knoxville, TN.

136. Aubrey J. Wagner letters to William Ruckelshaus, Peter Flanigan, assistant to the president, and Governor Winfield Dunn, January 22, 1973, Chairman's Office File, 820, TVA Archive, Knoxville, TN.

137. Roberts and Blum, *The Choices of Power*, 39–40.

138. Aubrey J. Wagner to Roy Ash, September 5, 1973, Chairman's Office Files, 820, TVA Archive, Knoxville, TN.

139. Jamie Whitten to Aubrey J. Wagner, February 26, 1974, Chairman's Office Files, 820, 011B (Whitten, Jamie L.), TVA Archive, Knoxville, TN.

140. Russell Train to Bob Jones, December 11, 1973; Alvin Alm to the administrator, undated and appended. Chairman's Office File, 820. TVA Archive, Knoxville, TN.

141. Roberts and Blum, *The Choices of Power*, 58–61, 70–71.

142. S. David Freeman to author, June 15, 1992.

143. Ibid., 74–75. For good, highly specific accounts of this episode, see Durant, *When Government Regulates Itself*, and Rivkin in Hargrove and Conkin, *TVA: Fifty Years*. I have relied on these accounts in addition to Roberts and Blum, and Reichichar and Fitzgerald.

144. Durant, *When Government Regulates Itself*, 123–124.

145. Aubrey J. Wagner, speech, March 28, 1972, TVA Public Information Office.

146. Tom Ripley to author, July 31, 1989; Paul Evans to author, August 11, 1981; Gabriel Wessenauer to author, June 9, 1981, Chattanooga, TN.

147. Knop, *The Tennessee Valley Authority*, 172.

148. Ibid., 183–185.

149. Ibid., 185.

150. Ibid., 194.

151. Ibid., 194–196.

152. Roberts and Blum, *The Choices of Power*, 68.

153. Ibid., 72–74.

154. Ibid., 81–83.

155. Ibid., 100–101.

156. Ibid., 104–105.

157. Ibid., 110–112.

158. Ibid., 323–325, 329–332.

159. Ibid., 337–339.

160. Ibid., 341–344.

161. Ibid., 360–361.

162. Ibid., 363–365.

163. Ibid., 371–373.

164. Ibid., 373.

165. Ibid., 374–375.

166. Rawson, *The Process*, 155, table IV-2; Annual Report, 1970–71, Tennessee Valley Authority.

167. Gabriel Wessenauer to author, June 9, 1981.

168. Aubrey Wagner to author, May 13, 1981; Marguerite Owen to author, July 21, 1981.

169. Rawson, *The Process*, 82–84.

170. Ibid., 88–89.

171. Aubrey Wagner to author, May 13, 1981; Gabriel Wessenauer to author, June 9, 1981.

172. Statement of Aubrey J. Wagner to the Subcommittee on Flood Control, Rivers and Harbors, of the Committee on Public Works, *Reserve Bond Financing by the TVA*, 89th Congress, 2nd Session, 1966, 21–22.

173. Aubrey Wagner to author, May 13, 1981.

174. Rawson, *The Process*, 103.

175. Ibid., 96–99.

176. Paul Evans to author, August 11, 1981.

177. Ibid., 110–111.

178. Ibid., 112–113.

179. Larry Calvert to author, August 11, 1989, Knoxville, TN.

180. Rawson, *The Process*, 113–115; Annual Report, 1976, 61, Tennessee Valley Authority.

181. Rawson, *The Process*, 128; Roberts and Blum, *The Choices of Power*, 78.

182. Rawson, *The Process*, 129.

183. Ibid., 132–135.

184. Tennessee Valley Authority Oversight Hearings, part l, April 30, 1975. Committee on Public Works, Washington, D.C., 31.

185. Tennessee Valley Authority Oversight Hearings, part 2, May 8 and 12, 1975, 1203–1204.

186. William Willis to author, August 7, 1990.

187. Knop, *The Tennessee Valley Authority*, 203–214.

188. Ibid., 212.

189. Ibid., 212.

190. Ibid., 213.

191. Paul Evans to author, August 11, 1981.

192. Ibid.

193. Ibid.

194. Aubrey J. Wagner to Ned Ray McWherter, March 16, 1976, Office of the General Manager Files, 366, 171B (TN), A(1), TVA Archive, Knoxville, TN.

195. C. H. Dean, Jr., to Charlie F. Brumfield, director of Power Marketing, Tennessee Valley Authority, January 25, 1974, General Manager's Files, 366, 181A, A(2), TVA Archive, Knoxville, TN.

196. Richard A. Couto, "New Seeds at the Grass Roots: The Politics of the TVA Power Program Since World War II," in Hargrove and Conkin, *TVA: Fifty Years*, 245–246; Aubrey J. Wagner to J. Wiley Bowers, executive director of the Tennessee Valley Public Power Association, May 6, 1975, thanking Bowers for the TVPPA board of directors resolution commending the TVA nuclear program as meeting the energy needs of the valley. Chairman's Office Files, T, A(1), TVA Archive, Knoxville, TN.

197. Rivkin, "TVA, the Courts, and the Public Interest," 200–201.

198. Edwin Shelley, former director of personnel and assistant general manager, Memphis State Oral History Project, December 16, 1971, Knoxville, TN, part 3, 17–20.

CHAPTER 8

1. *A Time to Choose: America's Energy Future* (Cambridge: Ballinger, 1974).

2. Memo to President Carter from Rick Hutcheson, February 29, 1977, WHCF, Subject File, FG259, Carter Presidential Library, Atlanta, GA.

3. Memo to President Carter from John W. Yago, Jr., and Richard D. Grundy, professional staff members, Senate Committee on Public Works, February 11, 1977, WHCF Subject File, Federal Government, Organizations, FG208, Carter Presidential Library, Atlanta, GA.

4. Memo for James King, director, White House Personnel Office, from Philip M. Smith, Office of Science and Technology Policy. Copy of memo from Frank Press to Hamilton Jordan re appointments to the TVA Board, February 23, 1977, WHCF Subject File, Federal Government Organizations, FG208, Carter Presidential Library, Atlanta, GA.

5. S. David Freeman, Memo to President Carter, "Future of the Tennessee Valley Authority," March 5, 1977, WHCF Subject File, FG259, Carter Presidential Library, Atlanta, GA.

6. Jimmy Carter to Aubrey Wagner, April 15, 1977, WHCF Subject File, Confidential, FG259, Carter Presidential Library, Atlanta, GA. Freeman informed the author on June 15, 1992, Washington, D.C., that he wrote the letter.

7. Knoxville *Sentinel Journal*, July 19, 1977.

8. Ibid.

9. Gibbons had written a memo for the Carter transition team in December 1976 in which he described TVA's failure to keep up with the times and suggested new opportunities in energy conservation and environmental policy: "TVA Issues and Opportunities." Report prepared by the University of Tennessee Center for the Tennessee Environmental Council, WHCF Subject File, Confidential, FG259, Carter Presidential Library, Atlanta, GA.

10. S. David Freeman to author, June 16, 1992, Washington, D.C. J. D. Brown, former deputy director of the American Public Power Association, tells the story somewhat differently. He knew that Stennis was skeptical about the Freeman appointment and suggested to Stennis that the publisher, whom Stennis respected, talk with the nominee. The result was the same.

11. S. David Freeman to author, June 16, 1992.

12. S. David Freeman, testimony before the Senate Committee on Environment and Public Works, August 1, 1977, 2–12, TVA Archive, Knoxville, TN.

13. Knoxville *Journal*, August 16, 1977.

14. Nat Caldwell, "Freeman Comes to Valley to Listen," *The Tennessean*, October 4, 1977.

15. S. David Freeman, "Listening Sessions" with Knoxville Cooperative Conferences, October 11, 1977, TVA Technical Library, Knoxville, TN.

16. Ibid.

17. S. David Freeman to Lynn Seeber, October 17, 1977, SDF, COG-COM, EG-EZ, U.S. Archive, East Point, GA.

18. S. David Freeman to Lynn Seeber, October 27, 1977, OGM, SDF, SA-SL, TEN-TZ, U.S. Archive, East Point, GA.

19. S. David Freeman to Lynn Seeber, 302 (VF), A (1), U.S. Archive, East Point, GA.

20. S. David Freeman to Lynn Seeber, November 14, 1977, SDF, 302 (VF), A (1), U.S. Archive, East Point, GA.

21. S. David Freeman to Lynn Seeber, November 14, 1977, SDF, 302(VF), A(1), U.S. Archive, East Point, GA.

22. S. David Freeman to Lynn Seeber, November 30, 1977, OGM.SDF, FA-FZ, LE-LZ, U.S. Archive, East Point, GA.

23. Lynn Seeber to S. David Freeman, December 23, 1977, OGM, SDF, AM-RER, U.S. Archive, East Point, GA.

24. S. David Freeman to author, February 26, 1981, Nashville, TN; Wheeler and McDonald, *TVA and the Tellico Dam*, 184.

25. James Branscombe, "TVA Unveils New Projects," *Washington Post*, August 26, 1977.

26. Godwin Williams, Jr., to Lynn Seeber, October 20, 1977, SDF, COG-COM, EO-EZ, U.S. Archive, East Point, GA.

27. Herbert S. Sanger, Jr., to Lynn Seeber, January 2, 1978, General Manager Files, 103(C1), U.S. Archive, East Point, GA.

28. Lynn Seeber to S. David Freeman, January 5, 1978, General Manager Files, 103(C1), U.S. Archive, East Point, GA.

29. S. David Freeman to Lynn Seeber, January 16, 1978, General Manager Files, 103(C1), U.S. Archive, East Point, GA.

30. S. David Freeman to Lynn Seeber, January 31, 1978, OGM.AM-RE-RZ' Aubrey J. Wagner to Lynn Seeber, February 2, 1978, General Manager Files, 103(C1), U.S. Archive, East Point, GA.

31. Aubrey J. Wagner to H. N. Stroud, Jr., April 12, 1978, OGM, U-X-Z. U.S. Archive, East Point, GA.

32. S. David Freeman to H. N. Stroud, Jr., April 4, 1978, SDF, FA-FZ, LL-LZ; Aubrey J. Wagner to Stroud, May 7, 1978, S. David Freeman File, U.S. Archive, East Point, GA.

33. S. David Freeman to Lynn Seeber, March 13, 1978, SDF, COG-COM, EO-EZ; Seeber to Freeman, March 15, 1978, S. David Freeman File, U.S. Archive, East Point, GA.

34. S. David Freeman to Lynn Seeber, March 7, 1978, William Jenkins File, 302, 153, 141, 956G; Seeber to Freeman, William Jenkins File, U.S. Archive, East Point, GA.

35. Charles Mohr, "Carter Has Chance to Return TVA to Its Original Role," *New York Times*, May 6, 1978.

36. S. David Freeman to author, July 27, 1979, Knoxville, TN.

37. William Jenkins to author, May 29, 1981, Rogersville, TN.

38. John Bynon to author, August 2, 1989, Knoxville, TN.

39. Nat Caldwell, *The Tennessean*, May 14, 1978.

40. S. David Freeman speech to the TVPPA annual meeting, Biloxi, MS, April 4, 1978, TVA Public Information Office.

41. John Wilder to Jack Watson, April 11, 1979, and Watson reply, May 29, 1979, WHCF, Subject File, FG259, Carter Presidential Library, Atlanta, GA.

42. Durant, *When Government Regulates Itself*, 134. Durant evidently learned about Carter's call from an interview.

43. Ibid., 84–85.

44. Ibid., 92–93.

45. Ken Gray to author, May 26, 1989, Ethan, VA. Gray was head of the TVA Washington office at the time.

46. S. David Freeman to John Van Mol, TVA Public Information Office, about the TVPPA resolution, September 26, 1978. S. David Freeman File, 820. A(2), U.S. Archive, East Point, GA.

47. "TVA Forms Citizen Action Office," TVA press release, September 9, 1978.

48. Chairman's Office to John Van Mol, "Follow up Special Agenda for Chairman at Board Meetings Discussed at May 25 Staff Meeting," May 26, 1978; "Public Executive Sessions In Lieu of Board Meetings," to Heads of Offices and Divisions, by H. N. Stroud, acting general manager, May 23, 1978, OGM, 111, 920, U.S. Archive, East Point, GA.

49. James Branscombe, "TVA Returns to Limelight," *Washington Post*, May 18, 1978.

50. OGM, SDF, 302(VF), A91, U.S. Archive, East Point, GA.

51. Suggested Remarks for the Tennessee Municipal Electric Power Association, Gatlinburg, TN, July 14, 1978, TVA Public Information Office.

52. Memo for President Carter from Tim Kraft and James S. Gammill, May 20, 1978, Office of Staff Secretary, Handwriting File, 86, Carter Presidential Library, Atlanta, GA.

53. Richard Freeman to author, May 1, 1986, Knoxville, TN.

54. Jerry Campbell, executive director of the TVPPA, to author, May 27, 1992, Chattanooga, TN.

55. John Wilder to Sam Nunn, August 22, 1978, WHFC, Subject File, FG259, Carter Presidential Library, Atlanta, GA.

56. Knoxville *Sentinel*, July 23, 1978; WHCF, Subject File, FG259, Carter Presidential Library, Atlanta, GA.

57. Frank Moore to President Carter, August 22, 1978, WHCF, Subject File, Executive, FG259, U.S. Archive, East Point, GA.

58. Frank Moore to President Carter, May 18, 1978, WHCF, Staff Offices, Office of Staff Secretary, Handwriting File, 86, Carter Presidential Library, Atlanta, GA.

59. These summary comments about Clement are based on my conversations with TVA officials over a period of months and my observation of Clement in meetings with his board colleagues.

60. John Bynon to author, August 2, 1989.

61. Memo to the Board of Directors from Leon E. Ring, general manager, February 26, 1979. Reorganization, pp. 4–6, given to members of the Summer Study group, including the author, in July, 1979.

62. To All Management Schedule Employees from S. David Freeman and Richard M. Freeman, June 8, 1979. General Manager's Files, 101, 103(1), 103(2), U.S. Archive, East Point, GA.

63. Transcript, TVA Policy Conference Retreat, Fairfield Glade, TN, June 10–11, 1979, General Manager's Files, 101, VF, TVA Archive, Knoxville, TN.

64. A. J. Gray to S. David Freeman, April 28, 1978, OGM, 107G, 101, 131, A(1), U.S. Archive, East Point, GA.

65. David Patterson to S. David Freeman, September, 18, September 26, and October 11, 1979, OGM, AM-RE-RZ, U.S. Archive, East Point, GA.

66. The members of the Summer Study group were Vernon W. Ruttan (chair), Ralph R. Widner, V. Kerry Smith, Handy Williamson, Jr., Ally Mack, Richard W. Poston, Royce Hanson, Ralph D. Widner, Robert D. Dahle, Frederick L. Bates, and myself, Erwin C. Hargrove.

67. John S. Barron to S. David Freeman and Richard Freeman, June 14, 1979. Given to members of the Summer Study group.

68. Descriptions of meetings of the Summer Study group with TVA officials are based on the author's observations and notes as a member of the group.

69. S. David Freeman to author, July 27, 1979.

70. Richard Freeman to author, July 27, 1979, Knoxville, TN.

71. Interviews by the author with Tom Ripley, Sharlene Hirsch, Louis Nelson, Hugh Parris, and William Willis, July 1979, Knoxville, TN.

72. Discussions of the author with LeRoy Rogers, David Patterson, David Sherrada, and John Barron, July 1979, Knoxville, TN.

73. Transcript, TVA Summer Policy Conference, Lake Guntersville State Park, AL, October 9–10, 1979, TVA Archive, Knoxville, TN.

74. *The 1979 Summer Policy Study: The Role of TVA Programs in Regional Development*, March, 1981, TVA Office of Planning and Budget, Knoxville, TN.

75. John Stewart to author, June 26, 1990, Knoxville, TN; William Willis to author, August 7, 1990, Knoxville, TN.

76. Vernon W. Ruttan, "TVA Programs and the Development of the Tennessee Valley Region: An Introduction," in *The 1979 Summer Policy Study*.

77. William Willis to board, "Board Policy Option Papers," October 23, Office of General Manager, 101, TVA Archive, Knoxville, TN.

78. William Willis to Those Listed, Board Policy Option Papers, November 23, 1979, Chairman's Office Files, 101, TVA Archive, Knoxville, TN.

79. Office of General Manager to the Board, "TVA Priorities for the 1980's," Office of the General Manager, 101, 111. TVA Archive, Knoxville, TN.

80. John G. Stewart, "Overview of the Policy Option Papers," January 1, 1980, Office of the General Manager, 101, TVA Archive, Knoxville, TN.

81. S. David Freeman, "Overview of the Policy Option Papers," January 1, 1980, and Richard Freeman, "Reaction to the Chairman's Comments," January 7, 1980. Chairman's Office Files, 101, 131, TVA Archive, Knoxville, TN.

82. Final Report, Core Policy Analysis Group, June 20, 1980, in possession of the author, by request from TVA. TVA Archive, Knoxville, TN.

83. John Stewart to author, June 27, 1990, Knoxville, TN.

84. Dr. Billy Bond to author, August 2, 1989, Knoxville, TN.

85. John Stewart to author, July 26, 1990, Knoxville, TN. John Needy To author, August 3, 1989, Knoxville, TN.

86. William Willis to author, August 7, 1990, Knoxville, TN.

87. Allan Pulsipher to author, September 8, 1986, Nashville, TN.

88. S. David Freeman to author, June 15, 1992.

89. Craven Crowell to author, June 15, 1992, Washington, D.C.

90. Senator James Sasser to author, June 16, 1992, Washington, D.C.

91. S. David Freeman to author, June 15, 1992.

92. Ibid.

93. The TVA annual reports for 1979, 1980, and 1981 describe these programs fully. Also see letters from David Freeman to House members Lindy Boggs and Richard Ottinger, respectively, March 12, 1982, and April 18, 1982. SDF, 302, 011B1 (Boggs, Lindy: 302, 011B1 (Ottinger, Richard L.), U.S. Archive, East Point, GA.

94. *TVA: A Path To Recovery*, report of the Advisory Committee on the Tennessee Valley Authority, Southern States Energy Board, Governor Gerald Baliles, Chairman, 1987, table 6, section 3, 22.

95. S. David Freeman to President Jimmy Carter, May 31, 1979, 259, Subject File, Executive, Carter Presidential Library, Atlanta, GA.

96. Jerry Campbell to author, May 27, 1992.

97. Ibid.

98. Nat Caldwell, "S. David Freeman, The New Energy Czar?" *The Tennessean*, February 1978.

99. Ibid.

100. S. David Freeman to Senator Jim Sasser, September 26, 1980, 153, 370, 132B, D11A1 (Sasser, James) A(1). See also two news stories: "Pluses, Minuses of Electrical Vehicles Found in Year's Test," *News-Free Press*, Chattanooga, TN, August 10, 1982, and "TVA Testing Electric Vehicles," *Daily Herald*, Columbia, TN, November 9, 1982.

101. Christopher Madison, "Murphy Hill—Is It the Wrong Plant at the Wrong Time by the Wrong Agency?" *National Journal*, February 28, 1981, 347.

102. Ibid., 346–347.

103. Ken Gray to author, May 27, 1989.

104. Madison, *National Journal*, February 28, 1981, 347–348.

105. Ibid., 348–349.

106. See the Knoxville *News-Sentinel* for three descriptions of these projects on January 21, 1979; September 29, 1979; and January 29, 1980.

107. "Freeman Defends Nuclear," *Oak Ridger*, Oak Ridge, TN, May 25, 1978.

108. Remarks by David Freeman to the Tennessee Association of Press Broadcasters, Gatlinburg, TN, August 5, 1978.

109. "Freeman Sees TVA N-Programs Staying Within Debt Limit," *The Tennessean*, Nashville, TN, December 2, 1978.

110. Ken Gray to author, May 27, 1989. Gray exempted Representative Ronnie Flippo, Democrat of Alabama, from this criticism. As the senior valley member of the House Public Works Committee, Flippo held up the debt limit bill for several months. He and his aide Bill Rasco posed hard questions to TVA, but Flippo did not trust the answers he got from TVA on the nuclear program and did not trust the Freemans. According to Gray, Flippo only let the bill proceed after he was publicly criticized by the president of the TVA unions. Flippo believed that Richard Freeman had provoked this criticism and thereafter firmly distrusted the Freemans.

111. S. David Freeman to Jim Frey, October 25, 1979, File 259, Subject File, Executive, Carter Presidential Library, Atlanta, GA.

112. S. David Freeman to Howell Heflin, October 20, 1980, 366, 319, 011A(1) (Heflin, Howell) A(1), TVA Archive, Nashville, TN.

113. Howell Raines, "TVA's Chief after First Year," *New York Times*, May 29, 1979.

114. Lamar Alexander to S. David Freeman, April 29, 1980, 020 (Tenn Government), 366, 62A, 107C, TVA Archive, Knoxville, TN.

115. S. David Freeman to Lamar Alexander, April 29, 1980, 020 (Tenn Government), 366, 62A, 107C, TVA Archive, Knoxville, TN.

116. "The Tennessee Valley Authority Can Improve Estimates and Should Reassess Reserve Requirements for Nuclear Power Plants," *General Accounting Office*, PSAD-79–49, March 22, 1979.

117. Libby Warren and Dick Copper, "Angry Freeman Asserts Wagner's Accusations are 'Essentially False,'" *The Times*, Chattanooga, TN, January 31, 1981.

118. Channel 10, Knoxville, TN, Special Report, January 26, 1981. Transcripts provided by TVA Public Information Office.

119. Ed Gregory, "TVA Nuclear Commitment Becomes More Costly," *The Tennessean*, Nashville, TN, August 10, 1980.

120. "Long Range TVA Plans Cited as Need for Debt Ceiling Life," *News-Sentinel*, Knoxville, TN, February 10, 1979.

121. "TVA Debt Ceiling Doubled; Representation Hike Try Out," *The Tennessean*, Nashville, TN, June 6, 1979.

122. "Borrowing Limit for TVA Doubled," *Journal*, Knoxville, TN, October 23, 1979.

123. To the General Manager's Files from William Willis, April 23, 1980, Subject: OEDC Nuclear Construction Program—Cost and Schedule, Board Briefing on April 1, 1980, 103(16), 131, Robert Clement Files, U.S. Archive, East Point, GA.

124. John Stewart to author, June 26, 1990.

125. Robert M. Press, "TVA pushes ahead with giant nuclear power complex," *Christian Science Monitor*, April 4, 1980.

126. "Anger, Frustration Reflected at 7 TVA Rate Hike Hearings," *Tri-Cities Daily*, Muscle Shoals, Florence, Sheffield, Tuscumbia, AL, February 2, 1979.

127. Mark McNeely, "Legislators Criticize TVA Power Rates, Programs," *News-Sentinel*, Knoxville, TN, December 12, 1979.

128. "Industry, Consumer Spokesmen Critical of TVA Rates," *Tri-Cities Daily*, Muscle Shoals, AL, February 27, 1980.

129. William Stevenson, "TVA Rate Advantage by Rising Costs, Industry Says," *Commercial Appeal*, Memphis, TN, March 12, 1980.

130. Hugh Parris to author, August 15, 1979, Knoxville, TN.

131. "Clement Opposes TVA Rate Hike," *Journal*, Tupelo, MS, March 29, 1980.

132. "Users of TVA Power 'will bask' in Oasis of Power in the 1990's," *News*, Birmingham, AL, April 24, 1980.

133. "TVA chief predicts another rate increase," *Daily*, Decatur, AL, May 9, 1980.

134. Ernie Beasley, "TVA Hikes Rates 13%," *Journal*, Knoxville, TN, September 3, 1980.

135. "Sasser raps TVA rate 'excesses,'" *Journal*, Knoxville, TN, September 9, 1980.

136. "Baker asking Senate probe of TVA rates," *The Tennessean*, Nashville, TN, September 28, 1980.

137. "Power Board Hits Rate Standards Weighed by TVA," *Times*, Chattanooga, TN, October 16, 1980.

138. "TVA Residential Rates Rank Low," *Journal*, Knoxville, TN, February 5, 1981.

139. "Industries Ask Delay in TVA Rate Hikes," *Banner*, Nashville, TN, February 13, 1981.

140. "TVA Rate Hike Approved," *Journal*, Knoxville, TN, March 3, 1981.

141. "'Worst is Over' in TVA Increases Declares Chairman," *News and Guardian*, Tullahoma, TN, March 4, 1981.

142. William Willis to author, August 7, 1990.

143. Jerry Campbell to author, May 27, 1992.

144. Resolution Concerning Financial Subsidies to Customers of the Tennessee Valley Public Power Association, Adopted by the Board of Directors, February 20, 1978, Huntsville, AL, T, 366, A(2), TVA Archive, Knoxville, TN.

145. "EPB's McQueen Raps Freeman," *News-Free Press*, Chattanooga, TN, June 23, 1978.

146. James R. Cudworth to N. B. Hughes, September 13, 1978, T, 820, 4(1), TVA Archive, Knoxville, TN.

147. TVPPA/TVA Joint Board Meeting, Nashville, TN, January, 29, 1979, Chairman's Office Files, 366, 360, 350, 171A (National Energy Act), A(2), U.S. Archive, East Point, GA.

148. S. David Freeman to author, June 15, 1992.

149. S. David Freeman, *Banner*, Nashville, TN, May 7, 1980.

150. "A Shake-em-Up TVA Chief," *Washington Post*, Washington, D.C., June 2, 1980.

151. Jerry Campbell to author, May 27, 1992.

152. C-Span recording, March 29, 1983.

153. Ken Gray to author, May 27, 1989.

154. Senator James Sasser to author, June 16, 1992.

155. Ken Gray, May 27, 1989.

156. Ed Gregory, "TVA Accountability Up for a Debate," *The Tennessean*, Nashville, TN, August 31, 1980.

157. Richard M. Freeman to William F. Willis, "Article for *Inside TVA*," October 2, 1980, 366, 11B11 (Gore, Albert), 181B, 175, TVA Archive, Knoxville, TN.

158. Testimony of S. David Freeman, chairman of TVA, before the Subcommittee on Energy and Water Development of the U.S. Senate Committee on Appropriations, December 11, 1980.

159. Ed Gregory, "TVA Chairman Fails to Convince Sasser Utility Not Overbuilding," *The Tennessean*, Nashville, TN, December 12, 1980.

160. "Reagan Team Says Alter TVA Charter," from staff and wire reports, *The Tennessean*, Nashville, TN, January 1, 1981.

161. "'Right On' Freeman Claims Reagan Will Give TVA Blessing," *Tri-Cities Daily*, Muscle Shoals, AL, January 26, 1981.

162. S. David Freeman to a group of faculty members, Vanderbilt Institute for Public Policy Studies, February 26, 1981, Nashville, TN.

163. S. David Freeman, testimony to the Senate Committee on the Environment and Public Works, March 16, 1981, Washington, D.C. Y4.P96/10: 97–119, 8–14.

164. William Willis, testimony to the Senate, March 16, 1981, 15–16.

165. Doug McCullough, testimony to the Senate, March 16, 1981, 54–60.

166. James Sasser, testimony to the Senate, March 16, 1981, 288–289. Sasser told the author on June 16, 1992, in Washington, D.C., that it would have been a mistake to have opened the act when the Republicans were in the White House. They might have had the influence to change it in fundamental ways.

167. Robert Sanson, testimony to the Senate, March 16, 1981, 289.

168. William D. Towers, testimony to the Senate, March 16, 1981, 318–319.

169. Recommendations of the Committee, testimony to the Senate, March 16, 1981, 571–572, 577, 580, 584.

170. Ed Gregory, "Baker Believes Senate Moving to Up TVA Board," *The Tennessean*, Nashville, TN, March 19, 1981.

171. Ed Gregory, "Baker Wants Freeman Out as TVA Head." *The Tennessean*, Nashville, TN, April 29, 1981.

172. Craven Crowell to author, June 15, 1992.

173. Senator Jim Sasser to author, June 16, 1992.

174. S. David Freeman to author, June 15, 1992.

175. Ken Gray to author, May 27, 1989.

176. Libby Wann, *TVA News*, July–August 1980, Knoxville, TN.

177. Ed Gregory, "TVA Facing Mid-Life Crisis," *The Tennessean*, Nashville, TN, August 12, 1979.

178. Bob Poole, "TVA's Image Tarnished by Agency's Expansion," *Times-Dispatch*, Richmond, VA, April 27, 1980.

179. S. David Freeman to author, June 15, 1992.

CHAPTER 9

1. Ernie Beazley, "KUB Chief Pushed For Top Post," *Journal*, Knoxville, TN, April 9, 1981.

2. Charles H. Dean to author, June 26, 1990, Knoxville, TN.

3. Ibid.

4. Ibid.

5. John Stewart remembered that David Freeman continued to function as de facto chairman but also confirmed the observation of many that Richard Freeman was a very strong influence upon David, who would not act without his friend's support. After David Freeman left the board, Richard Freeman was the dominant influence until he resigned in 1986 in opposition to Admiral White's appointment.

6. Herbert Sanger to author, March 14, 1988, Knoxville, TN.

7. Allan Pulsipher to author, March 14, 1988, Nashville, TN.

8. William Willis to author, August 7, 1990, Knoxville, TN.

9. William Mason to author, August 2, 1989, Knoxville, TN.

10. John Stewart to William Willis, "TVA's Nuclear Construction Program Strategy: Considerations of Continuity, Consistency and Constituents Support," September 29, 1981, S. David Freeman File, 319, 201, 3, U.S. Archive, East Point, GA.

11. S. David Freeman to author, June 15, 1992, Washington, D.C.

12. TVA news release, March 4, 1982, S. David Freeman Files, 319, U.S. Archive, East Point, GA.

13. S. David Freeman to editor, *News and Guardian*, Tullahoma, TN, March 17, 1982, S. David Freeman File, 319, 312, 956G, A(1), U.S. Archive, East Point, GA.

14. H. G. Parris to William F. Willis, "Recommendations for Cancellation of Certain Deferred Units and Related Considerations," July 16, 1982, S. David Freeman File, 319, 210, U.S. Archive, East Point, GA.

15. Wendell Rawls, Jr., "TVA at 50, Drafting New Role in Region's Future," *New York Times*, May 15, 1983.

16. "TVA's Freeman reflects 'I feel I have made a difference,'" *Jackson Sun*, Jackson, TN, April 22, 1985.

17. Charles H. Dean to author, June 26, 1990.

18. James Robert Durall to author, August 9, 1989, Knoxville, TN.

19. S. David Freeman to Marvin Bailey, Memphis State Oral History Project, March 3, 1984, Knoxville, TN, 10.

20. Ibid., 27–28, 22–23.

21. David Dinsmore Comey, "The Incident at Browns Ferry," in *Not Man Apart*, published by Friends of the Earth, San Francisco, CA, 1975., 6.

22. Brett Gage, "How safe is a 'good neighbor,'" *News*, Birmingham, AL, April 6, 1979.

23. Howell Raines, "TVA May Restrain Its Nuclear Effort," *New York Times*, May 8, 1979.

24. S. David Freeman, "TVA May Restrain Its Nuclear Effort," *New York Times*, May 8, 1979.

25. Jim Dykes, "TVA Tightens Safety Rules for N-Plants," *News-Sentinel*, Knoxville, TN, June 3, 1979; Nat Caldwell, "New N-Safety Plans for TVA Being Drafted," *The Tennessean*, Nashville, TN, May 13, 1979.

26. Ed Gregory, "TVA Facing Mid-Life Crisis," *The Tennessean*, Nashville, TN, August 12, 1979.

27. Ibid.

28. Ibid.

29. Charles M. Carver to TVA Board of Directors, September 12, 1979; reply to Carver from Robert N. Clement, October 10, 1979. Robert N. Clement Files, 319 (Watts Bar), U.S. Archive, East Point, GA.

30. Unsigned, undated memo in the files of Robert N. Clement, 103 (4–32), Robert N. Clement Files, U.S. Archive, East Point, GA.

31. John R. Emshwiller, "Nuclear Industry Tries Self-Regulation to Reassure Public but Skeptics Remain," *Wall Street Journal*, December 13, 1979.

32. S. David Freeman, the "Today" show, National Broadcasting Company, March 28, 1980.

33. Theodore Barry and Associates, *Management Performance Review of OEDC, Tennessee Valley Authority*, December, 1978, Chapter 7, 5, U.S. Archive, East Point, GA.

34. Ibid., chapter 2, 2.

35. Ibid., chapter 2, 3.

36. Ibid., chapter 2, 11.

37. Ibid., chapter 5, 15.

38. Ibid., chapter 2, 4.

39. Ibid., chapter 3, 2–5.

40. Ibid., chapter 5, 5.

41. Libby Wann, "NRC Criticizes TVA Safety Policy and Bureaucracy," *The Chattanooga Times*, Chattanooga, TN, February 7, 1981.

42. H. N. Culver to William F. Willis, "Watts Bar Nuclear Plant-NRC Inspection Closeout Meeting," July 30, 1981, Office of S. David Freeman, 054, U.S. Archive, East Point, GA.

43. "Browns Ferry Safety Examined." *The Chattanooga Times*, Chattanooga, TN, February 2, 1982.

44. H. N. Culver to W. F. Willis, "Browns Ferry Nuclear Plant—NRC-OIE Citations," January 20, 1982, Office of the General Manager, SDF, 319 (Browns Ferry), U.S. Archive, East Point, GA.

45. H. G. Parris to W. F. Willis, "Browns Ferry Nuclear Plants—NRC-OIE Citations," January 20, 1982, February 2, 1982. Office of S. David Freeman, 319 (Browns Ferry), U.S. Archive, East Point, GA.

46. "TVA Delays Loading of N-Fuel," March 12, 1982 and "Watts Bar Delay Will Cost 'Millions'," May 5, 1982, *News-Sentinel*, Knoxville, TN.

47. "TVA Overspends Estimates of $20 Billion, GAO Says," *News-Sentinel*, Knoxville, TN, April 25, 1982.

48. Discussion Paper by S. David Freeman, for the Executive Session on Nuclear Power and Energy Availability, Harvard University, Cambridge, MA, May 17–18, 1982, TVA Public Information Office.

49. H. G. Parris to W. F. Willis, "Semiannual Nuclear Activities Board Briefing, Division of Nuclear Power," May 16, 1983, S. David Freeman Files, 313, U.S. Archive, East Point, GA.

50. "NRC Hits Hard on Browns Ferry," *The Tennessean*, Nashville, TN, June 6, 1983.

51. "David Freeman hits Nader study of nuclear plants," *The Chattanooga Times*, Chattanooga, TN, September 2, 1983.

52. "New repair bill at Browns Ferry hits $122 million," *Journal*, Knoxville, TN, December 9, 1983.

53. "TVA: Browns Ferry Violations Technical," *Times*, Huntsville, AL, March 1, 1984.

54. "TVA nuclear staff to move to plants," *The Chattanooga Times*, Chattanooga, TN, April 17, 1984.

55. George W. Brown, "N-Plant to Come Back in Stages," *News-Free Press*, Chattanooga, TN, March 28, 1985.

56. George W. Brown, "TVA Announces Changes at Browns Ferry," *News-Free Press*, Chattanooga, TN, April 5, 1985.

57. "Finally, TVA Acts Tough," *News*, Birmingham, AL, April 1, 1985.

58. Libby Wann, "NRC to TVA: Get It Right or Give It Up," *The Chattanooga Times*, Chattanooga, TN, July 6, 1985.

59. Ibid.

60. Peter Coburn, "Directors Place Blame for Browns Ferry Woes," *Times*, Huntsville, AL, July 15, 1985.

61. Jeff Powell, "Dean Feels TVA 'Can Cope,'" *News-Free Press*, Chattanooga, TN, August 23, 1985.

62. Libby Wann, "NRC Questions Watts Bar Welding Records—TVA Lays Off 1600 Workers Until Problems are Resolved," *The Chattanooga Times*, Chattanooga, TN. August 24, 1985.

63. James W. Brosnan, *Commercial Appeal*, Memphis, TN, September 15, 1985.

64. William J. Dircks, Executive Director for Operations, Nuclear Regulatory

Commission, to Charles Dean, September 17, 1985. United States Nuclear Regulatory Commission.

65. Ibid., Enclosure 1, SALP Board Report, 1–6.

66. Randell Beck, "'Nuke Czar' Proposed to Watch TVA," *Journal,* Knoxville, TN, October 2, 1985.

67. Bob McMillan, "TVA Chairman 'Shocked' by Safety Problems," *Herald Citizen,* Cookeville, TN, October 3, 1985.

68. Randell Beck, "TVA Votes to Create Inspector General," *Journal,* Knoxville, TN, October 19, 1985.

69. Sandra Seeley to author, June 22, 1989, Nashville, TN.

70. Nuclear Safety Review Staff Overview, February 20, 1980. Office of the General Manager, 1980–81 File, 103(2), U.S. Archive, East Point, GA.

71. George Kimmons to William F. Willis, July 18, 1980, Robert N. Clement Files, 304, U.S. Archive, East Point, GA.

72. Handwritten, undated note to Robert N. Clement by Tony Valentine, attached to paper by R. F. Keck, dated July 28, 1978, Robert N. Clement Files, 304, U.S. Archive, East Point, GA.

73. Memo for QA Management Review Team to G. H. Kimmons and Godwin Williams, Jr., July 1, 1977, entitled "Final Report—Management Review of TVA QA Program" quoted by R. F. Keck, Robert N. Clement Files, 304, U.S. Archive, East Point, GA.

74. Ibid., 6.

75. H. N. Culver to W. F. Willis, "Overview of Quality Assurance Program in TVA," September 30, 1981, S. David Freeman File, 304, U.S. Archive, East Point, GA.

76. Ibid., 11–12.

77. Ibid., 25.

78. Ibid., 26.

79. Ibid., 30.

80. Ibid., 31.

81. Ibid., 32–33.

82. Ibid., 37–40.

83. H. N. Culver to William F. Willis, "Meeting with Nuclear Regulatory Staff of Inspection and Enforcement (NRC-OIE) in Atlanta, GA, December 18, 1981, S. David Freeman File, 319, 842 F, U.S. Archive, East Point, GA.

84. George F. Dilworth to William F. Willis, "Organization of a Corporate Quality Assurance Organization in the Office of the General Manager," March 20, 1982, S. David Freeman File, 103 (2–8), U.S. Archive, East Point, GA.

85. George Dilworth to author, August 9, 1989, Knoxville, TN.

86. Dan De Ford to author, August 10, 1989, Knoxville, TN.

87. Herbert Sanger to author, August 3, 1989, Knoxville, TN.

88. William Mason to author, August 2, 1989.

89. Sandra Seeley to author, June 22, 1989.

90. John Bynon to author, August 2, 1989, Knoxville, TN.

91. Ibid.

92. Ibid.

93. Larry Edwards to author, August 2, 1989, Knoxville, TN.

94. William Willis to author, August 7, 1989, Knoxville, TN.

95. Dan De Ford to author, August 10, 1989.

96. William Willis to author, August 7, 1989.

97. Ibid.

98. S. David Freeman to author, June 15, 1992.

99. John Waters to author, August 7, 1990, Knoxville, TN.

100. John Bynon to author, August 2, 1989.

101. Sandra Seeley, *Mancour Guity* v. *Tennessee Valley Authority, an Investigation*, April 28, 1986, U.S. Department of Labor.

102. Ibid. 4.

103. Ibid., 5.

104. Ibid., 6.

105. Charles H. Dean to Edwin A. Wiggin, March 29, 1983, S. David Freeman File, 319, A(2), U.S. Archive, East Point, GA.

106. Ibid., 6.

107. Charles H. Dean to author, June 26, 1990; John Waters to author, August 7, 1990.

108. Charles H. Dean to author, June 26, 1990. Dean also told the author that if the NRC and INPO had major problems with TVA nuclear units before 1985, they were discussed with executives below the board. Dean attended INPO conferences each year, and TVA plants were always presented to be satisfactory in INPO discussions. He speculated that TVA employees below the board were afraid of sending bad news up for fear of reprisal. Personal communication, September 14, 1993.

109. Herbert Sanger to author, August 3, 1989.

110. Richard Freeman to author, May 1, 1986. Freeman was very aware of the weaknesses of the TVA engineers working on the nuclear program. He saw them as complacent, riding on past successes and resistant to board exhortations to improve their operations. His hope had been to win congressional support for raising the TVA salary cap so that people could be fired and new and better engineers brought in to replace them. He is not impressed with my theory that the organizational culture of decentralization was a major cause of technical failures. But in the absence of new engineering leadership, the organizational culture was too strong for the Freemans. Dick Freeman and I will have to disagree here. Personal communications, September 14 and October 12, 1993.

111. John Stewart to author, June 26, 1990.

112. William Willis to author, August 7, 1989.

113. Ken Gray to author, May 27, 1989, Etlan, VA.

114. Senator James Sasser to author, June 16, 1992, Washington, D.C.

115. S. David Freeman memo attached to memo from John Stewart to the board, "Analysis of Options for TVA Oversight," March 13, 1982, S. David Freeman File, 175, 011E, A(1), U.S. Archive, East Point, GA.

116. Jonathan Cotten to John G. Stewart, "Report on Senator Sasser's Hearing," April 17, 1982, Memphis, TN, S. David Freeman File, 175, 011A1 (Sasser, James), 366, U.S. Archive, East Point, GA.

117. S. David Freeman to author, June 15, 1992.

118. Ken Gray, Appendix A, "Questions from Congress, Comprehensive and Specific Congressional Oversight of TVA, Calendar Year 1981." All the documents cited by Gray are from his reports to TVA, given to the author.

119. Ken Gray to Larry Edwards, "Corporate Situation Assessment," October 3, 1984, 2.

120. Ibid.

121. Ibid.

122. Ibid.

123. Ibid.

124. Charles Dean to author, June 26, 1992; John Waters to author, August 7, 1990; Herbert Sanger to author, August 3, 1989; William Mason to author, August 2, 1989; and Craven Crowell to author, June 15, 1992, Washington, D.C.

125. William Mason to author, August 2, 1989.

126. Herbert Sanger to author, August 3, 1989; Billy Bond to author, August 2, 1989, Knoxville, TN; John Baron to author, August 4, 1989; and Sandra Seeley to author, June 22, 1989.

127. Charles Dean to author, June 26, 1992; and Herbert Sanger to author, August 3, 1989.

128. Charles Dean to author, June 26, 1992; John Waters to author, August 7, 1990.

129. Steven White to author, May 25, 1989, Charlottesville, VA.

130. Ben A. Franklin, "TVA Troubles Worsen as Rescue Effort Falters," *New York Times*, October 19, 1986.

131. Steven White to author, May 25, 1989.

132. Ibid.

133. Ibid.

134. Ibid.

135. Ibid. The summary of White's report on his experience at TVA that follows in the text is all derived from the author's interview with White.

136. Randall Beck, "Discord, distrust, imperil Sequoyah restart, official says," *Journal*, Knoxville, TN, March 26, 1987.

137. Robert Dannavant, "TVA's White gives order to shape up," *The Tennessean*, Nashville, TN, June 19, 1986.

138. "NRC Creates Expert Team to Monitor TVA N-Plants, *Journal*, Knoxville, TN, February 11, 1987.

139. Libby Wann, "TVA Board OK's engineering contracts worth $170 million to cure nuclear ills," *The Chattanooga Times*, Chattanooga, TN, April 22, 1987.

140. Steven White to author, May 25, 1989.

141. J. Patrick Willard, "White: TVA needs 7 years to restore N-power program," *Journal*, Knoxville, June 19, 1987.

142. Charles H. Dean to author, June 26, 1992.

143. John Waters to author, August 7, 1990.

144. Dan De Ford to author, August 10, 1989.

145. George Dilworth to author, August 9, 1989.

146. Herbert Sanger to author, August 3, 1989.

147. William Mason to author, August 2, 1989.

148. Sandra Seeley to author, June 22, 1989.

149. Ibid.

150. *TVA: A Path to Recovery*.

151. Clifford Russell, director of Vanderbilt Institute for Public Policy Studies and an environmental economist, was a member of the committee and believed that its proceedings were intended to help TVA, not kill it. Personal communication.

152. *TVA: A Path to Recovery*, section 3, 2–3.

153. Ibid., section 3, 6–7.

154. Ibid, Executive Summary, 4.

155. Ibid., Executive Summary, 9.

156. Ibid.

157. Ibid.

158. Ibid, Executive Summary, 10.

159. Ibid., Executive Summary, 11–14.

160. Alex Radin to author, June 17, 1992, Washington, D.C.

161. Ibid.

162. Ibid.

163. Ibid.

164. Laura Simmons, "One Person, Not a Board, Should Run TVA, Chairman Says," *News-Sentinel*, Knoxville, TN, August 31, 1987.

EPILOGUE: PART 2

1. David Halberstam has described Runyon as one of the most innovative production managers at Ford and tells how and why Runyon left Ford and went to Nissan because of his frustration with the Ford company management. See Halberstam, *The Reckoning* (New York: William Morrow and Co., Inc., 1986), 497–502, 619–623.

2. Anne Paine, "TVA must increase N-Power to compete: Runyon," *The Tennessean*, Nashville, TN, February 17, 1988. The debt figure was obtained from William Malec, executive vice-president and chief financial officer, TVA. Personal communication, November 16, 1993.

3. Phil Williams, "Peace in the Valley," *The Tennessean*, Nashville, TN, March 22, 1992.

4. Marvin Runyon to author, October 26, 1990, Nashville, TN.

5. According to Alex Radin, Runyon had been urged by members of the Valley congressional delegation to take the job, and they then felt it necessary to defer to his decisions, such as instituting bonuses, in spite of their previous opposition. Alex Radin to author, June 16, 1992, Washington, D.C.

6. Marvin Runyon to author, October 26, 1990.

7. Ibid.

8. Ibid.

9. Ronald Smothers, "TVA Slashes Work Force and Holds Off on Two Plants," *New York Times*, June 30, 1988; Phil Williams, "Peace in the Valley," *The Tennessean*, Nashville, TN, March 22, 1992.

10. J. Voris Williams, "Runyonitis Infecting TVA? Symptoms Sound Awful, But Malady May Heal Agency, Workers Say," *Journal*, Knoxville, TN, April 15, 1988.

11. William F. Willis to author, August 7, 1990, Knoxville, TN.

12. Craven Crowell to author, June 15, 1992, Washington, D.C.

13. Jerry Campbell to author, May 27, 1992, Chattanooga, TN.

14. Allan Pulsipher, "Will TVA Survive Marvin Runyon?" Working paper, March, 1992, Center for Energy Studies, Louisiana State University, 1–6.

15. Ibid.

16. Jerry Campbell to author, May 27, 1992.

CHAPTER 10

1. The conception of leaders uniting purpose, politics, and process in a personal style is set out in my book *Jimmy Carter as President*.

2. J. R. Kimberly, "Issues in the Design of Longitudinal Research," *Sociological Methods and Research*, 1975–76, 4: 321–347.

3. Ibid., 11–13.

4. Ibid., 26–27.

5. Kimberly et al., *The Organizational Life Cycle*, 42.

6. Erwin C. Hargrove, "David Lilienthal and the Tennessee Valley Authority," in Doig and Hargrove, *Leadership and Innovation*.

7. There is a parallel here between Stephen Skowronek's typology of presidents and my categorization of TVA leaders. Skowronek's presidents of Reconstruction create new political regimes out of the ashes of old ones: Jefferson, Jackson, Lincoln, and Roosevelt. Lilienthal had the task of construction as a founder of an organization, and the work was essentially the same as that of a president of Reconstruction in that a system of political support for a new policy regime had to be created. Runyon was presented with the same possibility. The president of preemption is the president of a minority party who wins office and successfully governs despite the fact that his coalition is not that of the dominant party regime. Grover Cleveland, Woodrow Wilson, and Dwight Eisenhower fit this mold. General Vogel was a leader of preemption in TVA, the only outsider chairman before Runyon, who was successful in imposing his policies on the organization and the political environment. But to a great extent Vogel led against the grain, when compared to his predecessor, Clapp, and his successor, Wagner. Clapp belongs in the Reconstruction period, much like James Madison, Martin Van Buren, and Harry Truman. Wagner and Freeman resemble closely Skowronek's presidents of articulation. Such leaders attempt, and often succeed, in reviving the creative politics and policy of the Reconstruction period. They breathe new life into an old party regime. Theodore Roosevelt and Lyndon Johnson were such presidents. But the revival of old alliances is very likely to place strain upon them. Success may be its own undoing because the resolution of old problems may generate new issues that divide the old coalition. Thus the Great Society programs of civil rights and social welfare created a backlash among many traditional Democrats and created the political possibilities for wedge politics by two Republican presidents, Richard Nixon and Ronald Reagan, to divide the Democratic coalition. The same

kinds of divisions developed among TVA constituencies in the Wagner and Freeman periods. Finally, Dean matches the presidents of disjunction who preside at the end of a party regime period when the political resources available to a leader have seriously eroded. Presidents of disjunction, according to Skowronek, were John Quincy Adams, James Buchanan, Herbert Hoover, and Jimmy Carter. See Stephen Skowronek, *The Politics Presidents Make: Leadership from John Adams to George Bush* (Cambridge, Mass.: Belknap Press of Harvard University Press, 1993).

8. Miles, "Findings and Implications of Organizational Life Cycle Research" in Kimberly et al., *The Organizational Life Cycle, 443.*

9. Marshall W. Meyer and Lynne G. Zucker, *Permanently Failing Organizations* (Newbury Park: Sage Publications, 1989), 83, 93, 95–96.

10. Thompson, *Organizations in Action*, 145–146.

11. Arthur L. Stinchcombe, *Constructing Social Theories* (New York: Harcourt, Brace and World, Inc., 1968), 114.

12. Ibid., 114, 117.

13. Ibid., 120–123.

14. Ibid., 112.

15. Ibid., 162, 196.

16. Barry M. Staw, "The Escalation of Commitment to a Course of Action," *Academy of Management Review* 6, 4 (1981): 578.

17. Ibid., 580–83.

18. Ibid., 580.

19. James G. March, "Footnotes to Organizational Change," *Administrative Science Quarterly* 26, 4 (December 1981): 569.

20. Charles Perrow, *Complex Organizations: A Critical Essay*, (Glenview, IL: Scott, Foresman, 1986), 145.

21. Robert H. Miles and W. Alan Randolph, "Influence of Organizational Learning Styles on Early Development," in Kimberly et al., *The Organizational Life Cycle*, 51–52.

22. William U. Chandler, *The Myth of TVA: Conservation and Development in the Tennessee Valley, 1933–1983* (Cambridge, MA: Ballinger Publishing Co, 1984), chapter 4.

23. Meyer and Zucker, *Permanently Failing Organizations*, 23–25.

24. Ibid., 93, 95–96.

25. Ibid., 110–111.

26. Ibid., 121–123; March, *Administrative Science Quarterly*, 26, 4 (December 1981): 571.

27. Meyer and Zucker, *Permanently Failing Organizations*, 134.

28. Ibid., 109, 112.

29. March, *Administrative Science Quarterly* 26, 4 (December 1981): 572.

30. Meyer and Zucker, *Permanently Failing Organizations*, 134–135.

31. Richard A. Couto, "TVA's Old and New Grass Roots: A Reexamination of Cooptation," *Administration and Society* 19, 4 (February 1988): 462–476.

32. Meyer and Zucker, *Permanently Failing Organizations*, 128.

33. Thompson, *Organizations in Action*, 151–152.

34. Ibid., 152–154.

35. Ibid., 145.

36. Ibid., 147.

37. Ibid., 148–150.

38. Karl E. Weick, "Management of Organizational Change Among Loosely Coupled Elements," in Paul Goodman and Associates, eds., *Change in Organizations* (San Francisco: Jossey-Bass Publishers, 1982), 385, 405.

39. Todd R. LaPorte and Paula M. Consolini, "Working in Practice but Not in Theory: Theoretical Challenges of 'High-Reliability Organizations,'" *Journal of Public Administration Research and Theory* 1 (1991): 1, 37.

40. Ibid., 43.

41. Thompson, *Organizations in Action*, 154–155.

42. Todd R. LaPorte and Craig Thomas, "Regulatory Compliance and the Ethos of Quality Enhancement: Surprises in Nuclear Power Plant Operations," unpublished paper, May 18, 1991, 5.

43. Ibid., 10–11.

44. Ibid., 4.

45. Ibid., 14–18.

46. Ibid., 24–27.

47. Diane Vaughn, "Autonomy, Interdependence and Social Control: NASA and the Space Shuttle Challenger," *Administrative Science Quarterly* 35 (June 1990): 225–257.

48. Ibid., 225–226.

49. Ibid., 228, 243, 245–246.

50. Ibid., 230–232, 238–240, 247–251.

51. Gregg Easterbrook, "The Case Against NASA," *The New Republic*, July 8, 1991, 19.

52. Annemarie H. Walsh, *The Public's Business: The Politics and Practices of Government Corporations* (A Twentieth Century Fund Study, 1978), 37.

53. John Gaus to Draper Committee, March 29, 1937. See chapter 4, note 33.

54. Walsh, *The Public's Business*, 45–46. Walsh poses a conflict between "centralist" public administration theory, which argues for the reintegration of public corporations in the regular departments of government, and "decentralist" public administration, one of whose champions was David Lilienthal.

55. Thompson, *Organizations in Action*, 154–155.

56. Ibid., 162.

57. Wilson, *Bureaucracy*, 237, 250.

58. Thompson, *Organizations in Action*, 155.

59. Ibid.

60. Ibid., 156.

61. Ibid., 162. In *The Public's Business*, Walsh reports that interviews with the executives of public authorities indicate that many see themselves acting solely on the basis of objective efficiency. They do not see themselves as making policy (p. 50). Walsh contends, however, that such executives work in far greater secrecy than is the case in private corporations and that their ability to place a personal stamp on their organizations is greater than that of all but the most "extraordinary" government executives. In her view, such executives have "a low tolerance for competition and conflict" (p. 209–210).

62. Walsh, *The Public's Business*, 7.

63. Ibid., 11.

64. Ibid., 24.

65. Ibid., 25. Walsh adds that "most of the written works discussing public corporations are tightly woven in the fabric of progressive symbols."

66. Ibid., 337.

67. Ibid., 338.

68. Ibid., 340–341.

69. Jameson W. Doig, "To Claim the Seas and Skies: Austin Tobin and the Port of New York Authority," in Doig and Hargrove, *Leadership and Innovation*, (1990, abridged edition).

70. This is analogous to the profiles in Doig and Hargrove's, *Leadership and Innovation*, in which the individual career line is the unit of analysis. Leadership effectiveness and ineffectiveness are captured in the changing contexts of careers.

71. Doig and Hargrove, " 'Leadership' and Political Analysis," in Doig and Hargrove, *Leadership and Innovation* (1990, abridged edition).

72. Wilson, *Bureaucracy*, 370. Wilson sees the possibility that a "gifted executive" may appear at times to lead a new institution to develop a "distinctive competence" and a "strong sense of mission" but concludes that it is hard to create such an agency today because public agencies are too constrained by cross-pressures (p. 367–368).

73. Ibid., 277.

74. Hargrove, *The Power of the Modern Presidency* chapter 5; Doig and Hargrove, *Leadership and Innovation*, chapter 1; Hargrove, *Jimmy Carter as President*, chapter 6; Hargrove and Glidewell, *Impossible Jobs*, chapters 1–3.

Index